CINEMA BOREALIS

Ingmar Bergman and the Swedish Ethos

Vernon Young

EQUINOX BOOKS / PUBLISHED BY AVON

D0943473

AVON BOOKS
A division of
The Hearst Corporation
959 Eighth Avenue
New York, New York 10019

First Avon Printing (Equinox Edition), July, 1972

EQUINOX TRADEMARK REG. U.S. PAT. OFF. AND
FOREIGN COUNTRIES, REGISTERED TRADEMARK—
MARCA REGISTRADA, HECHO EN CHICAGO, U.S.A.

Printed in the U.S.A.

CONTENTS

*"Definition of a classical artist:
One whose dementia is simply the occasion of
release for his talent."*

*"Definition of a romantic artist:
One whose dementia becomes his subject matter."*

W. H. Auden, *Notes to* New Year Letter

*"Ever since we liquidated the gods, we have been
talking about them constantly; we have all become
theologians."*

E. M. Cioran, *"The Evil Demiurge"*

To write about films is to be wholly dependent on those who produce, distribute or conserve them. It would be impracticable here to try listing every archivist, exhibitor or press agent who has shown me films over the many years during which I have assiduously hunted them. However, since the nominal subject of this book is the film production of Ingmar Bergman, it is obvious that my gratitude should principally go to AB Svenskfilm in Stockholm—Kenne Fant, president—where I have seen and re-seen Bergman's films, collected information, consulted scripts, acquired stills. Specifically, I should like to acknowledge the services of Olle Grönstedt, previously associated with SF, and those of Anne-Marie Hedvall who currently presides over the Press office of Svenskfilm. Fru Hedvall has extended her favors and her untiring courtesy far beyond the call of duty; to her my blessing.

All quotations in this book from the film scripts of Ingmar Bergman are either my own translations from the originals or directly taken from English versions supplied by the SF Language Department.

I owe a major debt of thanks to George Simpson, a former resident of Stockholm, now Somewhere in France, who researched a vast amount of factual material, supported by numerous interviews with Mr. Bergman, in the early Sixties, concerning the early years of the director's career especially, together with much background data up to the Fifties. This research was pursued for a work Mr. Simpson never completed; with great kindness he provided me with the fruits of his preparation. *Unless otherwise noted,* my sources for the early Bergman chronology and synopses of his earliest plays were supplied by George Simpson. Naturally, he is not to be held responsible for the inferences I have drawn from his data.

V.Y.   June 1970

INTRODUCTION

Two temptations have prevailed in the largely generous reception which, since 1956, has made Ingmar Bergman one of the most celebrated directors in the history of cinema. The first is to minimize Bergman's debt to his native sources, as well as to his predecessors in Swedish theatre and film; the second is to see Bergman as an *intellectual* filmmaker, a term as often employed to damn as to praise him.

For the first, the stuff of Bergman's films emerged principally from his child-rooted enchantment by the irreducible forms of theatre: the magic lantern, the puppet play, the pantomime, the farce, the ballet. These in turn were given a moral temper by the other form of theatre to which he was seasonally exposed, owing to his father's calling, the ceremonies of the Church: baptism, confirmation, communion, marriage, and burial. (As Santayana said of Dickens: "Religion lay on him like the weight of the atmosphere, sixteen pounds to the square inch. . . .") Intervening before ever he had engaged a career were the crises of early manhood which involved him simultaneously in what were to become the master subjects of all his expression thereafter—the agony of the couple and the equivocal presence of God. These are the prime movers to be recognized before moving on to infer literary influences from Strindberg, Hjalmar Bergman, Dostoievsky, Pirandello, or Kafka. Many of the latter connections were all too recklessly assigned to Bergman by French critics in the mistaken belief that they were flattering him by admitting him to the company of a literary aristocracy. They were victims of an abiding confusion in criticism of the arts: the failure to distinguish an influence from an analogy. Further, they were failing to acknowledge the force of unconscious influence, curiously enough preferring to imply that a conscious derivation was more to Bergman's credit. If, in any given film of Bergman, there are themes or turns of thought which resemble those in the works of literary masters, might it not have been more tactful to have assumed the possibility of his having educed them independently?

The contingent sources of Bergman's films—those that assist the plot or suggest the characters, the settings and so forth—are eclectic. Bergman's eyes and ears, his memory and his sixth sense, have picked up fleeting images, hints, rumours, tributary motives, from a hundred directions, among which are daily life, novels, plays, films, anecdotes, dreams, and wives. When under compulsion to locate Bergman's several points of departure it is wiser to hunt for them first in his immediate vicinity. It is better to ask, in short, which other films Bergman had at certain junctures seen, which plays of his own had like preoccupations, which plays by other men he had himself lately staged. You might, of course, ask more intimate questions, the answers to which, if you come by them, may or may not support your deductions.

The second comfortably held notion, that Bergman is an intellectual, whether or not the attribution has been favourably intended, is pure nonsense unless we are willing to define intellectual life so broadly as to constitute the life of reason in which every articulate being participates. But the stricter attribution Bergman himself would be the first to protest. By the most provisional definition, the concern of an intellectual is to pursue ideas disinterestedly. For him, events suggest raw material to be translated into verbally expressible concepts; he is moved, one might say, by an impersonal passion for speculation. Fascinated by correlations and consequences, he does not halt at the borders of what personally gratifies his sentiment. Argument is his pleasure, discrimination his raison d'être, and his normal mode of communication is discursive. If he is relatively unsubtle, he may announce the Truth as his object! Bergman does not inhabit that world, though sometimes he worries at its fringes. He is not an intellectual, he is an artist, that is to say, a maker of expressive forms. Initially he responds to images, provocations and fugitive visions. Thereafter he proceeds from creative intuition and personal bias, reacting to experience subjectively (not to say obsessively), selecting from phenomena those elements which alone can feed his immediate artistic purpose. A muddled interpretation of what constitutes intellectual expression must be responsible for supposing that because Bergman's best films appeal to our minds as well as to our emotions, a rare consummation in the cinema, they were therefore intellectually conceived. Art may comprise a degree of intellectual activity, but it is not a synonym for intellectual activity. Art is a formal embodiment of the imagination.

Film critics, especially those made nervous by a Frenchman over their shoulder, have accepted the premise reluctantly, evidently fearing that it will place the artist beyond the jurisdiction of their analysis. To them, there is something nebulous about criteria which make taste or imagination the testing values; they feel safer when scouting for "ideas," since ideas are esteemed as precision instruments, sacred to the contemporary mind. A generation has failed to assimilate the distinction formulated by T. S. Eliot:

> The poet who thinks is merely the poet who can express the emotional equivalent of thought, but he is not necessarily interested in the thought itself. We talk as if thought was precise and emotion was vague. In reality there is precise emotion and there is vague emotion.[1]

To be sure, this distinction is the more persuasive because it was uttered by a very intelligent poet! We need to be aware that it can be made to serve merely antiintellectual ends; what may appear to be an "emotional equivalent" of thought may on closer inspection be an emotional resistance to it. The more gullible critics of Bergman's films seem to have been victimized by rumour of their complexity. The nature of this complexity has seldom been clarified; critics have often taken for complexity what was superficially complicated or just morally confused. In any case, such writers have been intimidated by the assumption that complexity is strictly a consequence of intellectual ferment. Now, in the films of Bergman, structural complexity should not be confused with moral complexity: the latter may have been conveyed in films which are relatively innocent of involved relationships, double meanings, or elliptical visual devices.

Complexity is one of many modes attained by the artist in his attempt to express more than meets the eye. Art is forever complex because the creative prescience of the artist reveals a world of implication which the subject in itself cannot wholly contain. And art is forever classically simple because in any instance—here I speak of narrative and poetic art —the essential subject is normally reducible to a gnomic text, a general statement that satisfies our need to explain the moral power which the work of art exercises over us.

> "Whom the gods destroy, they first make mad."
> "The evil that men do lives after them. . . ."
> "The cause of suffering is ignorance of the way."
> "Love makes time pass, time makes love pass."
> "Everything that happens to a man is intrinsically like the man it happens to."

These are examples of the kind of concentrated answer we grope for when asked, or asking ourselves, "Just what is this film, novel, play really about?" Whether the artist felt precisely the formulation that satisfies us, and no other, is usually debatable, but it may be misleading to presume that if he did he realized it at the outset and began by framing such a proposition to himself as a point of departure. It is far more likely that his poetry has coincidentally embodied what for someone else might have been a theme for an essay on morals, or a conclusion arrived at by consistent reasoning. When journalists at a press conference ask a film director if his movie isn't about "the loneliness of Man," he must feel considerable embarrassment, not to say exasperation. The film in question may happen to be about the loneliness of Man, but that will barely suffice to distinguish it from fifty others, described by the same cliché; furthermore, the film may be about a lot of other things, closer to the director's heart. Any director such as Bergman, who has reached art by trial and error, by guesswork and divination, and but rarely by a conscious exposition of ideas objectively grasped, could do far worse

than to reply, when called an intellectual, "Flattery will get you nowhere."

Charitable opinions are often the fruit of misconception. Critics who
have largely admired Bergman's mature work are prone to find in-
dispensably precious every film made by the master. They invent a
consciously graduated order in the Bergman chronology, each film chain-
flowering from the one before in a steady efflorescence of vision, intelligence, and style. Such ingenuity, one suspects, is a critic's compensation
for his personal uneasiness with the object of his criticism. He is probably
aware, at least before breakfast, that the motion picture is too seldom
a vehicle of astute revelation. By imposing on a single body of film an
unfaltering unity of development he may be able to restore to the dubious
art of the cinema that stature the presence of which in private he gravely
doubts.

Viewed in panorama, Bergman's continuity does encourage the lauda-
ble falsification; his films readily appear to group themselves in evolu-
tionary sequences that irresistibly invoke seasonal or diurnal suggestions:
hence, the division of his earlier periods, notably by M. Jacques Siclier,
into *films noir* and *films rose*.[2] Up to a point, this kind of classification
is harmless. Titles chosen from among the films themselves would as
conveniently serve the same end: *Music in the Dark,* the apprentice
period of Youth, Love, God and the Devil; *Summer Interlude,* transitional comedy and mature skepticism; *Winter Light,* a feebly illumined
return, sadder and wiser, to the original grievance, Man without God.
Upon closer scrutiny, however, such categories are simpler to invent
than to justify consistently; they can be supported only by a pretense
that the dividing lines are absolute, that no sequence was radically
modified by the appearance within it of a film seemingly irrelevant.
What we thought was Bergman's Winter may turn out to have been his
Autumn (a phenomenon, by the way, coextensive with the Swedish
climate). The excessive importance with which, for example, *Fängelse*
(*Prison*) has been endowed can only be maintained, if at all, by supposing that its production followed immediately upon its conception
in Bergman's mind and that the film we see was the issue of a disciplined
moral intention. This was not the case.

There are many other films that circumvent a short answer to Bergman's order of progression. Clearly he developed artistically, but certainly not without hesitations, grave errors of judgment, tentative reversals, periods of blankness or self-contradiction, wasteful rebukes of criticism he might better have ignored or, in some cases, taken to heart. To minimize the evidence of his prolonged struggle and his uncertain tenure of the insights ostensibly gained from it is to do him less than justice. Like other men, Bergman is fallible, even if, at his greatest, he is a film artist firmly distinguishable from most of his contemporaries. At which point he became a filmmaker, committedly, rather than a theatre man who made films on the side, remains a matter for criticism to decide, since he seems rarely to have been certain himself.

For some years after the release in 1951 of *Sommarlek* (*Summer Interlude*), in which film Bergman believed he first acquired complete artistic control of the medium, he was nonetheless contending that the theatre was his wife, the movie his mistress (a metaphor which anyone might interpret with an evaluation of his own).[3] In 1956, he revised the implicit priority, asserting that film was his natural element, a basic need like hunger for bread, that he made films as others might climb mountains, beat their children or dance the samba.[4] This was perhaps a rhetorical self-indulgence, for at the end of 1959, after completing *The Virgin Spring,* he assured me personally that theatre had the primary appeal for him; that film production, by its very nature, was an absurd enterprise. Again, in the speech he wrote, delivered for him by Kenne Fant (president of SF—Svenskfilm) at Utrecht in 1964 he virtually repudiated the honor there bestowed on him (sharing the Erasmus Prize for Cultural Achievement with Charles Chaplin) by defining all contemporary art as worthless when weighed in the scale against society's indifference and its preference for more elementary diversions. In September of 1967, at a press conference held on the island of Fårö, before shooting his twenty-ninth movie, *The Shame,* he repledged his allegiance to filmmaking and dismissed, not without tears, so to speak, the validity of theatre for contemporary audiences. The chapters that follow will, I trust, provide several clues to the reasons for the discrepancy between Bergman's performance and his public proclamations.

While I should prefer to engage my subject, Bergman as film-maker, at its finest hour, with fewer preliminaries and parentheses, I should not expect to clarify the subject adequately if I did so. First things first. Since the belief lingers that Bergman invented the recent Swedish film single-handed, I think any such notion should be corrected. The Swedish film industry, and the Swedish film as art, was already a definable presence when, in 1944, Bergman's contribution to it was invited.

THE PRECONDITIONS

Ingmar Bergman was born in 1918 in the university town of Uppsala, just north of Stockholm. When he was six years old he accompanied his parents to the capital city where his father, a clergyman, assumed duties as chaplain at a nursing home and, some years later, acquired the ministry of Hedvig Eleanora Church, in Stockholm. This much everyone who has read film biography seems to know. What escapes many is the significance of the birth date. To have been born in Sweden in 1918 was comparable to having been born in England or the United States, other differences allowed for, about 1890. Sweden was rural, pious, and remote in 1918, the year Stiller was making *Sir Arne's Treasure*. Stockholm could have hardly been a very urbane capital, though in certain quarters it was probably a great deal more gracious than it is now. Nineteen eighteen marked the end of the First World War. Bergman was born at the close of one war; he came of age at the outbreak of another; he came of age again, as a film director, shortly after the termination of the second war—two wars, moreover, in which Sweden had not fought. When personal traits and collateral circumstances are blended in the biography, the importance of this span of time embracing the definitive years of Bergman's development cannot be exaggerated. The sequence guaranteed a horizon of anxiety at climactic moments, even had other provocations been lacking.

As a child, Bergman commuted frequently between his parents' home in the city and his grandmother's house in Uppsala, the latter an indelible furnishing of his memory, a defunct mansion, so to speak: capacious, mysterious and opulent in an older fashion, loaded with chandeliers, tiled stoves, paintings of Italian cities, a forest of portieres, rhetorical furniture and genteel bric-a-brac. We know that he was quickly impressionable, tyrannically sensitive to atmosphere, solitary by inclination yet fascinated by things theatrical—that other world of artifice which many of us instantly learn to prefer if the "real world" is not compatible with our wish to manipulate it—among which were the Biblical tales painted on the vaults and ceilings of the country churches he visited with his father. One of his most cherished acquisitions was a small Oriental shadow-theatre given him by a guest at his grandmother's; when a little older, about ten, he was entrusted with a toy cinematograph for which he etched cartoons on a roll of film. The future was all around him. Taken, at which age I'm not sure, to a production of *Red Riding Hood* staged by the young Alf Sjöberg, he allegedly sobbed so loud at the girl's fate (or at that of her grandmother?) that he had to be removed from the premises.

During his adolescence he was enrolled in a private academy, the customary solution resorted to by parents when a youngster doesn't want to go to school in the first place. Theatre was Bergman's chosen school, then and thereafter. By whatever theatrical expression was offered in the Stockholm of the Thirties, whether drama or operetta, he was enraptured and displayed a strong taste for the bravura style of entertainment. He had a Wagner phase, a Nietzsche phase, and a Strindberg phase. Every Swede has a Strindberg phase: it lasts from the cradle to the grave. At the age of sixteen in 1934, Bergman saw the first of Olof Molander's now legendary productions of Strindberg at Dramaten (Royal Dramatic Theatre), an experience that has remained memorable for him to this day. The extent to which Strindberg has permeated the nervous tissue of his films is almost too self-evident to be pointed out. At seventeen he passed his Student Examination, indispensable requirement for admittance to the University, but he suffered such binding anxiety at the prospect of failure that he avenged himself for the fright while recovering by writing the story which eventually became the script of Alf Sjöberg's film, *Hets* (*Fury* or, in the United States, *Torment*, by which title I prefer to designate it hereafter).

Bergman spent the summer of his nineteenth year on an island of the Stockholm archipelago, commonly known as The Skerries; by his own confession, it was a harrowing season. He lost the girl he loved, he lost his faith in revealed religion—in which order we can only assume. Given his background, it would seem likely that if the circumstances attending his separation from the girl were sufficiently bitter, a failing trust in divine support would have followed. At nearly the same time, though Bergman is unable to place the event—his memory for the chronology of those years is by now confused—he also lost by death a very close male companion. This sequence of tragedy and shock, together with a patent element of guilt, is incorporated or at least suggested in almost all the plays and film scenarios he wrote or in which he had merely a hand during the years immediately following. The girl in question, whom he first named Marie, appeared in his work in so many contradictory

guises that Bergman himself has subsequently been hard put to explain
which was prototype and which a figment suggested by or transposed
from the original. We had best assume that the actual circumstances
were never literally reproduced in any of the films; it is their general
configuration which is conspicuous, recurring again and again with the
characters thereof split, reversed, modified, compounded, surviving in
one film, perishing in another.

I assume I have not to underline the grave importance, for the son
of a clergyman, of losing or believing he has lost his religious fidelity,
and with all allowance made for a degree of self-dramatization which
has seldom been absent from Bergman's personal declarations. From
time to time rumors have been broadcast that Bergman hated his father,
not a surprising imputation when you realize what a clear field his
movies represent for the Freudian examiner. Just as inevitably the in-
sinuation has been denied. His elder brother, who is in the diplomatic
service, and his sister, who lives in England, both have protested that
there is no truth in the assertion and Bergman has stated for Swedish
publication that he once inflated his rebellion against authority with
damaging implications for his father and mother which he subsequently
regretted. While nobody outside a given family circle, nor very often
inside, knows what concealed animosities or terrors may be harbored,
there would seem to be ambivalence enough in Bergman's relation to his
father (of his mother we scarcely learn anything) without a Karamazov
complex being introduced. Nonetheless, that the attitude toward the
father is the atitude toward God, Dostoievsky, before Freud, assured us.
In our post-Freudian age few filmgoers can be unaware that in Bergman's films undue place is given to rivalry with or mollification of a
father-figure, and paramount emphasis is placed on the theme of God's
dereliction from his obligations toward Man. Bergman told Vilgot Sjöman during the shooting of *Winter Light* that when he was a boy the
customary penalty for domestic offenses in his household was to be
stood in a closet. For milder breaches of conduct he was totally ignored;
his parents refused to speak a word to him. Bergman confided that he
is now offended by nothing so much as being ignored when he addresses
someone. Sjöman readily made the connection between this reminiscence
and a prevailing lament in Bergman's films that "God is silent."[5]

It does make psychiatric sense to infer that Bergman's attitude toward his father would have been equivocal. If a boy feels an initially strong obligation to admire the parent, and if furthermore he is humorless, which at heart Bergman appears always to have been, grief may well be the penalty for equivocation. We may imagine, without presumption in this case, that once the boy in question begins to see his father not as a haloed vicar of the All-Powerful, but as a mere man with habits and idiosyncrasies and irritating restrictive rights like all other parents, he will next begin to doubt if such a man is in truth divinely sanctioned to bring consolation to the souls of others. Remorse will be the consequence; since father is kind and instructive, when he's not condemning Ingmar to a dark closet and silence, taking him on nature-study walks and narrating the vivid stories of the Bible, the boy's doubt must be sinful. In his grandmother's house, peopled with magical presences by this boy's agile fancy, one may well believe that demons were supposed by him to lurk behind the clock or in the chandeliers at night, demons like those in *The Dance of Death,* painted on the vaults of country churches, demons that might carry him off and stand him in a black closet if he impenitently persevered in his heathen misgivings. Childhood, for the introvert who is without specifically religious ambivalence, is a stifling enough ordeal. Time is interminable—a minute an hour, hours days, punishment an outrage, a normal fear an eternity of horror. The child whose imagination is in excess of his talent for venting it lives a deferred life, waiting for the unbearable pressure to lift when he will be able to liberate, express, and avenge himself. By the time he has reached something like maturity he breaks surface into the daylight like a swimmer who has been forcibly held under. His reaction, if by nature he lacks a proportionate sense of things, will be often vindictive and not infrequently illusory, for he has long cultivated the secret vice of believing himself threatened, suppressed, injured. If, at the next decisive threshold, he meets love and death at the same time, it is small wonder if his ensuing attempts to reconcile them are unbalanced and obsessive. From such victims are derived our neurotic legions, a good part of our criminal fringe, our political tyrants, and occasionally our artists.

In Bergman's earlier films, seemingly unrelated to the God-is-absent complaint, there is a distinct note of sexual hostility toward the older men depicted. Conceivably, a radical modification in his response to his father was henceforth transferred to another adult (later, almost certainly, to the critic) with whom he had become competitively involved. I say conceivably because I am always prepared, in the investigation which follows, to cancel my speculations at the borders of the personal. I should prefer to discuss Bergman's films without touching his personal life at all, but not only do the films more often than not make this a difficult discipline, Bergman himself vitiates one's sense of discretion by the provocative egoism he has so often displayed. Beyond the more obvious connections, however, without which his films can only academically be analyzed, I shall make an effort to be diffident. His marriages, for instance, are in my opinion completely forbidden territory for the critic. I do not believe it important for us to determine Ingmar Bergman's nuclear conflict; it is sufficient to observe that Bergman's efforts to resolve it artistically are, if sometimes confused, almost invariably interesting.

After military service, a duty he did not find distressing, Bergman entered the University of Stockholm; his major study was ostensibly Literature and Art. Today he confesses that he was bored by most of the literature he read. Dostoievsky seems to have been his single literary passion, always excepting Strindberg. Clearly he could have derived but scanty intellectual advantage from this institution, for he was soon and busily engaged with theatre. Invited to stage plays at a Christian organization in Stockholm, where what had been a church was now a theatre, (so often life conspires with our drift) he produced for his first program Sutton Vane's *Outward Bound,* that veteran stock-company item of yore, in which the passengers on an ocean liner discover that they are dead. Bergman himself played God, or rather, strictly speaking, God's steward. His second directorial contribution was *Lucky Peter's Journey* by Strindberg, a play with which he had been familiar since childhood. Dramatic irony continued to play into his hands. During the Spring of 1940 at the very hour when, for Scandinavia, the War began in earnest with Denmark occupied and Norway mobilized, Bergman was staging *Macbeth,* in which he played the role of King Duncan.[6]

These productions earned him an invitation in 1940 to direct plays at Student Theatre, which was not wholly collegiate in makeup for it employed professional actors. For his introductory production, he chose

The Pelican, which Strindberg had written as an inaugural piece for his Intimate Theatre in Stockholm in 1907.[7] When he left the University he found part-time engagement without pay at the Stockholm Opera where, though he was given a fancy title, he appears to have functioned as a prompter and errand-boy. The experience rewarded Bergman's curiosity; he became familiar with the world of backstage apparatus on a large scale. Otherwise he was far from idle, at one period directing plays at two theatres simultaneously.

His most fateful encounter during these seasons was with Elsie Fisher, a Norwegian dancer trained in England who was appearing in a program for which she had composed her own choreography. Bergman, duly impressed, asked her to help him stage a pantomime ballet for children with which he was momentarily occupied. She consented, not long thereafter consenting also to become his wife. The marriage lasted five years. Bergman's writing had so far been confined to stories; the first Mrs. Bergman encouraged him to try plays. With alacrity he took her advice and among the first he wrote was an item called *The Station,* never published or produced, but to which he had unfortunate recourse later on for the film script of *Eva,* directed by Gustav Molander.

The first of his plays produced, by Bergman himself at Student Theatre, is well worth our noting, since it contained in solution, as it were, the Bergman cosmos. *Kaspar's Death* was developed from an earlier adaptation he had attempted of a Hans Christian Andersen tale about Death and a Traveller. The achieved version assumed a sort of Punch-and-Judy style with choreographic elements. The gist of the matter consisted of Kaspar's doomed effort to escape the pallid felicities of marriage by revelling at a tavern. Forced by his fellow bibulants to dance on the table until he collapsed, he was then carried away by Death in a large black coffin. Brought before the Lord to be judged and disposed of, Kaspar pleads eloquently to be excused from going to Heaven, for that would repeat precisely the kind of existence with his Kasparinna from which he had in desperation escaped to the joys of the tavern.

Marriage as an ordeal, the world of fellow-players as a creative escape, Death standing by, an Old Testament God to whom, with a certain suspension of disbelief, one may plead—here are nearly the essential dramatis personae of Bergman's future theatre and film. All that's needed beside another female is a devil, and that personage he was very soon not only to supply but to become attached to with exceptional tenacity. *Kaspar's Death*, slight as it may have been, was Bergman's nuclear creative deed from which the larger consequences would follow. It was his projection of a moral scheme of things to which he would make perennial return, a theatrical scheme of just this order—a morality, a farcical interlude, a fairytale—used as an *entr'acte*, a play-within-a-film, whereby he would appeal nostalgically to the naïve, enduring microcosms of a fading belief.

At the chronological moment, however, this modest pantomime play was crucial in Bergman's career for reasons more pragmatic. Its production was received with generous approval by its limited audience and by a critic on *Svenska Dagbladet*, who found especially poignant and macabre the moment when Kaspar, sitting in his grave, sings to drive away fear. As a direct result of this press notice, Bergman received a telephone call from the enterprising Stina Bergman,[8] then head of the script department at Svensk Filmindustri. Would Mr. Bergman be interested in submitting a story idea for a film? Yes, he certainly would be. The sequel to this invitation from SF, after their rejection of seven other manuscripts he offered, was their acceptance of his story *Hets*, or *Torment*, to be directed by Alf Sjöberg.

The Background

For almost fifteen years before *Torment* introduced Swedish film to a limited international audience, there had been an interrupted but never wholly cancelled effort to restore the art which had been lost when Victor Sjöstrom broke his own stride as a director by going abroad and when Mauritz Stiller emigrated, returning only to die. The crying need for Swedish cinema, after this long dark night of twenty years of anonymity and a level of production rarely above mediocrity was a genius, or at least a talent, who would reconnect Swedish film expression with that of the world at large, then being inadequately aped in a succession of dreary farces, bucolic cliché and uninspired adaptations of regional literature: a need for somebody who would raise the essentially provincial heritage to the status of an image instead of a local anecdote.

It goes without saying too emphatically, perhaps, that the scope of a country's subject matter is determined by the character of its social environment and its cultural saturation. And the quality of whatever experience an artist finds in that environment or recalls from a cultural memory will, of necessity, be distorted creatively by the imposition of his personality and the resources of his medium. Art arises authentically when experience is transfigured as, from the flash of observation, the artist creates a style. The unconscious struggle of the Swedish filmmaker in the Thirties and Forties, waged in a cultural atmosphere of low vitality, if of high mental disturbance, and a minimum of social nuance, was the struggle to discover a style independent of any earlier achievement and consonant with a uniquely Swedish subject. Sjöstrom and Stiller had long ago made such a discovery, but in these decades of Social Democracy, increased urbanization, and a tempting international film market the force of their so-called National Romanticism was diminishing, especally among those who considered themselves progressively in tune with the obligation to inhabit and express a more complex world. The development of filmmaking nearly everywhere else in the years when Swedish studios had been asleep offered a beguiling profusion of subjects and treatment for those who could learn how to duplicate them. Hence, the Thirties in Sweden are marked by cinematic false alarms, by opportunities unrecognized or not followed up. Quite simply, the problem was deficiency of manpower. Two men had put Swedish film on the map to begin with and until those two were matched by others of comparable talent there could be no film industry to meet the requirements of any but a local consumption. Sweden was a small country with no pictorial tradition and with a theatre establishment that characteristically thought of film as, after all, an auxiliary and inferior art. The probability of a cinematic renaissance must have seemed remote! From a later perspective it is perhaps self-evident to see that given the talent for executing it the authentic Swedish area of expression was indeed to be found somewhere between Stiller's *Sir Arne's Treasure* and Sjöstrom's *The Phantom Carriage*—between, that is to say, a species of Nordic primitivism and the earnest climate of reformist realism in the contemporary society.

Surveying the period chronologically, with close attention to its several productions, there is no doubt that a fruitful direction was first dramatically indicated by Alf Sjöberg's film debut in 1929 with the silent film, *Der Starkaste* (*The Strongest*). A young theatre director who had put himself to school under such continental influences as the Habbimah Theatre of Israel, which he had seen on tour, German Expressionism, and Soviet Russian innovations, Sjöberg proved that he could confidently handle the raw material of a Nordic adventure story and at the same time evince an uncommon mastery of composition and dynamic continuity. The story of *The Strongest*, of no great moment, concerns the rivalry and eventual rapprochement of two men who want the same woman, enacted against the background of an Arctic expedition. What is notable in the film even today is the combination of formal values and the tang of documentary. The many occupational details are alive; Sjöberg succeeded in capturing the rhythm of manual activity: of woodcutting operations, haying, casting-off ship, rowing, and of a bear hunt over the ice floes. On the verge of sound film, however, with international models of professed sophistication to overtake, Swedish film interests were not taken by the elemental flavour of Sjöberg's movie. They evidently missed as well the integral power in Sjöberg's treatment of an initially unpromising scenario. Since it was not then the custom, as it is frequently today under the auspices of the Swedish Film Institute, to hand 100,000 kronor to an eager apprentice (eagerness is often the most conspicuous qualification) with the injunction, "Make a second film!", Alf Sjöberg returned to the theatre for another decade. Rune Waldekranz,[9] whose authority on this subject is incontestable, believes that this hiatus in Sjöberg's career was a serious impediment to his sustained development as a film director; henceforth, Sjöberg was under stress of translating a theatre-trained sensibility to meet the demands of moviemaking. The strain is nearly always evident in Sjöberg's films, magnificent as some of them are. He succeeded splendidly in his *Miss Julie* of 1951; twice before he had been more than equal to the task, but not again, not wholly, in any of the films he has made since the early Fifties. Nevertheless, his position in Swedish cinema between 1940 and 1952 was unrivalled, even when his lesser contributions are taken into account. Arne Sucksdorff, in a special genre, was his only peer.

A brilliant curiosity appeared in 1931; the film, *En Natt* (*One Night*) was directed by Gustav Molander in a style almost wholly derived from the Soviet shock-cutting technique perfected during the Twenties.

Molander's roots were in the Stiller-Sjöberg era as a script-writer; he had been a director as well as a scenarist since 1923, adapting and re-adapting the novels of Selma Lagerlöf and in general imbued with the spirit of the older masters. He is a curious case, for he bridged the old and the new Swedish film, in some instances creatively, but he seems to have had no style of his own, turning out a half-dozen notable films under the authority of someone else's conviction. *One Night* is to a great extent the product of a young man, Gösta Hellstrom, who had studied the Soviet film at close range and, as production adviser to Molander, had impressed the veteran with his enthusiasm for the method of Eisenstein and his experimental contemporaries. While it is easy to disparage the derived treatment and melodramatic content of this film, it should be acknowledged that under the circumstances it was a phenomenal case of filmmaking in the context of the early sound movie. No film made in Sweden at that period, before the return of Sjöberg, had anything like its pace, its adroit metaphors, or its handsomely graded light effects. What makes it seem rather phantasmal when viewed today is, I think, its expression of a technique perfected for the symphonic film within the limits of a personal anecdote. The period story is one of those love-and-duty gambits. An officer is allowed a night's leave to see his woman who is distant miles away, but he must return to his regiment, word of honor, by the next morning. In the teeth of many contrived difficulties, he manages to do so.

The montage organization, the cutting-for-contrast, the witness points of the camera, the arbitrary selection of closeup details, all are reminiscent of Eisenstein or Pudovkin, and the sound trickery may have come from Fritz Lang or from the Hitchcock of *Blackmail*. A few entries from my notes will suffice to indicate the style. "Cut from scream of train whistle to overhead shot of couple embracing . . ." "tickertape machine announcing War becomes the sound of a train . . ." "tilted shots of railway tracks, crescendo of soldiers' song, abrupt cut to bridge being blown up . . ." "a cantering horse implied by closeup of rider's leg, only . . ." "a love scene in which faces and hands are the principal features" (an economy to which, one wishes, more directors would return) . . . "soldiers dancing to carnival music, cut to rifles aimed at a target, the target bulls-eyed and a painted soldier-effigy raising its arm to blow a bugle which, in turn, reminds the hero of his dwindling parole . . ." "direct shot, when hero is hiding in the woods, of his pursuers reflected in the camera lens."

Naturally, this idiom could not easily have been acquired by directors taking their first empirical lessons in the arts of the camera and the cutting room. Nor was it compatible with the Swedish way of viewing things, much the more likely reason for its not being adopted in even a modified fashion before Sjöberg incorporated the method upon his return. Soviet montage as a rationalized method was designed to illustrate in film-narrative form the ethos of the Soviet political dialectic; inevitably it suited film that concerned mass movement and counter-movement or the antagonistic interplay of individual characters and social forces. Except in the work of Sjöberg, whose international curiosity was professionally grounded, if not always temperamentally appropriate to his immediate subject, this style of antithetical cutting in a rapid tempo was never found sympathetic by Swedish filmmakers. One can only say, in reference to *One Night,* that it might have served as an object lesson, if nothing else, in the making of a movie, instead of filmed theatre. It was not so utilized. Hellström, after making a very sharp little film with a trick ending, called *Tango,* died of tuberculosis at the age of thirty—a tragic curtailment of a highly gifted young artist.

If you have read histories of Swedish film, especially those published in the Fifties, you will have encountered references to certain films of the Thirties reputed to have marked a turning point. Among them are usually included *Ett Brott, Swedenhielms, Valborgsmassafton,* and *Intermezzo.* Overevaluation is the chief professional hazard of all close readers of a period or genre in art. If you keep your eyes riveted day after day, film after film, to a continuity within a limited period, you are bound to observe minute improvements and infinitesimal felicities barely visible to the eye of someone who sees your sample discovery out of context. A moment of acting here, a piece of business there, the lighting a degree more subtle, the dialogue a shade less banal can seem revolutionary to the cataloguer who has neglected his cross-references, who has in fact forgotten that he's all alone in a tiny room with a viewola and a filing cabinet. In 1936, for example, when Molander's *Intermezzo,* a quasi-Hollywood triangle story with "continental" settings and dreadful histrionics, was in Sweden considered the brilliant new thing, Capra's

Mr. Deeds Goes to Town was Hollywood's film of the year. It was no marvel, but a more vital approximation of social actuality than the synthetics of *Intermezzo*. The New Deal documentaries were under way with *The Plow that Broke the Plains;* in Europe, Alfred Hitchcock attempted the Conrad underworld in *Sabotage;* Sacha Guitry made his egocentric and radically inventive *The Story of a Cheat,* and Leni Riefensthal produced that sinister documentary masterpiece, *Triumph of the Will.* Comparison is a brutal if indispensable instrument when recapitulating the history of an art form. The truth is that with her first efforts in the sound film, Sweden retrogressed more noticeably than most countries. For years, *Ett Brott* (*A Crime*) was considered a milestone in Swedish filmmaking, because it dramatized a public scandal with which every informed filmgoer was familiar and morbidly concerned. The dialogue of the film was laudably adult, the main roles were harrowingly acted, at least, for the period. Yet seen today it is a shocking example of the kind of closet drama to which the early sound film was for too long confined—static, cumbersome, dramatically stilted, with the camera frozen at sound range.

Unquestionably the Swedish movie moved again under the dispensation of Alf Sjöberg, who came back in 1940 and before 1942 made three films—*Flowering Time, They Staked Their Lives, Home from Babylon*—which, while certainly not memorable otherwise introduced to Swedish film the art of what one should call Baroque movie-making, assimilated by Sjöberg from Soviet Russian and German precedent. These films coincided with the outbreak of the Second World War, Sweden's established neutrality, and the acute anxiety consequent upon that position. They reflected Sjöberg's personal tendency to prove he wasn't confined to the proscenium arch of theatre by overstating every opportunity he could contrive for manneristic angles, symbolic placement, and supercharged energies of transition even when the content resisted such treatment. They reflected as well his militant sympathy for certain political struggles raging outside Sweden. Accordingly, there is something strained and unreal about these films, the agony of the nonparticipant; their intensity suggests the histrionic sympathy and guilt feeling of the romantic revolutionary who thunders his case far from the field of struggle. They illustrate pertinently Yeats's definition of rhetoric as "will trying to do the work of imagination.'' And of course they are initially characteristic of, if superior aesthetically to, most Swedish films produced during and immediately after the war years. They were the protest products of what shall henceforth be referred to here as spectator neurosis.

If we suspend such considerations while reviewing early Sjöberg, we can still readily grant that these films were technically adventurous; they echoed, less slavishly than *One Night*, the Soviet film grammar (Pudovkin was Sjöberg's favored Russian director) and they incorporated the psychological overtones of the German style, exemplified in the work of G. W. Pabst, F. W. Murnau, Von Sternberg, and perhaps the early films of Max Ophuls. Within the following years of emerging Swedish talent it was virtually impossible for anyone in Swedish studios to be unaware of Sjöberg's example. To emulate it was another thing; the new directors were either insufficiently versed or unsuited by temperament to utilise the Sjöberg film language: the art of decisive cutting, the bold use of architectural space and of accentuated forms in the picture frame, the sinuously moving camera, the enlisting of scenic objects as hyperbolic comments or as undisguised symbols. Eventually one or another of these elements became standard usage. In the Swedish film of the Forties we cannot be sure whether the improvements increasingly visible (with whatever hazards attended) were derived from Sjöberg directly or from the films of John Ford, Julien Duvivier, Jean Renoir, Gustav Machaty, Alfred Hitchcock, or Marcel Carne, all of which were, depending on the susceptibility of those subject to them, in vogue. All we can say for certain is that it's highly unlikely for inexperienced film-makers to have been unconscious of the single most professional talent in their midst.

If we are looking for new determinants of a national style, the key year in Swedish film was 1942, when Molander made *Rid I Natt* (*Ride Tonight*) and Sjöberg crowned his experimental phase with *Himlaspelet* (*The Road to Heaven*). *Ride Tonight*, adapted from a novel by Vilhelm Moberg, projected a theme of tyranny from seventeenth-century Swedish history in the fond hope that an analogy with the contemporary battle against Hitler would thereby be felt. It is a period piece which most film critics have tended to laugh off or to relegate as a circumstantial

product. Circumstantial it was and from that angle perhaps not altogether convincing, for a rural insurgence of Smålanders, oppressed by
the baliffs of Queen Christina, is hardly of the same stuff as war against
the Third Reich and its allies. What the film could boast, positively,
beside a well-knit plot and, save from the actresses!, many credible
characterizations, was a lustre never so confidently achieved by
Molander in his earlier films. The film was a poem of northern darkness,
shot through with pastoral touches which yet remained subordinate to
the stern drift of the narrative. It was Sjöstrom and Stiller, preserved
in Molander's memory; the Moberg story gave body to the opportunity
and the atmosphere was in no small measure the contribution of the
cinematographer, Åke Dahlquist, who had served Molander and Hellström admirably in *One Night* and who, by 1942, had thirty films to his
name.

In spare outline, the film is about the refusal of an obdurate peasant,
Svedje, to pay excessive taxes to the German squire representing Christina. Branded as an outlaw and forced to hide in the rock-and-forest
wilderness, he is hunted down by his own neighbors and killed like a
dog by the professional hangman, with whom he had once refused to
drink. His fate after the fact inspires the community to postponed
rebellion; a flaming cross is sent by relay through the back-country,
signifying *Ride Tonight*. This heroic denouement barely mitigates the
murder of Svedje by "neutrals," nor the incidental execution of his
betrothed, thought to be a witch. There are radical weaknesses in this
film, principally in the love story and in the handling of the musical
score. These are more than redressed, it seems to me, by the generally
firm sense of place and people, by the unsparing evaluation of Svedje's
fellowmen as bone-headed, superstitious traitors. Many visual touches
in this film, such as strained sunlight on a clearing in the woods, shots
of a log-house interior framed by a low, heavy-lintel doorway, and a
portrait composition of the dour executioner wearing a flapped headgear
to cover the place where his ears should be, strongly suggest a provenance
for similar effects and closeups in Bergman's *The Seventh Seal*. Since
the elements are common to the setting of both films, this may well be
merely coincidence. In any case, *Ride Tonight* can be seen as a forceful

precedent of the woodland mode to which, each in its own way, both *The Seventh Seal* and *The Virgin Spring* belong.

It is overshadowed quite by Sjöberg's *The Road to Heaven*. Tiresomely exploited today for the tourist, the north-central province of Dalarna has long been noted through its traditional houses, dances, costumes and customs for the conservative retention of old folkways. Rune Lindstrom, a very fine actor and writer in his prime—his active period in film attained its peak with the best scripts ever supplied to Arne Mattsson, in the early Fifties—had created a play to be staged outdoors in Dalarna annually, derived from themes in nineteenth-century wall-paintings of the region. These paintings depicted Old Testament stories with a local flavor; the characters were dressed in the Dalarna style of the period and earlier. Lindstrom's play has the simple narrative quality of a morality or a ballet, modestly designed for the resources of community staging. Matt, a wide-eyed but quite spirited peasant, takes the road to Heaven in order to upbraid the Lord (an old Dalarna pastor) with sundry human ills and evil visitations. On the way he encounters numerous Biblical characters, is exposed to age-old human vices and betrayals, and, at the end, is received by the Lord in his stovepipe hat and reunited with his sweetheart in a super-Dalarna cottage.

When filming this ingenuous story, on the basis of a scenario supplied by Lindstrom, the first thing Sjöberg did, inevitably, was to baroque-ize the story material. His film is epic in scope and in manner. The simple pilgrimage over Dalarna hill and dale becomes a fantastic journey through some of the most voluptuous episodes of Biblical story, during which Matt is transformed from a gullible peasant, bewildered by the fatal events which start him on his quest (a scourging drought and the burning alive of his sweetheart as the witch who is responsible for various local calamities) into a pitiful victim of the worldly temptations put in his path and finally into a monster of avarice who acquires power and riches in the most dastardly tradition of capitalistic venality. Consequently, when he meets the Lord face to face, he is in no position to question the origins of cupidity and injustice among men.

The film is a tour de force: a spectacular display of realism, bewitching pastoral conceits, anachronisms deftly handled. Into it Sjöberg put everything he then knew about filmmaking, which was considerable. The result, free of quasi-political tensions, was a completely liberated territory for Swedish film. I would still include *The Road to Heaven* among the most sheerly beautiful films ever made, not overlooking, in the years that followed, Cocteau's *Beauty and the Beast,* a dozen Japanese films, nor, on related ground, the wilderness films of Arne Sucksdorff. To Swedish critics in 1942 its splendor was not self-evident and the public was not unanimously charmed. While some were impressed by the scenic magnitude and the disciplined sweep of the crowd scenes—a sequence of revelry at Solomon's court and a mad torchlit sleigh ride over the ice was generally admired—most seemed unaware that here was the most dynamic step taken in Swedish film since the days of Stiller. Many resented the simple folk elements being expanded to fit Sjöberg's inordinate purposes. Those who in any case were bored by regional themes, preferring to see Swedish editions of Soviet ideology, French pessimism or American big-town lowlife, regarded the film as irrelevant to the hour. Of course it was, if one is judging film by the pertinence it has to one's immediate history. For some time the attitude toward this film was begrudging; only within the last eight years, when it has been revised on the television for a larger and more variously conditioned audience, have some of the younger critics recognized its visible loveliness. However it may suit anyone's prejudice to dismiss it, *The Road to Heaven* stands today as the film, if one had to choose a single example, with which Swedish cinema craft was redefined in a context rootedly Swedish. Sjöberg pointed the way for other filmmakers to find in their own surroundings, whether their treatment was to be realistic or fanciful is beside the point, the substance for their inspiration.

In 1942, however, other factors were mandatory. The War was on, life-and-death issues were being engaged, outside Sweden at any rate. Other filmmaking countries were suffering from limited production opportunities. Swedish film producers were anxious to contribute internationally acceptable films to a limited, if profitable, market, and at the same time supply the home audience which was expanding precisely at the moment when the imports were being curtailed. Now, for export purposes, historical and legendary material within a sylvan setting, even if as competently managed as in *Ride Tonight* or as dazzling as in *The Road to Heaven,* was not likely to be a profitable commodity. Further, by 1943, the Axis powers had made clear at the Venice International Film Festival and through more direct agencies that films from Sweden about the War, even by implication, or those likely to incite revolutionary sentiments, were not tolerable. Swedish filmmakers tried to supplement their literary sources with city-based melodrama, with Social-Democrat treatments of back-country life,[10] and, increasingly, with excursions into psychopathology, crime, and crises of religious belief.

Hampe Faustman, over-long hailed as a director of promise who in fact never qualified for international status, made *Night in the Harbor* in 1943, a dockside crime story of seamen on the loose; in 1944, *The Girl and the Devil*, a witchcraft tale far inferior to the achievements of Molander and Sjöberg; in 1945 a locally situated version, not very inventive, of Dostoievski's *Crime and Punishment*. Hasse Ekman made an uncertain beginning with a war film, a political film, and a gloomy drama which in point of departure resembled Noel Coward's *Brief Encounter*, filmed two years later by David Lean, before settling into a sequence of films largely inspired by deviated mental behavior. Arne Mattsson left engineering for film-making, and before striking his native vein of tough-men-in-the-wilderness scored an early *succès de scandale* by filming an exposé novel based on fact, concerning a prominent Swedish citizen who had been railroaded into an insane asylum. Two of the most extraordinarily successful films of the period were grounded in religious idealism (the Lutheran ethos) tinctured, respectively, with madness and fanatical abnegation; these were Gustav Molander's *The Word*, 1943, and Anders Henrikson's *Blood and Fire*, 1945. The former, based on a play by the Dane, Kaj Munk, received a more spacious, open-air treatment than Carl-Theodor Dreyer's filming of the same work in 1955. Rune Lindstrom, who had played Mats in *The Road to Heaven*, gave another of his impressive, idiosyncratic performances; his ecstatic pastor was a being all air and flame. The Henrikson film, about a Christ-like Salvation Army officer, was distinguished solely by its director's acting; it was otherwise refulgent with heightened shots of rain-glistening pavements and every window-transom was a crucifix in memory, no doubt, of *The Informer*.[11]

If Ingmar Bergman saw many of these films, during the very years when he was in transit from theatre to moviemaking, his attention to them was much more likely to have been casual than focused, since he was subject to so many other influences. He denies any influence from them. A corpus of Swedish film existed, this much one can say. Necessarily, his own could not have been widely divergent from the demands of the film industry nor from the climate of things which he shared with his contemporaries. This climate was naturally not conveyed by cinema, alone. Normally, the movies represent but a shadow, or a popularization, a shadow of a shadow, of a country's guiding beliefs. Since the war years were those in which Bergman entered theatre, then film-making, the mental atmosphere of the time was contagiously modified by the international situation and by the reaction toward it of those articulate in the areas he inhabited of theatre and of literary talk. The parental figures, Strindberg and Hjalmar Bergman, prevailed. But fashionable during the stress of the Forties were a number of poets who projected the guilt-feeling of Swedish neutrality or, commonly, a reflexive desire to become completely neutral, metaphysically neutral, with no quarter given, one infers, to political imperatives or the implications of history and with no consolation forthcoming from nature, philosophy, art, religion, or their friends. Contingently motivated by the claustrophobia of the day, such literature did not differ radically from its predecessors; it was the vehicle of a characteristically Swedish amazement at the operations of history and the given conditions of human existence.

The spokesmen of this attitude came to be known as the *Fyrtiotalists,* that is, the Forty-ists. Karl Vennberg, who, with Erik Lindegren, published a *Fyrtiotalist* anthology in 1947, probably summarized their viewpoint concisely when he declared that to live was "to choose between the indifferent and the impossible." A comparable alienation was expressed in the title of Lindegren's 1946 publication, *The Man Without a Way,* which included verse written six years earlier. The most extreme symptom of the movement—or should one say stasis?—was the brief revulsion of Stig Dagerman, who wrote a handful of overwrought stories and a play which were outcries of perplexity and nausea, before his suicide at thirty-one. It has always seemed to me that Dagerman's essential tragedy, and in Sweden he is not unique in this respect, consisted in his inability to distinguish for himself the prison which was Sweden from the prison he believed to be the world. "To admit one's terror is the first step towards gaining a victory over it,'' he announced. He was unequal to his own challenge (Bergman has followed this cue rather more successfully) and one wonders if his literature would today in Sweden be valued so highly if he had not become a martyr to his own suffocating and uncomprehending anxiety. Much of the contemporary inhibition and resistance was a heritage from the spiritual defeatism that characterizes Swedish literature; much, to be sure, was induced by the predicament of a country full of people sitting under a blackout, with nobody to fight but themselves.

Bergman was too young to qualify as even an associate member of the *Fyrtiotalists*. However, on the perimeters of university circles and in theatre greenrooms he would have been exposed to their masochistic doctrines. Ten films, a half-dozen plays and five years later, when the poets themselves were learning another refrain, Bergman appeared to be recapitulating their earlier burden in a context where it was no longer urgent; he was a belated *Fryrtiotalist*. In this he was not alone; nor does his lagging infection wholly account for the tortured content of his plays and early films, to say nothing of the later ones. While the terrified proclamations of the Forties cannot be overlooked as contributing factors in Bergman's more suicidal self-expression, factors quite as indelible had already been established: further back, deeper down, and closer to home. When a man, seriously dedicated, writes his first books or makes his first films he is the sum of all the forces which have made him, but these forces are not consciously available to him in expressive forms. Immaturity, restriction of his liberty to express himself, self-indulgence —any of these may inhibit or divert his acknowledging what the forces may be. He is not prepared to recognize what in his experience is essential and what may be a subterfuge for evading the subject peculiar to him. That subject may be growing inside him, yet he will live with it for years without being able to give it clear expression. In short, his art suffers because he doesn't himself know who he really is; it suffers just as much if he too strenuously makes this a primary question, with a blind eye for all those other mortals and toward a world in which he is of no more account than a blade of grass. This was certainly Bergman's case: an overweening preoccupation with his own pains and an overwhelming innocence of their real source. If it may be said that his total production has been a nagging adventure in self-revelation, the earlier films and plays scarcely transcend that definition, whereas the later films are often works of art.

The real sources of Ingmar Bergman's films were in himself, but what is a self? An accumulation of temperament around the living cell of a culture? The sources of the Bergman films were in his local Swedish inheritance, with all that implies of external conditioning and personal reaction. The matter of the films, whatever else came to be included, represents the strategies with which he met the consequences of his inheritance.

THE DEVIL TO PLAY

Before the gates of Stockholm, in 1542, a company of players performs an interlude depicting the Creation as having been a mere sport for a minor demiurge who calls himself God. His creatures pass their lives in a state of agitated ignorance until given the apple of knowledge by Lucifer, whereby they learn that they are playthings, victims, animated for the amusement of a higher power. The sum of their life on earth is pain. To countermand God, the Devil provides them with the liberating gift of death. God, in turn, retaliates with gifts of illusion to keep them alive. The most potent of these illusions is Love.

The play does not delight the spectators. They break it up and overturn the stage.

If I were to claim that the above was an outline for a film scenario never written, there is scarcely a knowledgeable reader who would not assume that its author was Ingmar Bergman. In fact it is the summary of a work by August Strindberg, the epilogue to his second version of *Master Olof*, 1877. That Bergman read and/or saw this play and henceforth adopted not only the message but the form of its epilogue for his own purpose, with no previous attraction toward such subject matter, is far from my intention to suggest. I trust I have made

"I was not wholly alone with my command, for there was that stranger in my cabin".

Joseph Conrad, *The Secret Sharer*

clear that Bergman's complusion to question God, fear the Devil, confuse each with the other and with parental authority had arisen early in his life. I simply find it to be a striking coincidence that this play-as-annex-to-a-play should so markedly bear the accent of Bergman's preoccupations. Since numerous coincidences of this sort may be disclosed I want briefly to engage the Strindberg confluence, a better term than influence, because it is crucial, and briefly since it is so obvious. To hunt for analogies, in the plays and films of Bergman, with the plays, stories, and biographies of Strindberg may well become a future assignment for those who write Ph.D theses to prove what is baldly evident to everyone else; it will be like demonstrating the presence of Bergson in Proust or classifying the ironies in Thomas Hardy. It is too easy. Given the personalities, the circumstances and the interests of these two men, it would only be surprising if there were no visible resemblances in their work. All the same the principal life-gestures of each are so startling in their similarity that one is tempted to believe in the operation of the uncanny, either that or to suspect Bergman of *willing* himself to repeat every stage of Strindberg's distraught, creative journey.

Both Strindberg and Bergman were brought up in an atmosphere of

Swedish Lutheranism which all but smothered them, against which they reacted militantly and from which they were unable to liberate themselves. It has been carelessly pointed out that Strindberg's final plays show him to have been in quest of God, whereas Bergman in his later phase is busy rejecting Him. Yet we have all read Francis Thompson's "The Hound of Heaven". To flee Him down the nights and down the days is to acknowledge that there is a Him from whom to flee.

Both Strindberg and Bergman are notorious for the self-crucifying ambivalence of their relationships with women. We need not pretend astonishment or superiority (pardonably, we may laugh out loud from time to time!); their problems in that direction are far from being unique. What is unique, or at least what imposes itself in the art forms of each man, is the overbearing intensity with which he has expressed the problem—August Strindberg, with misogyny almost unsurpassed, Bergman with a degree of solicitation so morbid as to make us wonder if it might not conceal a secretly rooted enmity.

Both Strindberg and Bergman wrote principally for the theatre (speaking broadly, film is theatre). Hence, they were encouraged by the medium, even more than would have been the case if they had been primarily writers of novels, to appeal to an audience for vindication of their agonies and at special moments of stress to advertise themselves, if not directly in the plays and films, by way of manifestoes, program notes, essays for the defense, court proceedings, interviews, public belligerence toward the critic, or whatever. Traditionally, drama has been the most impersonal mode of fiction. Strindberg, more than anyone before George Bernard Shaw, made it an instrument of the ego; and Bergman shares with Fellini and Jean-Luc Godard the dubious distinction of having transformed the most public of the arts into a confessional lined with mirrors.

Both Strindberg and Bergman exercised their talent in a country obdurately disinclined to listen to either of them until largely forced to do so by foreign critical attention. However, Bergman's struggle is in no way comparable to that of Strindberg, neither for recognition nor in any other area, and the deduction then follows that unconsciously Bergman would have preferred to have Strindberg's miseries, obstacles, and provocations in order to ratify the volume of his protests. Among many ironies that Bergman is unlikely to perceive is that he behaves like a genius who has been wantonly neglected, while actually he has probably had more attention paid to him than any personage in the history of movies except Charles Chaplin and Greta Garbo!

Finally, I had better say recently, Bergman's transition around 1960 to a type of "chamber-music" film, increasingly subjective and, from time and setting, dislocated, bears a close resemblance to Strindberg's terminal sequence, that of forms of theatre which only with difficulty the theatre could contain, forms which baffled his contemporaries even more than his preceding output, forms in which he enshrined the antipathies, fears, and self-aggrandizements of a lifetime.[12]

To return to the Strindberg item I summarized above (I could have chosen any of a dozen equally apt), my belief is that since Bergman must have been aware of that epilogue long before entering theatre himself it probably confirmed a tendency already distinct in his preferences. If you are sympathetically addicted to a special treatment of the human estate in art, in Bergman's case the Morality and its related forms, and if you arrive at the brink of professional life with a pronounced attitude toward its contradictions for which you are seeking the appropriate vehicle, you will naturally find encouragement in the fact that a great predecessor has anticipated your own proclivities. At the same time I am not minimizing the presence of Strindbergian echoes in Bergman's work. For the first ten years of his career it is impossible to avoid. What I believe to be more interesting than his annexation of any given motif in Strindberg is the adroitness with which he eventually turned it to personal account and the stages by which he liberated himself from the dependence—from the presence, never; from dependence, yes.

The omnipresence of the Devil or his surrogates in Bergman's world is a more complex business. To rest content with the explanation that he retained a conventional element from a fearsome childhood experience and thereafter simply played sets of variations is far too ingenuous. In a statement made in 1958, Bergman recurred to that childhood story, with a fresh emphasis on one of its components.

The devil was an early acquaintance, and in the child's mind there was a need to personify him. This is where my magic lantern came in. It consisted of a small metal box with a carbide lamp—I can still remember the smell of the hot metal—and coloured glass slides: Red Riding Hood and the Wolf. . . . And the Wolf was the Devil, without horns but with a tail and a gaping red mouth, strangely real yet incomprehensible, a picture of wickedness and temptation on the flowered wall of the nursery.

If he had already made the Devil's acquaintance in the frescoes of country churches, why was there further "a need to personify him," to, indeed, substitute him for the wolf, especially if he represented "wickedness and temptation"? Without cavil, we can all answer that up to a point: evil is attractive because it is vivid. And if he was prepared to make capital of the creature with his magic lantern, why was he so upset when faced with the same Wolf in Alf Sjöberg's youthful production of the tale? The short answer may be that Sjöberg's wolf was more grandiose, hence inducing a traumatic shock. Actually, the question is necessarily rhetorical, for one can never be sure if Bergman has not unconsciously rearranged the sequences in his growing-up to make their progression more dramatic. All of us are histrionic some of the time.

One thing at least is clear. The growing Bergman was less anxious to banish the Devil than to incorporate him, to visualize him, a strategy whereby moral discomfort was remedied by aesthetic adjustment. There followed a nearly life-long compulsion which first assumed public shape when in his early twenties Bergman created, for a series of sketchy stories he published in minor magazines, a "Jack" figure, suggested by Jack the Ripper. This Jack appeared again at the crime-serial level in his first film; then, still so named, as the author's alter ego in his second play, which was prepared but not produced, in 1943. Naïve in its conception and in its stagecraft, if one may judge from the available synopses, *Jack Among the Actors*[13] is a more important thematic crucible than *Kaspar's Death*, for it introduced the Merger Principle of God and Devil which, whatever its personal origin, was to supply Bergman with a crude dualistic cosmology in nearly all his early efforts for theatre and film.

Kaspar, the Swedish name for Punch, and Jack are now combined as Jack Kasparsson. This character, young and damned evidently, joins a theatre troupe supervised by a "director" whom none of the company has ever met. Finally confronted with this awesome personage, at the

end of the play, Jack asks him, apprehensively, if he is not God. "Why
not?", counters the Director. "I thought it wouldn't be a bad idea
to control things, create a little world for a few people. . . . You must
admit that I've succeeded." Jack nervously agrees that he has indeed.
The Director preens.

> And I have sat there pulling the strings. . . . And the people have hopped
> and danced like puppets for my amusement. . . . I'm a unique director. . . .
> But everybody is a little bit of a director and has his own little stage. The
> difference is that I am unusually human . . . If there is or ever has been a
> God, he was a criminal. You people pitifully cry out, "God is kind!" Like a
> call for help because you know there is no God! I think He committed suicide
> when He saw what a universe He had created. . . . Well, I shall die soon.
> But I was great while I lived. Great! Powerful! I shall be remembered by
> many. I was their God and their Devil. I was great and I was ugly. . . . Good
> night-my friend!

Jack is left alone on an ominously darkening stage, with thunder and
lightning that increase as Jack cries out his last imploring speech. "God
in Heaven, help me! *You who must be somewhere.* . . . you must help
me . . . not because I deserve help, not for any reason except that I can't
stand it . . . *Help me to find a way out.* Let it be lighter so that I can see
something and understand!"[14]

The numerous transformations and fissions involved here are quite
extraordinary. First, Bergman creates a half-devil figure, Jack; then he
confronts him with a Director who plays God (recall that Bergman himself had played a God-character in *Outward Bound,* which he directed).
The director next announces that God is dead and leaves Jack to his
doom. A creature half-God, half-Devil, by his own boast, functions finally
as Death. Confused theology it appears to be and it recurs, with variants,
early and late in Bergman's *oeuvre.* In a more articulate guise it may
be seen in *The Seventh Seal,* where the Knight also addresses his questions to Death.

We should try to distinguish, whenever possible, a theatrical solution
from a private strategy. For the moment I am trying to uncover the
provenance of Bergman's flirtation with the diabolic, not his sophistication of it in his matured art. Something of the psychological sequence
may be inferred. The climax of Bergman's creeping disbelief in divine
mercy which had so shattered his teleology at the age of nineteen was evidently too dismaying for him to bear without drastic editing. Through-

out his growing years, he has confided, he was recurrently visited by sensations of utter nothingness, as if a great black emptiness were settling around him. Among sensitive natures who feel their egoes threatened by a neutral immensity, or by a universe of rivals, this is not an unusual visitation. The feeling is naturally amplified by the shock of a major frustration, by a crisis of guilt, or by the loss of someone loved. Typically, the experience precedes a religious conversion or reversal, or an access of creative energy. Luther's fit in the choir and Dostoievsky's first epileptic attack are spectacular instances of a condition otherwise not uncommon. D. H. Lawrence has described with beautiful simplicity an ordeal of this nature, at a later age than that of Bergman's conflict, which followed the death of his mother.

> Then, in that year, for me everything collapsed, save the mystery of death, and the haunting of death in life. I was twenty-five, and from the death of my mother, the world began to dissolve around me, beautiful, iridescent, but passing away substanceless. Till I almost dissolved away myself and was very ill: when I was 26.
> Then slowly the world came back: or I myself returned; but to another world. . . . I used to feel myself at times haunted by something, and a little guilty about it, as if it were an abnormality. Then the haunting would get the better of me, and the ghost would suddenly appear, in the shape of a usually rather incoherent poem.[15]

For Bergman, one might add, the ghost would appear in the shape of a rather incoherent play or movie. Meanwhile, unable to live with the absence of God, therefore with Nothing, he substituted the active presence of Satan. The next step, if despair was to be effectually routed, was to *identify* himself with the demon, to make him in any case his familiar —an authentic Lutheran solution if one remembers how vividly the great Protestant testified to seeing devils perched on his window-sill and at the foot of his bed. Bergman has certainly employed this persona in excess of the sanction given either by Lutheran idiosyncracy or artistic license; for years he signed his name with a small fork-tailed devil beneath it. As late as 1960 he was still expressing, if with forced jocularity, a fellow-feeling for the creature in *The Devil's Eye* and in Stravinsky and Auden's *The Rake's Progress,* which he staged in 1961.

Again, the shadow of Strindberg looms on the wall of Bergman's cave. That troubled soul complained constantly of the Powers (*makterna*) by which he was importuned—no passing metaphor; under stress he felt them to be bodily present—but there is good reason for presuming that he was not altogether averse to their company. It should not be conjectured, however, that Strindberg and Bergman had simply inherited the obsessions, together with the theology, of Martin Luther. One assumes there are thousands of Lutherans who go through life unencumbered with secret-sharers. My conviction is that the Devil was invoked by them both as a psychological defense against despair, a conviction fully confirmed by Sigmund Freud's discourse on this subject. The substance of his theory, as it applies here, is that the Devil presents himself as a saviour when the anticipated rewards of faith and virtue are seen to be groundless. If devotion to an inscrutable Good yields nothing but anguish, relief is immediate when the opposite allegiance is adopted, since the favors of the Devil can be savored without delay and tokens of his rule are everywhere apparent. In the language of psychoanalysis the Devil is the suspended super-ego, that part of the individual which permits him to violate the precepts of the active super-ego. In the religious context that super-ego is God, and if God, following the inferences of Freud and certain schools of cultural anthropology, was originally an exalted version of the father then

It requires no great analytic insight to divine that God and the Devil were originally one and the same, a single figure split into two bearing opposed characteristics. . . . *The father is thus the individual prototype of both God and the Devil.* The fact that the figure of the primal father was that of a being with unlimited potentialities of evil, bearing much more resemblance to the Devil than God, must have left an indelible stamp on all religion. (My italics.)[16]

That it left an indelible stamp on Lutherans there is no gain-saying. Russell Hope Robbins alludes to them, in his encyclopedia, as "devil oriented" and amusingly points out that in Luther's Greater Catechism the Devil is named sixty-seven times, Christ only sixty-three. If we find the Freudian argument persuasive, and obviously I do, we can with it more satisfactorily account for the histrionic role played by the Devil in Bergman's psychic life: like those dark powers of Strindberg (and somewhat more successfully) it warded off, even if it did not expel, the forces of dread. In neither man would the super-ego remain suspended. Strindberg, after circling close to insanity and toying with the notion of entering a monastery, turned in his last years to a protracted and unavailing journey toward Damascus. Bergman, having played God definitively by recreating the miracle in *The Virgin Spring*, and having surrendered the Devil to the status of a joke, has relapsed into a more bereft state than before, fumbling in the dark for that split image which will convey with final authority the schizophrenia of modern man.

There would be no pleasure in having pursued this line of inquiry if my object were merely reductive. The psychoanalyst asks what the raw material of hallucination has done to his patient and from whence did it come. The critic asks what the artist has done with the raw material of hallucination. Ingmar Bergman's evolution as an artist does not, as I see it, include a cure; it simply brings him to the stage where the silence of God and the insolence of the Devil is raised from a prosaic level of antithesis to the dignity of poetic metaphor.

Torment

If we went no further than some writers we would pounce eagerly on *Torment,* the first film bearing Bergman's name, as dramatic evidence of Satan apotheosized in the person of "Caligula," the school teacher who dominates that masterpiece of claustrophobia with his virtually criminal neurosis. When we investigate the origins of this film closely, however, we find parenthesis within parenthesis, an abundance of circumstances that frustrates our wish to construct an orderly contention. To begin with *Torment,* as one sees it, is not Bergman's creation, it is Alf Sjöberg's; this must be stated categorically. Some years ago, when Bergmania was at its height, I was sent a clipping from an American film-club publication in which the local entrepeneur announced with impenitent confidence that this was of course Bergman's film and that Sjöberg's part in it was purely nominal. The temerity with which such an opinion is delivered almost arouses admiration. In 1944, Bergman was a nobody on the protocol of Svensk Filmindustri, a precocious, perhaps promising, student-theatre director whose script (what there was of it) they had been gracious enough to recommend to the attention of the top filmmaker in the business. Bergman had no authority whatever to take a hand in or to suggest a single camera movement, assuming he had had the know-how to make suggestions to Sjöberg. Bergman was the script girl on that production and while he was gratified at having what was little more than a story idea filmed by so important a director, he was not intimidated or spellbound. Not long ago a contemporary script-girl at the studio told me she had seen the clipboard Bergman had used on this occasion. Penciled in the margins of the shooting script were such parenthetical remarks as ''Good God, this is boring!'' ''Is he going to retake that shot?'' ''When do we eat tonight?'' and so forth.

The writer I have cited above, if pardonably ignorant of the conditions under which films are made, should have been convinced by internal evidence alone that *Torment* reveals the style of Sjöberg completely from beginning to end. Every scene, every transition, every arc of movement, the whole architectural feeling and the point of sight from which the camera is leveled, the baroque repetition of formal motifs—in particular, the steps and staircases where so many critical sequences are played —all is Sjöberg. I do not mean that Bergman's contribution can be discounted; the primary conception was his, born out of fright and the spirit of revenge, as I noted earlier; the psychological blueprint was his; his the tensions and the pity implicit in the story. But the eye and hand that controlled the story-telling was Sjöberg's and in view of the fact that for many years subsequent Bergman spoke slightingly of Sjöberg's mannerisms, it is unlikely that he would have filmed the matter himself with anything like the emphasis it has. That emphasis we find inevitable, in the absence of an alternative style. Simply as a study in suspense, the film is exemplary, showing up by contrast the shallow issues to which Alfred Hitchcock's technique is commonly dedicated.

There was no explicit suggestion of the Devil in the story treatment which Alf Sjöberg was handed, on the basis of which he personally developed the character of ''Caligula.'' Ingmar Bergman's tyrant, whether modeled on an actual schoolmaster or invented by way of fidelity to Strindberg (who was subjected to just such a martinet at Clara School in Stockholm a century before!), was at least conceived without horns or a tail. He is a product of the unlived life and puritanic suppression; he tortures boys and females instead of flies. It was Sjöberg's whim, not Bergman's, prompted no doubt by spectator neurosis, the neutral's burden, that Caligula should suggest an embodiment of the

Third Reich. Stig Jarrel had previously played Hitler, wearing a comic mustache; as the Latin professor he was made up to resemble as closely as possible Himmler, chief of the Reichsfuhrer SS.

I cannot regard this as one of Sjöberg's more fortunate inspirations. Caligula, as adumbrated, needed no extra shadow of meaning to exist in his own miserable right, for his evil was as personal as his despair. If it was thought that he should be seen as a type it was an evasion to pretend he was a type produced only on foreign soil. The political implication was superfluous and misleading. Himmler was an enfranchised thug in the service of a nihilistic organization pledged, under the guise of Socialism, to destroy a traditional system, root and liberal branches. One might, to be sure, imagine Caligula serving as a spy in a fascist society, but the eventuality is not relevant to his role in the film, that of a pathetic sadist in a sealed environment where he has been given authority and found no community. Sjöberg's device in any case misfired; to this day nobody outside Sweden realizes that Jarrel was supposed to invoke Himmler and the knowledge would make no appreciable difference to his reception of the film.

Many who saw *Torment* when it was first distributed outside Sweden felt that the pedagogic tyranny represented was oddly out of date, even out of place, that the atmosphere of suffocation altogether suggested Prussia, or Central Europe under the Habsburgs, rather than Stockholm of the 1930's. Quite apart from any expressed animus toward the National Socialist regime, hence toward Germany, the impression was established by the continental-chiaroscuro style reconstructed by Sjöberg from German films of the preceding decade, such as *The Blue Angel* or *Girls in Uniform*. The imposition of this style upon what we'd otherwise call a Bergman world is precisely what gave the film its strange, taut cohesion. If Bergman had been given a free hand to direct the film himself, say, five years later, when he made *Prison,* who knows what tautologies of plot, auxiliary symbols, and supernumerary characters might have accrued? Later than that he would have no longer been interested.[17]

The derelict girl, Berthe, is a slave to Caligula for reasons, or even in what particulars, we never find out; the hint of perversions never explicitly rendered makes the film a horror tale of unusual intensity. Erik

Vidgren, the student, soon discovers that his competition with Caligula for the favors of the girl is quite futile; he has stepped into a viper's tangle of sick dependence and sadomasochism. Berthe fears and loathes the older man, yet is unable to reject him. She dies, one may as well say, of a broken spirit, killed by Caligula, certainly, if not in such a way as to make him legally responsible. Erik, partly in retaliation for his treatment by Caligula in the classroom (the teacher accused him of cribbing), charges the vile man with torturing the girl, strikes him, and is expelled from school before the final examination. Erik and the teacher are eventually fellow-sufferers, since both are left isolated by the death of Berthe. Yet when Erik, living in the girl's empty room, finds Caligula blubbering on the staircase he ignores the man's entreaties and walks out resolved if alone into a darkened world.

The later Bergman is clearly foreshadowed here in the sinister older man, the slavery of the flesh, the barriers of incomprehension. But under Sjöberg's guidance, *Torment* is classic in its composure, the development pitiless and objective. Not for many years would Bergman acquire such artistic stoicism. The scene is blocked in, the damned trinity established, the screw turned; schoolboys run up and down stairs, three people cry out, no narrator breaks the spell by whimpering that God is silent. Sjöberg's visual treatment is at the same time frugal and wonderfully fantastic. Dreadful encounters take on shape in a Hoffmanesque place of animated shadows, distorted by the low ceiling of Berthe's attic room, of endless rain streaming down the classroom windows, shutting off all belief in a merciful outdoors. Caligula paces between the desks, master mariner of a slave ship. Thunder and lightning accompany the valediction address of "Try to see her [the school] as she is, a stern nurse, an exacting mentor—perhaps not always just, yet. . . ." And again there is rainfall, reflected on the walls. Rejoicing boys hurl themselves headlong down the stairs to an equivocal freedom, an anonymous girl is buried under a lowering sky, and the last words, those of Caligula, wring from us too late a gust of compassion for him. As Erik Vidgren descends the dark staircase at Berthe's house, a kitten under his coat, Caligula, huddled in a corner, begs for absolution from the heeedless boy.

I didn't want things to be like this . . . I've been ill. . . . I didn't do it purposely! I have nobody. Four walls, bookshelves, bed, writing desk—charwoman, schoolboys, waitresses. No one cares for me . . . They're afraid of me —but always I'm afraid of myself. . . . Turn on the light—don't leave me alone. Turn on the light! *Vidgren—turn on the light!*

At this moment, as in others, the film explores a depth of loneliness and animal suffering never again fully realized in the films Bergman himself directed before *Gyklarnas Afton (The Naked Night)* in 1953.

If any doubt remains that Sjöberg was the master mind of *Torment*, one has only to compare this film with the inceptive achievements of Bergman as director. How much familiarity with the craft Bergman acquired from Sjöberg and, in the course of time, learned to utilize, remains a touchy question. Except for his statement in the preface to *Four Screenplays*—"Alf Sjöberg. . . . taught me a great deal"—which appears to be a purely political performance,[18] Bergman has never acknowledged any influence from a Swedish director younger than the late Victor Sjöstrom. He counts Sjöstrom's *The Phantom Carriage*, 1920, among vintage films which most seriously impressed him. In an interview given in 1967 he reiterated that whatever he learned about film-making came solely from talks with Sjöstrom, who was Artistic Advisor at Svensk Filmindustri in the Forties, when preparing his first film and from his sympathetic association with the late Lorens Marmstedt who produced four of his early movies. Criticism is nonetheless justified in maintaining, since works of art have their origin at a level below consciousness, that artists are infrequently aware of the sources that have prompted them.

Be that as it may, there is scant trace of Sjöberg's skilled touch in the film with which Bergman made his debut as a director. Encouraged by receiving an award for his "scenario" of *Torment*, he sumbitted five more story ideas to Svensk Filmindustri, meanwhile taking over the directorship of the Hälsingborg theatre. (It is quite likely that he was, as report has claimed, the youngest director of a state theatre in Europe at that time.) Of two stories he personally favoured, one developed, by stages, into the film, *Sommarlek;* the other featured as its leading character a perverse, sick-minded liar, a simulacrum of his diabolic Jack. Open to his proposal that he direct a film, Anders Dymling, then President of Svensk Filmindustri, was not attracted by either of Bergman's story outlines—he wanted something more wholesome, more agreeable to a wide public. Finally they agreed on Bergman's adapting a Danish play he had produced, but not personally staged, in Hälsingborg: Leck Fischer's *The Mother Animal*. Bergman conceded because he wanted to make a film of something; from Dymling he won the proviso that he could write in a part for Stig Olin. Dymling's approval sprang the booby trap.

Anxiously, Bergman wrestled with an adaptation for which he had scant appetite; at one moment of panic he telephoned Dymling long-distance, intending to call the whole thing off. That unsuspecting gentleman calmed the young man's fears and extended the deadline for the shooting. Though the film was late getting under way, Bergman managed to complete it on schedule without alienating his actors or his cinematographer, Gösta, *The Road to Heaven*, Roosling. They recalled later that he had been commendably patient with them; he was not famed for his patience. If Anders Dymling had read the script which Bergman had at the last minute posted to him (in view of his surprise later, he could not have read it), the film might never have been accomplished without storms, for the original had suffered a rough sea change. The play, designed for simple staging, to say nothing of a simple audience, comprised the unarresting subject of a young provincial girl who leaves the home of her adoptive mother for that of her real mother in the city. Seduced and abandoned, she returns to her foster-parent, sadder and probably no wiser. As the seducer himself never appeared in the play, Bergman seized the opportunity to provide one for the film; who better than that same disreputable Jack, as constant a companion to Bergman as Mr. Hyde had been to the good Dr. Jekyll? Whether or not Leck Fischer's play had compensatory vibrations absent from the synopsis I've read, I couldn't say; if it hadn't, I think we can agree that a spicier ingredient was called for.

Kris (Crisis), as it was now titled, was directed with a fairly crisp, if mannered, style, suggesting here and there any number of American-cum-Hitchcock movies beside those of a Frenchman or two. The Danish no-place-like-home morality became a cynical melodrama wherein the girl is seduced by her mother's lover, Jack (Stig Olin), an ex-actor, a crook, a megalomaniac. He likes to see people dance to his tune, as they do literally in one scene, "like marionettes". If he wasn't as criminal as he wildly declares himself to be—he mixes a drink called a Jack-the-Ripper—he was mad as a hatter, for he did a great deal of gun-brandish-ing and after his "old sinner," Nelly's mother, interfered with his progressive seduction of her daughter he stepped into the street and blew his head off. This episode was played in the semidarkness of a beauty parlor, after hours, sounds of gaiety sifting in from a dance hall. A cinema advertisement flashes on and off outside the window; coiffured heads watch the rape of Nelly from behind a gauzy curtain, one of them the real thing, wearing the vigilant, outraged stare of Mother. In the last shot of this sequence, Jack lies on the street outside the theatre, a newspaper covering his considerably impaired face. On that newspaper is a photograph of Ingmar Bergman and a subhead announcing the death of the local theatre director.[19]

Rising above the temptations this film offers to one's talent for depreciation, I recall a few single shots or brief sequences which, because I had seen later Bergman films, appeared more significant, perhaps, than they might have done without that experience: a double-exposure nightmare on board a train, when Mother senses that Nelly needs help; an explosive quarrel between the two mothers over Nelly, waged as if they were fighting for the favors of a man; a shot in which Jenny, the real mother, stares at herself in a mirror, with surprise and dawning disgust. I was diverted by Stig Olin's jaunty performance of Jack, the demon lover, and amusingly struck by his resemblance, in face and mannerism, to Douglas Fairbanks, Jr., in that suave, wry product of Hecht and MacArthur named *Angels Over Broadway*.

Ship to India

Mr. Dymling was not amused. Nor, I gather, was any massive section of the Swedish audience. Nobody prophesied that a future genius had just made his first film. Far from indifferent to the negative reception (he had been cooly informed that there would be no directing assignment for him at Svensk Film in 1946), Bergman was eager to redeem the lugubrious impression he had given press and public. To this end he approached Lorens Marmstedt, president of the newly organized Terra Films, with whom he had once been incompatibly associated in a theatre venture. Marmstedt was hospitable; after they had telephoned the amazed Mr. Dymling for permission (he was then out of the country), Bergman was engaged to prepare, under the supervision of Herbert Grevenius, the scenario of *Det Regnar På Vår Kärlek* (*It Rains on Our Love*), from a play by Oscar Braathen. Grevenius, a theatre critic and playwright, is probably the closest professional friend Bergman ever had. Both their continued collaboration and their friendship were initiated with *It Rains on Our Love*. I should like to be able to add that this film was a rich fruit of the association. Honesty and a jarring memory compel me to say that it's as boring a film from a director subsequently eminent as I have ever seen.

David and Maggi, perhaps my aversion begins with those names, as cute a two-against-the-world as you've ever encountered, are having a rough time rehabilitating themselves; he has just come from prison, she is a Fallen Angel, pregnant by some vanished Jack. They take refuge in an unused summer cottage while David works at a greenhouse; abused by the neighbours, threatened with eviction by the owner of the cottage, and accused of theft, they are watched over by an elderly guardian— Gösta Cederlund, with wings pinned on him, like the angels of *The Road to Heaven*—carrying an umbrella. When David is brought to trial for assaulting a Social Democrat evicter, the illicit past of the young couple is exposed. They are rescued from the limits of prosecution, however, their counsel for the defense is their winged guardian, the man with the umbrella. This is all performed in a murderously light-hearted way, accompanied by arch symbolism, undertones of anguish that never reach the surface, and a prodigious number of smirks, double-takes, and winks. Cinematically, it has less energy and tension than *Crisis*. Its only surprise is the coincidence of its content with that of later films for which Bergman wrote his own scenario: young couple outfacing the world, an elderly mentor, a hint of Christian grace. Presumably, these elements attracted Bergman's attention to the script in the first place—these and his immediate necessity for capturing a larger audience.

I used to have difficulty in separating one early Bergman film from another in my memory, because I first saw them all in a single retrospective screening within a week. Revisiting some over the years, I realize that a major cause of my perplexity was the fact that Birger Malmsten was the leading juvenile in too many of them! If you follow the Bergman film chronologically to 1952, when Malmsten was jettisoned for many years thereafter, together with other tokens of Bergman's trial-by-water, you will expel a sigh of relief, as though with your own eyes you had seen the Ancient Mariner delivered of his albatross. Malmsten was not only David in *It Rains on Our Love* but also the more radically impeded hero in each of the two Bergman films that followed; he was hunchbacked in *Ship to India,* blind in *Music in the Dark.* He was then released during one film in the succession, no doubt to recover the full use of his faculties before being required to enact a mere paranoid case in the next piece.

Ship to India was first a play, by Martin Söderhjelm; Marmstedt, having seen it in Helsinki, believed it to have film possibilities. Bergman must have warmed to it immediately, by reason of its resemblance to a type of Strindberg embroilment: father-and-son rivalry over the father's mistress, sharpened by the father's neglect of his wife. The waterfront milieu was a staple of the Swedish-anxiety film, initiated by Hampe Faustman in 1943 and recapitulated by him in 1948 with *Foreign Harbor.* The chiaroscuro atmosphere, the marginal existence, the suggestions of escape or homecoming, the proximity of dirty deeds, the half-hearted sympathy with a workers' world, the implicit symbolism of water— these were the potential properties, salted with reminiscences of Duvivier's *Carnet du Bal,* Marcel Carné's *Hotel du Nord* or *Port of Shadows,* and John Ford's *The Long Voyage Home.* Bergman expressly intended to do a film in "the sombre French manner". He had visited France that year, his first venture outside Sweden except for Denmark. *Ship to India* is, by all means, a sombre film, pregnant with imported atmospheric effects, on the whole successfully assimilated. Göran Strindberg was in no small measure responsible; finding the port settings more conducive than those of *It Rains on Our Love,* he supplied Bergman with murky light and an obediently mobile camera. Herbert Grevenius was again assigned to supervise the adaptation yet the film, for all its division of labor and derivative taste, seems very distinctly to display a personal touch.

Bergman here initiated the quiet opening which was to become characteristic of his method. He used just atmospheric and occupational "business," a ship dropping anchor, shots of Stockholm, some strains of siren music—images and sound only, to concentrate the eye and ear, establish the key, and perhaps to allow for the talkers in the audience to settle down. There's a love scene in a deserted windmill, one of those constricting Bergman things he was to do even better, e.g., the brother-and-sister embrace inside a rotting hulk, in *Through a Glass Darkly*. So far as the story is concerned, it was made vivid principally through the strong performance of Holger Löwenadler, as the accursed father-figure, Captain Alex. While you watch the actor, who gives immense physical credence to his role, you are compensated for the overdrawn psychopathology employed to make the fury-governed character believable. The sunken wreck which the frustrated Captain is trying to raise from the depths of the harbor, in which he expects to sail to India, is as rough-hewn a symbol as may be found in Eugene O'Neill at his lowest tide. The Captain is going blind, an affliction he refuses to acknowledge, and is doubly enraged at fate when his girl Sally, whom he had salvaged from a music hall, actually prefers the attention of his crookbacked son (a mere subaltern in the legion of the handicapped). Jealousy takes him to the brink of murder; when Johannes, the son, goes down in a diving suit to work on the wreck, he tries to kill the youth by cutting off his air supply. His embittered wife saves Johannes; the Captain commits suicide when arrested by jumping through a window.

The story line does not proceed by normal chronology. Bergman had become enamored, like many others, with Marcel Carné's renovation of the flashback in the cyclical form of *Daybreak*, 1939. In the more advanced Hollywood films from around 1945 to 1950, it was simply not de rigeur to begin a film at the beginning. Nothing is new; the practice has recently been revived. *Ship to India* opens with Johannes returning from somewhere, later than the events described above; he is looking for Sally. While she is trying to decide if she should continue to reject him, out of false pride and humiliation, he revisions the tragedy of seven years before. As one among many period items, this movie has no great importance; but with it, Bergman was learning to make film; the peripheral theatre scenes and the devil masks among the Captain's seafaring souvenirs, cf. Jean Vigo's *L'Atalante*, were atmospheric paraphernalia which had yet to be integrated. *Ship to India* was sent to the Cannes Festival in September of 1947, where it caught the attentive eye of the critic Andre Bazin of *Cahiers du Cinema*, for which it had a "Northern mystery and intensity." This notice was a forecast of Bergman's future more valuable than substantial rewards at home, for it was the inception of that serious, if sometimes over-rhetorical awareness of Bergman which, in the late Fifties, reached in France a summit of adulation.

Between 1946 and 1948, Bergman staged three plays of his own authorship—the first at Malmö, the others at Gothenburg—which, even through the unsatisfying form of synopses, are profitable for us to inspect, since they are not unrelated to the films he directed and, later, wholly conceived, during the same period and thereafter. There is small doubt that for many years, no matter what his opinion may be today, Bergman believed his theatre commitment, as director and as playwright, to be a truer expression of his gifts than his film-making. In this conviction he was encouraged by the fact that in the theatre he worked independently. On this subject I can only deliver partial judgments, since I never saw a Bergman theatre production before the Sixties. So far as his own plays are concerned, and judging as I must from synopsis, from quoted dialogue, and from the several points of view expressed by Swedish critics (conscientiously selected by Henrik Sjögren),[20] I would affirm that the plays of Bergman suffer excessively from the very characteristics supposed to have endowed them with vital interest. They are monomaniacal, they are solipsistic, they follow theatrically the worst possible line of descent from August Strindberg without, of course, Strindberg's great powers and without the excuse of having been written between, say, 1880 and 1907.

The first of the plays mentioned above was *Rakel and the Cinema Attendant,* a somewhat volcanic restatement of the simple Marie story, alluded to previously; at the same time it comprises the situation which became the concentrated first episode of the film *Waiting Women,* 1952. The names of the important three characters are the same as those in the film: Rakel, married miserably to Eugen, and Kaj, her lover of a long-ago summer. In the play, Kaj has a pregnant wife, eliminated in the rewriting for the movie. Kaj and Mia, the wife, are guests of Rakel and Eugen. Kaj and his hostess go sailing together and later on she admits, impulsively, to her husband, that she has been unfaithful to him, for she has loved Kaj, though she doesn't admire him, since "that summer." As later in *Waiting Women,* Eugen explodes in a futile expenditure of violence, in this context fatal. Seizing a hunting rifle, he is then unsure whom to kill, his wife or the lover. When the servant tries to take the gun away from him, it goes off and kills Mia, Kaj's pregnant wife. There seems to be little logic in this denouement, which may or may not have been Bergman's design. Unlike the later version, the play was intended to reveal dark, occult implications. Early on, the maid had referred to Kaj as "the Devil's emissary"; when Eugen insists pathetically that the gun wasn't loaded, Rakel confirms his protest with the solemn explanation, "There was Someone waiting outside. . . . and *he* came and took Mia's arm." Poetic injustice, one was expected to infer, has been dealt by the Devil, who sacrifices an innocent female bystander and her incubus, apparently to demonstrate that the scheme of things is under universally perverted control. Though I have obviously made no attempt to convey anything but the essentials of the plot, I can assure the reader I have also refrained from retailing certain strange detours of debate involved in this play, as well as the incredible anticlimax which brings it to a close.

The critics took this play with a good deal more seriousness than I would have expected. On the negative side there was fairly general agreement that Bergman's thought was foggier than his stagecraft, a viewpoint neatly summarized by a Stockholm reviewer, when he wrote, "As a writer, Bergman is still in his puberty. As a director he is a mature artist." This distinction was not unanimously agreed upon, but it does indicate the area of controversy.

The Day Ends Early produced sharper dissensions among the men on the aisle. This play was another argument for the supremacy of Satan in the battle being waged between him and God for moral dictatorship. A half-dozen people are visited by a little old lady who assures each in turn that he will die on the morrow. Impressed by the mysterious stranger's conviction and by her other-world air, the six allegedly doomed characters assemble in consternation at the house of Miss Jenny, an aging rich woman. A morality play is staged by a puppet master, commenting on the vanity of things and of those present. At the end of the second act it is revealed that the visitor was an escaped lunatic. Nonetheless, Miss Jenny, remaining disturbed, consults a minister of the church. He has no consolation to offer, simply asserting the belief stated above that in the battle between God and the Devil, the latter is winning.

She takes her problem to a psychiatrist, who is equally unhelpful. These interpolations would appear to be time-wasters, a subterfuge for getting said what Bergman rarely tired of saying, since at the end of the play the appointed characters do indeed die. And there was evidently a sort of stylized death dance before the curtain fell for the last time. Again I have drastically simplified the content in the interests of conceptual summary, but the action does seem to have been distracted by a number of red herrings. Dimly, we can now descry certain germinal themes or encounters which will appear in later Bergman films such as the identification of madness with revelation, an hypothesis by no means special to Bergman, and the inadequacy of the Church when confronted with an assumed hour of Judgment. The critical reception was what can be safely described as highly controversial and again it was reiterated that Bergman the theatre man was in conflict with Bergman the moralist, although individual writers disagreed as to which was the greater hindrance to the other.

The following autumn, 1947, Bergman staged another *drame noir* at the Gothenburg Municipal Theatre entitled *Mig Till Skräck* (*To My Terror*). This title came from a text which, in times past, adorned the stocks and gallows: *"To My Terror and as a Warning to Others."* In all probability, the anxiety motif of this self-nagging exercise was inspired by a fear of failure comparable to the mood in which the original story of *Torment* had been produced. Paul, the play's hero, is a creative writer who fails, winding up as a schoolmaster and a textbook-compiling hack, alternatively tyrannical and morbidly sentimental toward the younger generation. Domestic warfare helps spin the plot, with bitter quarrels between Paul and his childless wife. Paul takes a mistress, his wife disappears; whether for Paul's convenience or for some more vindictive reason is evidently never explained—she vanishes abruptly between the acts!

By favorable reviewers the play was compared to its advantage with the dramas of Ibsen as well as of Strindberg, and Ebbe Linde, within my ken one of the more reliable theatre critics in Sweden, added Chekhov to the comparison. He described the atmosphere of a terminal scene in which Paul turns, with a mixture of bitter resignation and spite, to the arms of his mistress, as worthy of the Russian master, "depressing but fascinating." In the opposite direction, this play was subjected to a scathing attack by Olof Lagerkrantz, now chief editor of the "liberal" *Dagens Nyheter* in Stockholm, who was in those days the drama critic of the conservative *Svenska Dagbladet*. Lagercrantz charged Bergman with highhandedness toward the public, the actors, and the theatre, with busying himself clumsily over "a handful of clichés-mother complex, the Devil, a Sunday-school God, the noble female, Solveig style." The dialogue was as sloppy as any the critic had heard in the theatre, for "nothing was clear, nothing was properly thought through."[21]

The unabated hostility with which Lagercrantz has opposed Bergman ever since has its origins in this period and has been perennially fanned by Bergman's preoccupation with religious belief, a subject which, above all, Lagercranz positively abhors. As a consequence he seems never to have been able to acknowledge that Bergman, the world-famed movie-maker, is a whit superior to Bergman, the presumptuous and muddled author he castigated in the Forties. In all fairness it is not difficult to believe that Bergman then merited more adverse criticism than he received. There is no question, whatever one's verdict might have been on the quality of his writing or direction, that he was hellbent on self-advertisement in a manner not calculated to win for him the respect of critics who might have preferred to encourage him. When his *Torment* story was acquired by Peter Ustinov who prepared a dramatic version for presentation on the London stage where, in the following year, it opened and closed with humiliating celerity, Bergman was so gratified by this attention paid him from abroad that he announced the glad tidings in a printed program for *To My Terror*, together with a bibliography of everything he had to date written, published and unpublished. This gesture followed another solecism which scarcely endeared him to the serious literary world. For a popular magazine that wanted to publish his film story of *Woman Without a Face*, directed by Gustav Molander, he contrived a version in the form of a novel, which he entitled *The Puzzle Represents Eros*. Patently, this novel was intended to supply motivations which had been either absent from or unclear in the script of the film which in 1947 was enjoying what can best be called a salacious success. Before resuming the chronology of films directed by Bergman after *Ship to India*, it is appropriate to double back, as it were. *Woman Without a Face* represents a confused aspect of Bergman's psychology but perhaps no more confused than certain other examples I have the occasion to pass in review here. It should not be considered irrelevant simply because Bergman did not personally take a hand in its production.

From a special point of view, *Woman Without a Face* is significant as a solitary parenthesis in Bergman's repertory of obsessive themes. Its subject, the timeless one of an ingenuous man's truly damnable infatuation with a worthless woman, is never again dominant in a Bergman film. The subject is peculiarly congenial to the modern mind; novelists and playwrights have repeatedly engaged it and in numerous instances have endowed it with clinically unsparing insights. Bergman, oddly enough, has managed to avoid the subject except as a subordinate episode. There is a personal bias to his psychological inquest of the disharmonic couple. While he has from time to time recognized in passing the common-garden variety of bitch, he has never focused his full attention on the subject of Woman as Medusa. His male animals tend to be miserably unworthy of their women and his females of the species are more often sinned against than sinning. In this respect he seems quite arbitrarily to have reversed the Strindberg coin. Woman is a victim of Men; Men are victims of God—or of the Devil—and, in his latterday questioning, of God alone knows what.

In *Woman Without a Face* he worked unconvincingly to conceive a female who should have been next of kin to, say, Hardy's Sue Bridehead, to a legion of women in the plays of Ibsen or (it goes without saying) of Strindberg, or to Miriam in *Of Human Bondage*. Evidently he hadn't, in 1947 or whenever he first stumbled on the idea, the patience, the comprehension, or the zeal to concentrate his recognition of the type into a feasibly motivated individual woman. Instead he fell back on hearsay and on a few fragmentary hints from the Freudian canon. Whatever effectiveness reaches one from the screen is partly due to Gunn Wallgren's ambiguous performance and in part to our own familiarity with the generic creature. If Gustav Molander, as a director, had been as assured in his own right as Alf Sjöberg, he might have insisted on a renovation of the script with a view to making it more relentless, more consistent, and much less redundant. What the film principally required was the grim, spare articulation of *Torment*, since the story is essentially composed of a single tense coil: the embrace in which Martin and the pathological Rut are locked as they advance into "a night without limits."

At this phase of his precocity, however, Bergman was unable to drive to the heart of a matter; he needed side issues, supplementary histories, supporting explanations from too many directions. Because Martin is supplied with a wife and child, his heedless desertion of them must be doubly explained; Bergman was not content with explaining; he temporized. Martin, it seems, had married Frida only because she was pregnant, three years before the encounter with Rut, the implication being that he hadn't really loved her. But since that is an obviously insufficient justification for the extent to which he is engulfed by Rut, we are told by way of a confession he makes to Rut herself, highly unlikely, that he had grown up as a mother's boy, an attachment disastrous to the maturity required of him. Moreover, he doesn't desert merely his wife. The situation is placed in the War years; Martin dodges his military service, hence providing himself with a yet more cogent reason for attempting suicide when Rut abandons him. Rut, a compulsive maneater, is saddled with a burden she tries in vain to unload—Ragnar, Martin's friend, calls it "trying to get the monkey off her back." She claims to have been molested by a man when she was twelve, a characteristic plea from a type more often than not in retreat from latent Lesbianism. (My gloss, not Bergman's.) To compound the indignity of this source, and to bring it in line with the congested rationalizations of Strindberg-when-he-nodded, the man in question is still in the offing; he is her mother's lover, and Rut describes him as, to be sure, the Devil.

All these cross-purposes and too readily Freudian alibis are framed for distance within a series of cutbacks from the bemused narrative of Ragnar, delivered to Martin's wife, Frida and sometimes from Martin, explaining himself to Ragnar. Frida is the most neglected character in the story, assuming no dimension and registering no marked relationship to her erring husband. Anita Bjork ("Miss Julie") is required only to appear at intervals, cooly inconsolable, murmuring baffled sympathy for Martin's flight into darkness.

"I remember everything about her," Martin tells Ragnar, referring to Rut—"breasts, hips, arms, legs—but she's without a face." This is good, and Gunn Wallgren, unequipped with the obvious appeals of amplitude, was convincing largely, I'd say, by default. She didn't define Rut so much as she suggested her, a power of darkness with piquant mouth and glittering eyes, and Molander wisely allowed her to work within her own limitations. A woman without a face, though it's her face you exclusively see in focus. Sexual domination is a more elusively engineered matter than most Swedish filmmakers have understood, with their strip-downs, magnified breasts, and closeups of tongue kissing. Rut is pervasively hungry, deceptively winsome, owning the deadly art of surrendering herself completely without leaving any of her soul, possession of one assumed, in the man's arms. She waits and works to be rejected, then strikes to the core and moves on. The cycle is endless, the victims numberless, for predatory women never lack men pleading to be swallowed whole.

No question but that Bergman had caught a glimpse of something behind his back as he turned a dark corner. This is one demon he didn't fervently confront, or perhaps his failure to do so was no more than glib workmanship. It took several years for him to learn Arthur Schnabel's lesson, "Play nothing before you hear it." He sketched this story, plotted it perfunctorily and left it, with a host of loose ends, to someone else's mercy. Most regrettable of the weak afterthoughts is Martin's escape to America at the end with money from Dad, and Rut, of all people, at the station assuring Frida that Martin will come back—to his wife. As a whole, I can assure those who haven't seen it, the film was better to look at than my captiousness might leave them to think. Molander, importantly assisted by Åke Dahlquist, made the most of the scenic possibilities. Many scenes remain distinct in the memory, those especially in an empty warehouse loft—Bergman early learned to favor deserted buildings of one kind or another—high above the street where the two sensually bound fugitives look down upon a frozen Stockholm, always more exotic in a melancholy Nordic way when in the white clutch of mid-winter. "They've moved to a palace beyond the sun and moon which you can only find if you're mad," Ragnar informs someone, half-believing in the romance of this hopeless escapade. There are other moments in the film like this, when the successive stages of Martin's consent to degradation, enthralled by a nymphomaniac with spiritual undertones, are almost converted into passages for a poem by Baudelaire. I should concede that Martin himself might have been a great deal less believable if played by anyone then available except Alf Kjellin, who had an ingratiating knack for playing breakable young idolaters, as he had already proven in *Torment*.

Music in the Dark

Between September and Christmas of 1947 Bergman, after getting *To My Terror* off his chest and on to the stage, made another movie for Terrafilm, *Musik I Mörker* (*Music in the Dark*; British version, *Night is My Future*). Göran Strindberg was at the camera again. Malmsten was the leading sufferer, a blind musician named Bengt. The script was written in collaboration with Dagmar Edquist, author of the widely popular novel on which it was based. Bergman was determined to make the film as popular as the book. Father, in *Ship to India*, had been going blind, and perished with little sympathy from anyone related to him. Here to Bergman's hand was a chance to atone for destroying Captain Alex with a *youth* who is blinded and to venture, at the same time, an essay in the virtue of stoicism. Young Bengt is blinded by rifleshots when he tries rescuing a puppy in the line of fire. Note how an antiwar message is smuggled gratuitously into the argument. He drifts, darkly, from one humble job to another: organist, cafe musician, piano tuner. Meeting Ingrid (Mai Zetterling) when he plays the organ at her father's funeral, he spoils his first prospect of being looked after by this angelic girl, who simply wants "to serve", by making a slighting remark about her social background. After a round of dreary occupations he meets her again; she is engaged to another. Retreating to his own world, Bengt befriends a man, sightless like himself but happily in love. In an accurately painful scene, Bengt goes with him to see the girl, whereupon the lovers ignore Bengt for their own happiness, in contact with each other. Bengt stumbles around the town in a suicidal manner; he is coincidentally discovered by Ingrid on the railroad tracks. Her suitor also shows up—I can't remember the excuse given for his equally improbable presence—and finding the pair in a tender embrace he knocks the youth down. "Thank you for treating me like a normal man," says Bengt politely. The conjugal ending was predictable and, to a majority of the audience, acceptable.

As paraphrasable content, *Music in the Dark* is a mawkish, contrived narrative. Considered as film art, it is not a wholly negligible item in Bergman's development. Critics have usually commented favorably on the delirium montage when Bengt is undergoing an eye operation; consisting of immersion in mud, siren voices, tropical fish, girls, and deep-sea bubbles: all very ingenious but ingenuity was not just then Bergman's crying need. Worthier of our regard were certain grubby-social scenes, one in a café kitchen where a gluttonous boy who has attached himself to Bengt gorges himself while the musician and a friend perform a duet. A distinctive Bergman talent, his faculty for getting responses from actors, clearly begins to emerge in this otherwise tedious and complacently morbid film: Mai Zetterling was quite moving, out of all proportion to the general tone, in one beautifully directed moment when she gazed deeply into a mirror, caressing her face to learn how she must have felt when touched by the fingertips of her blind lover. Bergman has been exclusively credited with exploiting the mirror for psychologically extensive purposes. In Swedish film, however, it was Sjöberg again who showed the way, which is not to say that Bergman's mature use of the device was not inventive.[22] Briefly and emphatically, but not as sensitively as in the confrontation I have described above, Bergman had employed the mirror in each of his preceding films. He tried a playback of the Ingrid moment in *Hamnstad*, which he directed following *Music in the Dark*, in which a much plainer female stares at herself with affectionate resignation and writes with a lipstick across her reflected image the single word, *Ensam* (Alone).

The moral message of *Music in the Dark*, enunciated by Ingrid's mother—"Pain is to be accepted as part of life"—was a purely histrionic flourish, whether contributed by Dagmar Edquist or not, and fairly insulting to the imagination when you recall that in 1947 some millions of Europeans had been mortally struggling with this truth for many years. I feel compelled to add that Bergman has never, by the evidence of his films, accepted pain as part of life. There is nothing in his or the Swedish-at-large moral economy to support so heroic an attitude. Bergman has rarely ceased, in his own terms, to accuse a diffident God of allowing pain in human existence. *Music in the Dark* is not to be contested at this level, however, for the Dagmar Edquist story was obviously set up to blackmail the viewer with stock emotions. Owing to the previous fame of this novel, Bergman's film aroused popular interest and proved to be commercially profitable.

Flushed with victory, Bergman approached Svenskfilm again, where Anders Dymling was now in the mood to welcome him back. Before proceeding with his next directorial assignment, Bergman worked up from his first unstaged play, *The Station*, a script for *Eva*, to be directed also by Molander. It was released in 1948, the same year as *Hamnstad*. I said worked up because it's an excessively rigged business. Once more, Gustav Molander was guilty of forbearance; he should have been despotic, insisting that the script be cut to ribbons. Because he wasn't, the tolerated result has as powerfully negative a value as *Woman Without a Face* for those fascinated by Bergman's more wooly aberrations. Critics have tended to settle on one or another of his early films in which they find the principal themes in solution, or profusion, an occasion fraught with discomfort which they nonetheless agreeably pursue; it affords them such pleasure to identify the ingredients. *Eva* should serve them as well as, for example, *Fängelse (Prison)*, if thematic hares are what these hounds are after. Bergman seems to have been constitutionally incapable of using the wastebasket. *Eva* not only 'forecasts, it recapitulates. In it will be found the traveling players of Bergman's fairy-tale beginnings and of three later films and a play: the father-son hostility, as well as the homecoming-and-flashback, of *Ship to India*; blindness, from the two preceding films; the War-induced spectator-neurosis reflected in *Music in the Dark*, *Woman Without a Face*, and *Thirst*, and reverted to in *The Silence* and in *The Shame;* the encircling narrative employed more-or-less psychoanalytically, as in *Woman Without a Face*, *Somnarlek* and *Wild Strawberries;* the subsidiary couple united sadomasochistically, also utilized in *To Joy*, *Prison*, *Smiles of a Summer Night* and *Wild Strawberries;* the fantasy killings of *Prison*, *Thirst*, *It Can't Happen Here*, and the radio play, *The City*, the declaration that "God has forsaken mankind" which was advanced prodigiously in the earliest plays, as we have seen, and thereafter revived in *Prison* and in a number of God-is-silent films beginning with *The Seventh Seal*.

The traumatic episode that launches this multiplex of woe is the death of a small blind girl, member of an itinerant yodeling trio, with whom, after a dispute with his father on the subject of his abused mother, the twelve-year-old Bo has run away from home. He steals a locomotive, the monster is derailed, the child is killed. We are apprised of this calamity in flashback; at the opening the adult Bo—Malmsten, wouldn't you know?—is on the way home, remembering it all, or trying to resist memory, anxious to recover his human usefulness in the arms of his childhood love Eva, now grown into a sympathetic, if not elated, woman. The malevolent dreariness of the story is happily refreshed for the eye by numerous social anecdotes that introduce a variety of characters and places.

Most of Bergman's early scenarios have at least one engrossing passage-at-arms, for he was becoming a connoisseur of domestic sordidness; in *Eva* there's an authentically nasty interlude when Bo is housed temporarily with a married friend, a jazz-orchestra musician, Goran (Stig Olin). Goran's wife, Susan (Eva Dahlbeck) is patently on the make for Bo, a manoeuvre to which Goran appears indifferent; when in his cups he even seems to enjoy the spectacle. "Suppose we fall in love with each other?" Bo taunts him. "You won't!" sneers Goran happily. "*I know Susan*—I know you, too." His belligerence takes another direction as he continues to drink until, finding a provocation, he punches Bo on the jaw. Fairly drunk himself, Bo passes out and into a nightmare; he dreams of helping Susan to kill Goran by leaving the gas-jet open. At the strategic moment he revives, when Susan, now chastened, is going to bed with Goran. The musician can only be stimulated sexually by jealousy of his wife. (There's a more cryptic explanation of such cross-relationships but I'll rest content with the surface motives provided by the film.)

The remainder of the script is characterized by gratuitous pessimism and a coda that affirms life no more persuasively. Out in the skerries, Bo and Eva, she now pregnant, are brooding on the cruelty of it all. Upon seeing a corpse washed up from the Baltic, "possibly from a German destroyer," Eva wails that birth is, after all, meaningless, for "God has forsaken mankind!" All the same she has her child and suddenly Summer has come back! Bo, abruptly relieved of his demons, realizes— or should I say he dutifully mumbles?—that "Death is part of life . . . . no other explanations are necessary!" Many members of the audience were less easily fobbed off. Nor could they have been requited by the final montage of retrospective shots of the lethal train engine, of the blind child, of Susan and Healing Nature, reshuffled summarily and supported by music which, throughout, had been exhaustively editorial.[23]

Rarely has the invention of the scissors been so ungratefully ignored. *Woman Without a Face* and *Eva* were written but not directed by Bergman. Hamnstad (*Port of Call*), 1948, was directed but not conceived by him. A principle, triumphantly illustrated, should follow; but I have none to offer. *Port of Call* proves only that Bergman was in the wrong company. Certainly the film is better constructed than the two scripts assigned to Molander; yet it seems to me to have been a mistake for Bergman to have been identified with it. The Gothenburg writer, Olle Lansberg, who prepared the basic story, was moved by sociological impulses; he wanted to air the specific problem of abortion and say something sharp about the obligations of a social-welfare system. What Bergman wanted to say is not clear; one suspects he found the outlined story merely instrumental, for he announced his intention of doing a film in the Italian *neo-realismo* style complete with proletarian level and natural location, in this case the port region of Gothenburg. The naturalism of the best postwar Italian films, however, was touched by poetic fatalism and shot through with old Meditteranean memories of ritual. *Port of Call* is simply hard-edged realism, exceedingly garrulous, with a distinct ambience of frustration, mainly Bergman's.

There are good things in this film, at odds with difficulties which were beyond solution. Bergman's interests simply do not lend themselves to portraying characters from a submerged social station in the contemporary world. Only once, in *A Summer with Monika*, has he successfully concerned himself with such a mileu. There was the rub, for his leading male—a sailor, Gosta, played by Bengt Eklund—is not very bright and lacks the sensitive tissue of the striplings appropriate to the personality of Birger Malmsten; nor is he complex in the half-mad fashion of the Captain in *Ship to India*. Berit, the badgered girl, has a pretty limited consciousness, too; it is probably to Bergman's directorial credit that she was played by Nina-Christine Jonsson with sufficient veracity to hold one's attention. Bengt, however, was beyond his reach; half the emotional conflict of the film is therefore ineluctably hysterical.

Berit opens the film, stepping with grave concentration from a high dock into deep water, hoping to drown herself. Gosta, whose ship is just then tying up, saves her life, adding to his own problem the equally insoluble one of a character quite as mixed up as he. It transpires that his past is not altogether savory as viewed by the law. He learns Berit's story in a chain of flashbacks, all very familiar working-class-novel material of that era, involving low-class and low-morality upbringing (one of the best scenes in the film is a violent altercation between her parents in a cramped flat); apprenticeship in a millinery school; seduction by a happy-go-lucky bounder (Stig Olin); session in a detention hostel for running away from home and another affair, somewhat happier, with a nice middle-class lover, terminated by his parents after they have researched her dowdy origins.

Gosta fails to assimilate this history with compassion; his instinctive reaction is jealousy of the other men in her life. During his fuddled self-questioning on her account he runs stupidly amok. Meanwhile Berit, trying to cover up for a girl friend, gets herself foolishly involved with an unlawful abortionist; the law closes in, she is put on probation, and threatened with the detention home or the penitentiary if she does not supply the name of the abortionist. Frenzied by the constricting circle within which they are trapped together, Berit and Gosta decide to break her probation by fleeing the country—to Antwerp, a novel touch! On thinking it over further, they settle for limited security, acknowledging to each other that even if they have landed in a fairly hopeless mess, things were still worse a year before. Then they were alone; now, at least, they have each other.

I think we may assume that the closing sentiment was not the author's alone, for it rehearses the *faute-de-mieux* proposition of later films in which Bergman was struggling to meet the demands of intelligent reconciliation. For what it may be worth this film is the closest to being a social criticism, at the civic level, of any Bergman has made. The arid complacency of the probation officers was conveyed with candor; the scenes in the detention home had an air of credibility. At the time, he was bitterly attacked for misrepresentation, a small public flurry to which he could have paid very little attention—if for no other reason than that he hadn't the time—and it is hard to believe he was personally concerned for the sociological accuracy of Olle Lansberg's story. For one thing, by specifying a remedial grievance, the script had robbed him of the opportunity to attribute suffering to contentious powers of darkness. Hence, while the merits of the film are all in the interests of social-level precision, they express Bergman's authentic interests very little. As a discipline in moviemaking, the script was probably useful. On the whole it's a well-knit, unhesitating job. A dance-hall scene, shortly after the opening, is noteworthy for its rhythm and for the assurance with which Bergman shot and edited the varying perspectives. His luck with cinematographers held; Svenskfilm had assigned Gunnar Fischer who was, as they put it, "the best we can spare". Fischer had not yet earned seniority. In the years that followed, Fischer was so frequently associated with Bergman, until succeeded in favor by Sven Nykvist, as to constitute another of those inseparable teams in movie history, others of which are Sjöstrom and Janzon, Griffith and Bitzer, Eisenstein and Tisse, Fritz Lang and Wagner, Fellini and Martelli.

Bergman's fourth play, written for the professional theatre, was presented at the Hälsingborg City Theatre, December 8, 1948, directed by Lars-Levi Laestadius. *Kamma Noll* means literally "to draw a blank"; the phrase was derived from G. B. Shaw who wrote, in effect, that if you give the Devil enough play he will draw blank (give him enough rope, he'll hang himself). The Devil in this play is Gertrud, another version of Rut in *Woman Without a Face*, and apparently constructed with as few nuances. She attempts to wreck a household consisting of a music professor with whom she had once had an unfruitful affair; his wife, who is at the susceptible age before complete resignation to sexual fidelity sets in; the daughter who is at the awkward age of innocence, and her equally youthful fiancé, a visitor in her home on the crucial weekend which frames the drama. Ebbe Linde summed up the characterizations by saying:

> We have the uncomfortable feeling that Ingmar Bergman has slandered at least two of his characters and that we are accomplices because we sit silently and listen. This applies above all to Gertrud, but in a basic sense to the youthful pair who, with all their freshness, have been so obviously pre-sweetened.

He conceded that in certain scenes Bergman had written some of his most skilled dialogue for the theatre (*Dagens Nyheter,* Dec. 9, 1948).

Seven months later, when *Kamma Noll* was given a radio performance, another critic on the same paper (K.S-z) disagreed with Mr. Linde's generosity on this point. Under the title, "The Devil's Hairdresser," his review was largely a deprecation of the play's literary indolence: the dialogue smelled of the lamp and plainly proved that Bergman "had not strained himself" unduly to create a psychologically authentic drama. He objected strongly to the denouement. Evidently, the teetering situation in the play is saved by the girl, who has a religious inspiration while sitting in a tree during a hailstorm (DN, July 15, 1949).

Prison

At the end of 1948 three film ideas must have been jostling each other simultaneously in Bergman's consciousness. A story outline of *Fängelse* (literally *Prison*, but English distributors called it *The Devil's Wanton*) had been submitted to Svenskfilm before *Hamnstad* was in production, and while Bergman was preparing the film, partly in Stockholm, partly in Gothenburg, he was already conferring with Grevenius over the scenario for *Thirst*. Dymling, no doubt recalling his experience with *Crisis,* was inhospitable to the prospect of *Prison*. Marmstedt was willing to take a chance; when the tumescent conception had taken negotiable shape as a working script, the main shooting was accomplished in twenty-six days, while Bergman was staging *A Streetcar Named Desire* in Gothenburg. The unbelievably tight schedule may account for many of the maladroit fancies in the treatment. Critics have been generally over-eager to regard the film with clemency, if not with wonder, impressed by the fact that this was the first time Bergman had been given a completely free hand both in the scenario and with the direction. I think they have as often been persuaded that the film should be admired because it is so involuted as to be incomprehensible. I have never been impressed by it, I find it monstrously self-indulgent, morally meaningless, and inexcusably pretentious in its structure.

The main formal complication of *Prison* derives from the fact that you are seeing a film about someone trying to make a film, after which you are told that the film you've seen could never be made. A good deal of blither about the influence of Pirandello has been expended, whereas it seems more likely to me that Bergman had either heard of or seen a German film, released in 1948, with precisely this trick subject, handled as urbane persiflage—Helmut Käutner's *Film Without a Name.* Pirandello's drama, to which more recent films of Bergman may legitimately be related, is all too often invoked when justifications are needed for merely vulgar versions of moral relativity. The Italian's leading subject was the terrible ambiguity imposed on one by other people's conceptions of one's identity and motives; a corollary subject analyzes the equivocal status of fictions. Bergman's film is not about problems of identity, nor is its subject seriously the mystery of art. While it employs a device superficially recalling certain Pirandello plays, its Manichean subject would have shocked Pirandello no end.

The framing mechanisms of *Prison* introduce a professor, previously an inmate of an insane asylum (already this has a familiar Bergman ring), who has an idea for a film to be directed by a former pupil, Martin (Hasse Ekman). Bluntly put, the idea is standard early Bergman: the world is ruled by Satan. The film we are seeing thereupon becomes a test case for the professor's theory by way of a narrative instituted by Thomas (Birger Malmsten), a journalist friend of Martin, and centered upon or revolving around a doomed prostitute who is encumbered with the name, Birgitta-Caroline Söderberg. This daft innocent supports the man she lives with, together with his respectable sister, by the money she pleasurably earns. Thomas meets her after a quarrel with his own ''respectable'' wife, Sophie (Eva Henning), whom he believes he has killed, whereas in un-sober reality Sophie knocked him out with a bottle.

Since Martin, the film director, has been a witness to, or at least a sympathetic bystander in, this Thomas-Sophie-Birgitta triangle, one is never quite sure how much of the film-within-film is intended as real. The fate of Birgitta, however, is in all conscience grisly. First, her aborted child by Peter is destroyed by him and his sister. It is after Peter has been cleared by a police investigation that Thomas meets the girl. Birgitta spends the night with Thomas; her light-hearted moment is marred by visions of hell-fire from the open fireplace and by nightmares of murder. She rejects Thomas on the grounds that his bourgeois wife is after all what he needs, but her more compelling reason is her sickly persisting infatuation with Peter. She returns to her prostitute's life but when the first customer, sent her by Peter, treats her sadistically, she crawls away to a cellar where she kills herself. Martin concludes that such a film can't be made, for if it were true this would mean that the world is ruled by the Devil, and life would be simply insupportable.

I fail to understand how anyone could have taken seriously this congregation of pestilent vapors, which amounts to a sophomoric version of Gomorrah. On the whole Swedish criticism at the time received the film with a marked show of deference. French Existentialism was in the air; more than one interpreter found it irresistible to quote, from Sartre's *No Exit*, "Hell is other people". More than one have continued to find it irresistible. Yet, obviously, Bergman had not credibly proven that Hell was other people. The world of *Prison* is much too peripheral to be taken as an engrossing insight into common misery. Bergman offered us a handful of morally aimless characters who batten on each other, who drift into fantasy and vice with no comprehension of what they're doing, or where they're going at all. And his answer to the morass in which they find themselves is that if one can't believe in a choate God there is no answer except that Hell is the world we have. Which, if you ponder it, does yield an attractive medieval simplicity. Marlowe's Dr. Faustus murmured some such conclusion, did he not?

I will concede that the manner of the photography, the lighting, and the editing chimed with the Stockholm-Gothic subject matter, that Bergman showed no little ingenuity adapting German Expressionism to Birgitta's hallucinations of the phallic trees and the doll that becomes a fish. Only yesterday, Bergman was still denying that his head had ever been turned by the art of United Films Associations—an astounding repudiation, the more so since in the year he made *Prison* he purchased the first items of a private film collection. Among his earliest acquisitions were *The Cabinet of Dr. Caligari* and E. A. Dupont's *Variety*.[24] For this and other reasons I do not believe in the integrity of Bergman's symbols, nor in the sacred flame with which, according to numerous critics, not all of them French, this film was illuminated. Bergman did not conceive *Prison* in a rush of decisive inspiration. When he submitted the first draft of his script he called it "A True Story". I'd be not at all surprised to learn that any single situation in the film was taken from "life," either observed by Bergman or reported to him in the days he frequented *Gamla Stan*, the Old Town of Stockholm, which is quasi-Bohemian. But for the purposes of art a true story is not always a good story; when truth is stranger by far than fiction, it may be irredeemable as fiction. In point of fact, Bergman's prostitute was a very minor character at the outset; she met a variety of fates as the script altered its direction and hers.

Almost to the last, Bergman intended Birgitta-Caroline to join the Salvation Army! Grevenius was on hand at this juncture to protest so saccharine an eventuality. Instead, Bergman had her open her veins with a large knife. Whether this was more acceptable to Mr. Grevenius, a convert to Catholicism, I don't know. I should think it might be an unresolvable dilemma for a Roman Catholic to have to choose between the Salvation Army and suicide.

During the solemnities of the press reception a glint of humor was introduced by the Swedish journalist who maintained that only Bergman would have named a prostitute Birgitta-Caroline, for it sounded for all the world like his father's church, Hedvig Eleanora. The bells of that very church were heard in what is surely the most talked-of scene in the film, when Thomas and Birgitta, in his attic apartment, find an old cinematograph and project a farce—devised by Bergman, himself, à la Melies—wherein a slapstick romp is broken up by Death in skeletal form. It is easy to exaggerate the importance of this interlude as a symbolic comment on the nature of Reality and Illusion and of Death as part of Life. (Cf. *Eva* as well as *Sommarlek*) The film was over-equipped with suggestions to that end. Later works of Bergman provide examples less obtrusive. This particular sequence in *Prison* is memorable for the pure enchantment of the mood, which for a moment dispels the chaos which has gone before and postpones the bathos which is to follow. The strange gnome-like beauty of Doris Svedlund had much to do with the fey impression; elsewhere she seemed to me an implausibly piquant representative of her profession.

Thirst

Torst (*Thirst*) went into production immediately following the completion of *Prison* in March, 1949. While the stories by Birgit Tengroth, combined to make a feature-length film, were the chief responsibility of Grevenius to adapt, the script shows predominantly the idiosyncracies and thematic conjunctions of Bergman. The original tales were designed to exemplify Mrs Tengroth's conviction that "Every woman is destroyed by some man"—Hell is half of other people? Yet there is far too much going on in this film to leave one in the sole company of so unmodified a premise. *Thirst* is a genuinely intricate affair, overweighted by ironies of chance, yet worked out with musical fluency and many skillful overlaps in the narrative. Bergman here uses the train journey in a sustained manner for the first time, that dependable *mise-en-scène* wherein movement and confined drama may ideally supplement each other. As a bickering young married couple make their way home from Basel to Stockholm, shortly after the war, each is further revealed through flashback, and another extension of reference is added by Viola, the ex-wife of Bertil, who is shown advancing to her pitiful fate in Stockholm as the couple arrive in the city. Hence there are two principal journeys going forward in space and time, so to speak, intercut with backward excursions into the biographies of the protagonists. It is really not as confusing as it may sound.

Rut, the wife on the train, is a ballet dancer suffering from frigidity; as the result of an abortion undertaken after her desertion by a married army officer, she fears she is barren. Always on edge, frustrated, suicidal, Rut is intensely irritated by her husband's complacent interest in his precious-coin collection, a hobby that interjects, sententiously, the film's governing motif. Bertil's most valued coin depicts Arethusa, a goddess transformed to escape the amorous advances of Alphais, a river god. The Greeks believed that the river dug itself from the ocean to merge with its fugitive object, now a Sicilian fountain. Pure fantasy, Bertil admits wryly, for the sexes can never, never be united. The subject of metamorphosis by water is prepared by the first image of the film, a whirlpool, and sardonically completed by the final shots, following a death by drowning, of a dissolve through the image of the coin to the sea breaking on the shore.

The scenes featuring Bertil and Rut are not, however, portentous, despite their often repressed violence and Rut's impulsive offer to throw herself off the train. More often than not they are in a spirit of high needling comedy, by contrast with the retrospective passages. Bergman was trying to work out a lighter vein of marital discord, of the kind that was to serve him well in four films of the Fifties. The double tone was a difficult thing to bring off and in this film it is not consistently successful. It is supported or, in many cases, covered by sheer sleight-of-hand and diversions: an abundance of cutting for irony, cross-references from a remark made in the present to a similar one made in the past, and much lap-dissolving of objects such as Rut in a hotel bedroom reminded of her hospital confinement by a water carafe.

As the narrative progresses and the northbound journey nears its end, the various stories overlap or confront each other. At one stage of the Bertil-Rut story the train, briefly halted, is drawn up alongside another train, headed in the opposite direction; across the tracks the couple exchanges greetings with their old friends Raoul, the officer, of whose affair with Rut we have already been given knowledge at the opening of the film, and his wife. Our attention is then refocused on Viola, in Stockholm, drifting toward despair and death. She finds no help from a callous psychiatrist whose theraputic advice is that she go to bed with him and in this way transfer the quite illusory love for her lost husband, Bertil, which she believes is devouring her. "Criminal upbringing, silly marriage, distorted affairs. Wake up, woman!" When Viola rejects his advances, he shrugs cynically, assuring her she will go the regular way—to an insane asylum. She rushes into the street, and a cut to Bertil and Rut, homeward-bound, interposes an episode from Rut's past when she had been defended from a nagging ballet teacher by a danseuse named Valborg. The teacher hated Valborg, contending that the girl's future was sitting in her eyes "like a devil!"

Back in Stockholm, the teacher's remark is instantly and much too glibly illustrated; the distracted Viola actually meets Valborg. They too, had gone to school together. It is Midsummer Eve, there is dancing in the street; Viola goes to Valborg's flat and as the two women converse, drink and listen to music, Valborg's intentions are plain. Having persuaded Viola to dance with her, she tries to caress the older woman and Viola, as from the psychiatrist, breaks away in panic and flees the house. The scene fades with the violin melody on the gramophone and a closeup of the bereft Valborg. After a brief return to the homecoming train there is a flash of Viola desperately circling a group of dancers in the street, a cross-cut of Valborg alone, Viola again, walking grimly to the end of the waterfront street, with undersound of gull chatter, concertina sounds from the street dance, camera angle from a bowsprit, and then a smothered splash. The train bearing Bertil and Rut arrives; the film ends with their reconciliation.

Their concluding dialogue echoes a sentiment from *Port of Call* and will be more resignedly confirmed in *Waiting Women*. Oddly enough, the fantasy-killing in this instance referred to was not merely a Bergman retake; it took place in the Tenroth story.

> "I've been dreaming that I killed you," Bertil tells Rut. . . . "You don't say anything. *I killed you!*"
> "I'm not surprised."
> "It's better as it is—*now*."
> "Well——but you would have been alone and *independent!*"
> "I don't want to be independent. It's worse."
> "Than what?"
> "Worse than our hell. After all, we have each other."

Nobody would describe this film as austere; many have found its compound-complex grammar wearisome, the rhyming of theme and image glib, the symbolism gratuitous, the coincidences intolerable. Personally, when these solecisms have been duly listed, I prefer the film to any precedent effort of Bergman. There are light, air, movement, and geography in *Thirst*, as well as sickmindedness and implausible intersections. The person of Viola was compassionately realized and warmly, touchingly acted by Birgit Tengroth herself. Speaking cinematically, the inventions in *Thirst* are livelier than in any Bergman movie to that date, although they did not involve such abstruse effects as were boiled up for *Prison*. Viewers who have forgotten much of the film can probably recall the moment when, somewhere in Europe, a mob of people storms the train for food and on the window which Bertil promptly closes there is cast the reflection of a city gutted by bombs.

Prison and *Thirst*, taken together—the very titles are symptomatic— confirm a landscape of attitudes which can already be thought of as a Bergman world, even when the deduction has been made that contemporary Swedish films were almost unanimously haunted by marital discord, suicide, abortion, and murder. Bergman simply kept company with his phantoms more exclusively. I'm sure it has been said that *Prison* is a film only Bergman could have made, *Thirst* is a film anyone might have made, a gross simplification designed to justify overconfident young filmmakers who feel they should be here-and-now and without limits indulged, though they have little to express but their immaturity. If in the Forties Bergman had been condemned to work under circumstances that suppressed his finer insights or his most *unheimlich* private visions, one might be readier to concede that *Prison* was an intrepid, if distraught, effort to break the conventional mirror and reveal the fractured image man fears to face. Those who have argued hopefully for such an interpretation have radically overestimated the potency of Bergman's revelation; furthermore they have written in ignorance of Bergman's career. He was given a quantity of chances to promote his muddled philosophy in the scripts he wrote and the plays he produced before 1952, and he received a generous share of critical encouragement. How many times should an audience be asked to embrace aberration as a subterfuge for truth or, let us say, for art—which is not the same thing as truth?

The best that can be said for *Prison* is that in it Bergman began to learn how to abstract, from the sordid topical subject, forces and relationships which, being so abstracted, might transcend their prosaic origin. Since he didn't really know what he wanted to say he said too much incoherently. Abstraction that represents no clear principle is invariably thin, monstrous, or laughable. The worst that can be said for *Thirst* is that it was aimed at being commercially suave and intellectually esoteric at the same time, with all its Classical name-flashing and the titillation of Bohemia with Lesbian agony and an effete psychiatrist. If it can be said that there would have been no major Bergman without the sick, furtive probing into mental recesses exploited by *Prison* (the postulate comes from critics who seem to have been unaware of all the other films and plays in which Bergman had furtively probed), it is equally demonstrable that there would have been no major Bergman without a measure of consent to the real world—of other countries, other times of day— which, however submerged by special effects, was at least recognized in *Thirst*.

To add that *Thirst* made more money than any Bergman movie up to then may very well damage my defense of it for those who believe that box-office success is an infallible index of compromised film-making. To such a view, film history gives no consistent support. And if certain tabulated ingredients known as "human interest" are supposed to ensure success, I would expect to learn that Bergman's following film, *Till Glädje* (*To Joy*), 1949, was even more profitable than *Thirst*, but it was not.

To Joy

While certain of the mixtures as before were contained in this script, written wholly by Bergman, their context was far less cerebral than that of *Prison* or *Thirst*; moreover, the narrative was easier to follow and the inspirational doctrine pursued by it might be thought to have recommended the film to readers of womens' magazine stories, the Swedish equivalent of American soap opera. I can only conclude that *To Joy* was not sufficiently experimental for the Bergmaniac and too nebulous, in its proffered consolation through music, for the general audience. Beethoven's Ninth Symphony opens and closes the story; the "Ode to Joy" movement gives the film its title. Called to the telephone during a rehearsal of this symphony as the film begins, Stig, a violinist (Stig Olin), learns that his wife Marta and one of their two children, passing a summer in the Stockholm archipelago, have died as the result of an exploding oil stove in their cottage. The customary backward movement in time rehearses the marriage, Stig's professional struggle, the birth of their children. Bitterly humiliated when attempting to become a soloist (he had made a mess of a violin concerto), Stig has been unable to accept the fact that he is not a genius; increasingly he resorts to the aching assurance of his wounded ego, rejecting Marta's comfort with bleak refusals. "One is never two!" he selfishly reminds her. "The essence of it is that one is always lonely. . . ." They had bickered vehemently over a woman who was supposed by Marta to have consoled Stig; she had not, but after another of their altercations she does. Husband and wife finally arrive at an improved understanding too late. When Stig feels most devoted to Marta and most penitent for having struck her violently in their climactic argument, the fatal accident occurs with which the film opens.

Certain transitional passages in the story of Stig and Marta are merely narrated, an awkward device, by old Sonderby, the orchestra's conductor (Victor Sjöstrom) who appears as an avuncular figure, much like the man with the umbrella in Bergman's second film; he it is who urges Stig, after the tragedy, to transfigure his pain in the world of music, in that movement of the Ninth "where the celli and the basses sing for joy . . . a joy so great it lies beyond pain and despair". The suggestion that personal grief could be dissolved in the imaginative life of art was a new theme in the prison-and-thirst world of Bergman; regrettably it was all too close to the kind of answer given in numberless hackneyed vehicles of this sentiment. Not only that, to allow a musical performance to usurp the expressive assets of cinema itself leaves the film with a conclusion which depends very largely for its emotional effect on the values of another art. While I don't find this unforgivable, I do feel that it constitutes a kind of evasion. However, I should add that the sequence in the film was directed with obedient sensitivity to the double demand of Beethoven and the film continuity. And I think there is no doubt that conscious attention to an orchestral passage of such complexity was a vitally important experience for Bergman. It sharpened his attention to one of the most delicate problems in the craft of film: the nature and degree of a musical accompaniment. I find that most filmgoers are quite unconscious of the extent to which their emotions are edited by a musical score unless it is crushingly obvious as, for instance, the theme of *High Noon* or *Doctor Zhivago*, the sustained Mozart and Vivaldi recitals which cover the inherent deficiencies of films by Agnes Varda and Bo Widerberg, the injection of rock ballads when a crime film is about to go flabby. They are seldom conscious of there being no musical score at all. Yet, since the mid-Fifties, film music has for the most part been submitted to as rigorous a discipline as film editing, with comparably improved results. Among the pioneers of the intelligently handled and severely reduced film score, Bergman is in the forefront.

The better moments of *To Joy*, dramatically speaking, were the intimate scenes between Stig and Marta, between Nelly Bro and Stig or her husband. Mai-Britt Nilsson's candid face and disarmingly innocent reactions were never more appropriately exploited; a brief scene in which she is trying to play down her birth pains and Stig is experiencing them vicariously is memorable among my recollections of the light touch in early Bergman. The wife-of-a-chum in sexual pursuit, which Bergman had utilized in *Eva*, was recapitulated in *To Joy*, performed with properly embarrassing conviction by Margit Carlquist. Despite these compensations, the film is periodically tedious, a rather tepid venture in refurbishing obsessive problems and no end feeble in its attempts at philosophic distance. When, at the rehearsal that ends the film, Stig's surviving son sneaks in to watch Daddy play—Life goes on?—one feels that *Hearts and Flowers*, rather than Beethoven, is called for.

Sommarlek

Bergman's struggle to express a more sanguine acceptance of life's wounding contradictions is better illustrated at this point by *Sommarlek* (United States, *Illicit Interlude*; England, *Summer Interlude*), which was not released until October of 1951. In Bergman's career it is something of a milestone and for this reason has perhaps been overvalued by critics who know this because Bergman has so often said it was. Before making this film Bergman had been through another divorce, an experience by his own account as upsetting as any he had survived. Whatever intensity this may have supplied to his emotions of the hour, which is, of course, centrally important, there is no direct reflection of the matter, so far as I know, either in *To Joy* or in *Sommarlek*. Any biographical elements in them would appear to have been rooted in the earlier paradigmatic experience of Bergman's nineteenth year. Having treated this reminiscence with a nervous combination of sadism and the occult in the play, *Rakel and the Cinema Attendant*, Bergman now returned to it with a deeper respect and with no compulsion to substitute rhetoric and supernatural baggage for a more direct engagement. He acknowledges the constructive partnership of Herbert Grevenius in this enterprise of recovery. Grevenius, unemotionally involved, was in a better position to see what was irreducible and viable in the original version. *Sommarlek* was not Bergman's farewell to bad dreams (it only appears to be if his filmmaking chronology is taken as the sole evidence) but it was the most refined condensation of them at that period of stress. If familiar thematic patterns reappear in *Sommarlek* that is simply because those patterns had their origin in the nuclear story. *Sommarlek* was the seed as well as the flower of many plays and films that went before.

A ballet dancer, Marie (Mai-Britt Nilsson), is helplessly unable to commit herself to the man she loves, an admiring journalist, until she has relived and become reconciled with a crisis of sixteen years earlier when her first youthful love affair came to a terrible end. Henrik had dived from a high rock, where beneath there was no water, dying like a mashed lizard before her eyes. In the depths of her bitterness and misery she had given herself lovelessly to her "uncle" Erland, an aging bachelor in whose cottage she had been staying. In one draft of this scenario the film was to end soon after this misalliance, with Marie self-disgusted and spiritually broken—another accusation of the malevolent powers that destroy youth, hope, and the will to recovery. The final version is, however, affirmative. After reexperiencing the loss and the shame of that blighted summer by reading Henrik's diary, given to her by Erland, and by returning in the flesh as in her fearful imagination to the actual scene of the calamity, Marie is enabled to reassert the suppressed vitality which has, after all, kept her alive and at least professionally involved with the world. She returns to Stockholm prepared to acknowledge David's claims on her, if he will first read the diary himself and begin to understand why she has been so out of love with life. Like *To Joy*, the end of *Sommarlek* is a beginning, in this case the opening scene of a ballet. Marie has rejoined the concert of things, while David looks on from the wings, enraptured, his own hope now becoming fruitful.

I must plead with some regret, since I understand that this film is dear to the hearts of many, especially to Bergman's, that I have never found it altogether convincing. Visually it is almost flawless, atmospherically it is provocative; psychologically, it seems to me, it lacks the ruthlessness demanded by the experience represented. I saw it for the first time in 1955 and at that time I made the comment that the script sounded as if written by a high-minded woman who was attempting to conceal an intense carnal frustration behind an opalescent cloud of poetry and the kind of wisdom which is substituted for a passion one no longer feels. Today that description might still serve as the negative share of my opinion but I would not therewith dismiss the film. I did not dismiss it in 1955 either, but I did get the impression that something very personal, inexpressible, perhaps something untranslatably Swedish was buried in the story, something which was never quite conveyed in what my eyes received. There is of course nothing more difficult to project convincingly than the resurgence of life in a stricken human being, without recourse to a concrete event such as birth, another passion, a professional crisis. Bergman staked everything on mood, depending on Mai-Britt Nilsson's vulnerable, expressive face and on the suggestiveness of a given land-scape. To undergo a moral recovery by reading the words of the dead or by immersing oneself in nature is much easier to bring off in literature. On film, the requisite foreshortening of time is a hazard. An intense con-centration of means is called for, under the aspect of a selective order of poetry: the pangs of remembrance, the movement of growth and light in the natural world, associative images that link up in space and time. If these fail to cast a spell, the personal resolution of a grief may simply remain an interior climax which we, in the cinema, must take on trust.

Too much of the burden here was placed on Miss Nilsson and I still maintain that she was unequal to it. Her performance, in its lighter and more wistful phases, was without question acceptable, but she did not convince me that she could have exposed herself to a masochistic rela-tionship with a much older man which thereafter made her feel degraded. I am of the opinion that Miss Nilsson has little imagination of evil, which may well endow her with ingratiating life-qualities but is a drawback when she is called upon to evince the finer terrors in the theatre. Apart from this speculation, I found the journalist David, played adequately enough by Alf Kjellin, an insufficient reward for the agony this girl had allegedly suffered; he simply isn't, as written, anybody but "a journalist".

Nonetheless, the film has an ambience that repudiates many logical reservations which might be advanced. It *is* film poetry, of a kind. Berg-man, himself, remembers with great satisfaction that here, for the first time, he felt, the medium had obeyed him. To be sure, we can all recognize in this film a new, radiant sense of space; within the individual setting there is a significant physical distance and relationship between objects, between people, and with it a renewed feeling, on Bergman's part, of how light can be orchestrated to more subtle ends. Not that he was un-aware of his instrument before; he was familiar with it technically. In *Sommarlek* he is beginning to breathe with it. I can't help but repeat an assertion I have made earlier, that whether or not Bergman was con-sciously susceptible to the influence of Alf Sjöberg, that influence ap-pears to be present in the formal clarity of the closeups, oblique angles of vantage, the floor-perspective shots to enlarge or to make expressionis-tic the figures in focus, in, above all, the use of mirrors, which themselves amplify the space effect, for contriving antithetical compositions and implying antithetical human attributes. In the long run, the essentials of Sjöberg's style were of little use to Bergman, for the dynamics of the two directors were worlds apart. Sjöberg's technique is one of attack. His camera pursues and encircles his prey, his editing emphasizes shock, he cuts from one moving shot to another, changing tempo with the cut; in *Miss Julie*, 1950, he mingled past and present actions within the same frame without ghosting the characters.

Bergman's camera does not typically assume the role of a questing participant, although he is quite capable of making it do so. More characteristically it is an intent but stoical witness. Sometimes he gives one the feeling that his camera is a stranger who has blundered at the worst possible moment into the privacy of someone's life. Fearful of attracting attention, it either tiptoes away to a discreet position or simply freezes while the person intruded upon, all unknowing, exposes without reservation the torment or the absurdity he had hoped to conceal. Bergman usually depends far less than Sjöberg on movement within a scene or on sequences of short-duration cuts. I'm sure he would give implicit agreement to Chaplin's article of belief that "*placement* of camera is cinematic inflection"[25] (italics mine). So might Sjöberg, of course, with a different sense in his nerve ends of what for him camera placement means.

The symbolism in *Sommarlek* has been much remarked by critics writing with an acquired knowledge of this level of reference in Bergman's later films. To have seen *Sommarlek* in its chronological place, however, was to be less conscious of certain prophetic metaphors such as the theatre makeup as a token of false identity, the lights that go out in the theatre as Marie prepares to rehearse, the owl that hoots when Marie playfully tells Henrik that she will become Erland's mistress, and the woman dying of cancer who crosses Marie's path. If these touches seem immodestly prominent now, it is the fault of our foreknowledge; they were not gratuitously imposed. Surprisingly, there is no Devil in the film. Bergman clearly resisted a temptation to which even a year before he might have succumbed and a year later, in the theatre, he did. Erland, for example, is not conceived as a senile, conscienceless seducer. He is a fallible, burned-out, lonely man; he is Autumn, which is no season for

Marie, but if for her he is a kind of death he retains the lineaments of a human being. As played by Georg Funkquist, he wears a sort of bankrupt but gentle majesty, which does indeed take some of the edge from the self-loathing Marie is presumed to experience. On the other hand, the ballet master is patently an allegorical outrider, a figure of premonition, not baleful but insinuating, grotesque, friendly. His image in the mirror mocks that of Marie, juxtaposed, for she too wears a mask; his is only more comic, a false nose instead of false eyelashes. And his sexless kiss is as sharp a reminder that time is wasting as the lights that stammer and fail. The text of the film is here, where life is quickened by the kiss of death.

It Can't Happen Here to *The City*

Early in 1950 it became increasingly apparent that Swedish film studios would be forced to close down unless the government either reduced the admission taxes or granted a subsidy. Studio executives, understandably anxious at such a moment, were wary in their choice of scripts as well as with their releases. *Sommarlek* was not released until more than a year after its completion, but a film Bergman made later was distributed earlier. Always commercially realistic, Bergman anticipated the shutdown, knowing that if it lasted for the predicted two years he would find himself out of pocket. There were children to whose support he contributed; he expected to marry again; he was constant in his obligations to his parents. For this reason primarily, one hopes, he made *It Can't Happen Here,* 1950, a source of embarrassment for everyone connected with it. On all quoted credits you will find the script ascribed to Herbert Grevenius. He insists that if the original story is consulted it will reveal itself as wholly the inspiration of Bergman. A few years ago a friend of mine who wanted to have the film screened so that he could write something about it was actually told by someone at Svenskfilm that he must have been mistaken; Bergman had never made such a film. He made such a film.

It Can't Happen Here is a political melodrama unabashedly modeled on the work of Alfred Hitchcock, taking its point of departure, topically, from a very nasty incident in Sweden's political history. After the Second World War, the Soviet government was busy rounding up refugees from their captive countries, especially those who had assisted Germany, even if unwillingly; agents in Sweden were implacably hunting Esthonians, Latvians, and Lithuanians who were oddly reluctant to share the largess of Matushka across the Baltic. The Swedish government did nothing to frustrate this activity; on the contrary, in 1947 it delivered a shipload of these trans-Baltic unfortunates into Russian hands, knowing full well that it was sending them to death or imprisonment. This was the basis of the Bergman-Grevenius script, or should have been. Since, at the awkward hour, Svenskfilm was in no position to flout the government from which it expected favorable adjustments, the writers were asked to soft-pedal the circumstances. They did better than that; they ignored them. Hence, in the film, the foreign power is of course not named. The incidents of the story are in any case sufficiently improbable, in the espionage-film tradition, as not to be taken too readily for kissing cousins of the grim actuality.[26]

The plot as such concerns the sinister Natas, played with dour heavyweight persuasion by Ulf Palme. Natas arrives in Stockholm by airplane and at night (much purring of engines, spotlights on vigilant faces, cars that shadow him), with incriminating papers from his homeland, en route to defection and asylum in the West. He entrusts these papers, inventories of industrial sites and installations in northern Sweden, to his wife, Vera (Signe Hasso), to whose hotel he goes upon arrival. (That she lives in a hotel had something to do with the plot, not with the housing problem.) Vera had given him up for dead long ago, and good riddance; with some prescience she is now engaged to a Swedish police lieutenant (Alf Kjellin). During their reunion Natas discloses that to save his own skin he had betrayed her parents to the centurions, back in Soviet Ruritania. The wife is not a research chemist for nothing. With the steady nerves of a black-widow spider, she goes to bed with Natas and in the passive aftermath kills him, or thinks so, by plunging a loaded hypodermic into his arm—loaded with what is for medical students to deduce. A full synopsis is scarcely indispensable. Suffice it to add that Natas is carried off and revived by his countrymen, that Vera, who has sent the "important documents" to the police, is eventually kidnapped and post-eventually rescued from a foreign ship in the harbor, owing to the sagacity and enterprise of her cop and lover, and that the burly Natas meets his death when escaping his pursuers for the second time by jumping from the terrace of the Katarina lift (on Sunday morning the lift is not in operation), a tourist-famed structure overlooking Stockholm harbor.

The genuine Bergman touch could be felt in the hotel bedroom scene; otherwise every shot, chase, switch, and audiovisual irony is referable to earlier Hitchcock. There are reflections of a pursuer on the beveled surface of a headlight, the beating of a traitor behind a movie screen onto which is being projected a Donald Duck cartoon, and church bells tolling as Natas finds his escape route cut off. Locally, the chief attraction of this film seems to have been the opportunity for Stockholmers to identify the locations. A not inconsiderable snarl of resentment was voiced by local pro-Soviet journalists; even in a fairly recent review of *The Silence* the writer referred *en passant* to *It Can't Happen Here* as "a propagandist picture in McCarthy style".

Shortly after maligning the defenseless Union of Socialist Soviet Republics, Bergman turned in two scripts for films he did not direct. Had he done so, the extent to which they might have been vindicated remains in doubt. I think we can say that they would have had more style. His contribution to *Franskild* (*Divorce*), 1951, which related diffidently a triangle situation in which a lady of advancing years becomes disastrously infatuated with a young man, seem to have been a minor one. Directed turgidly by Gustav Molander, it starred Sweden's official favorite actress, Inga Tidblad, and has memo value only for noting another recurrence of Bergman's morbid distaste for love between couples of uneven age.

Medan Staden Sover (*While the City Sleeps*), 1950, written in collaboration with Per Anders Fogelstrom, dealt with one too many of the Jack personae, here named Jompa, from Bergman's receding apprentice years. Toward this deliquent werewolf, the writers had opposing views. Fogelström saw him as "a victim of his environment," to which Bergman responded with a thanks-but-no-thanks, leaving Jompa to the mercies of Fögelstrom and the director, Lars Erik Kjellgren. Jompa is pure jackal, an intensification of the lout devised by Bergman for his first film, *Crisis.* He pockets the loot of a robbery, in which his friends have participated with a stolen car, marries a girl he has made pregnant only after threats from her father and the award of a cushy job, steals from his employer's safe, doesn't appear when his wife is delivered of a baby, becomes henchman to a veteran crook just out of jail, informs on him with the result that he is rejailed, moves in with his mistress and tries robbing another safe to get her money for a fur coat, loses the swag, and unintentionally kills a policeman. Etcetera. When he is at last eliminated from the social scene, a speech delivered by a regretful associate states the preposterous sociology Fogelström had insisted on retaining. ". . . . there was something we should have done and didn't do. Or that I should have done. And that's what we ought to think over a hell of a long time and try to do something about . . ." It should not have taken prolonged thought to realize that the most decisive possible solution would have been to plunge a loaded hypodermic into Jompa's veins at an early age.

If the film can't squarely be laid to Bergman's account, it does give some slight indication of the left-overs in his mind or in his script drawer, and it reveals a pretty naïve conception of the Stockholm underworld. He can at least be commended, however, for not insulting our intelligence with the explanation that Jompa was a victim of society's negligence, nor even of God's. Yet, despite the transfiguring gesture of *Sommarlek,* he had not reached the deepest layer of Pandora's box. He reached it, during the year and a half before the studios reopened. The wonder is, in view of the stress which is conspicuous in his prevailing choice of subject, that he never broke down physically. Quite to the contrary, his industry was tireless; he produced plays in Stockholm, Gothenburg, and Norrköping, he married again, he concocted a number of *reklam* films, those short advertising features that precede the movie nearly everywhere in Europe, and he pursued his demon suicidally, one might say, in two bizarre plays of his own devising. It is not irrelevant to note the content of three plays he directed in Stockholm at this season, thoroughly in the groove of his preposessions: Brecht's *Threepenny Opera,* where he was accused of turning Peachum into a Devil, Jean Anouilh's *Medea,* four children murdered, and Hjalmar Bergman's *The Shadow,* a father murdered. His personal contributions to dramatic literature included a drama for radio, *The City*, evidently a revision of material which had already undergone a variety of mutations. The Narrator and distraught hero was given the same name as a character in one of Paul's books, in the play, *To My Terror*. In 1949, during Bergman's second visit to Paris, he wrote a play called *Joakim Naked*, which has never been published or produced and of which I have only an unreliable summary. I can only report that it sounds even more subjective and more ghoulish than *The City*, which was derived from it, if that is possible.

This radio piece, as well as *The Murder at Bajärna*, staged the next year, 1952, at the Malmö Municipal Theatre, where he initiated his long directorship, are pivotal to an exposition of the crisis that separates Bergman's early period from those of his predominantly filmmaking years. They are far more crucial, seen in that perspective, than *Prison*; they upset the simplified notion that *Sommarlek* was an unqualified transition, a crossing of the shadow-line, to use Conrad's figure. We can justify, if we will, *It Can't Happen Here* and the scripts Bergman wrote for Molander and Kjellgren as hostages to fortune. *The City* and the Bajärna play were deadly serious personal commitments.

I was fortunate to hear a rebroadcast of *The City*, fifteen years after its first performance, on February 20, 1966. Fortunate, because the excellence of the production, directed originally by Olof Molander, did much to mitigate my extreme distaste for the script. As a play conceived for the radio medium it did not seem as experimental as it was reported to be in 1951, naturally enough, but the sincerity of the actors and the intelligence with which Molander had modulated the spleen of the content endowed the occasion with more conviction than I supposed would ever be possible. It may be appropriate to insist here that the occasional attendant at a Bergman play or film over the years has not the same experience as a critic who has the whole corpus of Bergman's effort before him, so to speak, or who, in the line of duty, sees ten Bergman films in a week. The unprofessional viewer sees each performance in itself and is not likely to connect the several exhibits, one with the other, as reflecting the director's unifying and eventually monotonous problems. Hence, to the national radio audience in 1951, *The City* was probably a novel experience, unrelated in most minds to Ingmar Bergman's journey perilous.

The city in question was ostensibly set in France, an unnecessary subterfuge since if it is not indeed Uppsala it is substantially everywhere and
nowhere, like the city in *The Silence*. Joakim opens the narrative drama
with a soliloquy. "I want to know where I now stand, what has happened
to me. Let me see . . . I escaped from everything. . . . I couldn't lie any
longer." The ensuing action consists of Joakim's wandering through "a
town of memory's ruins" which gives every hint of being inundated
from some turbulence beneath which is straining and cracking the pavements and creating thunderstorm weather, hot and electrical. Joakim
hears that his wife, Anne Schalter, has been condemned to death for
murdering their four children. The executioner, Oliver Mortis by name,
permits him to see Anne in her cell where, when the couple is alone, Anne
tries to minimize the savage discordancy of their marriage and its bloody
result with a last pitiful plea. At least, she maintains, *despite* the lies and
accusations on both sides, they have been *loyal* to each other, haven't
they? "No!" Joakim answers her brutally. "I betrayed you with women
and you slandered me to your friends!" They wrangle bitterly over this
subject, then abruptly she asks him if he's happy with the woman he now
lives with. "Yes, I am," he informs her cruelly. "We do quarrel, of course,
but she's far milder than you!" In desperation, Anne begs for something—
a scrap of mercy—to hold on to. Doesn't he believe that, after all, their
common suffering has been worthwhile? Joakim, enraged at her colossal
dishonesty, storms in reply, "*No*, it hasn't been worthwhile! *Nothing* in
the world is worthwhile!" They attack each other again, wildly, but
before they part Joakim assumes a change of tone. Motivated by a touch
of remorse, no doubt, he asks Anne to forgive him. Now it is her turn to
be outraged and unrelenting. She screams abusively at him, branding him
an egotist and a liar, and concludes the fray by spitting in his face.

After this holocaust of emotion, Joakim again drifts through the city,
noting that the thunder has died down and the heat has been dispelled.
The sun is shining on drifts of snow. Unaccountably but to his unquestioning relief he finds himself at his grandmother's house, the crucible
and nest of his childhood, where he finds toy soldiers, a teddy bear, a
magic lantern. He remembers the shadow-sails that moved across the
ceiling, more real to him then than anything he knows now. And grandmother is there, reproving but merciful. She listens patiently to his self-
abasement. "I have buried myself in women, in religious ecstasy, and

I have believed in the activity called 'artistic'. All in vain! Now I give up, completely. I declare myself bankrupt!'' He is grossly exaggerating, Grandmother assures him; in fact he believes in himself, limitlessly! His emotional bankruptcy is a pose, since in reality he finds pleasure in an abundance of good things such as children, music, food, and books. She sums up his problem with the observation that to her it seems little different from the problems of others. He nourishes his guilt-feeling with conceited satisfaction, for it makes him feel better in his own eyes by preventing his seeing himself as but a small cog in the vast machinery of cause and effect. And she concludes: ''It is your insignificance that troubles you, my boy. . . .''

Suddenly Anne Schalter is there, arriving to fetch the children. This has all been only an evil dream or hallucination. *Or has it?* For now the flood is certainly rising; they hear that everything of value must be removed from the house. Garden Street will be spared the major disaster but there may be a long, long interval before the New City is built.

''Will there be a *new* one?'' asks Joakim, incredulously. ''What a damnable anti-climax!'' While the toy soldiers play a lively funeral march, the city sinks beneath the waters.

This extraordinary salad of self-exposure, perfunctory self-analysis, masochism, and willed nightmare reached the ears in May, 1951, of a nation-wide audience of Svenssons largely uninitiated by attendance at Bergman's theatre and far from prepared to hear avant-garde anguish by way of the radio. One wonders what the average listener made of Joakim's imagery when the city perishes by flood: ''. . . . hundreds of severed hands floated on the water. They moved and swam like animals; sometimes they crept up on one another and copulated, and at times they fought until the water foamed.''

The Murder at Bajärna

The Malmö audience for *The Murder at Bajärna* was probably better equipped to take Bergman at his most excessive. Lars Levi Laestadius, the theatre director, who had associations with the Fyrtiotalists, was an old admirer of Bergman's plays. Each had first attracted attention under similar circumstances: Laestadius by directing student plays in Uppsala, Bergman, nearly a decade later, by directing plays for student theatre in Stockholm. Their careers in one department were again to run parallel, for Bergman became Director of Dramaten in 1959, Laestadius the chief of the Stockholm City Theatre in 1960.

The Bajärna drama, which was staged in Malmö by special invitation from Laestadius, had its setting in the province of Dalarna, cf., *The Road to Heaven*. Allegedly, the style of its execution was robustly in tune with its character, that of a primitive ballad. Lusty but direly haunted, the central personage, a pastor in a remote nineteenth-century community of Dalarna, is strong enough to geld a stallion single-handed, demented enough to see visions resembling those recited by Joakim in *The City*, sheerly Bosch: the sea belching snakes and fragmented humans on to a dead landscape, women giving birth to pieces, only, of children—a hand, a foot, a head; a black sky punctuated by faces of half-animal, half-human features, "shining with a sick light". To this holy but seriously deranged man comes doom, brought by a troupe of players, among them a bewitched and pregnant actress whom her good companions succeed in cajoling the pastor to marry. This possessed woman is animated by the maleficent desire to pervert the pastor's Christian integrity and forbearance into evil, to lure him into the circle of her own depravity. Her black magic, or her powerful carnality, brings the wretched man thoroughly under her spell; when her demonic child is born, he pronounces a curse upon it. Even then she is insatiable. Since this malign gesture is insufficient to prove that she has destroyed his soul completely, one thing remains. She must provoke him to kill her, which he does, by strangulation. Thereafter, as the play ends, he castrates himself with an axe—in the woodshed offstage.

As usual, more of the critics than not were ensorcelled by the staging and intimidated by the half-baked ceremony of tragic purgation. Those who responded with gravity, if not awe, outnumbered those who were merely affrighted. Ivar Harrie, of *Expressen* (Stockholm), was stout-heartedly skeptical, declaring that he was sympathetic with those members of the audience who laughed at the improper moments. Ebbe Linde, writing for *Dagens Nyheter*, concluded his review of the saturnalia with what seems to me to have been, under the circumstances, an ingratiatingly balanced judgment. Such plays, he wrote, were "ejaculations of lava, personal documents which first acquire their true interest when seen as chapters from the author's inner biography. It [this play] is not pleasant. But it is done with frenzy and flaming talent." The latter statement we must take on trust, conceding, for the sake of an argument which we lack the evidence to defend, that frenzied execution can be effective in the theatre. I should add that I am quite aware of the possibility that two generations of playgoers inured to, even enthusiastic over, the lurid solipsism of, for example, Eugene O'Neill, Tennessee Williams, Jean Genet, or Edward Albee (a score of other names could be supplied) may experience no great perplexity as they read the summaries I have provided of *The City* and *The Murder at Bajärna*.

For those who are more alarmed than inured, who are genuinely baffled by Bergman's startling regression on his way to the stars, I should like to point out that we can best evaluate the phenomenon—after suppressing our readiness either to recoil in disdain or with Mr. Harrie burst into laughter—if we acknowledge that the mind often makes life decisions with which the psyche is obdurately unprepared to agree. My personal inference is that in such films as *Thirst,* in part, *To Joy* and *Sommarlek,* Bergman's mind-knowledge, in thrall to the public-oriented task of film-making, was far ahead of, or at least on a different level from, his pulse-knowledge which he stubbornly exploited in the self-indulgent arena of the Swedish theatre. Probably it seemed reasonable to him, even mature, perhaps, for his couples to become reconciled with each other or with life at large, for Stig or Marie to be reborn out of pain, through music, nature, and the dance. Against his own bitterly unstable experience he wanted to believe that coupling boys and girls are invincible, that a damaged relationship can recover and go forward lyrically, unimpeded and without eruptive misgiving. The artist managed the rest, giving to *Sommarlek,* at the last, an enveloping atmosphere of confidence and dawning light.

Yet in his soul, he was unreconciled. The other absolute, the death wish, remained inside him, like a genii in a bottle; he was under constraint to try again and again the rancorous backward journey. From an essay, long since irrecoverable, by Nicolas Calas, I have salvaged a rhetorical figure which I find enormously suggestive as a key to Bergman's predicament. Calas was commenting on Edmund Burke's definition of the Sublime: "... whatever is in any sort terrible, or is conversant about terrible objects, or operates in a manner analagous to terror, is a source of the sublime and productive of the strongest emotion which the mind is capable of feeling." Calas adds that the tendency of numerous modern artists, as well as of Freud, has been "to emphasize depth rather than elevation, anxiety rather than will, vertigo rather than light...." Further, and here's the pull of the rope:

> The need for perfection and beauty arises from a desire to recapture the lost objects of love who people the Oedipal world of early childhood. The sense of profundity corresponds to the attempt to reach this goal *negatively,* through a vertiginous death-plunge.[27]

The italics are mine; I am impressed by the pertinence of this image to Bergman's plunging detours through the black forest and into the whirlpool.

Truths, also, live in whirlpools and forests. Bergman was not then as free to find them and return with expressions safely beyond sophomoric egotism and the pseudo-primitive orgy. Yet, with *Bajärna,* the diabolic spell was for a time broken. Followers of Bergman's autobiographical theatre were relieved by one important circumstance, one that seemed to augur well for the future: the wife had been *in fact* murdered! The fantasy killings were perhaps to be discarded! And, to be sure, this particular delusion was not resorted to in his subsequent work. When the studios reopened, Bergman's next film was more comedy than not. For a period he was willing to work by wit and not by witchcraft.[28] This was no sustaining answer, though it gave all of us some matchless comic interludes. But beyond *Waiting Women* was *The Naked Night* and still far off, beyond *Smiles of a Summer Night,* was *The Virgin Spring.* The passage from *The Murder at Bajärna* to these peaks of Bergman's achievement marks a journey, however faltering, from hysteria to tragedy, from phantasmagoria to art.

MAN CAME LATE

During the late Fifties, when Bergman's career was being overhauled with a view to upholstering the films he had made with a pattern of consistency, it could not escape notice that in the first thirteen film scripts Bergman wrote and/or directed there were six suicides or suicide attempts; in four films a girl was seduced by a much older man; one wife died from the alleged neglect of her husband; three children perished, one murdered at birth; three wives and one sexual rival were murdered in fantasy; there were three abortions, apart from those referred to in *Port of Call,* and of the young men represented as heroes two were crippled, one a homicidal maniac and a number certainly infirm of character. If, to the above, the situations from Bergman's drama are added, the sum will be a rising litany of despair. Many French critics, as I have more than once said, wrote with high effusion about this state of affairs, for if Bergman suffered so much, read the inference, he must have a great spirit. A supplementary deduction was made by Jacques Siclier when in 1960 he added up the abortions and births in Bergman's films to that date; he saw the preoccupation on Bergman's part as evidence of a deep and tender solicitation for life. I need not

"Be sure, this world of nowhere will expel
All who seek here a chance outlandish spell
That any place could offer just as well."

Alan Hodge *The World of Nowhere*

point out too vociferously that the nature of these conclusions was radically unsound. Within the frame of film fiction, the insistence on destroying women or robbing them of their children could as well point to an unconscious motive of quite another kind. I shall leave this subject instantly, as I wanted only to point out errors in logic from denizens of a country reputed to be superlogical.

As for the obsessive character of Bergman's films, taking them for the moment no further than 1951, the preceding pages have in some measure provided an explanation. But the implication that Bergman was quite uniquely mad, or at least possessed, up to then will not survive inspection. There was a quantity of Swedish film produced at the end of the Second World War period, uninfluenced by Bergman's example—though later on, his successes may have inspired a recurrence of the earlier hysteria —wholly taken up with self-alienation, social persecution, religious phobias, sexual molestation of girls, incest, abortion, marital failures, That Terrible War, and so on and so on. We have already seen that the literary climate was characterized by the *Fyrtio-talists* and that films made by Hampe Faustmann, Anders Henrikson, Arne Mattsson, and Alf Sjöberg reflected, each in a personal way, the fact of war or the stress of those not at war. More unflinching and much more hopeless than any early film by Bergman was a film made by a young experimenter, Rune Hagberg, in 1947, *After Twilight Comes the Dark,* an imperfectly executed but quite frightening study of the inexorable approach of inherited insanity. Gösta Folke made two claustrophobic films about city life but he was surpassed, as was any filmmaker including Bergman, by Gösta Werner who, having already made in 1946 a short film titled *Midwinter Sacrifice,* which attempted to recreate a primitive blood-cult in a Nordic setting, directed two films which appeared in 1949 and 1950—the first *before* Bergman's *Prison,* entitled, respectively, *The Street* and *Backyard.* These two films alone are a fantastic anthology of the whole War-anxiety period.

Technically, they were ingenious, if monstrously overloaded. They included every conceivable element from the syntax of the Expressionist heritage, they were as energetic in their movement as they were morose in temper; they employed flashback and delirium fadeouts, false-inference cutting, analogy cutting, leit-motif cutting, kaleidoscopic images and overlapping sounds. Their common ground was a flight-and-pursuit plot, manipulated by unbelievable coincidences, within a texture of paranoia and unrelenting social cruelty. *The Street,* alleged as a documented chronicle, dramatized the fate of a burgeois heroine who attempted the rescue of a criminal character with no more conviction in the telling than there would be in *Wild Birds,* directed by Alf Sjöberg, five years later. *Backyard* located the source of moral evil in the sexual molestation of a minor and consequent Lesbianism.

I have read in the literature of the clinic that, for example, attacks on little girls by old men is among the conventional fantasies brought to psychiatrists. Whether or not the frequently sordid sex experience of Swedish film and fiction is authentically derived from the Swedish scene may be arguable. In any body of film, one tries to distinguish between social veracity and the uninventive resort of a scriptwriter in search of saleable sensations or simply following a tested trend. However, I don't believe any such ambiguity can be too readily dismissed; if the artist in question is occupied with the unlikely, we should next ask why the specfic data of the fantasy are being projected. I have no doubt at all that the personal life of any of the directors I have mentioned would reveal a significant connection between his biography and the kind of fiction he has chosen to adapt or to construct. But things do hang together, for even without such knowledge it is sufficiently plain to see that all these films, everything else being unequal, were governed by the unifying principle of anxiety, spectator neurosis.

Whatever judgment may be passed on the position of a neutral in a world at war, that position is not an easy one to maintain. Up to a point, a spectator is in a more vulnerable situation than the participant of an embroilment, since the participant has no time in which to think; he is too busy participating. The bystander is wholly at the mercy of his imagination and his fear, so that for him the suffering which someone else endures is exaggerated in its magnitude. Once you are overtaken by calamity, nature establishes in you the mechanism necessary to resist it. This may seem to be a cold statement; I do not for a moment mean that suffering induces sufficient complacency to still the pain but it does bring into play a complex of resistance, resignation, resolution, camaraderie, and the saving grace of action, all of which is denied to those who are not involved. The neutral is harried by remorse. The citizen of a non-combatant country may go about his business, secretly blessing his government's policy for saving his skin, but he cannot altogether ignore as the years go by that for whatever reasons to which he tries to rise superior other countries are waging desperate war for their existence and ultimately for his.

Swedes sat under a blackout for years, toward the end I mean, under official blackouts, beside the normal blackout of the Swedish season, which is two-thirds winter. Denmark was under the heel and shipping them refugees, Norwegian fugitives from the German invasion appeared in their midst, but not many, for Norwegian prisoners of the SS rarely survived torture. In the Baltic, Swedish shipping was sunk, Scandinavian Airlines planes were shot down over the North Sea, and twice during the War German troop trains were permitted to cross Sweden to Finland: at night, to save the Swedish face. Such experiences, especially for those Swedes who did not feel that Sweden's impartiality was morally justified, must have exerted an unbearable strain. They had not even a blitz attack with which to contend, which might have diverted them from their own imprisoned psyches.

The motion picture, therefore, in the immediate postwar period was in one respect a mighty release of pent-up tensions, guilt, confessional orgasms, and a belated protest, unconsciously, that although Swedes had not fought in the war, they had by all means suffered—and here was the evidence. This being so, one could expect, when the pressure was released, that filmmaking might be resumed at a level where moral issues would be engaged less mutinously, without the hysteria by which the war-conditioned product had been distorted. Let us look for a moment at some characteristic Swedish films of the 1966 season, twenty years after the War and two years before that of the great juvenile plague which swept every continent.

Hans Abramson disinterred a novel, *The Serpent*, by Stig Dagerman. In a published interview in "Film in Sweden, 1966" Abramson assured everyone that he wanted to connect the anxieties of today with those of the Forties, when the story had appeared—Why?—and that the two principals, a waitress and a military trainee, A.W.O.L., were suffering from the human failure of communication and from inability to make contact with each other. What he showed us in the film were two hellbent young illiterates with nothing to communicate save hatred and sexual hunger, lacking any shade of human sensibility which might indicate a need for contact. If memory serves, the girl killed her mother by pushing her off a train and the film elsewhere interminably exploited sexual masochism and French kisses with the camera at tonsil-depth, and a snake that periodically hissed, "I am the title and my name is Sigmund!" Anyone trying to assay the talent of Stig Dagerman from this adaptation would have concluded that his view of life was sordid and inane.

Arne Mattsson filmed *Yngsjömordet*, with a script by Eva Dahlbeck from a documented chronicle by Yngve Lyttkens, derived from a criminal case in southern Sweden at the turn of the century. Mother and son, incest-bound, murder the young man's wife. The *piece de résistance* in the film was the mother's execution by beheading, with a fantastically simulated head being sliced off and bouncing around like a football in the prison yard! Local critics praised the film as an exemplary argument against capital punishment.

Mai Zetterling followed up her first film, *Loving Couples,* handsomely derived from every master of the Swedish film, with *Night Games,* even more eclectic, but with closer attention paid to continental models. The subject matter involved the Oedipus complex, the loathsomeness of being female, birth as hideous, willed copulation, together with pyromania, as certain release from an incestuous fixation and as revenge against an aristocracy with which the author was never acquainted.

My Sister, My Love. Incest in the eighteenth century, suggested, so said author-director Vilgot Sjöman, by Luchino Visconti's Paris production of a Jacobean play. The incest situation was obviously chosen to entice the spectator, since no shadow of moral analysis appeared; the relationship was embraced without a struggle at the opening of the film and depicted as pleasurable, but the sinners were punished in the end.

Jag (I, Myself) was made by Peter Kyllberg, a young man in his early twenties, with a half million kronor from the Swedish Film Institute. As I remember, the film was premiered in mid-summer and ran for less than a week. The iridescent scenic views—Kyllberg had experimented with color film for ten years, I was told—were muddied with a silly, symbolically loaded story about a newly wed young Svensson who hates his wife. He tries to cheat on her and she shoots him. But it all turns out to be a dream. Does it sound familiar?

Ingmar Bergman's contribution for that year was *Persona,* on which subject I shall eventually discourse. For now, suffice it to say that if it transcends the foregoing items it is, at root, undivorcibly related to the social ethos that produced them.

The fact is that if you follow the Swedish film from the Second World War to the present day you will observe that strain is *always* present; the immediate provocation will vary, but not the temper, at least not for long. An assertion is being made, not necessarily agonized but invariably an assertion, that the Swedish filmmaker is *au courant* with the movements that are shaking the world, that he is more haunted than anyone by the contradictions of life, that he is more liberated than anyone else because he is sexually uninhibited, on film, that he suffers more than you from the pain of exploited Africans two thousand miles away, that religion maimed his father's childhood and father, taking to drink, ruined his, that Iago's definition of Love is the only one thinkable and that Capitalism is original sin. At the same time he, or his brother who writes copy for overseas consumption, assures you that Sweden has solved

its internal problems, there being no external problems, or that it will
have when Royalty is no more and the Church has been liquidated and
the genders are indistinguishable. In the teeth of all the misery conveyed
by Swedish film and the rising figures in Swedish society for rape, sex
murders, and venereal disease among the young, Ingrid Thulin tells a
Venice Festival interviewer that "in Sweden we think of sex as a happy,
natural thing!"

The contradiction is superficially easy to analyze. Spectator neurosis
afflicts first and foremost those who are in any influential way concerned
with maintaining a Swedish profile for the rest of the world, and this
means dominantly editors and journalists, theatre and film people, Leftist
youth groups, refugees who overcome their doubts about Swedish society
because they're glad to be alive, politically oriented executives, such as
the chief of the Swedish Film Institute. The unendurable fear that
Sweden may not be as progressive, as updated, as socially indignant, as
sophisticated or as pugnaciously liberal as some other country induces
a frenzy of overstatement which coexists, visibly comic, with the normal
and preferred existence of the Swede.

Let it be understood clearly, since without this premise nothing else
makes sense. Sweden is a prohibitive society. Root, stem, and branch it is
prohibitive. It is a society of the armored personality, it is a never-on-
Sunday society, it is a society whose doors are locked before 9 P.M., a society of no dialogue, a society in which hospitality is merely a word. It is the
only society on earth where you can leave someone's house in a suburb at
two in the morning, with the temperature below zero, and be assured that
it's only a ten-minute walk to the Underground because your host doesn't
want to take his car out of the garage. It is in short a puritan society
and let no one tell you differently. A seasonal correlative to complement
that movie image of they-loved-one-summer is the Salvation Army singing on the snowbound street. The rest—what you may believe contradicts
this picture—the sex magazines and films, the drug traffic, the hippie
gatherings, the political rallies, the headlined charity toward starving
millions in Asia, is of course overcompensation, a flight from boredom
on the part of a minority not yet tamed to the wrist, or an expression
of guilt for living in safety. Deep down perhaps, it is the desire of a
stodgy people to protest that in actuality it has a nostalgia for chaos,

since chaos at least implies a collision of forces, a condition of disorganized vitality. Deep down that desire must be, however, for the immediate strategy is to avoid making waves, to incite no undue passions and to keep concourse at arm's length or further, whenever possible. Every aspect of living is designed, with unconscious calculation, to discourage prolonged meetings and for every instance there is a rationalization to defend it. If, on a winter night at ten o'clock you can't find a cafe open, save one with international-luxury prices, that is because it is a winter night when everyone goes home early. If in the summer only half the cafes in town are open, that's because in the summer Swedes leave Sweden for as long as their budget permits. If they can't manage or prefer not to visit the continent they will head for the skerries or the lakes to get away from all those others in town, even though in summer Stockholm, for example, is as deserted as Pompeii. When all else fails, they pull out the telephone jack; this device is, I suppose, a composite international invention but I wonder if in any other country it is so precious a psychological convenience.

Operation Suicide

A foreigner on brief visit to Sweden may feel satisfied that he has been the recipient of conventional courtesies; if he extends his stay he will soon be confounded by something he'll be hard put to name, something very like bad manners. Yet, in the same way that we distinguish between the immoral and the amoral, we might describe the Swede at large as a-mannered. Exchanges for which there are rules he can negotiate; beyond them he seems to have no instinct and little schooling. You can learn consciously to say how do you do without faltering, to command your children to curtsey or bow to adults, to toast your companion on the left at the right moment, to say *tak för maten* (thanks for the meal), and any of these prescribed habits have been acquired by Swedes, to a pitch of boredom, but there are other moments for which a response is not taught. If it is, I think few of us can remember when we consciously assimilated the rhythms of impulsive courtesy. Example collaborates with inclination, but in Sweden one concludes they lack the inclination.

Notoriously, they cannot make small talk which, in its inception, is simply the instrument by which we try to discover to whom essentially we are talking. They express no desire to warm an encounter, otherwise impersonal, by suggesting a cup of coffee—certainly not by suggesting a drink! They reveal no inclination ever to drive a conversation beyond the pragmatic limit of the immediate subject; if you do so, their consternation or their boredom is instantly apparent. They have no art of letting you down easily if they have occasion to refuse a favor; they have no natural response—in fact they have a positive aversion—to tales of bad luck, to implications that you could do with their helping hand in a contact, to suggestions that you are troubled by something which you'd dearly like to chat about over a glass of water. The mere prospect fills them with horror, you can feel the machine of the mind desperately working to invent an escape, for they can no more bring themselves to say no, imperatively, than to say yes. Either yes or no is a commitment, and commitment they fear, as I fear typhoid or death by drowning. They struggle and gasp, clearly resenting the fact that you have placed them in a position where they feel obliged to say yes or no. If you don't take them off the hook by saying ''Forget it, it was just a thought,'' you have a distinct feeling that they're going to have a stroke or foam at the mouth.

What makes this all so unnegotiable is that their signals are not clear as, for instance, those of the Japanese are. You can fairly quickly get accustomed to the fact that an excessive grin on the Japanese face indicates Oh No!, while he's saying yes-yes, or that he forgives you for being such an ass as to display candor, or simply that you've had it! But with a Swede you're never quite sure. He looks like us, he dresses like us, he speaks English better than many of us, he appears to subscribe to the assumptions of a liberal Western society, but he does not, and until you've acquired a technique for sensing when you've opened the window too far (I never acquired it) you will be constantly baffled or outraged, depending on the elasticity of your threshold. If he says, with seeming cordiality, ''Do telephone me some time and we'll have an evening together,'' you must not believe him. To take him literally is to expose him to misery (not too high a penalty, perhaps) and yourself to repentance. He will shortly make it clear that you are a tyrant for having imposed on him a gesture he never expected to complete; probably he will evade the engagement for the moment and assure you that in a few days he will return the call and follow through. If you catch him so unaware as to leave him with no alternative except the proffered invitation, the effort he will then expend to make his hospitality convincing will be excruciating and, except to a professional sadist, is simply not worth the enterprise you have shown. But make no mistake, he will never forgive you.

Much I describe here may appear to be the normal symptoms of xenophobia, but such a diagnosis would be too simple. It is not toward foreigners alone that Swedes offer resistance or overreact. They display spectator neurosis whenever they are challenged or believe that they are being challenged. They can be challenged by your mere presence if they recognize that it conveys assumptions with which they are not prepared to cope, but they are most seriously disturbed when they meet a challenge which they have created themselves. This, at least, is the principal inference to be drawn from a valuable psychiatric investigation carried out in the early Sixties by an American, Herbert Hendin, M.D., *Suicide and Scandinavia.* The popular belief that Sweden, or Scandinavia as a whole, has a high suicide rate is among the received ideas which more exact definition will not sustain. On that subject, the inaccuracy of the terms we use, the sociologist Jack D. Douglas has provided eloquent and documented testimony.[29] I should have thought that a country as dedicated to self-preservation as Sweden would be self-evidently not a country whose inhabitants commit suicide by the gross. Probably the fact that anyone at all commits suicide in a society that advertises itself as virtually utopian is what has prompted the rumor. Dr. Hendin's study was undertaken to discover the motivations behind the suicidal act and with the express hope of discovering in what respects and to what extent such motives can be differentiated culturally. Toward this end, he conducted psychiatric interviews with a number of Danes, Norwegians, and Swedes who had attempted suicide, in order to learn what motivated them. In the course of his analysis he inevitably uncovered the basic social assumptions underlying their character and their behavior since, at the same time, he closely studied their reactions to his inquiries. His specific conclusions seem to me unimpeachable and the distinctions he makes are, I believe, indispensable to our more refined comprehension of the Scandinavian. My brief summary of his work here will be principally restricted to his analysis of the Swedish situation. Among Swedes, the impelling force toward suicide Hendin calls "performance anxiety," which I take to be the individual exhibition of what I have generalized as spectator neurosis, except that the audience to be impressed is the audience within. As distinct from the Dane, who is usually undermined by the loss of an object depended upon, or from the Norwegian who is beset by guilt-feelings which follow aggressive, antisocial behavior, the Swedish would-be suicide is brought to his pass by the failure of rigid performance expectations, accompanied by a strong self-hatred for that failure.[30] The imperative, Hendin found, was traceable to the customary early separation in Sweden of mother and child; the male child, especially, is expected by his parents to proceed on his super-ego and he spends the rest of his life intently so doing unless a crisis in self-esteem reveals the insufficiency. When the crisis arrives, and this is sadly interesting, the Swedish male withdraws from his woman instead of going to her for solace, his attitude being, quite without resentment, "She can't help me so why should I tell her about it?" Beside suicide, he has other ways of handling what Hendin calls "retroflexed aggression": these ways being alcoholism and hypochandriasis. But not sexual infidelity; at least, among the patients Hendin was questioning, this outlet had not been sought.

On the side of the women, however, repeated infidelity was resorted to, usually in retaliation for being slighted, but it was not a successful counter-measure. In other words it did not reduce anxiety and it did not stave off catastrophe. For women, the major precipitating cause of suicide was disappointment in the marital relationship. Hendin does not stress marital, he says "relationships between the sexes". The woman, from Hendin's account, is doomed to repetition. She grows up resentful of her mother for being unloving, demanding, and critical. When she receives the same treatment from her husband she attempts to strike back by suicide if all else fails. I presume that when she does not take this way out she completes the cycle by a compensatory self-assertion over her own children. In any case, the defensive female is a familiar figure on the Swedish scene.

Hendin further observed that his Swedish patients were by far the hardest to reach. In any discussion of emotional problems, for example, it took him four to five hours to get the same amount of information or the same degree of response from a Swede as he could get in two hours from a Dane. At the second or third session the Swede was embarrassed at having revealed so much of himself. Danes, on the other hand, were anxious to confide what they had previously forgotten. Hendin claims that the Swede was characteristically unaware of the nature of his own feelings; therefore it was extremely difficult for him directly to express anger or open criticism. And he remarked something particularly note-worthy, in view of Evald's negations in Bergman's *Wild Strawberries*, that many of his Swedish patients were preoccupied with the feeling of being already emotionally dead. Of further interest to the student of Bergman's films, half Hendin's subjects admitted to a belief in God, but of these only half believed in an afterlife and there was far more shame attached to believing than to disbelieving. In this, as in other ways, the merely negative contribution of the past to the Swedish present is suggested. The surliness with which the contemporary Swede rejects all cultural continuity derives from the unnutritious nature of whatever continuity one thinks to locate in his history. Paul Britten Austin has exactly defined the religious climate of the nation.

> The God whom modern Sweden has rejected was, one feels, above all a sombre bogey-God, whose chief role was to forbid men to get drunk and beat their wives. Christianity has been as much a part of Swedish history as of any other European people's. For centuries, indeed, the church had a virtual dictatorship, if not of the political scene, certainly of the moral. Moralism, perhaps necessarily, was one of its chief traits. In the Söder of Bellman's day it struggled valiantly against all sorts of devils. Go back less than a century earlier, and we are in the age of witch-burnings and hysteria. . . .[31]
> As he appears to the revivalist sects, such as the widespread Filadelfians, or the puritanical Schartauan wing of the State Lutheran Church (very strong among the fishing communities of the Bohuslän coast, and the villain of *One Summer of Happiness*) this old monster does not seem to have reformed his ways. Any discussion of "religion" with the average Swede swiftly reveals that, as far as he is concerned, what is here in question is a repressive type of moralism. Which is why he makes no bones about having rejected it. The God of humanistic, cultured Christianity, the inspirer and lover of mens' souls, never seems to have had much of a look-in.[32]

All told, I think that Hendin's findings are of immense importance. It is only a pity that he did not add Finland and Iceland to his Operation Suicide, in which event we should have had a vivid clue to the entire Nordic syndrome, as it were.[33] One would like to see such an inquest carried out on a large scale; it would be an immeasurable assistance to our understanding of the ways in which the cultural presupposition determines the crisis of the individual. Swedes, however, insofar as by Swedes we mean the press and the bruised specialists, were not gratified by Mr. Hendin's enlightenment and I believe the Danish and Norwegian receptions of it were no more generous. As journalists and medical writers rushed to the defense of their national equanimity, thereby confirming Hendin's proposition, they emitted a blood-curdling cry of pain. To be sure, the deportment of a man who has just tried unsuccessfully to kill himself is not likely to enlist his most endearing qualities; hence, the general conclusions at which Hendin arrived were taken as insults to the national character. Under other circumstances, no such category would be conceded. The predominant reasons given for impugning Hendin's relevance were first, that the evidence was drawn from an insufficient number of cases and secondly, that crisis situations tell you nothing of normal behaviour, which of course begs the whole question of Freudian methodology. The objection to numerical insufficiency of cases was plainly a subterfuge. For we know that if Hendin had had 5000 patients instead of 600, or even 50,000, and his picture had remained as unflattering, Swedes would have all the same repudiated him. And if he had had far fewer but concluded that the Swede was kind, obedient, brave, trustworthy, and passionate they would have extolled him with banner headlines on every magazine cover and newspaper front page. Incidentally, Hendin predicted that performance anxiety would inevitably increase rather than diminish, since Sweden, despite the internal restrictions of a Welfare state, is becoming more than ever a competitive society.[34]

Climate As Environment

It is a commonplace to observe that the Swede is the way he is because of the physical climate in which for centuries he has dwelled. That climate shapes the man is axiomatic, if inadequately tested. As a correlation broadly considered it is superficially obvious. Anyone visiting Sweden in the winter quickly observes the grim, set, pulled-down-at-the corner mouths, the neutral eyes, the contained, wrapped-tight body movements, all conditioned by the severity of the weather, which is merciless, incessant, protracted. In October the sun sets at four in the afternoon in Central Sweden, in December at two o'clock. Farther north, the situation is too scandalous to be the subject of discussion. Darkness at noon is more than a figure of speech. The object of daily life is to endure the outside since you cannot alter it and to learn not to expect relief for many moons. Beyond this is a sequel which few short-term guests are in a position to appreciate. While from time to time there is a resplendent summer which compensates for the long heartless night sheeted by snow ("beautiful" for the first ninety days) or infernally animate with wind and incremental ice, just as often this summer never arrives or malevolently drops in for a chat, long enough to arouse false hopes of clemency. June, if not May, will explode with heat and tulips; sailboats, suntan oil and open-air annexes will make their appearance. The southward doors of country stugas will be opened wide. Then July may close it down tightly, brightness falls from the air, balcony geraniums resemble shrunken heads, tethered rowboats fill with rainwater, love grows pale and spectre-thin and dies. August will resume the boycott and as the tang of Autumn spikes the air the sun returns faintly to speed the fading month of September, reminding one bitterly of what one missed by not migrating.

What does this do to a people over a period of, say, a thousand years, if we consider the Swede to have made a definitive appearance when the Viking impulse in the North had spent itself and those who remained became a forest-lodged folk, no longer belligerent and expansive? I once held the view that the diffidence expressed by the Swede toward the world out there, the resolution with which he makes security the key to every deed and attitude, and that fatal termination of friendships and loves which is more than a cliché in his literature and films—this, it seemed to me, was an inhibition of resources derived from the futility of expectation. No matter what else transpires, no matter what governmental mode is regnant, or what international dangers are avoided, no power on earth can modify the seasonal solstice; no floodlighting can banish the perennial darkness; no technology can altogether make casual one's opposition to the stony onslaught of the cold or induce the white nights to last another week. Surely, I thought, this endless fugue of disappointment molded the temperament, created that grudging reception of any felicity, established a psychic conviction of being in advance defeated by immovable objects and irresistible forces. And since man's attitude toward woman is bound up with his attitude toward nature, might not the Swede's refusal to expect anything of Her reenforce on the woman's part the belief that she has nothing to bestow? I said above that I once held this view. I have not completely abandoned it, but I am all too aware that it will not stand unaided. Climate, in itself, can never be the sole shaping factor in a people's destiny.

Within the very region I am discussing, the generalization falters; Norwegians, Swedes, Finns, and numerous Russians live at the same latitudes and experience the same winter severities, yet clearly there are marked differences among these nationalities. Wright Miller has pointed out that in Russia the climate has been a fundamental force in determining the lot of the peasant, because also the nation was remote for centuries from outside influence. Incarcerated in forests, held by despotic power, the Russian folk alternately plodded through existence and broke out in bursts of undirected energy.

> Yet Finns in a climate scarcely less severe had bred individuality as early as the 16th century. Medieval Finns lived in patriarchal "great families" similar to the Russian, though somewhat looser; but by 1520 almost the whole of Finland was divided among individual free-holding peasants who lived as a rule and by choice widely separated from each other, while in Russia the shackles of serfdom were being fastened more and more firmly on the villages.[35]

To an important extent, qualified also by imponderables, the terrain of Sweden has been responsible for certain broad tendencies in its history which is, in one sense, as Michael Roberts has convincingly defined, "the history of the conflicting influences of forest and water."

> The forests divided and isolated; they ruralized industry, impeded traffic, hindered invasion, preserved provincialism. The waters united—the immense indented coastline offered a highway by sea; the frozen lakes a winterway through the land; and both, it has been suggested, saved Sweden. . . . from

those internal barriers of tolls and customs which were the curse of continental countries. . . .[36]

Other internal barriers were not so easily removed. Because of the infertility of the land, the cruelty of the soil, the omnipresence of that forest which was not until modern times productive, the introvertive habits formed by communal isolation, and in the late nineteenth century a climax of famine and impoverishment which led to wholesale emigration, the rural culture of Sweden failed to humanize life. Sweden has of course its own sentimental traditional of folklore, its very recent memories of a community existence better integrated, it goes without saying, than the urban life of today, and a fundament of regional customs and notably of folk music. Yet, when put to the test, there seems to be as much resentment toward as nostalgia for the country life of yesterday and although Swedish nature poetry is prolific and the happiest effects in films are often pastoral, one has scant feeling in Sweden, by comparison with other European countries, of a humanized, monument-haunted landscape, finds little evidence in their culture as a whole of anything but an abstract, and frequently melancholy adoration for the outdoors.

Since it was never easy and rarely profitable for them to till the soil they cannot love it; more often they love birch trees, waterfalls and the silence of glacial valleys, and since their society was not complex and their overlords seldom liberal there was no indissoluble continuity flowing from the lord to the peasant. Consequently, it cannot be said of Sweden as Geoffrey Grigson has said of England that

> the history, nature and necessity of the land comes to a kind of visible climax in every village, its cottages, its farmsteads, manor-house, mill, church, vicarage, village cross, its stop and pub and whichever corners or nooks are the favorite ones for evening lounging and gossiping.[37]

Though undergoing severe attrition, the substance of this situation is still available in England. In Sweden today, the "visible climax" is more often a tower-block sleeping suburb, neither rural nor urban, as uninviting as Stonehenge and with considerably less grandeur. The village church still stands, almost the only reminder that Sweden wasn't born yesterday, but the Swedish equivalent of a parish is largely a statistical registrar of the district and the churches would appear to exist largely for the sake of art historians who tirelessly accumulate the same details of fonts, weapons, sculptures, and armorial bearings for new editions of books they have researched before.

Climate in Sweden, as elsewhere, was a conspirator, not the prime mover. Faced with the mystery of a people's temperament and performance, we do well to remember an ambiguity phrased by Henri Bergson: that what we are depends on what we do and, equally, what we do is determined by what we are. His inference was that we are thereby remaking ourselves constantly; he could have as easily concluded that we move within confined compass. Did the Swede become isolated and passive *because* he was encircled, by the Danes to the south, the Norwegians to the West, the Finns and Russians to the east, or was he so encircled because his ethnic tendency was to remain isolated and passive? Geographical conditioning and political vigilance subtly interpenetrate. In earlier times, the most vigorous of Swedish efforts were spent in keeping the Danes at bay and the Baltic open. Otherwise, the Swede sat tight and hugged himself against the cold, learning how to adjust without conceding to importunity from foreign sources. The far-flung military ventures of Gustavus Adolphus, at the end of the sixteenth century, and those of Karl the twelfth at the end of the seventeenth were dictated by a combination of diplomatic alliances, imperialist policy, and personal vanity; they illustrated no fundamental urge of the Swedish people to embrace the ends of the earth. Toynbee's "challenge and response" principle is more actively demonstrated by the other Scandinavian countries.

The Norwegians, a coastal people, face the ocean and the West; the outward instinct of the Viking has been supressed or converted into forms of chaffing truculence and, under stress as during the Second World War, into an unbelievably heroic resistance to a ruthless enemy. The Finns have long had Russians to contend with and they have learned how to contend; the attempted suppression of their nationality made their retention of it the more militant. In different fashion, seemingly fortified by whimsy, the Dane inhabits what is essentially a peninsula, with auxiliary islands, of the German mainland, with no shadow on him of anything we know as Germanic. If he has little of the exuberance, the virility, and the ranging curiosity of the German, neither has he the German's fatal infatuation with what a Joycean character called "those big words that make us so unhappy" and which can lead with frightening celerity to the barracks and the concentration camp. Each Scandinavian country is, in the last analysis, responsible for the idiosyncracy of the other; if there had been a genuine Scandinavian union centuries ago, their several defensive mechanisms might be less pronounced. But *if,* as we contemplate history, is a frivolous word.

To whatever measurable extent Sweden's politics and trade have been governed by its climate, its neighbors, or the equivocal decisions of its ruling elites, the cultural character demands other considerations. Culture I understand as the gratuitous expression of a people, in other words the customs and arts, of no earthly use, without which man is a boor. And the peculiar culture of Sweden is a consequence of the phenomenon simply put by the historian Michael Roberts: *Man came late.* When, in the sixteenth century, Gustav Vasa banged mens' heads together and forced them to become a nation—forced them, that is, to trade with one another and to extend that trade—a barter economy was still dominant, as it had been in Carolingian France five hundred years before.

Man came late to Sweden; the Romans never came at all; Christianity did not finally triumph till half a milennium after St. Augustine came to Britain. Lying on the periphery of the world of the Western Church, rescued from heathendom only when the renaissance of the 12th century was in full flower, Sweden escaped the great clashes between *regnum* and *sacerdotum* which provide much of the dynamism of the medieval history of the West. For a true capital she had to wait till the mid-13th century; for a common law till the middle of the 14th. Provincial feeling remained strong for centuries thereafter; and was a political force to be reckoned with perhaps as late as 1743. Indeed the successive ascendancies of this province or that . . . . may almost be said to resemble the rise and decline of Kent and Northumbria, Mercia and Wessex, four or five centuries earlier.[38]

Sweden, in short, missed the Middle Ages in the richest sense of the connotation, missed the Renaissance and, except for the limited realm of the Court, missed the full force of the Enlightenment. The assasination of Gustav the Third at an opera ball in 1792 was an unnecessary symbol of the aristocracy's demise. Royal patronage had bequeathed its last refinements of rococo pavilions and French ballet.

Economic power had already been shifting towards the "Skeppsbro-nobility" [i.e. the wealthy shipping interests whose exchanges lined Skeppsbro—Ships' Bridge] of Stockholm, the naturalized merchants of Göteborg and the non-noble iron-masters. . . . The social and political functions of the aristocracy were passing to . . . . the professional men, small gentry, rural industrialists, non-noble civil servants—for whom the old division of society into Estates had been unable to find a place.[39]

The middle class had arrived. Within another century the transition was all but complete from autocracy and a rural population to a rapidly urbanizing democracy sharply inflected by an obdurate labor movement which, however, took the less dynamic and less apocalyptic road of social planning as opposed to the Marxist-Lenin imperative of revolution. Actually, the accumulated shock of this transition, under the given circumstance of Sweden's remoteness from the great European stir, is what we see reflected in the shuddering mind of the creative Swede.

For when Sweden consented to enter the modern world, you might say when it was impelled to do so by the urgency of economic survival, it entered at a point where European culture had reached its peak and was already fermenting with the vast technological revolutions, the rationalizing of life, and the submerged barbarism which among them would destroy it. The Swedish were prepared, or soon became so, for the mercantile involvements; they were almost totally unprepared for the rich contradictions suddenly facing them on a continent of countries centuries older than themselves. (The relative ease with which the nation adopted a compromise form of socialism was assisted by the fact that unlike England or the United States property in Sweden was not so widely diffused among prosperous freeholding farmers and small enterprising businessmen. Ownership was not a potential status for the bulk of the people; in fact social mobility was not even an ideal; protection was.) The multifarious shadings of class, a profusion of philosophies, arts and religious factions, an intricate and sinister power balance—these were altogether unnerving to a small country with a restrictive class system from which it derived little creative benefit, a petit-bourgeois morality rendered fanatical by religious pietism, a meager language, no philosophy, and by any worldly standard no arts. The creative personalities in Sweden of this period were confounded.

When the aberrations that everywhere in Western society followed in the wake of Romanticism are allowed for, the incidence of mental disease, erotomania, abnormal seclusion, drug addiction, and suicide among Swedish literary talent for over a hundred years is still remarkable. The situation, if infinitely more tragic in its personal consequences, is in kind not unlike that of the film-maker who discovered the wicked world on the verge of the Second World War. The poet of the earlier day, un-nourished by an exterior subject which a dense tradition and an intimate connection with another culture might have supplied, was left to contrive a world from his own fantasies, an alternative which was doomed to incoherence unless he had very great powers indeed. Furthermore, in the setting of nineteenth century Sweden, a macabre and dessicated travesty of the Victorian era of England, a supreme inflexibility reigned; society, when not indifferent, was inconceivably hostile to the deviates in its midst.[40] At the turn of the century a greater number of Swedish writers and painters traveled abroad. Some few remained, in Paris or London, but the majority expressed a reaction which became a fairly standard one thereafter. They took one steady look at Europe, recoiled in extreme horror, and returned to Sweden where nonetheless they were rarely able to tolerate existence because of their secret conviction that anything important in the world was happening somewhere else. I suspect it was then, if not earlier, that spectator neurosis was born.

The Pueblo

A small society depends for harmonious survival on the absolute cohesion of its members. Under special circumstances, which cannot be contrived for they are determined by nature and luck, such a society will achieve cohesion painlessly. Among the Pueblo Indians of the American Southwest the integral society can be seen in pure form, or could have been seen earlier in our century, and in my recollection was still visible twenty-five years ago. Within a single pueblo, such as Zuni, there is no discontent, no rebellion, since there is no disagreement on any fundamental issue; the goals, in our language, are limited. There is no separation of need from desire, no contradiction between religious feeling and legislative gesture, no disparity between the secular and the divine, and the tribal elders are assumed to embody the essential wisdom of the group. We do not know how many centuries of trial and error were required to arrive at this state of equilibrium; historically, the pueblos are probably unique among the societies of mankind and their like may never appear again on the face of the earth. Of their kind they are inimitable; they invite no judgement, for we are so totally on the outside that we have only subjective criteria by which to judge; we tend to falsify them with Romanticism, which is irrelevant to their conditions, or to disapprove because their existence is to us inconceivably monotonous. We know something, however, of the fashion in which they eliminate discontent when, very infrequently, it arises.

About every two hundred years, perhaps, a freak, unaccountably born into this seamless milieu pays dearly for the balance of the whole. This anomalous character grows up doubting; he cannot follow the rules; he questions the decisions of authority—which means of everyone, since decisions are only formulations of general consent. Perhaps he is skeptical of the cosmogony taught him by the elders. There are no gods on Zuni mountain; he knows, for he has hunted deer and fished for trout. Perhaps he disbelieves that dancing will bring rain for the corn, or he fails to respect the clan taboos when he casts his eye on a woman. If his behavior is merely odd, he becomes an object of ridicule; if he is openly hostile, it may be decided that he has been bewitched and he becomes the solicitous object of the medicine man. If he remains antisocial to an intolerable degree, he will be banished from the pueblo, a penalty which is likely to bring him to his senses, to *their* senses, because the pueblo is the world. If he is obstreperous beyond the reach of all sanctions, however, *they hang him.* The object of Swedish society is to avoid the necessity for hanging anyone and the method employed to arrive at this bland condition is substantially that of the pueblo: total incorporation. (No other comparison is intended or feasible.)

Swedes are united by a rationale of disunity. They hasten to bury their differences by denying the presence of difference. Truly, the Swede has a genius for noncommitment. This is why it is difficult to describe him in affirmative terms. You cannot find any ideal by which he lives, because his expression of an ideal always involves the absence of something. He has no philosophy; he has a policy. He is committed to non-commitment and disbelieves in believing. This is not skepticism, it is evasion, for true skepticism would be skeptical of so consistent a strategy. Ultimately, there is formed a solid pack of negative convictions by means of which everyone agrees with everyone else to be disagreeable.

It works. From the collective point of view, that of the race or nation, any trait which has survival value is to be respected. The Swedish system—as a political economy, K. A. Popper defines it as "interventionism"[41]—appears to have survival value. And describing the way it works Kurt Samuelsson, author of *From Great Power to Welfare State*, has explained, with impeccably Swedish moderation, that this system

> consists of enormous blocs of concentrated power which have largely achieved a state of equilibrium. On the one hand, augmented power is vested in the state and the Government, but on the other, the large organizations are better equipped not only to influence the central authority but even to thwart it. It can be contended that the new equilibrium was born out of equilibrium by the alliance which has existed all along between the Social Democratic party and the workers' trade unions.

The Swedish establishment, though more diverse in social origin than the previous order of a ranked society, is still a hierarchy: class divisions remain and are simply reclassified; wealth and family are not outlawed qualifications, but influence is the key to prestige. Samuelsson suggests that a typical list of guests invited to an official dinner would consist of cabinet ministers, party chairmen, parliamentary speakers, a few undersecretaries of state, ambassadors, directors-general in the civil service, the president of SAF (Swedish Employers' Confederation), chairmen of the wage-earners', salary-earners' and professional workers' unions, two or three generals, several professors, managing directors of top banks, a number of industrial giants and the editors-in-chief of the leading newspapers (all political parties represented, of course). This would seem to cover everyone but movie directors! The implicit slogan behind all this, "I'll sit on your board if you'll sit on mine," is a mercantile version of the advice given by the Touareg tribe of North Africa: "Kiss the hand you cannot sever".

Samuelsson confesses that the overall impression is that of "a society that has been rendered highly conservative by the countervailing force which different power groups exert against one another, each in its own 'sluggish' way". His very wording is an example of what he is euphemistically trying to define. The word sluggish is in quotation marks because it is one of the few emotive words he permits himself to use; it is a Swedish strategy to say something "through the flower," as if someone else had said what you are saying and you are deprecating the bluntness of the term. His use of "highly conservative" is equally interesting; what a Swedish writer on economics and government would consider highly conservative is food for speculation. The central contradiction of Swedish life is that the most politically leftward of European countries today, save possibly Italy, is characterized by attitudes and behavior for which the word "conservative" will not suffice. Rigid would be closer to the mark, or unyielding, for one does not call a seesaw flexible!

The master emblem of Swedish society might well be the sign on every escalator of the Stockholm Tunnelbahn, or subway: "Stä till Höger—*Gå till Vänster*". Stand on the Right; Move on the Left. This injunction completely exemplifies both the conscious and the unconscious strategies of the Swede, whether we are looking at his art, his morals, or his politics. He has achieved without recourse to revolution a society that lives in domestic equanimity; his popular press implicitly urges revolution on every country in the world where the probability exists. He pays lip service to the values of liberty yet he cannot tolerate criticism if he is caught in its searchlight. He thinks it outrageous that anyone in the world should suffer pain but he can't buy a pill strong enough to cure a blinding headache without a prescription. He laughs (moderately) at films such as Cousteau's which show him a school of fish that twitches in unison at the tap of a hammer; he stands in line to buy his liquor at a Government dispensary. While he admires, envies, and imitates American packaging and American business enterprise, to say nothing of American popular music and underground art, and has emigrated to America in larger numbers than to any place on earth, his government permits a Leftist tribunal[42] to prosecute the United States for its war on North Vietnam. *Justice?* It would never dare indict

Soviet Russia for its forcible occupation of the Baltic States or for crushing Hungary. In common with virtually every other country, to be sure, Sweden protested the invasion of Czechoslovakia. Following Kosygin's visit, however, the Social Democrats made a strong bid to recognize East Germany. Since Ulbricht's government was one of the few in the world that did not object to the invasion of Czechoslovakia, the logic here is obscure.

Swedish performance anxiety in all its dual ingenuity was conspicuous in 1968. The usual student and Left groups massed and screamed because such groups were screaming in every capital of the world. But when elections were held, the Swedish people, fraught with apprehension by the threat of any change in their own country, voted not to budge one inch leftward or rightward and retained the Social Democrats by a greater majority than they had ever granted them. The Höger (Right) party was smashingly defeated owing to a widespread fear, which is always being fanned by anyone Left of Right, that if in power they would in some sinister way remand the bounties of the welfare state, a perfectly idiotic notion. Political suicide would attend any party that attempted very far to liberalize the present hold of the government on every department of existence. That hold has for the most part been invited. Swedish capitalists do not typically defend the principle of business at all costs, and the Swedish welfare state can thrive only by encouraging business enterprise up to a controllable limit. The definition of that limit is of course controversial; it is the only controversial issue in Swedish politics. Therefore, and in other than political directions, it is not easy to understand the categories of Right and Left in Sweden. It is difficult enough, God knows, to understand them in many places today. The words liberal and radical have become interchangeable, just as in the populist mind the words conservative and reactionary long ago were fused. The world of intelligible discourse has thereby been alarmingly reduced to the hostile opposition of two wholly inadequate and uncharitable concepts.

So long as he is assured that everyone is being restricted, the Swede will accept restriction almost illimitably, it seems; he will not tolerate impositions of free choice if there is a risk of losing an iota of security. Without too much resentment, he will accept a decision from the State, let us say, of which he does not wholly approve, so long as the issue has been debated. The object is not to be swayed by one argument or the other, but to make way with a clear conscience for the arbitrary decision which he knows will anyway be implemented. After all, he will shrug, the matter was debated. Years ago the public was asked by plebiscite if it wanted to drive on the right instead of the left; the public answered no. The government bided its time, then instructed Swedes to drive on the right.

Hendin found that his generic Swede showed an exaggerated deference toward authority; for that statement, empirical evidence is plentiful. Deference may be thought of as a conservative impulse evoked by the presence of authenticity; in Sweden you feel no respect for truth behind the social reflex. While a Swede will accept pure rubbish from an "authority," especially on cultural matters, he will fail to recognize wit in the uncertified. The Swede has never killed the slave in himself; hence, he cannot meet another man directly. He has to know what rank and species that man belongs before exposing himself to the perils of challenge or reciprocity. He has no feeling for the intrinsic. If you refer, for instance, to a foreign writer whom you admire and with whom he is unfamiliar, he will not ask, "Is he good?" or "What is his view, essentially?" Invariably he will ask, "Is he *important*?" An imprimatur is required for every achievement. Several factors are probably involved here. For one, there is the famous "Royal Swedish envy," a traditional term; while no longer royal, envy remains endemic. Further, I suspect a survival from Old-Testament doctrine: the concept of a single father-figure, unrivaled and omniscient.

Stand on the Right; move on the Left. Even as he crooks the knee, the Swede of today pronounces Amen on anything older or more noble than himself. He shears off all ornament, all sentiment for the past, all expression of the gratuitous; he whittles down, levels out, and has put an end to the white-cap ceremonies of graduating students because it's a "class-conscious" remnant. He is ghoulishly hoping that the King will die before the Crown Prince comes of age so that, by some constitutional technicality which has been devised, the monarchy can be declared null and void. He is prepared to see Strindberg's house pulled down at the beck of commercial interests squeezing the city fathers, since to preserve it would be sentimental. Conservative? The Swede has little to conserve except his complacency, and it follows that he has no sense of history. If you despise what you have replaced, you will have scant respect for anyone else's traditions either. Like Hegel, who believed that past history was but a preparation for the Prussian state in which all potentialities had been realized, so the "liberal" Swede, at least, tends to believe that all history begins and ends with Swedish Social Democracy and that other countries are exasperatingly stubborn for not emulating the Swedish example tomorrow. Gunnar Myrdal's famous work, *Asian Drama: An Inquiry into the Poverty of Nations,* is more than implicitly built on this premise. If the book, which is formidable because of its bulk and data, had any tone, one might describe that tone as tacitly contemptuous of the centuries, since the astonishing pageant of India, alone, is treated as if it were merely the consequence of one long metaphysical error.[43]

Paul Britten Austin, using certain Bergman films as reference, among them *The Naked Night,* says with immense pertinence to the whole Swedish subject:

> In a highly schizoid way it is taken for granted that the social self is only a mask, that reality and value lie exclusively in the release of primitive impulses. Violence and *avslöjande* (being shown up) strip the soul of its disguises, and Eros, flooding the psyche (if only momentarily) with a plenary sense of being, rescues the ego from the shame of a merely social existence.[44]

Mr. Austin is describing the New Man, everywhere, but I can scarcely detour to stalk that imputation at large. The source, on Swedish soil, should not be mysterious to Mr. Austin, for he has located it in the very primitivism which he is tempted to admire: the Swedish love of the elements, the impatience with nuance, the pragmatic approach to arts and crafts. Civilized man perversely develops nostalgia for what he has destroyed whether that be innocence, culture, or power. Devoid of what culture he had, the Swede finds no resources to make life more graceful or subtle; he is without the context which would provide alternatives to relationships not comprised by the schizoid extremes which Mr. Austin has pointed out. Innocence is all the Swede has to regain. This is why there is such a short distance in his thinking between simplicity and a tasteless pragmatism, and in art between naturalness and violence or pornography. The predicament is tragic. When a Swede rejects the materialistic interpretations of his fellowmen, he has nowhere to go, for he has no rich intellectual frame of reference within which he might reconcile to his spirit the seasonal equivocations of living. He can retreat only into mindless nature—not as an accession to a reality which should humble him but as an escape from a reality with which he can't cope because it is too complex. To be innocent willfully is to refuse knowledge, which is to refuse maturity, which is to refuse conflict for conflict may lead to death. The Swede inhibits his life in order to escape death.

"Meanwhile there is beauty," adds Mr. Austin, "all this lovely furniture brought in to replace the unsatisfactoriness of the guests". Alas! I do not share Mr. Austin's proclivity for Swedish modern furniture and I am baffled by his serious belief that in Sweden one is dazzled by their effort toward perfection of decor. Perhaps he had in mind the sentiment, "Euclid alone has looked on beauty bare". The modern Swedish craft article, whether a lamp, a hanging bookshelf, a ceramic vase, is a highly rationalized product derived mentally, as Swedish vernacular art has always been, from provincial solutions where accidental charm did duty for style, combined with the minimum demands of an efficient international mode such as Style Nouveau, Cubism, or Bauhaus. If tidiness is perfection, the Swedish surround is perfect, but Switzerland is tidy too, and there you don't feel that everything was made last week.

Swedish Modern

Arriving in Sweden from anywhere on the continent, let me suggest, one has the impression that a contest has been strenuously waged to see who could construct not the ugliest town or building, for there is little in Sweden you would call downright ugly, but the most sterile: the decor or building-complex or unit least reminiscent of any historical vibration or of anything in nature. There is an unwritten law, one is convinced, against the wave, the crescent, the arch, the horseshoe. I can best describe Swedish architecture by naming it sexless. There is an unholy fear that any plastic component might suggest the feminine principle; on the other hand you would not call the atmosphere masculine. There is certainly no phallic thrust. It is neuter. Architects pursue unerringly the same plane geometry forms of the cube, the conic section, the quadrangle, the square, and infrequently the circle, but God forbid, never an oval! Since in Swedish practice form *only* follows function, their industrial architecture is often more vital than their domestic; for operational reasons they are forced to build a ramp, construct an overhang, contrive an ellipse, tent the roof, or observe a pleasing disproportion between a vertical element and its foundation structure. That form is shaped by movement, Leonardo's principle, is in Sweden a heresy. Once, looking at the scale model of a hospital site on a hillside, where ample space was available for adjustment, I asked the architect why a building façade couldn't have been curved. He answered, quite simply, "The question never came up". No, it never would.

As in all things, the object is to solve a problem with as little fuss as possible, not to express an impulse or capture a memory or simply to relieve the eye. The aesthetic argument of Swedish modern is reductive: safety lies in not taking a chance. Anthony West has pegged this spirit admirably in a review he wrote of a Norwegian novel, *Palace of Ice*, by Tarjei Vesaas:

> . . . if one wanted to be precise one would say that the book gives an overwhelming impression of the intellectual poverty of the Nordic culture that has adopted the slogan "Less is more" as its battle cry. *Palace of Ice* is indeed a manifesation in literature of the aesthetic of design, vulgarly known as Swedish, which evades all major problems of choice and preference by scraping everything down to the rudimentary minimum. . . . His novel is exactly like some ghastly provincial museum in which a tiny collection is surrounded by an excess of space and an atmosphere of reverence, and in which one's spirit faints from lack of nourishment—a formalist tomb in which the interaction that gives art its meaning is suspended.[45]

No generalization about a country can or should hope to catch the inhabitants without exception like helpless fish in a net. Logically, there are events and individuals of the Swedish scene exempt from the character I have sketched, but I have not been writing a personal memoir in which I might select only what delighted me or pleased my friends. I have been trying to present the dominant motifs in Swedish society in order to emphasize, with those in mind, the nature and difficulty in such a milieu of the creative effort and, too, of the social effort. On certain days in Sweden, you feel you should note in a diary that Someone smiled. You cannot reach these people with a show of affection; they distrust it, they are in this sense as touchy as Spaniards. You must wait, let the miracle happen, if you think it's worth waiting for, so that you have something with which to oppose the more salient impressions such as the vocal conceit and the slave mentality, the café sugar that won't melt, the degrading tyranny of those pornographic paperbacks strung from every kiosk, like chili-peppers shriveling in the sun, the class-hatred ethos of *Aftonbladet*,[46] and the valley of dry bones that is Stockholm's Museum of Modern Art.

There is an authentic note which you must strain to hear; it is so often locked up, muffled, walled in behind the defensive façade. You will catch that note, sounded in rudimentary fashion, in the surviving country dances and old songs; with quickened interest, in a locally trained ensemble singing angelically an oratorio of Handel or vespers by Monteverdi, in the phenomenon of a music critic who a few years ago wrote that during a Chopin recital played divinely by a young Italian he changed his seat during the performance because he didn't want his neighbor to see the tears coursing down his cheeks. You can catch the note in such homespun ballets as *Moon Reindeer* and *The Prodigal Son.* You can hear it clear as a bell, yet with undertones you are not sure you've identified, like the melodies of birds unseen in a summer-thick forest, in Harry Martinsson's wonderful book, *The Way to Klokrike,* 1948, the only Swedish novel I have read with heightened pleasure. It is hardly a novel, rather more a reverie, a peregrination, a social fable, a prose poem of which the guiding images are the smell of bog-myrtle, the flight of a jackdaw and "the fear of those who live in houses." Klokrike, though a real place, is, if you like, a symbol; the word means "kingdom of bells". Unrelated to the kind of abstract and unalluring fiction more common in Scandinavia, described above by Anthony West, *The Way to Klokrike* is warm with human hope and dread, soaked in earth like an oak-leaf which, pressed into humus by the rain, leaves an imprint. Set in Sweden of the turning century and no doubt autobiographical, insofar as this has any bearing on the social contingency and the informed magic of the observations, the book also casts a shadow before.

It has been prophesied, said Bolle, that the last professional tramp shall see the last windmill milling and after that a new happiness shall come to the world holding a new unhappiness by the hand. They shall dance across rich plains and spread the new happiness one day and the new unhappiness and doubt and death the next.[47]

Harry Martinsson's struggle as an artist was comparable to that of Arne Sucksdorff and of his natural successor in Swedish film, Jan Troell, the only other filmmaker since the ascendancy of Bergman to compel major consideration. This was the struggle to reconcile the innocence, of which Paul Britten Austin speaks, with comprehension and of course to convey it in a form which would not devitalize the primal source. Few people realize that the brief nature films made by Sucksdorff in the Forties were wrested from a background of anxiety as unrestful as any expressed by Bergman.[48] But in Sucksdorff's work, controlled by the documentary intention, there is no trace of the assailed ego to despoil the poetry.

Alf Sjöberg, likewise, is a pure product for whom certain reservations must be made. I speak of him now in the theatre, where his Swedishness might not be apparent to those who associate him with productions of Shakespeare, Sartre, or T. S. Eliot. In his vision there is a rawness, born of that Nordic chill in which man came late; it preserves his often lavish dramaturgy from any touch of the effete and by the same token it forces his hand. If Sweden had been physically connected with the European main, Sjöberg would not have had to impose his rhetoric with such a degree of spectator neurosis. In the last ten years he has lost touch with his actors, submerged as they have been by his Idea, largely the Social Democratic Idea; still, today, he can use all of a stage as no one else can and if theatre historians knew what they were about Sjöberg's theatre art up to 1960 would be securely ranked in the European continuity with that of Leopold Jessner, Jurgen Fehling, Erwin Piscator, and Gustaf Grundgens.

Where feeling rather than intelligence is demanded, Swedish artists are pretty well limited to lyric expressions, to those they can play by ear. And when a more complex and conscious structure is called for, their mind, a fairly blunt instrument, kills. They lack the steady perception that would make them masters.

So often, when trying to summarize Bergman's idiosyncracies, I have been met by the Swedish comment, especially from those who are not in sympathy with his work, "But Ingmar Bergman is not a typical Swede!" Of course, he is not typical; he has genius and no genius is typical. Yet no man can wholly transcend his culture and in his stress as in his grasp, in the nature of his rejections and in his fleeting discoveries, Bergman is quintessentially Swedish. We shall see him in the Fifties achieving his best work, hampered sometimes externally and confusing his own bent but creating, so that with every year, as it happened, one looked forward to a new Bergman film. During this period and with increased nervousness in the Sixties, he falters, to our surprise, when arraigned or snubbed by regional criticism, even though he has the rest of the world at his feet. We should not be surprised, for he is Swedish and the pueblo is the world.

LESSONS IN LOVE

Waiting Women

When the Swedish film studios reopened after a brief but worrying shutdown, commercial recovery was the inevitable requirement. Anders Dymling, president of Svenskfilm, hoped that Bergman might help him in such an enterprise and it can hardly be doubted that under the circumstances Bergman was prepared to cooperate. This seems to have been a principal factor in the four-story form of *Kvinnors Väntan* (*Waiting Women;* United States title, *Secrets of Women*), 1952, since, in the many multi-episode, multi-star films which were then current and popular, Dymling believed he saw a profitable model for Swedes to emulate. With a lively scenario, unified by Bergman's ingenuity, they could present a bouquet of Swedish talent, especially female Swedish talent, to the international market. Later, the obvious but in fact inaccurate deduction was widely advanced that the American film, *Letter to Three Wives*, was the source of Bergman's quartette. It so happens that he had not seen the film and one can scarcely imagine that he would have acquired very useful hints from it if he had; the milieux of Joseph Mankiewicz do not suggest ready transposition into those to which Bergman has a natural response. The form of three stories in one

"We wander on the earth or err from bed to bed
In search of home, and fail, and weep for the lost ages
Before Because became As If, or rigid Certainty
The Chances Are."

W. H. Auden, *Commentary*

he had already handled in *Thirst;* in *Waiting Women* he employed a simpler way of amalgamating them. At a summer house in the Stockholm skerries, which was becoming as familiar a setting in Bergman's films as Monument Valley was in those of John Ford, three women, waiting for their men, exchange intimate stories about the burdensome heaven of love and marriage, following which there is a coda, you might say, with a member of the younger generation heading for a similar destiny. The suggestion of using the wives themselves to recount the episodes of the film came from Bergman's third wife, Gun Grut.

As I noted previously, the first story was yet another fragment of the Marie fiction which had served the wavering motivations of that weird play, *Rakel and the Cinema Attendant*. The original names were retained: Rakel, the erring wife; Kaj, a former lover with whom she amuses herself again when he comes to visit; Eugen Lobelius, an antiquarian, the somewhat frigid husband. This version, if slight, is mordant in a more sophisticated way and is sufficiently touched with lyricism— as in the scene in a bathhouse where the lovers look down into the brooding, neutral world of gliding fishes—to leave an undertone of pathos after the tragicomic mess manufactured by wounded dignities and irresolute violence. The cuckolded husband, when the affair is blandly revealed to him, tries playing the masterfully injured innocent, a difficult position to maintain with any bite in it when Rakel and Kay wish to discuss it all rationally! Eugen's first action had been to seize a loaded gun, not quite knowing whether he should shoot his wife or the lover or both. But their insouciance renders him impotent to act in the traditionally aggressive manner.

Frustrated beyond measure, he locks himself in the boathouse, threatening with some conviction to shoot himself. Rakel is as cautious as she is skeptical and calls on his brother Paul to talk him into reason. Paul manages to appease the wretched man with the assurance that damaged as his vanity may be, "it is better to be betrayed than to be lonely." Later, when he repeats this to Rakel, he adds cynically, "I don't know if it's true or not but it sounded good." Eugen, a punctured bag of his former self, will now live in fear of another betrayal, with the sad conviction that he has joined a legion of manipulated husbands who would rather have it that way than risk the moral isolation of independence. Rakel has the last word, however, and one that must strike any male in the audience as inordinately smug. Asked if her marriage is less boring than it was before, she answers, "Not for Eugen, perhaps, but for me. Because now I understand the child in him. Our *only* meaning in life is each other. It's very simple." I recall now that before the second story began I grunted, "Not so damned simple!" But that's the way Bergman wanted to see it, and as touchy as I may have felt about this lordly mothering from a cooly emancipated Swedish female, I admired the crystal-clear fashion with which Bergman had transformed the wild original into a vignette which says something very pertinently, and with commendable economy, about the inexorable claims of marriage.

The second and longest story is more complex in its technique, shifting with fairly rapid cuts and editorial metaphors from Marta (Mai-Britt Nilsson) in hospital awaiting a child to scenes in Paris with the unknowing father, Martin, a young Swedish student whom she had never taken the opportunity to inform and who was too wrapped up in himself to notice anything odd. The relationship itself is barely developed, showing only the immediate consequences, for the episode is in fact a subterfuge for a crescendo of impressionism through the delirium of a birth sequence in which images are constantly lap-dissolving: stoppered bottles and dancing girls, macabre shadows, fragments of Martin's face, the sound of waterfalls, a sudden clear view of Marta, Martin and a child in a meadow, water again, then the cry of the new-born baby and Marta's life-trusting laughter. At the close of her narration, Marta's seventeen-year-old sister, one of the "waiting women," asks, "Why did you finally marry Martin?" And Marta replies simply, "I love him." Bergman was hunting simplicities in this film, that's for certain. No summary of this episode can salvage the inconclusiveness of the story content; the beauty of it is in the treatment. By contrast with the first and last items in this film, the Marta story is cinematically feverish, moving incessantly through flashback time and through the Paris streets, In one brilliant sequence, Bergman's editing and Gunnar Fischer's camera contrive a long, silent, eloquent journey, beginning with a love scene in which the lights of a room are focused on a Paris panorama on the wallpaper; dissolving transitions follow the lovers on their walks around the city, then to a gynecologist, and finally to Martin's studio. If my notes are accurate, nearly six minutes of film elapsed without dialogue.

The penultimate story is probably the best-known anecdote in a Bergman film, wherein Frederick (Gunnar Björnstrand), a businessman, and his wife Karin (Eva Dahlbeck) meet in the lift of their apartment house for the first time in months, so few are the personal claims they make on each other. He receives clients and goes to conferences; she goes to matinees, one supposes, and dull supper parties. (*I* don't know what neglected Swedish wives do with their time.) The lift sticks between floors and the married strangers are forced to spend a night with each other. Before long they are exchanging insults, in a light-fingered way. Karin, by advancing a sexual confession which may or may not be a joke, traps Frederick into boasting of his infidelities. One mood leads to another. They make love in the elevator, as ardently as space and shape permit. Comes the uncomfortable but hope-inducing dawn. Things are going to be different now; they have arrived at a more basic understanding. But when they are rescued from their trial by cage, Frederick is reminded that he has a conference at ten with a Brazilian delegate and life goes on as before. One of my favorite Bergman sallies is delivered during the above contretemps. Frederick, counting his assets against Karin's broadsides at his ego, announces proudly, "I have no *enemies*!" To which she responds drily, "You haven't any friends either!" Never was Swedish life contained in a tighter nutshell.

With the final section of the film Bergman points his moral and adorns his tales. Marta's sister runs away with Annete's son, Henrik, who has naturally promised the girl that he will be different from their flawed elders; he will be considerate, faithful, obedient, and all the rest. Marta wants Paul to pursue the youngsters and cancel their impetuosity. This time, however, he refuses to interfere, assuring Marta that "the important thing is that they do something they believe is forbidden. . . . *Let them have their summer*. Wounds and prudence will come soon enough." (Italics mine.) Since he doesn't add, as before, that whether or not it's true it sounds good, we can believe that here Bergman is speaking in his own person. Whenever Bergman has reached a point of temporary certitude, that moment becomes for him the whole truth; this is why many of his films, different in kind, carry conviction; it is also why we have a problem reconciling one of his personal manifestos with another that contradicts it. When he made *Waiting Women* he was trying to convince himself that an intelligent resignation to things as they normally are was the only feasible adult attitude. While we need to be cautious in supposing that any given film reflects Bergman's mood while making it (nobody in film business could expect such a conjunction of his inclinations with the demands of his producer!), we are safe in assuming, from what I know of the circumstances, that he was considerably lighter of heart in 1952 than he had been. He was growing up to himself as a film-maker, the expected film-industry crisis had not taken place, and he was remarried with the fresh illusions no doubt engendered by that condition.

The constructive feature of comedy, in the intellectual sense, is that it allows us the illusion that nothing in life is irrevocable. Or, as Osbert Sitwell once said, that life might be considered a comedy only if it were never to end. The comedies of Bergman's middle period were compensations for the less compromising vision of things which was native to his soul, a statement I feel is justified by the fact that *The Naked Night* erupted in their midst. Only because that film was a complete failure did Bergman return to comedy, and once this genre had enabled him again to impose his preference, the success of *Smiles of a Summer Night* being the liberating film, he turned instantly to the more probing questions of *The Seventh Seal, Brink of Life,* and *Wild Strawberries.*

It must never be overlooked that Bergman is as persistent a showman as he is a moralist. He is of the theatre, and while I should not want to declare that the one talent is all comic and the other—a preoccupation rather than a talent?—is altogether morose, I would suggest that there is a conflict between the two tendencies, between his desire to entertain and his instinct to preach, and that his masterpieces arise when the tendencies are virtually inseparable, when neither dominates the other, as in *The Naked Night, The Magician,* and *The Virgin Spring.* The sources of Bergman's theatre sense were, as I said at the outset, the stylized sources of religious allegory, moral fable, the puppet play, and the ballet. When Bergman saw a staging of Moliere during his sojourn in Paris, classical French comedy became one of his enthusiasms, for this too is a stylized form, a thing of masks in which the precisely representative character, whether misanthrope, miser, cuckold, overeducated young lady, or faithful servant, is embodied in a theatrical structure which derives its spirit from ancient forms of ritual.

One of the most fascinating problems of Bergman's development is his perennial return to the schematic disciplines of a primitive or classical mode, even as he is struggling to comply not only with the more fluid, less categorical, more musical medium of film, but also with the relativistic demands of the modern temper. *Sommarlek* was alternately pure movie, subjective, scenic, and time-compounding, and rudimentary classical theatre complete with symbolic attendants and exemplary characters such as crabbed age, hopeful youth, faithful companion, and the Manager as Chorus. *Waiting Women* was a breakaway experiment, not radical but indicative, like *Thirst,* a playing with contrary moods, a test of cinematic control—space, confined or illimitable; time, protracted or foreshortened. But framing it all was a convention, provided by the intrinsically Swedish experience, of the hippodrome of domestic incompatability and the false white nights of summer. Following his advice to Marta about the fugitive youngsters, Paul says, by way of a last word : "Come inside, now. It's getting cold".

A Summer with Monika

A Summer with Monika resumes this motif with quite another approach than any Bergman had taken in any of the skerry-setting films he had directed before. This is perhaps the least identifiably personal film Bergman has made and I know I am going against judgments indignantly pronounced when I add that I consider it one of his best. Not one of his most profound, for that's another matter; not one of his most revolutionary, yet there is paradox in that thought. Precisely because here he wasn't attempting new dimensions, symbolic extensions, or journeys into the maelstrom of the mind, this film is unique in Bergman's continuity and is an exercise in critical naturalism, lyrically executed and impenitently resolved, with not a whimper nor an accusation on the way.

An American critic wrote to me while I was composing this study to say he hoped I was going to explain why the French had overrated *A Summer With Monika*. I wouldn't dream of trying to explain any attitude taken by the French, but I suspect that what puzzled the critic in question is why the French had praised the film at all, which can only mean that he found nothing in it to admire. In my opinion the French, by which I mean French critics I have read, have overrated a number of Bergman films, for the same reason, very likely, that critics everywhere else may have overrated them: they have confused other attributes in them with their weakness for Swedish actresses. Perhaps my counter-question should have been why have critics outside France commonly underrated *A Summer With Monika?* I know some of the answers. Having been banned here and there upon its initial release, the film was later exploited for its sex features and in many cinemas of the United States and England it arrived long after the equally irrelevant fuss which had accompanied Arne Mattsson's *One Summer of Happiness*. Hence, in the view of critics who were by that time determined to take Bergman solemnly or not at all, *A Summer With Monika* was just another of those Swedish films making its way with a nude-in-the-open-air interlude.

Ingmar Bergman (1959)

Gunnar Fischer   Sven Nykvist

Doris Svedlund and Stig Olin in *Prison* (1949)

(Left) Evo Henning, Mimi Nelson and Naima Wifstrand in *Thirst* (1949)

Alf Kjellin and Mai Zetterling in *Torment* (1944)

Stig Olin and Inga Landgré (left) in *Crisis* (1946)

Stig Olin and Maj-Britt Nilsson in *Sommarlek* (1951)

(Right)Lars Ekborg and Harriet Andersson in *Summer with Monika* (1953)

(Above) Björn Bjelvenstam and Ulla Jacobsson with Gunnar Björnstrand (in rear distance) in *Smiles Of A Summer Night* (1955)

(Right) Anders Ek and Åke Grönberg in *The Naked Night* (1953)

(Right below) Helge Hagerman, Gunnar Björnstrand and Eva Dahlbeck in *A Lesson In Love* (1954)

The Seventh Seal (1957)

Victor Sjöstrom in *Wild Strawberries* (1957)

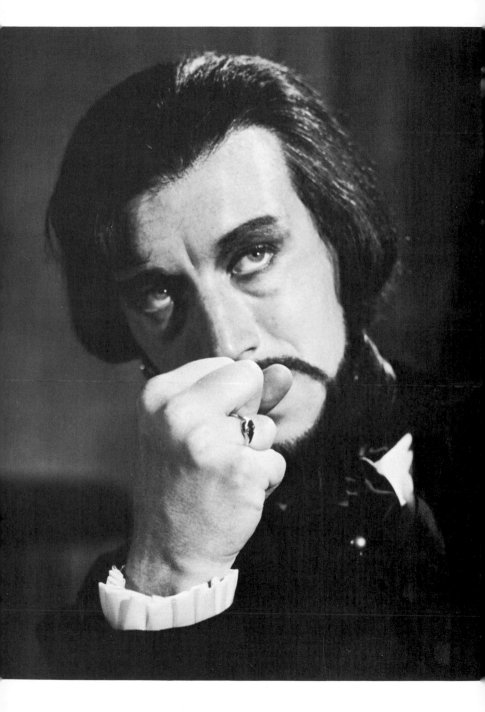

When this reaction was not involved, another, equally chilling, was. Around 1959 there began to emerge a steady stream of retrospective Bergman criticism, thought to be sophisticated, much of which assumed, a priori, that in every Bergman film there were manifold levels of meaning and a cryptic core. For the purposes of such criticism, *A Summer With Monika,* which was plainly about a sweet boob and a tramp who go for a summer-long picnic and get caught in the rain, was impossible to account for and too simple to admire. It revealed no maze for interpretation to wander through, no angst, no autobiographical insinuations, no theological dissension, no worthwhile clue to the modern failure of communication. John Russell Taylor's perplexity typified the general bewilderment when in 1963 he struggled to explain how the film ever got into Bergman's life to begin with. He was puzzled by its almost "documentary" treatment; he couldn't see how it was to be related to the Bergman films he was prepared to take seriously such as *Prison, Sommarlek, The Seventh Seal* or, above all in his preference, *Smiles of a Summer Night;* he concluded that "the film stands quite outside the course of Bergman's development from *Sommarlek* on . . .".[49]

Far from standing quite outside, *A Summer with Monika* is an integral part of Bergman's development. It is not paramount, to be sure, if you are considering the furthest reaches of Bergman's film art, but it is related; it is related simply because it is a film made by Bergman; it is specifically related, despite the difference in tone and social level— I should have thought this was obvious—to films he had made before in which a couple had spent a blighted summer on an island outside Stockholm, notably *To Joy* and *Sommarlek.* And the ending of *Waiting Women* all but predicts a sequel; the eloping couple is of an age with Harry and Monika. However, the direction taken by Bergman to arrive at this film was somewhat oblique. But for a trick of timing, he would have produced it before *Waiting Women.* Per Anders Fogelström suggested the idea to Bergman as a vehicle for collaboration while they were disputing the scenario of *While the City Sleeps.* Bergman thought of making the film as a pendant to *Sommarlek,* but circumstances diverted him; Fogelström then wrote a novel from the subject instead. We can wonder how the film might have differed if he had undertaken it before the intervening years, but we shall never know. It is fair to

Max Von Sydow in *The Magician* (1958)

guess that to its detriment it would have been more complex and even mirthless.

During the two years that elapsed, Bergman had a further incentive for reconsidering the Fogelstrom story. Viewers of *Sommarlek* had not infrequently reproached him for the sadness of that wrecked love affair, the earlier affair with Henrik. Bergman wanted to know if in actuality it might not have been worse if the couple had survived the summer, then, back in town, discovered that the other wasn't so beguiling as, under the seasonal spell, he had seemed to be. Something of this sardonic edge was supplied by the *Monika* story. By the time Bergman and Fogelström sat down again to resume collaboration they were more *d'accord* than they had been with the drawn Jompa between them. Fogelström remembers that Bergman "had the melody" from the beginning; his suggestions about cuts or elaborations in the development were more often than not acceptable to the author.

Never before had a Bergman film narrative been so directly conveyed, so free from sentimental editing or the director's moral imperiousness. The two principal characters are seen for what they are: confused, meagerly educated, unassisted by amenities at home, susceptible to movie-conditioned romancing, hence defeated, uncomprehendingly, by un-mysterious causes. Their veracity in the film is of course the creation, under Bergman's hand, of Lars Ekborg and Harriet Andersson, from whose performances all acting has been effaced. Behind the introductory titles and into a grave scenic prologue, we are shown the quay fronts of Stockholm in the early morning, a marvelous largo of shots in which the eye and ear seem to be waiting for something portentous, just such an effect as Antonioni would compose seven years later in *L'Avventura,* a breathless, expectant scrutiny of the unpeopled world before it awakens to the stir of commerce. In Bergman's film, however, the sleeping harbor implies no metaphysical concealments. It is simply the gateway to a more primal setting in which two very gauche and desperate youngsters will play a brief tragicomic role before resuming the life style of everybody else, never again to be touched by a transitory glamor.

Harry and Monika, both of whom work at stalls near the waterfront, are disgruntled with their occupations and no less frustrated by their indifferent or intractable parents. The preliminary scenes reveal con-

vincing samples of their home neighborhoods. In his house there is no
mother, father is in the hospital, a supervisory aunt presides over an
ugly decor of pseudo-period furniture, potted ferns, too many family
photos; at her's, a cold-water flat of a kind that looks and smells the
same the world over, kids are under foot in the area-way and her Dad
is a drunk. They go to an American movie with the prophetic title, *The
Girl Who Was a Dream*. Later, Monika leaves home after a row with her
father; she wants to sleep with Harry but since his aunt has a key to the
flat they take a sleeping-bag and spend the night on his father's motor-
boat under a city bridge. After Harry is fined for being late to work,
they decide to get away from it all, borrow some money, take the boat,
and live among the islands of the Skärgård.

For a while it's heaven. The weather holds, they cook in the boat, or
build fires on the rocky islets. They swim naked, dance to a portable
gramophone (this was before transistors), exchange childhood biographies, and become mellow about their tawdry lives. She admits that if
Dad is a bothersome drunkard he's fun, too, and Harry asserts he will
study engineering and get a good job. Their first serpent is a jealous
boyfriend of Monika's, Lille, who overtakes them (this is not too plausible) and tries to set fire to their boat. The ensuing scrap is decided by
Monika who bangs the intruder over the head with a frying pan. She
and Harry get drunk and make love; time passes and, as it will, brings
reckoning in the form of empty pockets and clouds from Norway. She's
fed up with mushrooms, they're out of groceries, with no more money
to buy any, and there's a chill in the air. Stealing apples from an orchard
on a skerry estate, Monika gets caught; while the good woman of the
house tantalizes her with a large roast, her man telephones the police.
Monika, suspecting the worst, grabs the roast and makes her way back
to the boat, terrified by the innocent pastoral darkness in which owls
rattle, spiderwebs threaten, and a fitful moon shows laden clouds. After
the roast, clarity sets in: no tea, no kerosene, Monica doesn't want to go
back, yet clearly they can't stay out in the weather with nothing under
their belts but desire.

They return to Stockholm, girding themselves to face the animal cares
of the normal life—a baby for her, a job for Harry, and the back of a
hand from fate for them both—which is character. The poor boy is made

of sterner stuff than she, for while he studies in his evening hours like the heroes in the success stories, she neglects the baby and feels the pull of her round heel. The climax occurs when Harry is away from Stockholm on a job and she takes the rent money, reverting to type. Harry comes back a day earlier than expected; there's someone else in his bed. This is very well done. We see only Harry, at the doorway; we know full well at what he is staring. He walks around the block, so to speak; later, he faces the inevitable showdown with Monika in one of those authentically barbed scenes of which Bergman is a master: reproach and counter-reproach; when vituperation fails, Monika cries; she teases his manhood, he slaps her away. When she tries again to provoke him sexually, he beats her, in a sequence skillfully shot through a fence of bedrails. She walks out on him forever and Harry is left holding the baby, which presumably his father and his aunt will raise as clumsily as may be. He has had his summer with Monika.

We shall pass lightly over the notoriety which sold the film and removed it from the attendance of the wary until they were persuaded to see it years later when the wolf whistles had died out. Those scenes in which Harry fondles Monika's breast and she trips into a rock pool, naked as a turnip, would raise a yawn today. (At least from me, for whom nudity has become as oppressive a cinematic cliché as the deathbed scenes and clinch fadeouts of the Silents, or the stop-motion shot of recent indulgence). In the Fifties they were the reason for this film running a year in Montevideo, being banned in Nice and Los Angeles and showing up at Skid Row palaces in a pirated print. They were probably the reason for a writer in *Le Monde* describing the film as "a classic depiction of Nordic pantheism". Far be it from me to rebuke the *aurora borealis* daydreams of a Parisian journalist, yet I do feel that this somewhat overstates the more precisely shrewd observations embodied in *A Summer with Monika*.

M. Beranger was nearer the mark when he alluded to Harriet Andersson, on the basis of this film, as "one of the most redoubtable erotic presences in the history of cinema," which may account for his otherwise curious opinion that alone among Bergman's films this one ended on a "resolutely pessimistic" note.[50] There seem to have been at the time not a few fellow sufferers with M. Beranger, put off by Bergman's, and Fogelström's, refusal to end the film with a lovely improbability; this is an instance of the Swedish myth in which so many people find false assurance. Long since corrupted by the Rousseau-Whitman heritage, they want to believe that undressing in the sun in itself confers character on those who have none, that sex in the great outdoors transfigures the subjects of it beyond the hour of their Eden-plucked-from-the-burning. Bergman knew better. If, in *Sommarlek*, Marie was healed by sources in nature, she brought to the experience a subtle consciousness and a will to share herself. Monika can scarcely be said to have a consciousness. Before the weather changes she is fleetingly endowed with an aura of pagan decency; her nature is purged of the urban subculture in which it more readily thrives. When the holiday ends, she has no further capacity for self-transcendence, for she is quite simply a slut. No other reading of her is possible; therefore no other end to the relationship would have been plausible.

If I have paid as prolonged attention to this film as to others of Bergman which are more ambitious, it is precisely because I believe the film has been taken for granted. I do not find it negligible because it lacks the refined indirection of *Sommarlek* or is transparently readable by comparison with, let's say, *Prison* or *Wild Strawberries*. At this stage of his filmmaking, I think it must have entailed considerable self-discipline on Bergman's part to leave his characters alone and let the story, inexorable and touching, tell itself. There is not a false foot in this film. Harry and Monika never say anything they couldn't say, never do anything in any style but their own. If not hay, they make poetry while the sun shines—their kind of poetry.

Between 1950 and 1953, while Bergman was hesitating at the brink of the real thing, Swedish film from the international standpoint, no other is an adequate criterion, was still eminently represented by three films of Alf Sjöberg—*The Road to Heaven, Torment,* and *Miss Julie*—together with the wildlife essays of Arne Sucksdorff which received their cumulative expression in his feature-length poem, *The Great Adventure,* released in the same year as *A Summer with Monika*. However perceptively a close student of Bergman's films may then have expected wonders, he would have had to acknowledge that so far Bergman had made no film to rival *Miss Julie* in beauty of invention, and that if you looked abroad he was no more than promising when you noted the outstanding movies of the early Fifties, among them some of the greatest in the history of the medium. From Italy, we were offered *Miracle in Milan, Umberto D,* and Fellini's opening salvo, *The White Sheik,* to say nothing of Antonioni's restrained advance into the company of those to be reckoned with in *Story of a Love.* From France, there was *Diary of a Country Priest, God Needs Men, Forbidden Games, Casque D'Or;* from England appeared, in the second release after litigation, Lean's masterpiece of Gothic energy *Oliver Twist,* from Brazil *O Cangaceiro,* from Buñuel *Los Olvidados,* from Japan *Rashomon* and *Ikiru (Living).*

In 1953, Alf Sjöberg made *Barrabas,* splendid to look at but empty at its heart; Gunnar Skoglund adapted Harry Martinsson's novel, *The Way to Klokrike,* a film which should be better known to film historians than it is; and Arne Mattsson redeemed the popularity which he had always found unwelcome for having made *One Summer of Happiness* by making the very unpopular film about the Finnish-Russian war, *Bread of Love,* an heroic effort with moments of weird poetry and corrosive power, the only Swedish fiction film of that year that wasn't reduced to impotence when placed beside Bergman's *Gyklarnas Afton (The Naked Night),* which had its premiere a month before and seven months after *A Summer with Monika.* Nobody could have foreseen, and certainly nobody was prepared for, the unhesitating grasp with which Bergman now seized the medium, after playing in the skerries with a pair of crossed-up juveniles. Taking a giant step, Ingmar Bergman doomed himself as never before; he could now neither repudiate himself nor retreat for long into less dangerous enterprises. With *The Naked Night* he had joined the company of the illustrious. He was an artist.

The Naked Night

Gyklarnas Afton is a fairly un-negotiable title if translated literally as "Twilight of the Jugglers". The French *La Nuit des Forains (The Night of the Clowns),* is a good approximation. *Sawdust and Tinsel,* the British title, is pointlessly awful. *The Naked Night,* while very probably intended to carry the connotation of Swedish nudity, in fact gets poetically closer to the world of this stark film than any title I know. For the story does take place during a night of the soul, the protagonists stripped to the bone of all saving pretense. Literally they emerge from night at the beginning and by a darker night, called a new day, they are swallowed at the end.

The setting is dawn, somewhere on a Swedish coast around the turn of the century. Anywhere is the place name. Bergman shortly introduces his shabby circus of agonists into a small town which is only an arena within which four characters, principally, enact and reenact a cycle of unavailing struggle and humiliation. The caravan is sighted, the waves roll on the shore, the camera lifts to the turning wheel of a coach, part of a circus entourage managed by Albert Johansson (Åke Grönberg). Kissing the armpit of his sleeping mistress, Anne (Harriet Andersson), Albert then joins his coachman on the driver's seat above. With the anecdote recounted by the driver, the film moves instantly into a dimension of the terrible. Jens tells the story, which you expect he has told often before, of a time some years ago on just such a coast as this when poor Frost, the circus clown, was exposed by his wife Alma, already fading toward desolation, to an excruciating ordeal before a company of soldiers.

The dreadful scene is visualised in a surreal manner, unnaturally flat and blanched as in old photos, and unnaturally silent, although you will swear later that you heard every panting breath and every scream.[51] Alma (Gudrun Brost) impelled by wanton motives—lewd assertion, self-destruction—goes down to the beach where the garrisoned soldiers are scattered among the rocks at rest, cleaning guns, preparing their gear, and swapping stories. There with all eyes on her she undresses herself, garment by garment, down to the flesh and followed by the whistles, the ribaldry, and the taunts of the men, she walks naked and absurdly provocative into the sea. At the height of the uproar that ensues, Frost (Anders Ek) comes, searching for his wife; he is a gaunt, anguished, grotesque man, the wraith of a man, himself his own parody, a man with a clown's face save only for the ghastly fact that on it there is neither a painted nor a human smile.

While the men jeer him on, the poor wretch pursues his Alma into the water, procures the floundering woman, and, not without a struggle, brings her back to the beach where he manages partly to cover her nakedness. Lifting her in his arms, he commences his staggering gauntlet of the soldiers, barefooted across the stony waste of beach. The soldiers sit and stare, some of them crowd him, mouthing words you never hear, for the scene is shot in silence, save for the ominous tatoo of a military drum that accompanies the clown's straining journey back from the sea: silent and bleached, so that the figure of Frost, bearing in his arms his monstrous wife as he moves with tortured feet over the boulders, seems like some apparition in a world itself impalpable, the sunlight white, the sky a nothingness, the soldiers unreal by token of their out-of-place reality—toys aping soundlessly the sounds of men. Time stretches unbearably while the slow drum beats and Frost, painful step by step, like a creature animated by a bungling Frankenstein who has given him locomotion and sweat but no blood, makes his way, the woman writhing, grimacing, and probably screaming imprecations in his embrace, her hair a tangle of sea bracken, her face, like Frost's, a chalky mask over which the eye mascara is now making runnels like paths of tears. Frost's eyes are glazed, his clown-wide mouth is fixed in a pucker that expresses pain on the verge of a laughter that never comes. At last he collapses from exhaustion and Alma, in her turn, bends over him to gather him up, one rag and motherly doll comforting the other.

So the episode passes; brutal, indelible, demanding. It must have taken supreme artistic confidence for Bergman to suppose he could plot the rest of the film at a pitch any less extreme and sustain the emotional attention of the audience. The remainder is wholly dominated by the prophetic terror of that prologue, for what one sees thereafter, conveyed in almost comedic terms, is an elementary equation whereby the burly, sensual Albert and his Anne strive desperately, unknown to themselves, to escape the ultimate beach across the stones of which Albert too may one day stumble, carrying a burden for which, he will believe, he never asked. They are characteristic victims of the love that cannot be without assurances; they must continually test and strain and provoke each other; centered on lust they experience the panic that accompanies desire, the frantic need to escape possession, the need to prove that they can escape, a need that infallibly transforms love into a species of revulsion that is yet insufficient to inspire in the victim a decisive act of rejection. The need to inflict is greater than the need to be free of infliction and in time the weaker of the two souls will be the slave of the other; yet even that distinction becomes meaningless since, whichever of the two may appear to dominate in the household sense, each is inextricably captive, the soul as dependent as the flesh on injuries begged for and returned.

When the wheels of the caravan stop at their temporary destination, other wheels begin to turn. Since the circus is drastically without funds and equipment, Albert and Anne, dressed in their best, go to beg or borrow costumes from a theatre company performing the classics, for it is Albert's thought to stage a parade and drum up an audience for the evening show. He is snubbed, not only by Thalia but also by the civic authority. Here the societies within society are mirrored, as in Carné's *Les Enfants du Paradis,* the little hierarchies on which self-esteem feeds. To the members of the theatre troupe, themselves on the perimeter of the human occupation, Johannsson's circus is a primitive specimen of the performing arts. Sjuberg, the theatre director, tells Albert scornfully, "You risk your lives, we risk our art"—an extraordinarily pregnant line, as it turns out. Yet Anne, imperious in her plebeian way, highlighted as she stands on the stage of the empty theatre, is no doubt as impressive as any ingenue the company would be likely to boast. Frans, the leading actor, seemingly effete and uncomfortably feminine, takes Anne's measure; he senses her price. Piqued by Albert's fussy resolve to visit his wife and children, whom he deserted three years ago, who happen to live in this town, Anne hopes to use Frans to glut her revenge, not dreaming that she is being used by an expert. Her baser motive is greed for an amulet the actor flashes before her eyes; if she can sell it, she can free herself from Albert.

These sequences at the theatre are lighted and angled as if the glamor of the setting was conjured and enhanced by Anne's point of view; in reality, nothing there is much more genuine than the paste amulet she covets. The theatre is a hopeful framework held together with shadows. Inside Gripsholm, a castle near Stockholm, one may visit a small Baroque theatre, designed for the private theatricals of Gustav the Third at the end of the eighteenth century. The semicircle of seats probably accommodates thirty-five people; the stage is larger than the house. As you step inside, however, a first glance reveals a sizeable theatre. Jointed mirrors from the seat level to the ceiling form a crescent of reflections which doubles the stage, compounds the chandeliers, and multiplies the platoon of seats into a regiment. It is one of the small masterpieces of interior late-Baroque in Europe. And it is this kind of spatial illusion which Bergman creates in the brief theatre scenes of *The Naked Night*. His boxfull of tricks includes masks, costumes, an overhead shaft of light, compositional asymmetry, mirrors that isolate, entrap and duplicate, profiles and sculptured darkness. Comparable to such shots in *Sommarlek,* these have greater force because they occur in a world already made unstable by the expressionist distortions of the beach setting.

In an effort to restore his dignity, seriously injured at the theatre and on the street, where the police forbid him to parade his circus-folk, Albert goes to visit his wife, confident inside his baby soul that all he has to do is show himself and she will immediately shelve the past, wrap up her knitting, and rescue him from the hazards of his world by falling at his masterly feet. She does no such thing; she receives him with the poise she has earned from independence, treats him hospitably, mends the button on his coat and gently but resolutely sends him packing like a child back to school. She has no need of him; her only reproach is that he should dare to suppose he could blunder back into her life and disturb her tranquillity with his male prerogative of vanity.

While Albert is pathetically courting his wife, Anne is as ingloriously betraying him with the sneering actor. Frans has no interest in her beyond his satisfaction at having guessed the price of her undressing. Albert sees Anne coming from the actor's dressing room and going to the jewelry shop to sell Frans' gift. At this moment, the military drum from the opening scene resounds in the background, a striking premonition; Karl-Birger Blomdahl's musical prompting, I would not call it a score, is throughout the film remarkably pertinent and subtle. The frustrations already imposed on Albert are increased. His agitations are fanned in a wild scene with Frost in which they both get drunk, brandish a gun, and separately bemoan their lot. Frost begs Albert not only to shoot the circus bear, a forlorn pet which Alma loves dearly, but to shoot Alma too, for that would be merciful!

Albert braces his masculinity to assert himself at the night's performance. When, before Anne's equestrienne act, the actor makes it clear by
his taunts that he had seduced Anne in the afternoon, Albert coaxes
him into the ring by snapping off his hat with a long circus whip. But
Frans knows a trick worth two of that; after provoking Albert into a
further show of mastery, he swiftly tosses sand and sawdust into his
eyes, kicks him in the face, and beats the helpless man unmercifully.
The crowd goes wild, the show breaks up; Anne, screaming, flings herself
on Frans, violently kicking and scratching in a vain attempt to repair
her own shame and defend her abject Albert who is on his knees, bloody,
all but blind, and ignominiously defeated. After a protracted and harrowing moment, alone in the caravan, where he tries to shoot himself
but fails, the wretched man bursts into the open air and shoots instead
the bear, hence releasing symbolically, and too late, the tethered animal
in himself, at the same time with an equally futile gesture rewarding
Frost for his humiliations by Alma.

Toward dawn the circus prepares to move on. Albert and Anne exchange looks, that is all, one of the most eloquent moments in the film;
for in that look everything is pledged: his need, her power, the helplessness of both before the fatality of their common bondage. The
caravan departs into a day, we feel, indistinguishable from night, into
a circle of purgatory around which, as in a circus-ring, Frost will stumble with his Alma and Albert will be beaten to his knees forever and
ever.

No film of Bergman expresses more ruthlessly the consequence of the
formulation by D. H. Lawrence, which I'm sure Bergman never had in
mind, that all human relationships are based either on love or on power.
When power flows the wrong way between the sexes, catastrophe is
inevitable. Critics who have admired this film, for many years they were
few, have often tried to assuage the stringency of its conclusion with
the unfounded hope that Albert, having reached his last oubliette, has
attained self-knowledge with which to sustain his future. "Life begins
on the far side of despair," said Jean-Paul Sartre, but not Bergman—not
in this film! I do not see, as others have seen, any comfort to be derived
from the fact that Albert and Anne are after all still united at the end
of the film. This is a fate worse than death, surely, else why would
Bergman go to the trouble of creating that macabre prologue and of

adroitly plotting each sequel, so that one after the other they move steadily through confirming circumstances toward the self-same direction, with Frost himself as memento and prompter? Albert and Anne become resigned to each other; which must mean that each is resigned to himself. Resignation is not love. Frost and Alma illustrate the polar limits of resignation. I suspect that the crux of the difficulty experienced by critics—male critics, at any rate—when reacting to this film is just that everybody wants an Anne and nobody wants to believe that time may change her into an Alma.

I would scarcely recommend *The Naked Night* as consoling, but then I don't expect a moviemaker to console me. I expect him to be authentic. I find the film authentic; it does not bear false witness. I cannot help but insist on what I implied earlier: *A Summer with Monika* was a timely contribution to the undismayed clarity with which, at this hour, Bergman was observing his characters, not hovering like a godmother or a schoolmaster. *The Naked Night* is Bergman's crystallization at the tragic level of the ineradicable civil war between men and women which he had been staging, with scarcely a truce, since his first play and his first movie. Here the subject acquires a classic ritual in a baroque style. Later, he was forced to retrace the ground and produce a classic formulation as comedy in *Smiles of a Summer Night*. Of course, the truth is that while he has discarded other motifs and other presuppositions in his films, this one— the failure of love, or perhaps I should say the bondage of love—he has never for long discarded. He is probably the obsessed master of the subject in our time.

Unusually, for a Bergman film, the men in *The Naked Night* are more cogently characterized than the women. Agda, you feel, has been dealt with in some other film, some other context; there was no point here in concerning oneself with the complexities of her situation; she is only required as the author of an anticlimax, then she is out. Alma is a complete wreck; any closer or more retrospective view of her would be unbearable; we can read the original architecture of her soul from the ruin that remains. Anne (the part was written for Harriet Andersson) is, if you like, Eros and therefore a presence rather than a dimension, a formidably embodied presence to be sure, owing very much to Bergman's magnificent sense of placement (I mean within the whole context and physically within the scene; for some years I was under the illusion that Miss Andersson was a towering, Junoesque woman). There are moments when Anne appears to be the pivotal figure but she is not; eventually she will be Albert's master because she is colder than he, but in the action we see she makes nothing happen; she is a contingency.[52] The principal and you might say maiming interest is supplied by the men, even by the smirking half-man, half-rat, Frans:

Does the bullfight indeed serve as a model for the Albert-Frans combat, as Rune Waldekranz once suggested, ''signifying the victory of the intellect over emotion''?[53] This is worth a quibble, since if the image is to be consistent it asks us to accept Frans, a ham actor with a back-street accumulation of little dirty skills, as a paradigm of intellect and generically as a matador. On this comparison I should like to hear the opinion of a Spaniard. Certainly, Albert resembles a bull in his blind charges against red flags flapped at him. However, I should prefer to treat the resemblance as but a passing simile, the more so because we have already a circus-ring as our correlative. Bergman is often enough explicitly antiintellectual without attributing to him one more doubtful instance. Albert is outwitted by the resources of a clever pervert. At large he is outwitted by the life-choice he dimly believes he has made and can control. The cause of suffering is ignorance. Albert is life-ignorant. Life destroys him.

Frost is indubitably the overpowering and most baffling presence in the film. His whole aspect is an equivocation. A mirthless clown—what could be more futile? This is really an ingeniously oblique conception, even if we remember that Picasso had painted lugubrious clowns, for traditionally the clown in literature and drama has been employed intellectually, as a foil to complacency, a critic of absolutes. The clown is conscious of what he is doing. ''The art of the clown is a calculated art which improvises,'' said Andre Suares. But Frost is no longer in possession of his vocation. We never see him performing and we cannot imagine his performance, since he is far more like the object and butt of clownery than he is the instigator of it. ''The clown ferrets out the eternal grimace lying beneath the most pious and domineering appearances. He is conscious of their vanity and they are not; he has no faith, and they have. In fine, he is their skeleton, carried about with them but unknown to them.''[54]

No doubt, Frost is Albert's skeleton, yet Frost himself does not appear to know it. If he has ever displayed the mocking omniscience described by Suares, there is no remaining evidence of that talent. He has *become* the "eternal grimace"; he is identified with the object of his ostensible mockery. As a clown, he's a dud. You would never take the kiddies to see him! As a motif in Bergman's circus, he is an inspired figment. We must not be too literal-minded about that circus or we shall catch ourselves complaining that the equestrienne never mounts her horse and there were no performing seals.

When *The Naked Night* opened in Sweden, the reaction was virtually a unanimous scream of incomprehension, outrage, and contempt. Not a single favorable review appeared in the papers and not until some months later, when Harry Schein wrote a sympathetic but unavailing defense of the film for the literary magazine *BLM* was there a voice raised in opposition. Internationally, the negative reception was repeated almost everywhere. As late as 1964 when, the French having led the way, criticism was prepared to reassess previous opinions, John Russell Taylor, while conceding that *The Naked Night* was a "complex" and "magisterially confident" achievement, could nonetheless summarize it as "Depressing, obviously; superficial, very probably; highly mannered, without a doubt".[55] D.H. Lawrence, who has said so many sensible things about our nightside and our mental falsifications, maintained that people are not actually afraid of a new idea—they can pigeonhole an idea—what frightens them is a new emotion. The outcry against *The Naked Night* was, I am sure, of this order, because the film touched off something in people that they would have preferred to conceal. It invited feelings with which they could not cope. Out of resentment and panic they rejected both the agency and the source of their disturbance.

It took ten years for the wheel to come full circle,[56] but the damage to Bergman's continuity could not then be repaired for in 1953 the public rejection had been decisive. Bergman was compelled to swallow his toad and confine his darker inspirations to the theatre where, in the six months following the premiere of *The Naked Night* he staged for requital, in Malmö, Pirandello's *Six Characters in Search of an Author,* Kafka's *The Castle,* and Strindberg's *The Ghost Sonata.* Having arrived at the art of film, definitively, by purging his exposed content of all compromise and factitiousness, he was obliged to laugh off the implications he had revealed and go backward to the circumstantial situations he had already comprised and surpassed. He made *A Lesson in Love.*

"A Comedy for Grownups"

I should like to believe that Bergman's subtitle for *A Lesson in Love*— "A Comedy for Grownups"—was a sardonic reprisal for the generally contemptuous reception of *The Naked Night,* as who should say, "If it's only fluff you want, I'll give you fluff!" But I fear that the film was the best he could do at what must have been a galling moment. I went to see the film again just before writing this reminiscence, for I wanted to see if it was really as bad as I believed it to be when I first saw it. Indeed it was, an embarrassment, few moments of which have survived the brief ravage of time. The few are those played by Gunnar Bjornstrand and Eva Dahlbeck in the train compartment. This and the following film, *Kvinnodröm (Womens' Dreams, Dreams* in the United states, *Journey into Autumn* in England) are to be viewed as expendable. Since Bergman was now to concentrate his talent on comedy, they represent rehearsals for *Smiles of a Summer Night,* by which they were subsumed, and they may therefore be appreciated by the tolerant for the hints in them of that superior geometry and superior elegance which orders and elaborates the later film. Seen in relation to the films before them, they are bound to appear secondhand and not a little desperate. Bergman's inventiveness is out of breath.

In both, Bergman rewords the sexual warfare of *Waiting Women,* without improving on the stoic cruelty of the first episode or the bland self-sufficiency of the couple-in-the-lift sequence; in both, there is a train, bearing someone toward an unresolved relationship; in both, absurd male animals are at the mercy of their age or their women; in both there is a daughter as *deus ex machina* or as *memento mori* and in both there is a kind of contrapuntal movement and structure. The train journey southward of *A Lesson in Love,* on which Erneman, a gynecologist, (rather a tasteless joke) and his wife meet and pretend not to know each other is interleaved with scenes between Erneman and an importunate mistress, played abominably by Yvonne Lombard, as well as scenes between Erneman and his daughter, Nix, these totally out of key with the rest of the film, whose candour impels him to recover his wife; she has been having an affair with a bombastic sculptor. Similarly, two fruitless love affairs comprise *Dreams,* the first between Susanne, a fashion-photographer, and a marriage-nailed businessman, Lobelius, and a complementary nonsense involving Doris, a model in Susanne's salon, with an aging Consul.

Whereas in *A Lesson in Love* Erneman is given a second chance and justifies it, by successfully rewooing his wife, in *Dreams* the second chance is an anticlimax. Susanne, who believes she wants to revive an embered affair with Lobelius, is defeated by the security which Henrik chafes under but basically needs; Doris, about to become the mistress of a wealthy benefactor, is defeated by the Consul's sheer incapacity for playing Don Juan, assisted by the scornful realism of his daughter who interrupts his amour with deflating reminders of his age and obligations. But these doublets or anitheses do not strike one as hilarious variations so much as ingenuity in search of an adequate object.

Here and there *A Lesson in Love* suggests a parodic version of the contradictions Bergman had exposed with unmitigated grimness in *The Naked Night.* Marianne Erneman coming to the rescue of her spouse in the slapstick fray which all but ends *A Lesson in Love* is a lame reminder of Anne, hysterically trying to defend Albert Johansson from the feline aggression of the actor Frans. In fact, the whole situation of Erneman reclaiming his wife seems to be a sheepishly conceived reversal of Albert's failure in the preceding film. Many critics, struggling to salvage something novel from this largely banal movie, have noted a single cinematic strategy whereby the camera, placed on one side of a Copenhagen canal, moves and hesitates and retracks in parallel with a quarreling couple on the far side. This was the only refreshing visual business in the film. Most of the time, Martin Bodin was trying to compensate for the stilted movement of the story with chiaroscuro effects better suited to one of those waterfront melodramas which Bergman had earlier contrived, or, for instance, by photographing from overhead the reverse-position faces of two conversing characters, a pretentious device because it lacked all psychological relevance to what was going on in the shot.

Dreams was an improvement, cinema-wise; as there was virtually no music in the film, Bergman was forced to create sequences in which sound and facial expressiveness built their drama unaided from that source. Perhaps the most decisive examples of this discipline were the opening scene in the fashion salon, pregnant with unexpelled irritation, and the shock-editing of Susanne's suicidal impulse on the train. But it might also be noted that the principal in each of these passages was Eva Dahlbeck, and that the film's cinematographer was Hilding Bladh, responsible for the most creative effects in *The Naked Night*. Unfortunately all this skill was of no avail in the long run, owing to Bergman's failure to maintain a tone either consistently flinty in a comic manner or on the other hand consistently autumnal. I should add, however, that there are situations and snatches of dialogue in these two films which, when dressed for another context, we readily accept. The rather strained jokes about the prison of marriage—"Marriage is a grimace that ends in a yawn"— and the failure of desire when the prison has been breached are only a little less sophisticated than those in, say, *Thirst* or *Smiles of a Summer Night*.

In the latter film they are the source of mirth; in the two preparatory exercises they seem somewhat mechanical. The vision of life as a train journey during which men and women, inherently incompatible, are handcuffed to each other for reasons they fail to understand or refuse to acknowledge was easier to accept in *Thirst*, before it was insisted upon, or in *The Naked Night*, where the train has been replaced by a caravan and the issue is closer to the knuckle-bone or, I might say, when the terms are transposed and enlarged in that frightening line of *Ansiktet*: "Step by step we go into the dark; movement is the only truth."

Suggestive, then, these two films may be if we are regarding them as imperfect fragments of that unity which Bergman inexorably builds with every film he makes, good or bad, constantly and compulsively reviving, eliminating, repeating, combining, and reversing. But such a preoccupation is interesting only to those who are concerned with the peculiar case of the artist; it will hold no appeal for filmgoers who simply demand to be entertained at the moment of their attendance. For them I do not see how, unless they are fanatically addicted to seeing Gunnar Bjornstrand and Eva Dahlbeck again and yet again as two sides of an identical and indivisible coin, either *A Lesson in Love* or its successor can today be found very amusing. If they have such an addiction it can be satisfied with scarcely a qualification I would hazard, by *Smiles of a Summer Night,* 1955, which, besides Mr. Bjornstrand and Mrs. Dahlbeck, who surpass themselves in a by-now-familiar juxtaposition, has many other inducements.

Smiles of a Summer Night

The interdependence for Bergman of theatre and film has perhaps never been more creatively demonstrated than in this period when his stagings at Malmö of Franz Lehar, of Moliere, and of his own play, *Trämålning,* unquestionably found their reflection in the scenic qualities of *Smiles of a Summer Night* and *The Seventh Seal.* For, as obviously unrelated as these two films may be otherwise, their raison d'être is decor. *The Seventh Seal* is as artificial, in the best sense, as *Smiles.* Life as theatre and life as allegory; we are saying the same thing. Both demand a style of the impossible while suggesting, in fun or in dread, the borders of the possible. *Smiles of a Summer Night* was shot in fifty-five days with a remarkably low investment, in Hollywood terms, of $150,000. In Sweden, however, the investment was considered to be a major risk which everyone concerned hoped to see justified by the international, if not the national, reception. Their hopes were completely fulfilled. *Smiles of a Summer Night* was the film, more than any other, which the world over replaced one Bergman by another as a household word among the knowing.

The period ambience in which *Smiles* was created was a direct inspiration from the costumes and settings, by Per Falk, of Franz Lehar's operetta, *The Merry Widow,* which Bergman had staged with huge success in October of 1954 at the Malmö City Theatre; and when describing his own conception of the film, Bergman expressed the hope that it would put us in mind of paintings by Renoir and Degas. "It is a mixture of operetta and comedy; all mental effort should slumber in a mild narcosis induced by music, color, light and festivity." It is interesting that he should have included color among the ingredients; the gamut of tones in this film, intense blacks, pearly whites, steel or dove gray, does indeed suggest a scale of polychromatic values. Yet it is difficult to imagine that in 1955 actual color would have enhanced his effects; the "white-night" feeling, with its inevitable undertone of melancholy, is better rendered by the subtleties of the black-and-white medium.

On the basis of Joseph Wood Krutch's definition—that tragedy judges man by his heroism, comedy by his intelligence—I once stated that if you discounted Bergman's early compulsive efforts to see life as tragically determined, you would conclude that he was essentially a creator of comedy, since nearly all his films had ended on a note, however wry, of reconciliation. Given the moment, long before *The Virgin Spring,* when I published the remark I daresay the claim was demonstrable. I have long since qualified this observation and I seem to recall it was upon revisiting *Smiles of a Summer Night,* his most successful attempt at pure comedy, that I did so. To my sense it is a wholly delightful film; under close scrutiny, however, it is exposed as a precarious act of tightrope-walking. The situations therein are so expertly contrived and carried off, the repartee is so calculatedly brittle, the final adjustments so sensible, that it does pass for heedless comedy, which is to say an antiheroic mode intended to provide pleasure rather than second thoughts. Yet the more often one sees it, such has been my experience, the plainer it becomes that in it the comic, which is to say the reasonable, point of view is sustained by a tense effort of will. And it was at this point that I had to remind myself of how histrionic Bergman's comic pose had always been, an art of defense forever at the mercy of something more habitual in the man's temperament, something closer to despondency, if not rancor.

However that may be, in *Smiles* the major balance is established; the erotic absurdities are staged and performed with mainly admirable levity and with entrancing style; at the end one heaves a sigh of relief, as one should in comedy : the surface of things has been repaired and the couples who substantiate the animating principle of the plot have been re-arranged as reason would have them. Obviously, to the eye of social common sense, Lawyer Egerman's young wife needs the more ardent at-tention of his son by a former marriage who has been mistakenly trying to transfer *his* suppressed Adam to the housemaid, Petra, a sensual but witless young lady who, since she needs nothing Henrik has to offer ex-cept masculinity, is better matched with the groom—with whom she in fact beds down in the hay during the midsummer night which comprises the climactic phase of the story. Quite as obviously, Egerman, who thinks he needs to be adored, even while he suspects that he is not adorable, will in actuality be the more content at the other end of a leash held by his disenchanted ex-mistress, the actress, Desiree, of whose cardinal attractions he is dreaming at the beginning of the film, hence initiating the complete game of musical chairs which is the subject. In *The Naked Night* Albert would have been spared destructive agony if he could have recanted with the assent of his wife; in comedy it is never too late and *Smiles of a Summer Night* assures us so more convincingly by far than *A Lesson in Love*.

Bergman adroitly employs the multiple view of things in this film. We see Egerman as he sees himself, as his too-young wife sees him, as his son sees him, as his mistress sees him, and as he appears when looked through, so to speak, by that fantastic military dummy, the sadist, Malcolm. Bergman even tries joking at Lutheran solemnity through the person of young Henrik fighting a losing battle with a priestly vocation, but at the fateful party, even while he asks us to believe that the guests of that old ruin, Mrs. Armfeldt, are acting under the sway of a love potion, he utilizes the boy's drunken surliness to reprove the amorality of his elders. Earlier, Henrik deplored his father's habit of treating everything as a joke. "So will you," returns Egerman with a twisted smile, "when you realize your folly and the insignificance of your illusions". Bergman is here passing on the counsel given to the hero of his radio play, *The City,* with no more personal conviction I imagine than before, but within the context of *Smiles* it carries all the conviction it needs.

When he tackles the sadomasochistic relationship of Charlotte and her asinine husband, Malcolm, the mask slips. In Charlotte's bitter knowledge of her carnal dependence, the film momentarily breaks down as comedy and the fragility of the structure so beautifully designed becomes apparent. Self-knowledge in comedy is rarely articulated with such savage repugnance. When Charlotte, played with stark poise by Margit Carlquist, confesses to young Mrs. Egerman how acutely she despises her husband, how thoroughly she loathes the male as an animal, how disgusted she is with her own thralldom to the physical act, something subterranean and repressed to that point breaks the marron glacé surface.

There is no question that in this scene the bite was intended; it was not an accident of overemphasis. Bergman places the splendid Miss Carlquist in the foreground screen right, with Ulla Jacobsson middle distance on the left, a passive audience to the declaration which is delivered face front to us, as if this were the theatre and the actress had been instructed to come downstage to the edge of the apron and project the speech into our teeth. "I hate him!" she insists, "I hate him! *Men are beasts*. They are foolish and vain. They have hair all over them. Love is a disgusting business!"

No other dramatic moment in the film is not at the same time funny. There is nothing funny here. The speech cuts like a knife and it tends to give a different color to the asperities which have gone before; it prepares us to flinch at those which may follow. For there is certainly little relief in this film from the spirit of masculine self-degradation which Bergman had been exuding in a sort of crescendo, beginning with *Waiting Women* and absent only from *A Summer with Monika*. Egerman, like his predecessors played by Gunnar Bjornstrand, while the most sympathetic male in *Smiles,* is nonetheless written—one might say written off— as the best representative of an inept species. As vehicles of intelligence or candor, the women have the best of it; if the film were not such fun, so lovely to look at, and so cleverly wrought into a form that combines lyric tenderness with asocial wit, one might find oneself bristling at Bergman's readiness to repeat that banality loved of women, that men are but contemptible children of a larger growth.

It is my belief that while Bergman was positively exhilarated by the challenge of staging two such comedic forms as operetta and neoclassical comedy, Moliere's *Don Juan,* the strain of holding the comic position in cinema, now his more personal medium, was beginning to tell on him. Even as he had at last, on film, all but perfected the comic formula, his thoughts must have been elsewhere. In September of 1954 he had already presented his medieval piece, *Trämålning (Painting-on-Wood)* over the radio. On March 18, 1955, barely a month before *Don Juan* opened, he staged it with the drama students of the Malmö theatre. Surely the awareness must have been churning in his mind or, if not yet, in his subconsciousness, that here was the subject of a major film. When the success of *Smiles of a Summer Night* at Cannes in the spring of 1956 confirmed the ovation it had already received at home, Bergman was ready to pounce on Anders Dymling (who initially rejected the script of *The Seventh Seal*) with the virtual demand of All right—now! Now that I've done my bit as an entertainer and rocked the world, let me do something nearer to my soul!

For the moment, however, in 1956, it was not Ingmar Bergman struggling with the higher questions who was abruptly made known to the world outside, especially to the Anglo-American world which was but vaguely aware of him; it was Ingmar Bergman, that new Swedish master of comedy. Three of his films had been seen in one summer of festivals by reporters whose reactions varied from admiration to ecstasy. The most eloquent among them were, of course, the French. By *Smiles of a Summer Night* they were altogether seduced, since it suggested, more conspicuously than any preceding Bergman film, that the Swedish director had learned more than a trick or two from the French drama. French critics are sometimes surprisingly gallant. They feel flattered when their arts are echoed by those of other countries, even when the echo is blatant and close to the limits of plagiarism (no reference to *Smiles* intended). This may well reflect the feeling of proprietorship to which they are charmingly prone, for as Horace Walpole once said, "If something foreign arrives in Paris, they either think they have invented it or that it has always been there". An international contest ensued, the object being to see who could produce, preferably in one sentence, the greatest number of eminent predecessors with which to compare Bergman. Perhaps Samuel Lachize of *l'Humanite* did not fire the starter's gun but he should be credited as a pioneer of the rhetoric which was now to be indispensable when addressing this subject. *Smiles of a Summer Night* put him in mind not only of Feydeau, Musset, René Clair, and Jean Renoir but also of Shakespeare and Gogol.

Five years later, Jacques Siclier in his study of Bergman[57] announced that *Smiles* closed and perfected Bergman's Rose Period and pointed out, with somewhat more precision than many of his colleagues, the vaudevillesque situations à la Feydeau, the incisive dialogue à la Beaumarchais, the pleasantries of Marivaux, and the élan of Jean Renoir with the reservation that in Bergman's film one searches in vain for that *overture spirituelle* which is almost always present in the work of Renoir.

Informing it all, he felt, was the "Strindbergian clarity" of Midsummer Night and the shadow of death. I suspect he was concretely recalling the film, *Miss Julie.* Of spiritual omnipresence in the films of Renoir, most of which in my opinion have been widely overpraised, I am not as confident as M. Siclier and I am surprised that he failed to acknowledge that in *The Naked Night,* of which he wrote so refined an analysis, Bergman's treatment of the sacrificial nature of theatre, therefore of art, was more profound by far than Renoir's in that piquant film, *The Golden Coach* (released in the same year, I believe). Perhaps *spirituelle* has a more delicate coloring than I have realised. If he only intended the Renoir comparison for *Smiles,* I would agree that it has not the critical acerbity of Renoir's *The Rules of the Game,* of which, from certain angles, it is mindful. But it has an enchantment all its own. Fairly inevitably, it was compared with previous masterpieces of comedy, since every comedy of good-or-bad manners in likely to remind us of every other we have admired. The artifice of the genre always entails the opposition of sense and sentiment, the rivalry of the generations, the combat of the sexes, the dialectic of the classes, and the paying off one fool by another, whether we think of Congreve, Moliere, Marivaux, Goldoni, or Ostrovsky. I still think critics in France worked too hard. Bergman said it himself in a nutshell when he said think Degas and Renoir.

By a kind of miracle or a kind of superior charlatanry, which in theatre is just what performs miracle, Bergman made this *jeu d'été* imply reaches of mood and space and consequence which are not, to the eye, fully contained in the material. Revisiting this film, I am always surprised at how static in a sense it is, how it seems always to return with relief from excursions here and there to conversation pieces, how a very few exterior shots were selected with such art as to leave us with the feeling that we have traveled far, commuting between villas, theatres, pavilions, and acres of spacious countryside, how even the funniest physical sequences—Derek trying to hang himself and instead releasing the mechanism which propels a bed into his room, bearing the sleeping beauty of his most illicit thoughts, or the Russian-roulette duel between Malcolm and Egerman—even these are primarily of the theatre. Yet the whole *is* cinema, for it creates illusion and, with a very few brief bucolic scenes where Petra and Frid expound the three smiles of love which gives the film its title, trails in its wake a palpable mist of nostalgia. This is not *spirituelle*?[58]

Last Couple Out

Before making *The Seventh Seal,* Bergman contributed a scenario of quite another kind, *Sista Paret Ut* (*Last Couple Out,* nominally a game played by children and, in country-times past, by adults) which reached the screen under Alf Sjöberg's direction and certainly with his amendments. Appearing at a moment when Bergman was again abstracting his subject matter and extricating himself from the social-debate level of theatre, this script, concerned with the always topical friction between youth and its parents, seemed so out of place as to be uncalled for, the more so since although intelligent by the standards of television for the home, let's say, it was neither a radical version of the subject nor cinematically engrossing. I once believed that Bergman had written it years before and kept it in his desk but my suspicion has not been confirmed. Of course, one can see connections in this film with *Smiles of a Summer Night,* as well as with *Wild Strawberries,* but connections can usually be discerned if one peers.

Parental negligence is the ostensible villian in this film, teenage confusion, the immediate issue. It does look as if Bergman had been assailed by bad conscience for having celebrated easy virtue in his preceding film, an impression which is strengthened by the prominent role now assigned to Björn Bjelvenstam, who in *Last Couple Out* speaks his mind as he had been unable to do with any coherence in *Smiles of A Summer Night.* As young Bo Dahlin, in a contemporary setting, he tries to mediate in a festering triangle situation composed of his father, his mother, and her lover without giving marked allegiance to any one of them and with little success by way of reward. He rejects the self-pitying advances of his father (Olof Widgren) and is rejected in turn by the cold sense of the lover, Ernst (Jarl Kulle) who reminds the boy sharply that he has been Susanne's lover for three years, which has not harmed her as a mother. This struck me as a reasonable point, yet Ernst was portrayed unsympathetically. Why? Is it simply that he was played by Jarl Kulle, whom I always find unsympathetic? He challenges Bo to break up his affair with his mother, if he thinks he can do so. The youth applies himself to this crusade, with the unexpected result that Mother (Eva Dahlbeck) simply packs her bags and disappears, intending, so she claims, to go off somewhere by herself.

Bo escapes to an adolescent party which occupies the middle part of the film much like a second act in the theatre. When the party gets out of hand, we know that we're clearly being instructed in the further consequences of the single standard, for Anita, the young hostess (Harriet Andersson) is unable to restore order by summoning her parents; they are having a bit of a time, themselves, in Gothenburg. In the confusion, Bo is commandeered by Kerstin (Bibi Andersson) who, jealous of Anita, takes the young man hopefully to her apartment, also parent-free at the moment. Bo, plausibly confused by the sexual labyrinth in which he finds himself, is unable to warm up to the girl. To cap his misfortunes, her mother arrives unexpectedly and berates the boy for taking advantage of the confidence she always placed in him. Bo, at the end of his patience, tells her what he thinks of her and of all absentee parents, whereupon Kerstin defends her mother by turning abusively on Bo. Returning to the party, now at its ebb, Bo announces to Anita, with curious irrelevance, that he is grown up. I suppose he meant he was fed up; disillusion does have the tendency to make one feel older in the space of an hour!

A characteristic Bergman interpolation follows, when Bo plays with a dollhouse, simulating the domestic ineptitudes of all the adults in his life. This scene terminates with surprising mildness, when you consider the swords-points at which Bergman's lovers are habitually engaged. Anita admits to Bo that she wants him but just now she is simply too mixed up to know what's she doing. Bo, as generously, complies with her mood and upon leaving tells her, ''All right, I'll call you—or, you call me, when *you* feel like it''. At this juncture, one reflects, Bo and Anita are scarcely ill advertisements of migrating parents.

The final scene, in the classroom where the film had opened, depicts Bo as having lost the equilibrium which he had displayed with his girl friend, for he blurts out his misery to a sympathetic teacher, announcing dramatically that there are only two ways out of his mess, either to run away from home or to commit suicide. From the teacher he receives advice of a kind not forthcoming to Erik Widgren (in *Torment*) seventeen years earlier, he who stood on a much darker threshold utterly alone, that there is a third alternative, which is to look into his own heart and guts and accept the fact that life is full of nasty betrayals and that he himself will be guilty of them as he grows up. "Then, what's left?" asks the disturbed boy. "Your will and your thought," the teacher tells him. "You will always have the privilege of searching your mind." Few critics in Sweden failed to recognize that the closing sentiment was obviously Sjöberg's, since Bergman has never expressed any undue confidence in the role of intelligence.

It is not so much the subject matter in itself that seems out of order in Bergman's chronology as it is the treatment inevitably demanded for such a script. *Last Couple Out* is barely a film; there is nothing in it which could not have been represented on the stage. Eliminate the dialogue and there is no self-evident episode. There is nothing about the script, therefore, which should have interested Alf Sjöberg who, of all directors, demands for his full effectiveness space, time, and the incensed clash of mighty opposites. Since his last two films had been commercial failures, I assume he was obliged to accept the Bergman scenario in the absence of any more suitable. He did what he could with it but the film is eloquent of his frustration; given no telling contrast of environment, no exteriors, no loud alarums, and no dynamic excursions he fell back on effects he had used in *Torment,* very self-conscious in respect to stairwells, rain on the windows, and such. I cannot today recall a single composition in this movie. I retain only a distant conviction that by the youngsters it was reasonably well acted. But is there actually any more tiresome debate after all these years than this between one generation and the next? Intergeneration warfare is one of the poisons of our age, and perennial crucifixion of the elders is a banal proposition, a protest glib on everyone's tongue against a condition no one has any intention of rectifying. Liberalism decided long ago to relax sexual morality, emancipate children, even from manners, and substantially reduce the principle of authority, not only in the school but in the home. Periodically, someone gets up and screams about an intergeneration problem, a marital problem, a venereal-disease problem, an alcohol problem, a birth-control problem. Since all those who scream are wholly committed to the system which has created the problems, the force of their outcry is somewhat unconvincing.

Not that Bergman was screaming in *Last Couple Out*; he would appear to have been trying to square himself in the Sweden of 1956 with an age group vaguely in revolt, although the conclusions to be drawn from the film would today provide no comfort to a new generation which, in most countries, has given up dialogue for moral blackmail, hedonism, or criminal assault. As a matter of fact, Bergman has never tried very hard to find a social scapegoat for his suffering juveniles. When he was young and groping he made films about characters who were young and groping but he seldom blamed adults as such for their ordeal. In *Torment,* notably, the most forceful critic of Caligula's foul behaviour was another teacher, even older, and the headmaster was tolerably kind to Erik. As I suggested earlier, Bergman was much too convinced of a diabolical human condition to be satisfied with merely social accusation. So, in *Last Couple Out,* as far as we can judge a script achieved in collaboration, he was honest enough to acknowledge while ticking off the parents that the whole domestic arrangement in our time is beyond the reach of simplicity; when you think to accuse one generation of having misled another you have opened up a complexity of human needs far from easy to resolve.

Insofar as this is Bergman's script at all, it does point to a peculiar recurrence. He has rarely stood firmly on a gained insight, then moved on to another level without looking back. In his own terms, he had exploited exhaustively the confusions of the young and in *A Summer with Monika* he had seemingly washed his hands of the involvement by seeing it as a casualty of life which he had no further obligation, cinematically, to lament. But he never has the grace to leave a subject so long as he has another manuscript unemployed. In *The Seventh Seal* and in *Wild Strawberries* he was still reluctant to take leave of the illusion, which he knew to be an illusion, that young love was a happy conspiracy of two against the wicked world.

THE MAGIC FOREST

Painting-on-Wood[59] was Bergman's farewell to play-writing; it is commonly regarded in Sweden as his best play, a back-hand compliment since it rather clearly defines his inability to write for the stage. His gift for dramatic encounter and human interplay, so remarkable if scarifying in his best films, was never successfully developed in the theatre. *Painting-on-Wood* is a masque, a series of tableaux, a *mise en scène* embodying, in low relief, the principal motifs from church paintings and sculpture which he had been carrying in his memory since childhood. In view of the fact that he had on numerous occasions before introduced The Dance of Death or some other Last Judgment element into his staging, the critics were unusually forbearing when, confronted with *Painting-on-Wood*, they did not exclaim, "What? That again?" Probably relieved at not having to grapple with Berg-man's capricious ventures into abnormal psychology, they made content with a colorful semipantomime. Their general murmur of approval emphasized Bergman's staging of the play, not its conception or its text; they waxed enthusiastic over its "line, color and form," not very high praise. Someone who had been directing plays for upward of sixteen

"The magic forest is always full of adventures. No one can enter it without losing his way. But the chosen one, the elect, who survives its deadly perils, is reborn and leaves it a changed man. . . . The forest is the antithesis of house and hearth, village and field boundary, where the household gods hold sway and where human laws and customs prevail. It holds the dark forbidden things—secrets, terrors, which threaten the protected life of the ordered world of common day."

Heinrich Zimmer, *The King and the Corpse*

years might well be expected to have mastered such rudiments of the scenic art as line, color, and form. While *Painting-on-Wood* is not without intrinsic interest, it is chiefly important as the ground plan for *The Seventh Seal* in which Bergman tested the Christian motifs in a setting that simultaneously conveyed the apparently real and, by fanciful leaps into another dimension, thwarted reality.

As narrative, the film is a simple progression toward death of an assortment of characters, chosen for their generic value, during a time of plague under the darkening aspect of what Johann Huizinga has unimprovably designated, "the waning of the Middle Ages". The action as such is so confined, the issues are so direct, the choices and resolutions are so little complex, that one can only react with amazement to the copious analyses, glosses, symbol-synopses and so forth which have been produced to explain this movie. For this reason, I shall not provide a detailed chronicle of what transpires in the film; I shall assume that everyone remembers the general sequence or has at his fingertips a dozen outlines of the episodical continuity. Everything that takes place in the film is illuminated or shadowed, as the case may be, by the moral dialogue of the two principal characters: the Knight, Block, and his squire, Jöns. Having returned from the last Crusade they are making their way homeward through a forest, where they meet various characters representative of the common human condition, most of them marked out by Death with whom, personified, Block plays three forestalling games of chess before his journey is over. The Knight seeks an answer to the question that unshakeably assails him. Why does not God, even in the shadow of death, reveal his tangible presence? The squire, for his part, asks no such question; he has long since become disenchanted of metaphysical promises or unquestioning faith. For an unguarded moment, appalled by the burning of the young witch, he asks, "Who watches over that child? Angels, God, or the Devil?" But he answers his own question with "Emptiness, my lord! . . . Emptiness under the moon."

As befits an allegory, there is no character development. Matters of life and death take place, to be sure, but those involved are mainly ignorant of cause or consequence. The Knight ends as he began, believing, but anguished by the silence of God. Ironically enough, he has been answered, but this he cannot know. For in his final game of chess with Death, he has enabled Jof and Mia, the young couple whose innocence has deeply moved him, to escape with their child. Hence, he has performed a more-than-Christian deed, if we allow an ellipse of time, since it is clear by the context that Jof and Mia are but translations of Joseph and Mary. Jöns, the squire, remains skeptical to the last trump, having performed his kindnesses (his defense of Jof and his rescue of a girl from the villainy of Raval, a corrupt seminarian) with no reference to an ulterior power. At most, the Church and all its works move him to outrage. The voices crying in the wilderness are those of an inquisitorial monk and a young girl burning in ignorance, convinced that she is a housing for the Devil. His own last words abjure the solemnity of death. "I shall be silent," he tells the Knight's wife, "but under protest."

To understand why this film should have been thought so esoteric as to inspire interpretations plentiful enough to fill a sizeable volume, we must recall again that it appeared between *Smiles of a Summer Night* and the equally successful *Wild Strawberries*. By the time it had reached the peripheries of criticism (the literary magazine, the lecture platform, and the art film societies), unveiling Bergman had become a strenuous exercise of intellectual prestige. Moreover, in the ostensibly godless purlieus of the university graduate seminar and in less exalted regions where their *explications du text* were obediently, if gracelessly, imitated, there were hosts of heathen, not previously habituated by T. S. Eliot, who evidently discovered in *The Seventh Seal,* as for the first time, how vivid the Christian drama and its derivatives could be. In their zeal, critics who would never dream of visiting a medieval church to look at its stained-glass windows rushed into print with admirable enthusiasm but often with patently familiar explanations, quite unnecessary for anyone who had been raised in the tradition, and lamentably often with quite ingenuous confusions of their sources. As an extreme, while not unique, example of where this kind of criticism can lead, I quote from a publication sent to me a few years ago. Since the pages were torn from the indicative context, there being neither date nor authorship, I have only the heading *Seventh Seal Panel Discussion* (*continued from p. 18*) and a plain reference to Washington State University. The object of the discussion seems to have centered on the meaning of the film and of its "ultimate symbolism" (ultimate, mind you; the attendant symbolism wasn't enough). My attention was riveted by the incredible observation that "Another example of self-evident symbolism occurs in the film's opening scene where the hovering bird —a vulture, or at any rate a bird of death—is contrasted with the ocean, a traditional symbol of life."

I find this completely hilarious. Where on earth or in the air did the writer think Bergman came by a vulture in Sweden? Directors often display extreme patience, and their production managers indefatigable enterprise, but I can't imagine even Bergman waiting around on location for a vulture to show up, in order to employ it as a symbol. Sucksdorff perhaps, Bergman, no. And *is* the ocean a traditional symbol of life? In which tradition? The ocean, like any element, may be utilized as a symbol of anything you intend, determined by the context in which you place it. Perhaps, to one born under Pisces, the ocean is instinctively felt to be a life symbol. What of those born under Virgo? Was the ocean a life-symbol at the end of *La Dolce Vita*? And if so, at the end of *La Strada*? With what distinction of emphasis? I shall not pursue the fallacy ad infinitum. I try to recall the impression I personally received from the film, prior to any further interpretation.

The beginning, characteristic of many Bergman films, was an atmospheric prelude, a preliminary hush here, the seacoast and Death. We are at the edge of things. *After the breaking of the Seventh Seal, there was silence in Heaven for about the space of half an hour.* Bergman's source, the Book of Revelation, justifies the images of empty sea and sky, which might connote eternity or neutral expanse, uncontaminated by the plague. But any such connotation must be made in retrospect, since it is what follows that enhances the value of what has gone before. For Peter Cowie, "the sea summons up resonances of hope, of arrival and departure. . . ."[60] How could it, before any issues have been raised with which to evoke a contrast?

Following this nest of misleading allusions, the writer I have cited above declares with fatal misapprehension: "Then, the eating of the wild strawberries contains crucial symbolism: the meal is obviously sacramental, in fact reminiscent of the Last Supper." The Knight, eating wild strawberries with Jof and Mia, reminds him of the Last Supper? How can this be? Shall we take this in sequence? During the course of the film it becomes increasingly recognizable that Jof, the juggler, Mia and their child, Mikael, are at the same time a recapitulation and a forecast of the Holy Family, though Bergman is sly enough to offer the suggestion obliquely. Jof is not a carpenter, he is of the theatre—here, Bergman sneaks in a little self-aggrandizement. If we take the boy to suggest Jesus in the future, he has not yet questioned the Elders, or become the Messiah or acquired the disciples who were with him at the Last Supper. Why in the name of this Jesus would the writer suppose wild strawberries to be the communion food when the Christian ceremony has not yet been born? He wants to ascribe intention to Bergman; why not assume, before learning differently, that Bergman's intention observes a certain logic within the fantasy? Sacramental the wild strawberries may be, if you disengage the word from too specific a designation. Bergman explicitly gives us the meaning of this repast in Block's words.

I shall remember this moment. The silence, twilight, the bowl of strawberries and milk, your faces in the evening light. I shall carry this memory between my hands as carefully as if it were a bowl filled to the brim with fresh milk.

The wild strawberries are a token of human kindness, of something shared, something the Knight will take with him into that darkness which he finds so appalling when tempted to believe that it may be an empty darkness. His image for the occasion, drawn from local tradition, is a lovely one and it is self-sufficient. I do not understand the compulsion for making it mean something else which, beside being inaccurately conceived, impairs its natural congruity.

If the interpretation I have been chiding is more comical than conjectural, it is not otherwise singular. Statements equally strained were made by experienced reviewers; among them, professional theologians contributed to the obscurity. For these gentry, a movie that dealt with the very stuff of their daily, or weekly, argument was a rare opportunity for them to vie with film critics in an area which they could not help but feel was securely within their jurisdiction. There is a delightful moment in *The Seventh Seal* when Jof tells of a dream he has had in which his boy achieves the ultimate juggler's trick of making a ball stand still in the air. This is a charming clue to Joseph's intuition that the child will be a miracle worker. Peter Cowie quotes approvingly, one must assume, a certain M. D'Yvoire, surely a critic-of-the-cloth, who asserts:

. . . . the trick in question symbolizes the interruption of cosmic movement, in other words the end of the world, the return to stability through reabsorption in the principle of Being: one more way of suggesting the comparison of the child with the saviour of the world, the only one capable of effecting this reintegration in the immobility of God.[61]

This goes a giant step further than the presumptions of the Washington State University writer who was attempting to define the symbolism of something *visible* in the film. Now we are being instructed in the significance of something *invisible*, an event referred to speculatively. I cannot believe that Bergman would be flattered by such ambitious reconstructions, for they do precisely the opposite of what they should be doing. They lead you away from the image instead of bringing you close to it. Here is a moviemaker trying to incarnate an abstraction for us, and what does this M. D'Yvoire do? He reconverts the iconic symbol into an abstraction, into a theocosmic proposition. I believe the viewer should be attentive to ultra-mundane nuances in a film, if he senses them, but I don't find this kind of transliteration helpful to anyone. Bergman is not a systematic theologian. He is an artist with an obsessive concern for the question of God's existence, too obsessively concerned, for my taste; if he makes art of the obsession that is agreeable to me; when I think he hasn't, I say so, but I do think it is unfair to transpose the expressions of his art into terms that nullify the art.

This, at least, Mr. Arthur Gibson does not do, in his recent analysis of seven Bergman films, *The Silence of God*.[62] Mr. Gibson, a professor of theology, renders in minute, often passionate detail the quality, the texture, and the atmosphere of each film he undertakes. Nonetheless, he plainly falsifies many aspects of these films in order to make them conform neatly to the *message* he finds in them. Part of his method is to ignore any previous expressions in Bergman's work of the doctrines or doubts he, Gibson, is at the moment scrutinizing. This is graduate-seminar procedure; in the interests of purely textual elucidation it demands from us dissimulation. We are required to pretend ignorance of the author's existence outside of the text under scrutiny. Mr. Gibson is intent on demonstrating that *The Seventh Seal* "formulates the problematic [sic] of the entire film series; and that problematic is the silence of God." What you wish to demonstrate you will demonstrate; hence, it is convenient for Mr. Gibson to imply that in *The Seventh Seal* Bergman was for the first time, to any point perhaps, posing the awful problem of a world without God. Mr. Gibson is particularly impressed with the dialogue in the chapel, when the Knight is unwittingly moved to confess his tormenting doubts to Death himself.

Knight: .... I want God to stretch out his hand toward me, reveal Himself and speak to me.
Death: But he remains silent.
Knight: I call out to Him in the dark but no one seems to be there.
Death: Perhaps no one is there.
Knight: Then life is an outrageous horror. No one can live in the face of death, knowing that all is nothingness.

Without enumerating all the other occasions in an early Bergman film or play when something comparable was formulated, I will simply note that this is substantially the viewpoint expressed by Martin in the film *Prison*. The terms are reversed; the reasoning is as dogmatic. If there is such hell on earth, there can be no God. If there is no God, there is hell on earth. In the earlier film, I found the sentiment fatuous. In *The Seventh Seal,* I can accept it because the historical context makes it plausible in the mouth of the Knight. This will never do for Mr. Gibson, but it will remain my view of the matter. Another line of dialogue that affected Mr. Gibson intensely is the Knight's outcry at the end of the film, his last words, I believe. ''God, You who are somewhere, who *must* be somewhere, have mercy upon us.'' The reader will recognize that these are all but the self-same words ejaculated by Bergman's alter ego character, left alone on the darkening stage, in *Jack Among the Actors,* 1943. ''God in Heaven, help me! *You who must be somewhere. . . .*''

I do not claim that these rehearsals invalidate Mr. Gibson's reception of their further presence in *The Seventh Seal,* and I can scarcely repudiate his emotional reaction to them in the context. I am contending that from my point of view the state of disbelief expressed in this film cannot be regarded as an astounding novelty and that therefore I am not persuaded by Mr. Gibson's description of the films he has arbitrarily enlisted as moving through a ''great arc'' from ''an initial oppressive uncertainty'' in *The Seventh Seal* to ''a terminal horrifying certainty . . .'' (i.e. in *Persona*). In fact, I believe that this part of his thesis is disqualified to begin with. For I cannot see how he can fairly describe *The Seventh Seal* as totally evincing the silence of God when its last word, so to speak, is the liberation of Jof and Mia who will ostensibly reinstitute, to use Mr. Gibson's phraseology, the Christian dynamic.

The character of Bergman criticism henceforth will consist largely and desperately of the attempt to impose a unitary logic on every one of his films or, by way of a reaction equally irresponsible, to deny them integrity when they are most integrated. In the presence of such desperation, one can only feel sympathy toward the predicament expressed on an earlier occasion by the late great James Thurber, when *The Cocktail Party* arrived in New York City. ''Ever since the distinguished Mr. T. S. Eliot's widely discussed play came to town, I have been cornered at parties by women, and men, who seem intent on making me say what I think *The Cocktail Party* means, so they can cry, ''Great God, how naïve!''[63]

I should like to restore to *The Seventh Seal* its status of a magical movie, more suggestive than definitive, more lyric than didactic. And the best way I know is to think of it as one might an orchestral suite for a small orchestra, in which certain themes from the motley life of a medieval community, threatened by death in the forest, comprise the various movements, with signature instruments for the principal characters: a viola for Block, a cello for Jöns, clarinet and flute for Jof and Mia, a bassoon for the flagellant leader, a harpsichord for Death, and perhaps an organ to enforce the harpsichord during the chess games and at the conclusion, that is, before a final brief rondo as Jof is scolded by Mia for thinking he has glimpsed the others in a death dance on yonder hill. If you heard a suite of this order, I think you would feel no compulsion to decide whether its composer was agnostic or devout; you would not think to translate the fugue into an ontological argument; you would more than likely miss the implication that those repeated triads symbolize the Trinity and while you might have a favorite movement you would not leave the concert hall asserting you had heard a piece of music which had infallibly pictured the misery of a world deprived of God's mercy. You would recall the spirited *allegretto,* when Jof, Mia, and Skat prepare for the festival, or the *scherzando,* representing the altercations among Plog, Lisa, Jof, and Jöns or praise, above all, the *largo* dialogue of viola and harpsichord in the church scene, punctuated from time to time by a derisive *glissando* from the cellist.

I think *The Seventh Seal* is a beautiful, harmoniously composed film with indelible pictorial effects but I do not feel that its questions disturb the universe.

Wild Strawberries

Wild Strawberries is linked to *The Seventh Seal* by more than its title image. There is in the earlier film a gratuitous attribute of the Knight's character which no one seems to have observed. At the beginning of that confession at the chapel, in which, all unknowingly, Block is addressing Death, he maintains that through his indifference toward his fellow men he has isolated himself and lives now in a world of dreams and phantoms. We are asked to accept this statement with no further reference to the

Knight's confessed disability; yet, if we think about it, the declaration becomes highly unlikely, since Block's responsiveness to the mortals he meets is unaffected, not at all the reaction of a habitually indifferent man. True, he is not shown in his particularities; he is little more than an animated question mark—which is accounted for by the customary sacrifice, in allegory, of psychological density to representative trait. Even so, we know something of Block, the man; he has been on a crusade and since he does not suggest the type that went along for the booty, we must believe that he was spiritually dedicated to the adventure. And the environment of a crusade would scarcely be conducive to the cultivation of indifference. Nor was there any implication that he went to the Holy Land to escape from his wife. This relationship is really quite nebulous and seems to have been introduced merely to give him a home to go back to. In my opinion, this superfluous self-denigration was awarded him by Bergman in a moment of absent-minded anticipation. Indifference is allegedly the tragic flaw of Isak Borg in the following film. I think Bergman may have faltered when he brought the Knight into that church; he had to find something for him to confess, beside his anguish that God remained silent. Jof, in the same film, does live in a world of dreams and visions, but not the Knight; he is all too awake in a world that is, fearful that there might be no other; this is why he insists that God should reveal himself in mundane form.

In short, the Knight is pretty clearly a mouthpiece for Ingmar Bergman; the confession he is making, except for its greater austerity, could be that of Joakim, in *The City,* forlorn in the presence of his grandmother. "I have buried myself in women, in religious ecstasy, and I have believed in the activity called 'artistic'. All in vain! . . ." In the mouth of a medieval knight, this theme of insufficiency reasserts itself in the Bergman film, to appear subsequently in oddly sublimated forms. As if restating Yeats' affirmation, "Players and painted stage took all my love/And not those things that they were emblems of," Bergman now pursues that self-questioning of the artist which receives its consummate expression in *Ansiktet* and its most enigmatic extension in *Persona.* Some of the more negative, self-wounding aspects of this sentiment are, however, transferred; they are projected into characters, not necessarily artists, who are depicted as being fatally remote from common humanity by virtue of the professional concentration to which they have pledged their lives. Anyone eager to accept, in Bergman's later films, his persistent indictment of the artist or intellectual as a shameful epitome of the man apart had better look closely at the character into which this feature has been smuggled, in order to decide how universally it can be interpreted, in what measure it can be adjudged a specifically Swedish style of response, and to what extent it records Bergman's personal, puritan unease.

The issue is conspicuously raised in *Wild Strawberries*. The contention of the film, what is thematically announced and, you might say, intellectually concluded, is contradicted by the action of the film. Bergman's confusion, for so I see it, arose from an error of love, which goes far to pardon it, but it was an error all the same. He wanted to make a film in which Victor Sjöstrom, for whom he felt inexpressible admiration, would have the leading role. At the same time he wanted to make a film about an esteemed old man whose personal life, empty and selfish, repudiates the esteem awarded him. The two intentions simply would not blend. Involved with an actor whom he admired as a person, Bergman was unable to make him sufficiently unsympathetic as a character to justify the accusations leveled at and the judgments passed on him in the film story. What should have been an increasingly ruthless self-confrontation by old Borg is considerably mitigated by the sentimental excursions he makes, en route to his lost childhood, and by the ambience of reconciliation at the soft-focus close of the film.

I am quite certain by now that the affection most people have for this film, an affection I cannot in any way share, is unconnected with the ostensible and certainly *verbalized* subject: the presumably terrible consequence of Borg's dawning recognition, as he enters a forest as dark and deathly as that of *The Seventh Seal*, (the tangled forest of his own evasions and subterfuges), that he is in cold fact a pillar of stone, a product of egoism petrified and the planter of it in his own son. On the contrary, I gather from those who express pleasure in the film that more often than not they minimize this feature of it and are chiefly warmed by the sympathetic performance of Victor Sjostrom; thus, they tend to take the film as if in it Bergman had been attempting the same kind of compassionate portrait of an old man faced with death as Vittorio de Sica had achieved in *Umberto D*, or Kurasawa in *Living*. This is not their fault of interpretation, entirely; in the long run, a diffused compassion is what Bergman proffers.

Bergman's devotion to Sjöstrom was rooted many years ago, probably further back than my knowledge informs me. I recall the intensity with which he answered me when in 1959 I asked him diffidently, since I felt it might be a banal inquiry, if there was a single figure in filmmaking whom, above all others, he admired. "Yes!" he exclaimed instantly, stabbing his finger vehemently at a picture on the wall over my head. It was, of course, a picture of Victor Sjöstrom. He had directed Sjöstrom once before, in *To Joy*, 1949, and there is more of a hint of old Sonderby, from that film, sitting with the young couple on the grass, in the unseen presence of Borg, in *Wild Strawberries*, espying Sara with his brother, Sigfrid, who replaced him as her sweetheart. I have previously quoted Bergman's statement that, except for Lorens Marmstedt, he owed no debt to any filmmaker other than Sjöstrom who, when Artistic Adviser at Svenskfilm, gave him invaluable counsel. The identification moves closer. In Bergman's first film, *Crisis*, the lights of a cinema marquee advertise the movie, *Ordet (The Word)*, directed by Gustav Molander, in which Sjöstrom played the character, Morten Borgen, changed, in the Swedish version of this Danish play, to Knut Borg. That name, in *Wild Strawberries*, became Emanuel Isak Borg. The initials are the same as those of Ernest Ingmar Bergman.

We may be sure that Bergman was not being arch. The names he gives his characters are frequently significant, although one must not look for consistency in this practice. However, when a character represents a *persona*, or even a phase of Bergman himself, he is likely to be named in accord with a previous instance or in some identifiable manner. That with Isak Borg, by a super-Lutheran leap of conscience, Bergman was already prosecuting himself as an old man, I would prefer not to insinuate, although I suppose such a thing is possible. But I am at least certain that while he was creating, or recreating from a real-life hint, a specific aged professor who would exemplify the unlived life, he was half-consciously initiating that severe inquest of himself, (of his self as an artist is all I am concerned with) which he would recapitulate in a sequence of excessively tormented variants from *The Magician* onwards.

The unlovable attributes of Isak Borg we are asked to accept without question; they are announced prosaically by the protagonist himself as the film opens.

> I have of my own free will withdrawn myself almost completely from society and therefore find myself alone in my old age. This is not a regret but a statement of fact. I ask only to be left alone and to have the opportunity to devote myself to the few things which continue to interest me, however superficial they seem. . . . I should perhaps add that I'm an old pedant, at times very trying—to myself as to those who must be around me. I detest emotional outbursts, the tears of women, the cries of children. . . .

Hardly a scathing self-assessment; it could even occur to one that he was listing the basic indulgences allowed to old age. But this was not part of the intent; with this deprecation, our attitude toward Borg is immediately edited. From there on the evidence against him is asserted by someone else. We learn from Marianne, his daughter-in-law, who accompanies him on the trip to Lund which utilizes much of the film and is parallel with his journey into the past, that he is a cold father, and that his son Evald has become an even colder replica. Marianne is at the moment in a deadlocked struggle with Evald, because he is repelled by her desire to have children. We learn, in a return-through-time sequence from Sara, the girl who married his brother instead, that he was a cold suitor. We learn by meeting his mother, largely by the reaction of Marianne to that meeting since the old lady is one of the few personable characters in the film, that he has come by his frigidity naturally, for Mrs. Borg announces matter-of-factly that she has been cold all her life. Moreover she makes it clear by her enumeration of the other sons, nine of them, all dead, that she had understood none of them, nor they her, and that her grandchildren never visit her unless they need a loan.

But the man, Isak Borg, whom we see, does not bear out the accumulated impression given by his accusers; he is a sweet, troubled old gentleman who in context seems to be the victim of an unreasonable amount of abuse from people who are mostly less attractive than he and inordinately self-righteous. I do not expect an actor, with every entrance, to underline his wickedness like the late Monty Wooley: "Sorry to be late but I stopped to throw stones at a small boy!''; even so, a man as mean and as curled on himself as Borg is, by private reputation, would certainly betray himself by his expression, by his involuntary movements, by the clothes he wears, by the disapprovals to which he gives casual voice, by the way he carries his hands. "My body is unwillingly the secret agent of my ancestors," as the poet Ruthven Todd once said. Of course, it is possible that Victor Sjöstrom was then too old to bear down on the minute shadings of the character, that Bergman did not insist, and that the opening poster of the film was to do duty for negations unexpressed.

In order to comprise a life-cycle, by selection, within a day-cycle in which Professor Borg goes to Lund to receive an honorary degree, returns home, and attempts to resolve his alienation from Evald and Marianne, the form of the narrative required a high degree of compression. And since the witness point was to be as often as possible that of old Borg, even as a youth, a strongly modified naturalism was in order. To my view, the problem was gauchely solved. The convention of allegory on which Bergman had relied in *The Seventh Seal* permits an easier coalescence of pretense and reality. Nothing seems strange because everything is strange; in allegory, as in high comedy, the possible is what you invent. But in *Wild Strawberries* the challenge was more difficult to meet, since the time and place made greater demands on the standards of the probable. I felt throughout an incongruity of effect, the real never quite real because of the stilted nature of the action, the fantasy never quite unreal in the right way, the inevitable way. The images in the surreal dream at the opening of the film when Borg meets himself stepping out of a coffin—a watch without hands that shows up again in the Mrs. Borg scene, an empty street in blinding light, the audible heartbeats —these are too crude to be graced with the term "symbols," and I found them unpersuasive in every way because the whole vision was inorganic, contrived by the will, unlike the hallucination which opened *The Naked Night* wherein reality was sufficiently distended to create from the event a spectacle and a gruesome prophecy. As I have said, Bergman dreamed this episode; its counterpart in *Wild Strawberries* he dreamed up. The Borg nightmare is a theatrical arrangement, like those macabre settings in *Prison* which, instead of convincing you that Birgitta-Carolina was indeed dreaming them, only wrenched you from the context with some such question as, "Where did he get that from? Pabst or Cocteau?"

There are other schemata in this film I find equally uncomfortable.

Consider the two students, Viktor and Anders, who epitomize the antagonism of Science and Religion, two calf-like boys who are bundled out of the scene by Sara, their bickering then summarized by her in a slang paragraph. This is glib and irresponsible, but Arthur Gibson accepts it as "a perfect paradigm of the argumentative man of principle, whether earnest theologian (like Anders) or doctrinaire scientist (like Viktor)". In a farce it might just pass; in a serious film we have the right to expect a more imaginative encounter than this to suggest the very important contradictions between science and religion. The contradictions are important, that is to say, if science and religion are offered as ways of looking at experience; logically, they can't contradict each other, for they are different orders of knowledge. I fail to see why Bergman needed this silly interlude, save as a hidden persuader he never develops that truth transcends partisan arguments. At one moment, Borg, with the theology student and Sara, recites a theistic poem (from which I quote in part):

> Where is the friend I seek for everywhere?
> Dawn is the hour of loneliness and care.
> When twilight falls I am still yearning
> Although my heart is burning, burning.
> I see His trace of glory and power,
> In an ear of grain and fragrance of a flower. . . .[64]

But I am not convinced that this is other than a passage of nostalgia, a transitional piety which should not be confused with the God-quest of *The Seventh Seal*.

Then there is the quarreling couple, Berit and Alman, who are taken into the car with Marianne and Isak Borg after a collision. We have already an embittered couple, Marianne and Evald; we don't need an echo of the situation to imply a universal incompatibility. The fact that this venomous interchange is one of the most passionately felt in the film only contributes to my suspicion that another Bergman preoccupation was here misplaced. Besides, it is a patent ruse for later employing Alman, the husband, as the judge in the fantasy trial at the penultimate ending, when Isak learns the last unpalatable truth: that his own coldness was responsible for his wife's infidelity.

Isak: And what is the penalty?
Alman: I don't know. The usual one, I suppose.
Isak: The usual one?
Alman: Of course. Loneliness.

Since the name, Alman, is obviously a variant of *allmän*, meaning general or public, Isak is in effect being tried by society; one may justifiably ask of this supercilious character, "Who are *you* to sit in judgment on Isak Borg?"—was Bergman's meaning supposed to be the loveless condemned by the loveless? But the film is loaded with mysterious divided allegiances. Evald, who wants Marianne to have an abortion because he thinks it is ridiculous to populate this world with new victims, opposes her moral argument with his statement: "There is nothing which can be called right or wrong. One functions according to one's needs; you can read that in an elementary-school textbook." In his preface to *Four Screenplays* (Simon & Schuster, 1960), Bergman, himself, writes that he was tremendously impressed philosophically by a book, which he does not describe as an elementary-school textbook, called *Psychology of the Personality,* by Eiono Kaila. "His thesis that man lives strictly according to his needs—negative and positive—was shattering to me, but terribly true. And I built on this ground." The invisible question mark is mine.

Further, Isak Borg's reencounter with Sara in the past, and the appearance of her twin and namesake as the young hitchhiker in the present, is flagrantly sentimental; with this involvement, which gives the film its title—the wild strawberries here represent a precious moment which has been lost forever, and the image has an erotic overtone—the force of Borg's self-scrutiny and subsequent damnation is substantially deflected. What had appeared to be an unfolding drama of exposure to a concealed and ugly truth becomes almost imperceptibly the tremulous search of an old man for the lost objects of love in the Vanished Garden. It is noticeable that those like Bergman, so redoubtable at portraying steel and stress in the male-female relationship, veer into a world of pink and sky-blue when they envisage a feminine ideal and a compatible couple. The conception of Jof and Mia in *The Seventh Seal* just misses the saccharine by virtue of the implied dimension which transforms them into Biblical reminders. Sara the First (like Mia, played by Bibi Andersson) is to my sense an inocuous, uninteresting young lady; with all allowance made for willing suspension of disbelief, I doubt that a seventy-year-old man, sifting the memories of his life, would be anything but relieved to have escaped from such a Valentine-picture-pussy as Sara. As for Sara the Second, she's illiterate.

The critical judgment which the whole narrative has portended is now vitiated and the conclusion, after Borg has been safely tucked into bed, as it were, unexpectedly minimizes the gravity of his insights: Sara, with her wild strawberries, calling to him across the abyss of time; Mother and Father, waving to him from the other bank, for whom he now feels forbearance because, presumably, he has arrived at a more generous understanding of their failings. How does he come by this understanding? By recognizing his own defections? In that case, he is at the last forgiving himself. A direction in which he might have been allowed to do so is totally muffled. The distinctions accorded this man of science are nowhere in the film a positive source of pride, an extenuating professional achievement. A man, such a man, is more than the sum of his deficiencies. Even assuming he has discovered what sham his emotional life has been, something might have been said for the gifts of learning which he must have shared with thousands of students during his academic lifetime. An irony was missed here. Henry James or Ibsen would have made it plain that Borg had already been punished and that in the punishment was the reward, the only wild strawberries he would ever reap: for intellectual dedication, which is a good in itself, may well exclude the vital satisfactions by which those more moderately endowed with mind animate their existence. It may well exclude, and this should be his hell, a proper regard for his own kin. The terms are hard and they are irreversible, but the film does not end on this note. It frays into wistfulness, because Bergman approaches his material subjectively; he can only bring to a conclusion what he has himself concluded.

Here is where Arthur Gibson sharpens his instruments; he is quite certain that the clandestine or real subject of the film is what he calls the failure of a "restrictive humanism". By humanism he does not mean humanistic studies, he means a human-centered world. If Bergman hadn't underlined the sin of being secular, Gibson will do it for him. Isak Borg is modern man, no less, and of modern man Mr. Gibson takes a very dim view. "Modern man," he complacently tells us, "must face the reality of his own dissatisfaction, lovelessness, sluggishness and instability. . . .''[65] That he has been facing it for a long time now is my first thought, since I can entertain a definition of Man, without the adjective, which, from a Platonic standpoint, would describe him as eternally dissatisfied, loveless, sluggish, and unstable! Gibson means Godless man but it is often difficult to know just when, in the sight of a theologian, man became godless irreparably. In the sixteenth century? The seventeenth? In 1899? Yesterday? While I cannot let myself be led into an extensive argument with Mr. Gibson over the depravity of modern man, I believe that the viewer of Bergman's films should be wary before accepting Gibson's conviction of what Bergman intended, unless it is more clearly discernible in the context of the film than in this case I think it is. Gibson is not alone with his platitude; two thirds of the critics I have read on the subject of *Wild Strawberries* have called Isak Borg modern man. Every time an en vogue filmmaker embodies some miserable victim of the human comedy, critics rush to invest the embodiment with the epithet, modern man: a tautology, if nothing else, for if the film is about contemporary life, the subject character will be ipso facto modern. All this aside, I think Gibson's interpretation of Borg's plight is presumptive. Borg, Doctor of Medicine, does not stand for humanism without God. Borg is not looking for God; he is looking for himself. He is not suffering because he has failed God; he is suffering because he failed humanism; because he failed to meet the challenge of a thoroughly virile selfhood.

My personal dissatisfaction with the film should not be construed as impatience because it was not intellectually consistent. Criticism is a method of rationally explaining the emotional experience one has already had. Truthfully, I was ever untouched by this movie. When, upon its first appearance, it aroused such clamant admiration and shortly evoked reams of candle-lit prose comparing it with the achievement of Marcel Proust and solemnly maintaining that it was one of the indisputable works of twentieth-century art, and such a deal of skimble-skamble stuff, I confess to having been intimidated. Conceivably, I told myself, I had been prematurely uncharitable. I had missed an experience. I procured a script, I went to see the film again, and after a suitable length of time, yet again. That was quite sufficient. I credit Bergman with an ambitious enterprise; the film presented a complex problem. I honor his affection for Victor Sjöstrom. Paraphrased as an idea, this movie always sounds good in the telling. Close up, for me, it is tedious. The absence of any felt rhythm irritates me, most of the minor characters are no end boring, the vision of country-cousin felicity is unappealing and I feel cheated of the deeper subject which, from time to time, can be fleetingly glimpsed in the haunted eyes of Victor Sjöstrom—the agony of contrition.

One direction in which I think Bergman succeeded, if unconsciously; he did define a Swedish predicament. In every country, to be sure, there are people who have abdicated from life, "the world forgetting and by the world forgot". But in no other country to my knowledge are there so many people who have turned their backs on society while remaining in it. This ancient ruin, Mrs. Borg, deserted by her sons and ignored by her grandsons, this undoting father who has made loans of money to his son at exorbitant rates of interest, and the son, declaring to his wife, "My need is to be dead. Absolutely, totally dead," are all familiar Swedish phenomena. So, at the end, Isak Borg is sentenced to loneliness; this comes within circumference of the joke. To no Swede would isolation be a capital punishment. *Ensamhet: loneliness.* Their favorite misery. They cherish it; they hug it to themselves, they write odes to it, they perch it on their wrists and feed it.

Brink of Life

Bergman made *Nära Livet* (*Brink of Life*), 1958, for Nordisk Tonefilm, to meet an unwritten obligation which had remained unfulfilled after an earlier project, a film version of *The Bridal Crown,* had been abandoned (see Note 28). The Social Democratic ethos of Nordisk Tonefilm appears to have had an influence on Bergman's treatment of this movie; in many of its scenes *Brink of Life* has a tentative sociological coloring which ill consorts with the private world of suffering in which Bergman is most at home, unreachable by outsiders and inaccessible to agents of social welfare. In *Brink of Life,* however, based on stories and a scenario by Ulla Isaksson, the indisputable presence of a hospital maternity ward had to be given some credit in the scheme of things. The result is a film without a distinct subject, unless you are satisfied that the value of life is its subject; I should prefer to think of this as a premise. A single relationship, that of Cecelia Ellius to her husband, Anders, is recognizably a modulation of the central conflict within the Borg family in *Wild Strawberries*; the remainder is only an attenuated effort to spin out the general theme of life and death.

Brink of Life is not otherwise in the same realm of discourse as the films that precede and follow it. This is no journey into the depths of the magic forest, though it might be said that in the Cecelia episode Bergman ventures further into the womb of time, if I may risk the expression, than most of us care to go, having so far emerged. I have never been able to experience this film with the requisite solemnity enjoined upon mere man by the awful mystery of childbirth. And my lack of complete reverence has been encouraged by the fact that most women with whom I have discussed the film are quite yawny about it. They have usually sensed, more readily than the critics, what has always seemed stridently obvious to me: that the anxiety with which Bergman was herein nursing the lot of women was so importunate that one is bound to turn the conception inside out (pun unintentional) and ask why, in film after film, Bergman so morbidly forces the agonies of women into merciless closeup. Apropos *Brink of Life,* I seem to remember that in 1957 owing to the distribution lag the universal opinion of Bergman had not yet agreed upon the loftiness and sobriety of his intentions; there were many filmgoers, as there still are, who insisted on enjoying him principally as the director of *A Lesson in Love* and *Smiles of a Summer Night.* Bergman definitely wanted to alter the impression that he didn't take womanhood with sufficient seriousness. And in *Brink of Life* one does have the distinct feeling that he is standing at one's elbow, thundering, "*Listen to me!*—WOMEN—HAVE—BABIES!

Except for the characterization of Cecelia (Ingrid Thulin), so anomalous and intense that it is a law to itself and deserved a whole other film to comprise it, *So Close to Life,* as the English know it, is too close to soap opera. Three women, rather schematically chosen for age and class, or social group, as the Swedes prefer to put it, fill out the material; as I suggested above, material rather than subject, because the film as a whole never rises to the level of the possibility implied by the word birth. Actually, no birth takes place. Cecelia is victim of a miscarriage,

Stina's child is sacrificed to save the mother, and young Hjördis is at the hospital to have an abortion.

There should have been drama enough in these three lives at a crucial hour to have nailed the spectator in his seat, but probably because Bergman did not have complete authority with an intention which in any case was fortuitous rather than creatively explored, two of the women, Stina and Hjördis, are but sketchily conveyed, which is not, I think, the fault of the actresses, Eva Dahlbeck and Bibi Andersson. Stina has one supreme moment, when she concentrates with all her nerve and mind on reaching for a glass of water, after the crisis which has nearly devastated her control; the expression in Eva Dahlbeck's eyes puts this moment among the great Swedish film closeups. But the expression does not belong to Stina, if I have any coherent sense of the woman as otherwise drawn; she seems to be a suburban sort with a very simple consciousness. It looked to me as if Mrs. Dahlbeck was having a difficult time giving this woman any inner, personal weight; she played her too broadly in her public moments to be convincing when in the grip of her private effort and grief; at this point the Dahlbeck of Strindberg and Lorca, on the stage, overshadowed the shopping-center psyche of Stina.

Hjördis, the third member of this natal trio, was apparently not in the original story (just the one I would have supposed had been!) and was supplied by Bergman, I would say, as an avuncular warning to young ladies contemplating abortion. As a result of her identification with Cecelia and Stina, in which there is more prescription than believable inner resolution, she decides to have her baby. The film thus ends with an unfortunately slick illustration of life carried on by the youngest. As is so often the case in Bergman films, the denial of life is more palpable than its affirmation. Cecelia and her repellent mate compel attention above all other characters in the film. Cecelia's fear that she cannot ever have a child is first insinuated as a consequence of the loveless, unvital union she experiences with her pedantic Ellius, who strongly resembles Evald in *Wild Strawberries*, but the real poignancy of her ordeal is that at bottom she feels guiltily in doubt of her own womanliness. Here, the psychological shading is astute and Bergman's direction of Miss Thulin was so forceful and incisive that nobody else in the movie comes within her emotional range. Beyond the Ellius couple, involving much painful dialogue between Cecelia and her somewhat epicene husband, played with admirably hideous precision by Erland Josephson—I won't here belabor Bergman's contemptuous notion of the intellectual—the film is drab, uninventively shot, and where least overwrought quite ponderous. The teeming, if efficient, background activity of society's most dramatic public institution is barely suggested; in this *Brink of Life,* the brink alone is where we arrive.

Over the Bergman subject in 1958, when the film was released, madness hovered. At a certain film-festival press conference, one character raved to the skies about how inspired Bergman had been to devise that touch of Bibi Andersson losing her slipper as she rushes to the telephone. Whereupon a still photographer from Stockholm in the know and emboldened, I am told, by a Martini or two rose to snort. This had been pure accident, he claimed, as Bibi's shoe did come off and Bergman was sharp enough to leave the accident as a take, which was included in the final print. An extraordinary number of critics seem to have no conception of the creative process, no idea that art can ever be anything but scrupulously planned. If it happens spontaneously, if luck is abroad, it doesn't sound difficult and they want art to sound difficult if it is to be something they couldn't dream of executing themselves. Odd that they never recall how hard it is to write five pages of readable prose, yet how often a solution presents itself which had nothing to do with the writer's conscious intention.

This effort to attribute to Bergman a concatenation of premeditated effects finds some of its wildest outlets on the subject of *Brink of Life.* As if to compensate for the parturitions that never materialize, certain critics have subsequently found everything in the film pregnant. Eugene Archer and Peter Cowie, writing respectively one year and seven after the event, were equally anxious to load their rifts with ore. What is the source of this anxiety? That you might make less of a showing than another critic? That you doubt the film is all that good and hence you redouble your labors? That Ingmar Bergman is over your left shoulder? Bergman, who of all people resents these triple-decker interpretations? Archer describes Stina's bellowing outcry as "a moment as revealing as Death's denial of interior knowledge in *The Seventh Seal*".[66] What kind of intellectual vulgarity is this that looks the other way during

Stina's birthpangs and tries to transfigure them in a simile as remote as it is irrelevant? Such a statement tells one nothing about Stina, shut in with her bull; there is nothing to be said, since the experience is irreducible. A critic has nowhere to go with it, beyond expressing his opinion that the moment in question is either affecting or that it fails to affect him.

Cowie, likewise.[67] There is absolutely *nothing* in the film he doesn't edit, working until steam rises off the page to bring this movie into line with *The Silence,* made five years later, cooking up a unity of stress which he claims Bergman places on "inanimate objects such as surgeon's gloves and electric clocks" which, taken together with a remark dropped by Cecelia, represent "a typical Bergman plea against the dehumanizing powers of scientific progress". "Dehumanizing powers" is a bit thick, isn't it? Birth, in our time, is a collaboration of nature and science. If it were not for surgeons' gloves and other "inanimate objects" among a hospital ward's equipment, none of us would ever get born, not even Ingmar Bergman. Cowie infuses the simplest living gesture with an overload of extrinsic meaning. Of Hjördis, he says, "Bergman reveals her latent femininity in the scene where she brushes Stina's hair and makes her up". Latent femininity? She's twenty-two, if she's a day; she's old enough to have a child; she probably brushed her doll's hair at the age of one and coiffured her playmate at one and a half. Females have been brushing each other's hair since they stepped out of caves. It's probably one of those built-in-and-conditioned mechanisms, like the pursuit of mice by cats, or those things that fish do when they think they're being observed by Konrad Lorenz.

The Magician

A halt or reversal in the fervor with which critics had been greeting Bergman's films was noticeable in the reception of *Ansiktet* (literally, *The Face,* and so called in England; *The Magician* in the United States). Not only when the film appeared but on later occasions when sufficient time had passed in which to reconsider hastily furnished opinions, mystification was stronger than affection and, since mystification often leads to animosity, an irritated tone informs many futile attempts to make sense of this film. Rereading many of these reviews today, I find pure impatience masquerading as common sense and I see critics fearful of being taken in; in some cases I note a flat refusal to make a simple effort, and only a simple effort is required, to divine what *The Magician* is all about—if knowing what it is all about is the only proviso for a critic's enjoyment of it! A certain kind of poetry, T. S. Eliot said great poetry, I believe, can communicate before it is fully understood. In these days of the humbug and the vague-minded, I would not depend on the principle, yet it might be a good one to invoke here. Critical viewers have swallowed, it seems to me, a vast amount of vulgarity and facile symbolism from, for instance, the films of Pier Paolo Pasolini (that dubious mixture of Catholicism, Marxism, the sacred epicene, and the godlike stud, all of it *mental*). They tend, often the same viewers, to get thoroughly confused, always at the wrong time, by Bergman or for that matter by Antonioni.

The Magician is an incredibly suggestive work; that it is also definitive is as much to my point, and this very suggetiveness has beguiled critical opinion into strange interpretations; equally it has tempted certain critics into suspecting Bergman of trifling with them, of indulging a taste for the occult which he then hopes to endow with a spurious morality.[68] I believe that Bergman has been many times confused, in his several films, as to how best to convey a moral or metaphysical ambiguity; I am of the opinion that in his latest films he has lost the power of discerning what is self-evident to an audience and what is absurd. I am convinced that he has ultimately unclear ideas about the nature of moral catastrophe. And it may well be that there are calculatedly hidden meanings in his later films; but I do not believe that he trades in gratuitous mystification and I do not believe that he manufactures effects which have no meaning to him. Frivolity is surely the last vice with which anyone should charge Bergman.

Above all, *The Magician* is not the film in which to expect irresponsibility, since the conscience of the artist is precisely the burden from which Vogler, the magician, is suffering. Perhaps I should not say precisely because Vogler is a necessarily imprecise figure, for a very good personal reason which, at the same time, cannot but lend interest to the character in the film. I may as well state at the outset of this exploration that when Bergman was working on *The Virgin Spring* he told me that he had not felt "quite right" about the two films preceding. As I recall, he was not including *Brink of Life,* which is quite another matter. With *The Virgin Spring* he felt absolutely sure of what he was doing. Now, in *Wild Strawberries,* I suggested, he was unable to see Isak Borg as cooly as the context warranted because of his respect for Victor Sjöstrom. During the shooting of *The Magician* I know that he was not altogether decided on the fate of Vogler. Should he rescue him, should he let him be crushed? His artistic shrewdness gave him the answer. You can't very well construct a film in which every appearance is stained with ambiguity, then conclude it on a note of doom, categorically sounded.

Vogler's fate is left open, as it should be; we have never been quite sure of his identity; it is fitting that we should feel unsure of his future although, for the moment, it looks rosy. There may be undertones, intensities, extremities of feeling in this film which cannot rationally be accounted for, but I sense no fundamental imprecision in the character of the underworld which Bergman was apotheosizing. Obscurity is one thing, mystery another. At the heart of *The Magician,* as in the heart of the magician, there is mystery, an onset of fright because people's definitions of each other digress so wildly, and a suspicion demoralizing by its enormity that the powers we hold to be most reliable are just those on which we cannot depend when the hour of exposure arrives.

Let us, as prosaically as the subject permits, recall the continuity of the tale. From the depths of a forest, perhaps for the last time in a Bergman film, comes that cry of players so often materialized before, usually a token that deeds not altogether savory and not apprehensibly real are about to transpire. Vogler and his outlaw company, including his wife disguised as a man, his "grandmother," who has all the appearance and jargon of a professional witch, and his factotum, the ridiculous Tubal, are on their way to Stockholm in the 1840's, where Vogler hopes to demonstrate his magic at the Royal Palace. We learn, from brief exchanges of dialogue, that these mercenaries of the occult art have been fined and jailed in some of the best cities of Europe for heresy, for blasphemy, for sundry dubious ventures in the realm of the cure-all. Traveling through the forest, they pick up a dying, or demented, and

certainly drunken actor, Spegel. At the entry to Stockholm they are
detained at the custom house for approval by Starbeck, the Chief of
Police, and invited by the "liberal" Councillor Egerman (he is open
to proof) to spend the night at his mansion where the royal Doctor
of Medicine, Vergerus, hopes to expose Vogler as a charlatan. Bergman's
first title for the film was *The Charlatans,* raising the obvious question,
"Who are the charlatans?"

During their stay at the mansion, the presence of Vogler and his
company stirs up a red-ant colony of frustrations, antipathies, concealed
impotence, and buried desires. Ottilia Egerman, wife of the councillor,
wants Vogler to requite her loveless life with her husband—their marriage
had collapsed after the death of their child, one of the few warmed-over
situations in the film—by explaining why the child died and by taking
her husband's place in her bed. Egerman overhears her trying to make
an assignation with Vogler, reveals to her later that he knows her intention and strikes her. Following which, in true Strindberg-Bergman
fashion, he asks her forgiveness. Vergerus too has an itch, for upon
discovering that Aman is Manda, a female, he tries to seduce her; when
challenged by the irate magician he calms his jealousy by telling him
wittily that he has nothing to fear; his wife's fidelity "borders on madness".

Meanwhile, the company downstairs is pursuing its own pleasures and
suggestions of supernatural visitors trouble the night; a spectral figure
steals the brandy jug. Tubal expresses what share he has of the master's
power by bedding the cook; Sara, one of the housemaids, given a magic
potion by Tubal makes love in the laundry room (where Antonsson's
corpse will later hang) with Simson, the Vogler coachman. Granny
shuffles to and fro, murmuring incantations, chalking a sign of exorcism
on the courtyard wall, and placating the younger of the two maids,
Sanna, who is confused by the whole menagerie, with a lullaby and
prophetic mutterings. Some of the nocturnal disquietude is "explained"
by the surreptitious return of Spegel who had vanished upon the troupe's
arrival in Stockholm. We are so occupied with Bergman flourishing a
handkerchief in his right hand that we forget to observe what he's doing
with his left. Spegel insists to Vogler that he is not yet dead but decomposing whereupon, soaked in brandy which he stole from the Egerman

kitchen, he falls lifeless to the floor. Vogler promptly puts his body into a casket among his stage properties.

The next morning, by invitation, Vogler, by now brought to a pitch of inchoate rage by the demands made on him and by the insensate hypocrisy of his hosts, a rage he dares not publicly express for he is supposed to be speechless, gives his performance. His first trick fails to convince, and to avenge himself he maliciously induces Mrs. Starbeck to disclose in ribald detail the undignified nature of her life with the Chief of Police. He then picks the Egermans' coachman, Antonsson, to be the victim of his mesmeric specialty, holding the man powerless in an imaginary vice. Antonsson, furious at this humiliating reduction to physical helplessness, flings himself on Vogler and presumably strangles him to death. After which, as we discover later, he hangs himelf.

This is the climax of the film. Vergerus takes Vogler's body to the attic, dissects it, decides that there is nothing unusual about the anatomy of this necromancer, and proceeds to write out his report. Suddenly the world turns eerie; a living hand is placed on that of Vergerus, a stopped clock begins to strike, blots appear on the writing paper, a mirror shows unbelievably the face of the freshly carved magician! For Vergerus, a nightmare follows; he is pursued out of the attic by the resurrected Vogler. Of course, the body anatomized by Vergerus is that of Spegel, which Vogler had substituted during the confusion attending his own "death"—a detail which disciples of Vergerus will simply have to accept as theatrical license. A final confusion ends the film. The troupe breaks up. Tubal and Sofia have found each other, i.e., she has commandeered a good provider, and Granny has decided to abandon the twilight career of a spellbinder; she has been hoarding money, she claims, with which to open an apothecary shop. Vogler experiences his final humiliation, begging Vergerus for money with which to leave town; unmasked, vocal, and in need his magnetism vanishes. "I liked *his* face better than yours," Vergerus, with recovered poise, tells him. Egerman is disdainful; even his wife, the hungering Ottilia, tells Vogler: "*I have never seen you before.*" Then, the denouement. Starbeck appears, thoroughly distraught but, in his official person, relieved, for he announces with awe that Vogler has been summoned by the King to give his performance at the palace. Under a beneficent shower of rain, Vogler is rushed off in a coach accompanied by his wife and by Simson with his new bed-warmer, Sara.

I should think that going no further than this synopsis, which I trust will revive the memories of those who saw the film, one would immediately sense the further reaches that lie beyond the bizarre turns of the plot. Previous familiarity with Bergman's films should readily evoke parallel lines of direction and similar conjunctions of profile. The casting, itself, is of assistance here. For to recall that Max von Sydow (Vogler), Gunnar Björnstrand (the skeptical Vergerus), and Bengt Ekerot (Spegel) played, respectively, the Knight, the Squire Jöns, and Death in *The Seventh Seal* is already to be in possession of a clue, if these relationships in *The Magician* are not self-explanatory; of a clue, not of a photo-copy. The Knight, infirm believer, was bereft by the want of visible assurance, but he had not made himself responsible for the salvation of others. Vogler is clearly tempted to believe, especially under the stress of confidence placed in him by foolish minds, that his powers may come from an external source, whether diabolic or divine he hasn't the courage to explore; up to now he has only toyed downward, so to speak. Vergerus, unlike Jöns, stakes his life on the positive content of rational demonstra-tion. The Squire was a genial stoic; for him, "Emptiness under the moon, my Lord," yet he was not dehumanized by the insight; one can-not imagine his being more tolerant of a Vergerus than he was of the defrocked priest, Raval, or the witch-burning monk. Vergerus expects a sign, a confirmation that "miracles don't happen," that there are no indefinable forces; his faith, like Vogler's, needs to be ratified.[69] He assures the Egermans, who are prepared to support the opposite view, that it would be fatal if scientists were suddenly led to accept "the inexplicable."

"Why would it be?" Egerman asks.
Vergerus tries to explain. "It would mean we should have to take into ac-count—we should be forced to—we should logically have to conceive a—"
"A God," supplies Egerman.
"Yes, a God, if you wish."
And Starbeck concludes for him: "A grotesque thought. Besides, it's not modern."

As to Spegel (the name, of course, like Spiegel in German, means mirror), he has nothing of the aloof dignity of Death, a figure from a masque, in *The Seventh Seal*; he has undergone a radical treatment from Naturalism. But, indeed, he is not the thing itself, he is Death's creature; he is more closely comparable to Frost, vis-à-vis Albert, in *The Naked Night,* a forecast of what another might become—and Volger is fully aware of that possibility. Spegel confronts him in the forest with the unsparing question, "Are you a charlatan who must hide his real face?" He supplies a terrifying thematic undertone with his weird appearances and disappearances. Has he indeed passed over, one reflects with a shudder, returning as a ghost palpable enough to perish again under the knife of Vergerus? His proclamation to Vogler that he is already decomposing introduces the most disturbing text of the film. *"Step by step we go into the dark. Motion itself is the only truth."* Without this consent to an underlying incertitude, without his unnerving remark before 'dying', "When I thought I was dead I was tormented by horrible dreams," *The Magician* might be thought a harmless, comedic exercise in the perennial Bergman duel of belief and unbelief. During the verbal sparring with Manda over the authenticity of her husband's act, Vergerus has occasion to ask, "Is that true?" and she quickly replies: "Nothing is true". Whatever alternative answers Bergman hopes to imply through one character or another, this, it seems to me, is the key and the burden of the whole film.

I should not argue against the opinion, held by those who are disposed only to see Vogler as himself, that his agitation is forced into a dimension too great for its vehicle, i.e, for the "real" level where a mountebank is on trial before obtuse judges. No question but that this intensity gets close to the creator of the film. Vogler is named Albert Emanuel. Albert is also the name of the circus proprietor in *The Naked Night,* Emanuel the first name of Borg in *Wild Strawberries.* The problem, which to my feeling increases the refractions of the character like planes on a mirror, is that Vogler is simultaneously a faithhealer in 1846 who would like to be genuine and he is the artist—modern, certainly—provoked by the gullibility of his audience into despising it and, alternatively, doubting and probing his own authenticity. Conscious of how much art and how much luck or meticulous timing goes into his act which so impresses otherwise unimpressible mortals, Vogler is intimidated by those who are irreversably skeptical of his art like Vergerus, those who would like to believe in it for reasons that have nothing to do with art like the Egerman's, those who are merely hypnotized by it like Antonsson, those who exploit it without an inkling of its intrinsic value like Tubal or Starbeck, those who blindly hate it, together with its maker, like Rustan.

The mystery of that touch which produces an effect out of all anticipated proportion to the cause must be a common experience among creative artists in every genre. You stage a farce of which you're so tired after three weeks of rehearsal you can't imagine how anyone might believe it to be funny; yet on opening night and for 136 performances thereafter the audience will have paroxysms of laughter at a sequence of interlocking tricks you feel ashamed to have organized. You introduce a French horn at the unerringly right moment and for two and a half seconds only; 875 inattentive listeners, with a rush of blood to their hearts, become a concerted moan of attention. You bend one outline more acutely, thicken a shadow, or deepen a patch of umber and respectably competent form is preternaturally alive. You accompany a piece of dialogue with a gesture timed to illustrate the point before you have verbalized it and you are credited with "a great reading"! Call it the magic of art, call it quick thinking; it is the *ding an sich*: intuitive skill, the power of make-believe. Bergman, haunted by this paradox, takes it with an impenitently bad conscience.

> When I show a film I am guilty of deceit. I use an apparatus which is constructed to take advantage of a certain human weakness, an apparatus with which I can sway my audience in a highly emotional manner—make them laugh, scream with fright, smile, believe in fairy stories. . . . Thus I am either an impostor or, when the audience is willing to be taken in, a conjuror. . . .[70]

Kierkegaard said of Martin Luther that he always spoke as if lightning were about to strike behind him! More contingently, however, Bergman's words suggest a paraphrase of Luigi Pirandello on the same subject, an example to which I prefer to advert when we reach the film, *Persona*, since there the whole question of apparatus, by which Bergman claims to be embarrassed, is involved to the hilt. In this context I'll just say that Bergman is begging the question; dourly and impossibly he seeks to refute the irrefutable. However, his instinct is often more sophisticated than his misgivings. In *The Magician,* which is about imposture, once you have accepted the ambivalent character of Vogler, you will see that the tone is right, the tenebrous atmosphere in which Bergman conjures and mocks his own conjuring has an awful symmetry.

Within this penumbra, the Bergman ensemble, whether or not it has played the same roles before, is totally interrelated and the performers display a marvelous reciprocity. Max von Sydow, as Vogler, has never been better in film. There is about him sometimes for my taste a touch too much of the unblastable pine tree; in this film he bends to the wind; he is properly tortured, he gnaws on his knuckles, he twists his handkerchief, he has the style of his role—I should say the styles of his role, for the poor man is many—beside the inner compulsions. His readings are of the essence. One of the most electrical moments in the film is his first articulation. Shortly before this moment, we have heard a servant of the Egermans saying viciously, "There's something about magicians—their faces make you mad . . . You want to smash them, tread on them! Faces like Vogler's . . .''. Then we are in the Voglers' bedroom. He is lying sleepless, his back to his wife. He stirs, tries to make himself more comfortable, and he speaks, he who has never spoken before in our sight. He puts no undue pressure on the words. "I hate them. I hate their faces— (pause)—their bodies, their movements, their voices.'' Another pause, and a sigh. "But I'm afraid, too. . . .''

Equally resourceful at playing a part which, with an infinite number of modulations he had so often played, was Gunnar Björnstrand; and all the other supporters, Toivo Pawlo, Naima Wifstrand, Gertrud Fridh, Erland Josephson, are completely tucked into the things they are. But sometimes you pause to ask, *"Who are they?"* Granny, for instance, seemingly a stock figure of senile clairvoyance, babbling such stuff as madmen tongue and brain not: "Wound in the eye, blood in the mouth, fingers gone and neck broken, he calls you down, he calls you forth, beyond the dead, the living and the living dead . . .''. She has the gift of foresight, she has an odor of the charnelhouse, she is vatic, and she is in the business. She is, within the scheme of *The Magician,* I would say, decaying religion as Spegel is decaying art. When religion decomposes it becomes mysticism and is often taken for profundity because it does, sometimes, arise from the depths; in such a state, the subject may well feel that he is an ark of revelation. "Mysticism is the most primitive of feelings and only visits formed minds in moments of intellectual arrest and dissolution."[71] Granny is thus a mixture of diabolic superstition, fakery and memories of Christian love, with which she sings the frightened Sanni to sleep:

"Love is trust and love is rest,
Love gives strength to the cowardly breast. . . ."

All the same, she has an eye to the self-preserving future, what for her remains; she is advancing into the age of science for she will become an apothecary. In her Vergerus will triumph. Tubal sums up her status shrewdly when he says that her tricks are old hat. "They're not fun any more; they can't be explained. Granny, you should be dead".

Tubal himself (Åke Fridell, with every mannerism in place) is the eternal sacristan who lights the candles and knows nothing of the mystery that is reenacted at the altar; the press agent who guards the personality of the artist; the film distributor who stands knowingly at the screening-room door and tells the more receptive exhibitor that "Of course you know this movie is really about the Loneliness of Modern Man"; the film-maker who infallibly misconstrues the example of the master by translating his visions of outrage or depravity, for example, those of *The Virgin Spring* and *The Silence*, into salaciousness for its own sake. Tubal explains everything to the others but he is as little astute about his own genitalic "power" over the widow, as the others are when faced by the magician. To steal a line from another movie, he is impotent everywhere but in bed.[72]

One returns to Spegel because he is, despite the scarcity of his appearances, as central to the mood as Vogler, himself, and for this Bengt Ekerot is in no incidental way responsible; he is almost unbearably outstanding; he is in such a convincing state of disintegration that you fear for his, Ekerot's, life before the film is well under way; you swear he will break up before your eyes and that someone else will have to play the part in the later stage of the story. To be sure, Ekerot is one of the most steadfast character actors in Swedish film, so infernally subdued to the role he plays that you forget how many times you've seen him and how unalterably alterable he is.

Concerning analogies with and sources of *The Magician* the fluffier moments, when the company backstairs recapitulates the sexual man-oeuvres of those above-stairs, reminded many critics of Renoir's *Rules of the Game,* an observation made also when Bergman produced *Smiles of a Summer Night.* Since, on the first occasion, he had not seen the Renoir film, I would assume that in *The Magician* he was very likely imitating himself, recognizably with those toothsome housemaids he invents. Among more distant references, Fellini's *Il Bidone* was called upon, with its squad of cheats, its theocentric morality, and the undisclosed ethical intent of the swindler played by Broderick Crawford. The mesmerizing of Antons-son and his "murder" of Vogler recalled to some the explosive killing of the hypnotist-dictator in Thomas Mann's *Mario and the Magician;* Mann is authoritatively the progenitor of a Bergman subsubject, the Janus-face of the artist. However, these are random, if interesting, attempts to locate influences of which I am personally skeptical. Closer to the predicament of Vogler is that of Pirandello's Henry IV in the play of that title, *Enrico Quarto,* forced to continue playing a role he had once assumed arbitrarily. Bergman himself told Sjöman, quoted in *L 136,* that the connection between his theatre production and his films was a close one and that, for example, intimations of Pirandello in *The Magician* should not be overlooked. On this occasion he did not, however, divulge the unarguable origin of the film; I don't know on which occasion he did so.

The direct source of the situation, the main-character scheme, is ob-viously Gilbert K. Chesterton's *Magic,* 1913, his only play, I believe, which Bergman had staged in Gothenburg, 1947.[73] Chesterton's setting is the house of an affable, none-too-bright Duke, where the conjuror, hired to entertain the guests, finds himself pitted against characters who repre-sent attitudes consistent with their professions: a liberal clergyman, a mundane young businessman, an agnostic. The conjurer's face is des-cribed as mask-like and he has, it follows, the disconcerting habit of mak-ing others feel unmasked. Patricia, the Duke's niece, nonetheless falls in love with him, though he tries to dissuade her from thoughts of marriage by telling her what a rough life his mother had undergone after marrying a wandering peddler. A believer in the supernatural, the Conjurer cannot explain his more lurid feats of magic. When he turns a red lamp green, the company is flabbergasted; Patricia's skeptical brother has a brainstorm.

The conjurer, who is nothing if not gallant, assures Morris that there is a natural explanation, which he proceeds to contrive, but in fact he had called on devils! It begins to sound like an early-Bergman play, but my summary tells nothing of the tone, which is that of Oscar Wilde (nobody ever says anything not intended as an epigram) mated with J.B. Priestley. "It is much more marvellous to explain a miracle than to work a miracle," says the Reverend Smith, if I recall. This is a fair sample of the whimsy comprised by the play. It is romantic, too; the Conjurer wins his aristocratic bride.

You can see at a glance what Bergman was able to appropriate from this play: the general bearing of the dialectic and a few diagrammatic stand-ins for worldly reason, science, and religion. He took a cue from Chesterton, an epidermis, if we need an image to suit his eventual subject; he had to supply the vital organs, himself. Chesterton's play is all skin. Typically, his characters speak of heaven and hell without ever, you feel, having glimpsed either. He scarcely distinguishes magic, a technique, from faith, a form of comprehension, and his mouthpiece, the liberal clergyman, is far too genial for Bergman's more sanguinary purpose. "You talk of religious mania!", he chides the Doctor. "Is there no such thing as irreligious mania? . . . Why can't you leave the universe alone and let it mean what it likes?" There are times when such a question might cogently be put to Bergman, himself; if he took it to heart, however, we might not have his best movies. We should certainly not have *The Magician*. He took Chesterton's do-it-yourself paradoxes and brooded on their implications until the borrowed characters, while remaining consistent with their original labels, were warped unendurably by the pressures to which they submit each other.

Like *The Naked Night*, to which it is indebted quite as much as to any extrinsic work, and for more than its circus, *The Magician* is an acrid hyperbole: a *comedie rosse*.[74] In the former, Bergman had first, with any power, split his protagonist into the two aspects of Frost and Albert; in the latter film, the fission is even more drastic and complex. Vogler sees not only the mirror-face of Spegel who begs, in his half-delirium, half-reminiscence, for a knife to remove his brain and heart, to cut away his tongue and his manhood; he sees also the face of Vergerus, that other colder self, ready to oblige. At the same time he is supplied with a feminine component, Manda—not very carnal, to be sure. In public he has already surendered his powers of speech; now he delivers his body, i.e. Spegel, to the inquisitive surgery of Vergerus, in order to retain more surely what is incorruptible. The self-mutilation of the artist has seldom been pictured with such audacity and in such a spirit, that of a desperate carnival. The progressive self-division of Bergman, dating theatrically from those early primers, like *Jack Among the Actors,* here reaches a kind of climax.

When you consider the wealth of sources, his own and that of others, from which *The Magician* was shaped, the marvel remains that the film is autonomous, a period fantasia which can be enjoyed, if that isn't twisting a euphemism, for its own sake, without concerning oneself with the subterranean occupants.[75] A world of sharp shadows, I would call it, and the shadows are thrown from the beginning. With frugality of means, the brief monitory sequence in the forest—at first, silence, wind-grieved faces, spaced chords from a guitar, a bird of ill omen, a fox—casts such a spell it is hard to realize that the rest of the film takes place inside one house. The remote forest, by the way, was a clump of trees not five hundred yards from the Svensk Filmindustri lunchroom in suburban Stockholm. And the scherzo that ends the film, the coach disappearing up a ramp and a lantern swinging in the final sunlit silence, was shot outside an official building near the palace where, if Bergman had swiveled his camera forty-five degrees, he would have disclosed a view of contemporary Stockholm. This is part of what Fellini meant when, some years ago, long before meeting Bergman, he remarked to our point: "He is a con-jurer—half witch and half showman. I also like his tricks, the spectacle made from nothing. . . ."[76] True, if *The Magician* is about the muffled voices of the dead and the maddening voices of those living, it is just as much about theatre, even as it calls theatre into question.

The joke on the actor is no longer a quip as it was in *Smiles of a Summer Night,* when Mrs. Armfeldt asks, "Who's coming to the party? If they're actors they must sleep in the stables," or again in *Wild Straw-berries,* spoken by the same actress (Naima Wifstrand): "I think this is Benjamin's locomotive; he was always so amused by trains and circuses and such things. I suppose that's why he became an actor. We quarreled about it often because I wanted him to have an honest profession. . . ." The joke on Vogler remains a bitter one. Vergerus is temporarily shattered.

Starbeck is stunned. The artist triumphs. Yet, but for the grace of—
whom?—he would have been an outcast; he would have been Spegel under
a bridge, aging in brandy. The man who rides off in a coach to give
a royal performance is the same who begged for a safe-conduct and
groveled on the staircase for survival money. Tomorrow he may be a
Messiah. Mrs. Egerman said, confidently: "You will explain why my child
died. What God meant". One remembers the wealthy and licentious
women of fifteenth-century Florence, spellbound by the personality, no
doubt erotic, of Savonarola, making bonfires of their velvets and tossing
their jewels into the Arno. Little in history changes except the icons:
the priest, the political demagogue, the social engineer, the film director.

To wit, an anecdote told me by a Swedish business executive. On one
of his trips to India, he was accosted by a Bengelese woman, associated in
some way with an emancipation movement, who exclaimed,

"You're from Sweden! I'd love to go to Sweden—for just one purpose!"

"And what would that be?" he asked.

Tense with excitement, she answered. "I would just like to shake Ingmar
Bergman's hand! *He understands our problem!*"

The Virgin Spring

"Motion is the only truth," said *The Magician*. *The Virgin Spring** tells
another truth. After making what for the sake of a ready image we might
call his Hamlet-work, Bergman made a film that concludes with Christian
faith. The inference should not too quickly be seized upon. We have seen
that for years Bergman was subject to a besetting dualism, which was
largely a histrionic convenience; his skepticism, either about morality or
the religious ethos, had never been wholehearted, even if his will to believe
had never been secure. His dialectical compulsion strongly resembles that
of the convert, in which disbelief is pushed to the brink in order to make
the recoil more thrilling. Consider Graham Greene; like Bergman's, the

---

* *Jungfrukällan; Die Jungfrauenquelle; La Fontana della Vergine; La Source;*
El Manantial; La Fuente de la doncella: The Virgin Spring. In almost every language
but ours, the title of this film is euphonious.

provenance of his religious awe was compounded from fear of the dark, revulsion from physical bondage, and an excessive consciousness of sin. Even so, the vehicle with which Bergman expressed a positive return to the foundations of Christian sentiment is an accomplishment of vital sincerity and of supreme cinematic art. If I remark that up to 1959 *The Magician* was Bergman's most intensively personal film, I avoid the charge of redundancy. Few of his films could be described as other than personal but my point is, I think, clear. *The Magician,* while it does not obligate us to identify in it Bergman the man, does speak, if in thaumaturgic accents, with a crucially subjective appeal. In clear contrast, *The Virgin Spring* is Bergman's least personal work. I do not mean that it would never be identifiable as a Bergman film if all the credits were lost. Palpably and totally it is Bergman's. But it is not visibly about Bergman and I think that can be said of no other film he has made except *A Summer with Monika.*

Let me put it that *The Virgin Spring* is the most selfless of his films. From a special view it is his most intimately and deeply felt; after brooding on the project for two years Bergman, certain of what he was after, was yet so subjectively involved that in order to keep his distance he handed the idea to Ulla Isaksson to prepare as a film. While we may be sure that he controlled the conception, this in no way depreciates the eloquent austerity of Miss Isaksson's share in the creation. An inspection of her manuscript is edifying. In a film script the dialogue is typed on one vertical half of the page, the running narrative on the other. In the Isaksson continuity you can read for pages at a time without looking at the lefthand column; in the other is description, dense, concrete and sensuous, the spirit of the old ballad which is the source of the film captured and retold with the art, common to novelist and filmmaker, of moving through time and space as an eye. I may say that Bergman had previously fought, with considerable frustration, for the privilege of handing in just such a scenario. When he had appeared at Svensk Filmindustri with his manuscript of *The Naked Night,* one third the conventional length, they protested, ''What! That a script? Where's the dialogue?''.

As I said, the most selfless film. Much for this reason, I would choose it as his masterwork, had I to name a superlative: the most lyrical, the most compassionate, the most lucidly constructed, metre by metre, and the film that most surely enters the heart and mind of the race, a film that should stir depths, I think I'm safe in saying, in anyone of North European ancestry who has not overlaid his feeling with a crust of disbelief. I do not speak here of belief in miracles or in the Christian response, albeit a concession to such belief is integral to complete sympathy with the film. I mean the credence we give to the characteristic myth shaped by our ancestors from an idea by which they were overwhelmed and from the elemental conditions of their lives, conditions which reverberate in our memory when we are shaken by the basic forms of essential emotions. One of the important things with which art is concerned is just the expression of the down-under permanent feelings present, if not accounted for, in all men, and in such a way that any other experience seems transitory, idle, and of no engraving importance. Art of this kind leaves a scar. There have been a few crystalline examples in the history of film: *The Passion of Joan of Arc, La Strada, Rashomon.* How many others? *Ugetsu? The Bandits of Orgosolo? Viridiana?* Perhaps not quite. I hesitate to place beside these any others for the qualities I have in mind, the classic qualities of direct appeal and delayed effect, proper distance, concentration of means, and an ambience of poetry that remains inviolable beyond all analysis to which it is submitted. Such films make their most profound impression some time after one has seen them, when the mind engages with a sudden flash of cognition what the emotions have been coping with; the real, evaded subject rises from the deep, like the body of a drowned man which floats to the surface after three days.

The source of this movie is the thirteenth-century folk ballad, *Tores dotter i Vänge,* thirty-two couplets, with quatrains fore and aft. Scarcely deviating from the matter of the ballad, the film continuity can be outlined in less time than it takes to read the poem. Young Karin, Herr Tore's daughter, is sent to church by her parents on a saint's day, accompanied by the girl of the house, Ingeri, who hates her because she's virgin; Ingeri is pregnant. Ingeri has put a live toad into the bread she has baked for Karin's noon repast. Ingeri goes as far as the bridge, over a stream, guarded by an old man who still worships the ancient gods, Thor and Odin. Karin continues her journey until intercepted by three herdsmen, i.e., two men and a boy. They are grotesques; the one man is tongueless, he can only slaver sounds, the other is gaunt and poll-shaven, the boy is gat-toothed. Karin agrees to rest and break bread with them; while they eat, she prattles in a flirtatious manner of her life in a great palace. The composition of this scene, with the two leering horrors flanking the vivacious girl, is like one of those richly painted, ghastly visions of Flemish art.

When the toad jumps out of the loaf, the original lecherous intentions of the unholy churls are fanned into superstitious anger, as if they had been affronted by Beelzebub, himself. Their rage enforces their lust; they rape the girl and, in an access afterward of fear and panic, they kill her by felling her with a club-like branch. Later that night they arrive, all unknowing, at the Tores' *gård*, where the mother, Fru Mareta, is already gravely alarmed by Karin's failure to return by nightfall. They eat with the family and bed down overnight. The Thin One offers Fru Mareta Kartin's shawl as payment for their lodging. With sinking heart, the woman conceals her recognition until she has locked the three into their stuga; then she confides her suspicion to her husband who, after a grimly prepared cleansing ritual, enters the stuga where the two men and the boy sleep and slaughters them, dashing the boy against the wall. With Ingeri, who has been guiltily skulking in the darkness, and his wife, Tore goes to recover the body of the girl. When they raise her from the ground, a spring of water gushes from the earth beneath her head. Tore kneels to God to ask why these evils—*"Varför, Varför?"*—but promises to build a church with his own hands—*"med dessa mina händer"*!—to atone for his perpetuation of evil by an act of triple murder.

I may as well say now, and get it said, since I think the film is otherwise perfect, that I cannot understand how Bergman could have brought himself to employ those angel voices at the end. The celestial choir is a *bête noire* of mine in the cinema and at this moment it was a nearly fatal artistic error. Perhaps he was following the admonition that the gods hate perfection.

Any critic who pretends that his initial reception of a work of art is not principally subjective is deceiving himself. This is the center around which most critical dispute unnecessarily revolves. If you do not feel the power and truth of a film such as this one, no argument can persuade you. One might argue about *Breathless* or *Accident* or *Last Year in Marienbad* (and I don't want to be there); you can't argue about *La*

Strada or *Bicycle Thieves.* I may be able in some measure to clarify what I believe to be the formal perfection of *The Virgin Spring.* I cannot impose, by intellectual urgency, an emotion you cannot share. There are some experiences at the border of which many of us halt. In these cases we try to be tolerant of each other's predispositions.

For me it was gratifying to see that in Sweden the entire critical fraternity was taken unawares by *The Virgin Spring* before it could muster a defensive spectator-anxiety or organize a secular resistance to the spring that never was. The reporters were swept off their feet by the telling power of a native feeling, the unarguably elemental images and an incontestable smell of countryside, seven hundred years distant. Only later among Bohemians, logically I suppose, did I encounter any of that begrudging attitude that infallibly follows a fear of self-exposure, a fear that they might have to grant that here was a root expression of Swedish art, that in art, as Zoltan Kodaly has said, you must be national before you can hope to be international. The German magazine, *Der Spiegel,* devoted no less than ten pages to Bergman on this occasion. It was in fact only or chiefly in Britain and America that puritanism, inverted, was cool or smart and shallow toward this film, or even shocked. In London a few lady critics were quite disseated by the blank terror of the rape and scuttled to assure their readers that Bergman was being naughty and prurient—as if he had designed a film from a medieval ballad about murder, vengeance, and redemption for the sole purpose of introducing to the screen a genuine rape. The irony was not slow to appear, for these same ladies have had since to swallow an abundance of filth, then unimaginable, and claim to find it nutritious in order to save their liberal faces.

The Seventh Seal is by comparison a charade. For all its talk of plague, desolation, and the fumes of burning flesh it does not draw blood. If at one moment you watch an actor, dressed as Death, sawing down a tree of life in which Skat is squealing, ''Are there no special rules for actors?'', you can't bring yourself soon after to be mortally frightened when Raval naturalistically dies of thirst. *The Seventh Seal* has its own subtle gravity and charm but *The Virgin Spring*, while utterly beautiful in its pastoral spaces, cannot be called charming. The actuality before the miracle is an immediate sensation of primal existence, of a world in which you can nose the woodsmoke and the sourness of clothes and the nearness of stinking goats as you eat, and feel the roughness of the table under your hand and the high-country chill which only mead and raw meat, when you can slaughter it, can ward off. Time rolls back. Out of thirteenth-century Sweden come the atavistic fears and beckonings we normally live without, which we have hoarded in our under-consciousness; I wouldn't want to say, with Jung, the racial unconscious, since this might simply be a cry from the nights of our childhood and the repository in which we keep with mingled pleasure and dread our memories of the Pied Piper of Hamelin, Rumplestilzkin, and The Pardoner's Tale.

In the fairy tale, everything that happens seems to have happened before; the form always has a moral purpose which obeys a familiar rhythm or is subsumed by the cycle of seasons, the hours of the day, a significant number, colors, and the hue of weather. The north is always fearful, the forest lures and threatens, flowing water tends to suggest hope, though it might harbor goblins; nothing in nature is neutral, everything is a promise or an omen. If you are not prepared to surrender with your nerve ends to the thematic simplicity of this assumption (think of the simplicities you *normally* assume at the movies!), you will not appreciate *Jungfrukällan*. It is not a fairy tale although it has the suspense and the setting of one, for there is nothing in it incredible to the educated mind until at the close nature obeys faith and imitates art. The only preparation necessary for this film is to put the academic part of your mind to sleep and to call on the faculty with which you read poetry, so that you sense rather than observe the numerical motifs, the antitheses, and the omnipresence of the four elements. The film begins with fire, Ingeri stoking the oven with a bellows, ends with water and earth; smoke is invoked by the clairvoyant beggar as an image for Karin, smoke idles into the outer air as Tore waits for the murderers to awake with the cockcrow. Pagan and Christian doctrines, opposed, are signified by the opening speeches. As Ingeri prepares the toad-filled bread which she hopes will bring misfortune to Karin, she calls on Odin, and the next speech, given by Tore, who is more "Christian" than his wife—she persists in the older custom of self-infliction as they pray before the crucifix—begins, "*Gud Fader, Son och den Helge*" ("God the Father, the Son and the Saints''). At a later point in the film, the repetition of the Christian grace, first spoken by Karin, "*O välsignade Jesus,*" is recognized by the boy when the herdsmen eat with the Tore household. This is one of the taut, brilliant moments in the film, brought off so swiftly many people fail to note it. The boy vomits on to the table and the Dumb One scoops up the vomit deftly with his bare hand while casting a look of apprehension and apology at his host.

Three is the fatal number, repudiating the Holy Trinity. When Karin awakes on the morning of her departure, she bubbles about a dream in which she had danced with—she holds up her fingers to illustrate—*one, two, three!* The old man at the ford tells Ingeri that if she wants what he wants she can hear voices in the water, three dead men riding north. And Tore, as he reverts to the law of an eye for an eye, cuts just three branches, from the birch tree with which he wrestles, for his purgative ceremony before murdering his guests. But the master image is the embrace, appearing throughout the film as a varied refrain. Karin is embraced by her father, too fondly for the taste of the mother; Ingeri embraces her falsely; the murderous embrace of the rape is foretold by the old man at the stream, trying to climb Ingeri; when we first see the *skurkar* (the Swedish word contains action and quality) in the deep woods the Dumb goatherd is sitting on a ewe to quiet it. Tore embraces the tree in that magnificent pre-dawn shot, as he soon embraces the Thin One while butchering him with his head in the fire. The prophetic beggar embraces the frightened boy, briefly, and spins him a cryptic little fantasy about the damned and salvation. Finally, Tore and his wife lift Karin from the ground to form a triple embrace. Everything in the film seems to move fluidly toward a single image that will crown and comprise all the others, like a sestina, that wondrous poetic form wherein the identities are teasingly in disunion until the envoi consummately enfolds them.

It has been told that William Blake, looking at a sketch shown him by Constable, declared, "Why, this is not drawing, it is poetry!" To which Constable rejoined drily, "I intended it for drawing." Tempted to exclaim that this is not filmmaking, it is magic, we do well to observe that it is the art of film narrative: consecutive images rhythmically related, luminous, perfectly edited, and, in the two murder sequences, a restraint of all but essential movement which is as masterful in this style as anything the cinema has to offer. The deliberation with which the ritual killing is rehearsed and with a violent paroxysm achieved is a peerless exhibition of flawless montage. When Tore enters the stuga, pauses to inspect the sleeping mens' gear, seats himself, plunges his knife into the tabletop as the cock crows and the smoke escapes into the dawn, all in that room which will escape, the whole passage of suspense is executed from a single witness point without cuts, the camera only panning slightly as Tore moves from the bed to the table.

Nonetheless, there is magic here, the magic of conception. Karin struggling to escape from the rapists and coming to rest for a moment in the boughs of a fallen tree, as if skewered there by a butcher bird; this has little or nothing to do with analyzable shot sequences. Another transcendentally successful achievement in this film is never noted in the journals and I confess that it was not until I saw the film for the third time that I concentrated on what before I had suspected but failed to verify. The boy —so conspicuous in the rape scene as he cavorts over Karin's body, if you saw the uncut print, sickens at the supper table, quails in the arms of the beggar, and rushes to the arms of Fru Mareta before he is seized and hurled to the wall to break like an egg—*never speaks,* not a syllable in the whole film.

This same boy is the occasion, further, of the strangest touch in the film before the miracle, of an image which is for me one of the most mysterious, entrancing, sorrowful images in all film art: like the moment, perhaps, in Dreyer's *Passion of Joan of Arc* when, after her suffocating sessions in the court and the torture chamber, Joan is taken into the daylight and the outdoors to be burned and her eye focuses first on a detail, focuses desperately and tenaciously on a bird, perhaps a dove, that flies from the prison roof to the church and back, helplessly free in its element; or in *La Strada* when Gelsomina, sitting on the curb at dawn waiting for her worthless Zampano, looks up to see incredibly a white horse plodding down the street, just an inexplicable white horse with no rider, an enigmatic intruder, absurd to the point of havoc, lumbering into the sad scheme of things; or the end of *The 400 Blows,* that other boy brought and held in arrested closeup, outfacing us with a Da Vinci smile as he dips his toe into the waters of the world, so that with absolutely upsetting conviction we feel that we have become the screen and the image is waiting for us to resume, to do something decisive (unfortunately, the image that touched with insanity the moviemakers of every continent) ; or the final shot of *L'Avventura,* the woman touching the shoulder of the shamed and weeping man, in the background the beautiful crumbling façade of a past glory he will never, never recover.

So in *The Virgin Spring* the murderers leave the boy seated by the dead body of the ravished Karin in the woods of the cruel afternoon; all nature stirs and in him produces a great shivering unrest which he tries to dispel by covering the girl's body with a little dirt. And at this minute of his growing panic, his unbearable vigil with the freshly dead, it *snows* : only for a second, a split second; a few flakes of benediction. An utterly fantastic inspiration! Needless to say, I trust, that I never had the heart to ask Bergman, or anyone, if he had planned this, knowing that northern weather in the spring might cooperate with his hope and squeeze out the necessary effect, or if it was one of those benign accidents which played to his advantage. There are some curiosities we should never work to satisfy.

I had never before been so certain, as when following the creative struggle of Ingmar Bergman, that the artist is in many ways the least free member of the human community and that the contemporary envy of the artist is one of the more groundless illusions that besieges mankind. Let the artist's work be admired; he, himself, should not be envied. For he rarely creates from a fund of illimitable options. His subject chooses *him.* This is only more evident in Bergman's case because he has made the problem the object of his discourse and his aired anxiety. I suspect that in most artists you will find this sacred dependency on monomania. Bergman cannot release himself from a compulsion either by willing to do so or by taking a deep breath; he has never rid himself of a nuclear irritant until he has exhausted the possible variations he can find for expressing it.

After *The Murder at Bajärna* the fantasy murder was banished, though in his latest films there are suggestive instances of latent belligerence. After *The Virgin Spring,* another worry disappears from his work; for five years, at least: the seemingly haphazard way in which birth takes place; women who don't want children bear them, those who want them are in one way or another deprived of them. The subject is basic to the play of malignant motive in *The Virgin Spring,* for it is Ingeri's unwelcome pregnancy that initiates the curse laid on Karin. When M. Siclier isolated the phenomenon of birth and abortion in the Bergman film, he put his finger, without doubt, on a unique obsession. In no other filmmaker is there such incessant emphasis on the subject. In all modern art and literature, I can think of only three other artists so involved with the image and the fact of fecundity, for presumably quite separable reasons. They are Henry Moore, Sigrid Undset, and Garcia Lorca in his plays. As usual, when discussing Bergman, the private concern should be related to the public ethos. The nation proposes, the artist disposes? Rational Sweden pioneers state-controlled abortion. Their most prominent spokesman in the arts repudiates the denial of life by reason. Is he exposing his country's bad conscience or expressing it? A subtle ambiguity exists.

Another text from *The Revelation* is germane here. "One woe is past; and behold, there come two woes more hereafter" (9.12). Faintly projected in *The Seventh Seal,* stronger in *Wild Strawberries,* explored and personified, at least in the nether reaches, in *The Magician,* the guilty status of the artist, which had always lurked in Bergman's vicinity, will now assume priority. The climactic vision of *The Virgin Spring* did nothing to dissipate the anxiety of this position, quite the contrary. It seemed to me in 1959 that with *Jungfrukällan* Bergman had put something to rest and at the same time opened out a richer world than any he had heretofore discovered. This is how it was, he said in the film, this is how it might have been, this lie more vivid than truth, this belief with such mingled consequences of good and evil. This is the answer to the Knight, the solace for Isak Borg if he needs such solace, and the refutation of Vergerus. Here was one answer to be found in the Magic Forest, that the destruction of innocence breeds an avenger who in turn perpetuates armed hostility. With the Christian dispensation, Man drops to his knees but he does not sheathe his sword; he builds churches instead. He preaches a gospel of humility and forbearance even as he continues to perish in his pride. And this is a magnificent irony; the artist, himself, has performed the miracle, created "the substance of things hoped for."

And with that creation, for Bergman, all belief, at that level, was perhaps drained away.

If this was so, I thought then, Bergman is freer than he has ever been. He might be able to see, with Santayana, that religion is "that splendid error" and turn his attention to a world in which, without the God of his fathers, or indeed without any God, he could celebrate, unconfused, the mysterious majesty of its design, the prodigious number of explanations it has called forth and the creature satisfactions that ensue when you learn that besides demons in the wood there are hamadryads, that nature itself is well-being enough and that there are now no corners to your subject matter. He was back on Swedish earth where, as anywhere else, suffering is sweetened by poetry, where what is good is positively good, where legends abound and history is thick with riddles, great deeds, incessant folly, sour solutions, ironic terminations, and life is possible if you want it to be. This is what I believed had happened to him. Now he can go anywhere, I thought. Now he is untethered—a hawk riding an updraft.

I was radically mistaken. Faced with a world in which anything was possible because that single answer had been proven impossible, Bergman denied multitude, cancelled all voyages, trod underfoot the root and the leaf, blocked all but one narrow path which led him from the bird-throbbing heart of the forest to a pile of boulders on a dead seashore. With the period initiated by *Såsom i en Spegel* (*As in a Glass, Darkly*), he moves to an island, closes the doors and windows, and turns out all the lights. Then he screams because he is in the dark.

THE ISLAND

Ingmar Bergman did not move to an island to live until 1965. Fårö means "sheep island", and is actually an island beyond an island; its mainland is Gotland, an island in the Baltic. The metaphor is almost too good to be durable. As you might expect, the familiar ambivalence is involved. Looking at the films Bergman has made in the last decade, learning that he removed himself physically from *staden* and remembering the antisocial outbreaks he has indulged and the imprecations he has launched during this period, you might conclude that the phenomena are all of a piece. They are; yet at the same time a counter-strategy was being performed. The state of mind expressed in a man's art is not necessarily a response to an immediate something in a man's life. We saw this disparity of timing in the early Fifties, when Bergman's life and theatrical arts were fighting a civil war. Again, during the Sixties, while he is retreating from society residentially, and in his films from any central identification with human endeavour as most of us know it, Bergman is at the same time as much as ever committing himself to the whole calamity of the private and public obligations of his world.

"An island, if it is big enough, is no better than a continent. It has to be really quite small, before it feels like an island; and this story will show how tiny it has to be before you can presume to fill it with your own personality."

D. H. Lawrence
"The Man Who Loved Islands"

"Island! prison;
A prison is as gaysome: we'll no islands:
Marry, out upon 'em! whom shall we see there?
Sea gulls and porpoises and water-rats
And crabs and mewes and dogfish! goodly gear
For a young ladie's dealing, or an old one!
On no terms islands; I'll be stewed first."

John Ford
The Broken Heart (II, 1.)

In 1959 Bergman married Kabe Laretei, a concert pianist, which half accounts for the musical nomenclature he gives to his films thereafter, in 1965 he married Liv Ullman, the Norwegian actress (he has children from both these women); as of 1970, that marriage, too, has come to an end. In 1963 he was appointed Director of Dramaten in Stockholm, a post he resigned three years later, though he continued to produce plays there. For three years he voluntarily gave his Saturday mornings to directing plays for children. He has staged plays in Oslo, written and directed plays for television and the radio, produced and directed a sixteen-millimeter documentary film about the Government's displacement of families on Fårö, gone so far as at least to deceive himself that he might make a movie with another director in another country (in this case, Fellini, but never credit such reports), capriciously consented to long interviews at the most unlikely moments and most recently chatted for publication[78] about his private life on Fårö where, by his account, he has become as domestic as a bullfinch. Stand on the Right, move on the Left.

To receive Bergman's films made between 1960 and 1970 without reference to the contradictions and rationalizations of all his other activities is to interpret them in a vacuum. Let us agree that critical discipline is first and last occupied with the specific content of the film as offered; even so, the Bergman film comes from the psyche of a man more than ordinarily conditioned by personal conflict. Approaching his later films, contemporary criticism has widely and fairly consistently attributed to them an autonomous and eremitic character which, even without extrinsic clues, a touch of intuition or common sense might have corrected.

Bergman's habit of deprecating his major efforts is recognizable in the so-called comedy he made as a relief from the solemnities of *The Virgin Spring*; yet how much relief could have been earned by an exercise so devoid of genuine levity one wonders. If *The Devil's Eye*, 1960, had been directed by anyone else we should not find it worth the lingering, although it is not as positively negligible as *Not To Speak of All Those Women*, 1964. The tragedy of a virgin is followed by a joke on virginity, together with a joke, equally labored, on Bergman's old friend the Devil. An unassailable virgin is a sty in the devil's eye; this is the quaint "Irish" proverb devised by Bergman to spike his half-pint of invention. The idea of Don Juan being sent from Hell in order to cure the Devil's sty by seducing a pastor's virginal daughter, who is, of course, twenty and Swedish, accompanied by his servant, Pablo, who will try his luck with the pastor's wife, is loaded with potential fun if the author were Bocaccio. Or if—well, there are many ifs. The perpetration of such a joke could only be vindicated, if not by brilliant handling, which it is not, by a surprise in the development. But Don Juan falls in love with his victim and is rejected by her, while Pablo has more success but thereby brings the pastor and his wife closer together. There is no surprise here, it is conventional morality; no surprise, no comedy. In my opinion a Don Juan played by Jarl Kulle would make any virgin's resistance easy; hence, there is no conflict, either. Nor was there any compensation from the scenic craft or from the camera which, in effect, was unusually immobile. Two actors contributed whatever amusement could be found—Sture Lagerwall, whose Pablo was a sort of lugubrious Figaro, and Nils Poppe as the plausibly discomfited pastor.

Bergman totally missed his subject. Anyone else, I speak in hyperbole, given the compass reading, would have been able to find sharp north. Since Don Juan is ostensibly a Mediterranean type, the girl, being Swedish, would have fallen for him without a push. Satan, to reward the Don for curing his sty, would have permitted him to remain on earth with his Nordic seedplot. And as the snow begins to fall, inexorably and forever, the film would end with Don Juan desperately entreating the Devil to let him come back to Hell.

The first of those works Bergman called Chamber films in emulation of the later Strindberg reminds one in fact of the other Scandinavian master, Ibsen, in a purely negative reading. The spaces that separate the people, like the spaces that separate the furniture, and offstage a comfortless space of nature at its most forlorn, recall the Norwegian's scoured and skimpy settings. But his critical insight is nowhere apparent. It is Ibsen at his most taciturn, of whom on one occasion Henry James wrote, "His subject is always, like the subjects of all first rate men, primarily an idea; but in this case the idea is as difficult to catch as its presence is impossible to overlook."[79]

The working title of *Såsom i en Spegel* was *Tapeten* (*Wallpaper*), because it is from behind the wallpaper of a room in a dreary house on an island in the Baltic that Karin, in her onset of progressive schizophrenia, hears voices and in this pseudo-floral and immured world where she hopes to meet God. (A wallpapered door was a feature of the setting in Strindberg's *The Ghost Sonata.*) No matter what Bergman says in a number of interviews during the Sixties about having given up the search for God or having surrendered an old conception of God in order to discover a new one, God is still the substantive in his serial declarative sentence. God is Silent, God is Absent, God is a Spider, God is the sum of all possible Love, and, by my deduction, God is the Artist. This is the succession of unclear hypotheses with which one must cope in most of the films Bergman has made since 1961, the year of *Through A Glass Darkly*, to give it the simplified title by which it is known in English. The latter film was alleged to be the first part of a trilogy but how early Bergman decided he had a trilogy in the making is not clear to me; in a conversation with Sjöman, recorded at the end of *L 136*, he pondered the subject of *Through A Glass Darkly*, next of *Nattvardsgästerna* (*The Communicants*; known as *Winter Light* in English), then of his forthcoming film *The Silence,* and suggested that together they might comprise, as he later formulated it, a reduction, "in the metaphysical sense."

In that sense a reduction would be a leading back, as it were, to an original source or unity, and in the films designated that source is certainly the primal silence; for in this trilogy there is plainly depicted a reducton of confidence in the presence of God, without drastically redefining Him and what is deplorable, cinematically, there is a reduction of observed life to as few elements and gestures as will sustain the viewer's attention without simply resorting to a series of still photographs. This is a form of cinematic arthritis known in the trade as the "Dreyer syndrome" or "Bresson's disease."[80]

Through A Glass Darkly is as sparse visually as any film Bergman has made. Before my disclaimer is misunderstood I'll make it clear, if I have not already, that I have no personal aversion to the principle in art of *multum in parvo*. I tend to admire films in which the statement is untrammeled, implicit, and simply and intensively organized on the surface. The late Bergman films, I except *Winter Light* from this generalization, are beyond this description; they have not in my opinion a sufficient degree of expressiveness to ratify the economy of setting and the paucity of action—to say nothing of the manic circumscription of their subjects. Austerity is one thing, but aridity is something more disagreeable. After the lights and shadows, the echoing woods, the power and terrible piety of *The Virgin Spring*, the world of *Through A Glass Darkly* is unflickering; nature is utterly stilled as if God had already quieted the elements, preparatory to being the next voice you hear. But there is no miracle here, there is no life, there is no wonder, except in certain lines of the dialogue more bromidic than awe-stricken. There are indications of a living earth in the script as written; all those bird cries and slidings of the nocturnal element tend to dissolve in the uniform passivity of the film's images. It is a fallacy to believe you best express spiritual devaluation by devaluating your artistic means. Antonioni's *L' Avventura*, from the same year, has also a moribund subject; the film is not scenically and humanly dead.

I can imagine a man in an inspired fit of melancholy making *Through A Glass Darkly*, suiting the visual diminution to the bleak conclusions of his script. I can imagine his devising *The Silence* in a moment of sardonic fright, in which two caged females would symbolize the internecine, mutually voracious pastimes of derailed moderns. What I find hard to imagine is how a man can plot steadily, year after year, films that chart a continuing decrease of human energy and vision, without ever being diverted by a change in his bloodstream or a qualification from his intelligence. These late films of Bergman are made with the will; they are the response of a man who is unable to find a creative alternative to a barren theme he is determined, for God knows what (irony acknowledged) deepseated reason, to exhaust down to the last filing of bone.

During one sequence of *Through A Glass Darkly*, when two characters are conversing in a boat on the sea, there is no natural undulation of the water under the boat. Wondering if and why, since he made much of the film on location, Bergman had used back-projection, I asked a member of the crew what had happened. I was informed that Bergman shot the scene with the boat beached, from such an angle that it would seem as if the boat were on the water. When someone suggested that the boat would have no movement, Bergman said it wasn't important and that nobody would notice the unreality. I have seen a number of reviews in which critics have claimed to see in such effects, here as in *The Silence*, an objective token of metaphysical foreclosure. I feel that my skepticism is justifiable.

To regard the first three films as a trilogy is incidentally a problem, for they are not, considered together, noticeably distinct from the subsequent films and they are not themselves uniform in their mode of conception. However symbolic certain aspects of *Through A Glass Darkly* may be, the work as a whole is not symbolically intended; you are not expected to translate the characters into abstract qualities, nor are you in *Winter Light*. The first film is about four ostensibly substantial people on an island; *Winter Light* concerns the faith problem of a visibly human and fully dimensioned pastor in north Sweden involved in a despairing struggle not only with his belief but with a woman he can't love who loves him. When viewing *The Silence*, on the other hand, it is patently implausible to remain at the realistic level and suppose you are witnessing a combat to the death between two literally depicted sisters—the Russians would call them "warm sisters"—in a hotel somewhere in the near future or at any time. They demand translation into their universal equivalents, comparably to characters in *The Magician* or in *La Strada* or *Viridiana*. *The Silence* is stylistically closer to *Persona* than to the preceding films of the trilogy.

In any case, *Through a Glass Darkly* is subheaded in the published scripts as *Certainty Achieved*. Which certainty you may have to decide to your taste, since God, in the final vision of Karin, is a spider; the image is immediately preceded by that of the helicopter which will take her to the hospital. Bergman describes it in the script as looking like a monstrous insect. However, since Karin is clearly divided between herself and her fair judgment, there is no reason for accepting as a finality her view of things that nothing will come from the sky but a gift, sinister in form, of technology. The film ends with her father's assurance to her fifteen-year-old brother, whom she has seduced into the incestuous act, that "*every* sort of love" implies God, the highest and the lowest, the poorest and the richest, the most ridiculous and the most sublime, the obsessive as well as the banal. This is an extremely generous definition: his further exposition is equally liberal. "We don't know if love proves God's existence or if love *is* God. In the end, it doesn't make much difference." This would seem to take care of the whole question by reducing it to a semantic shambles! For the time being, I prefer Spinoza's version: "Love is the feeling of pleasure *accompanied by our knowledge of the cause*". (Italics mine.)

No wonder this film has appealed to a part of the public that wants answers to excuse its errors and satisfy its nostalgia with a transcendental message that makes no demands on its ear for precise language. If incest can be washed out as merely evidence of a species of love this gives the audience, especially the Swedish audience, the benefit of having its smörgås and eating it too. I don't know what the latest findings are about the linkage of incest and hereditary insanity—when I last inquired, the experts were aggressively divided in their opinions—but I do know that the recurrence of incest and insanity in the context of Swedish film is too remarkable to be relegated as casual juxtaposition and I know further that social workers will unofficially assure you of the numerically high ratio of incest situations in provinces they will name. I stress this because I think the subject of incest used as a symbol of entangling spiritual alliances is highly questionable. And I see the subject of insanity,

(Above right) Gunnel Lindblom and Birgitta Petersson in *The Virgin Spring* (1960)

(Below) Axel Düberg and Max Von Sydow in *The Virgin Spring* (1960)

Lars Passgård and Harriet Andersson in *Through a Glass
Darkly* (1961)

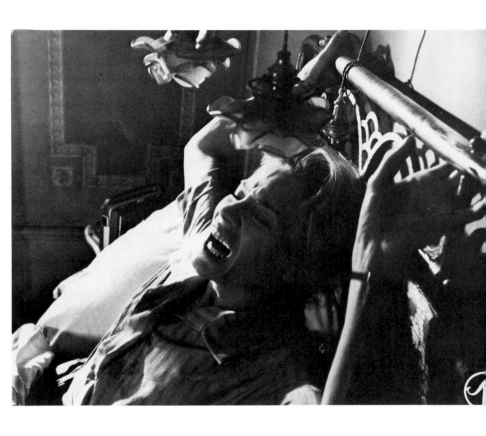

Ingrid Thulin in *The Silence* (1963)

(Next page) Gunnar Björnstrand and Ingrid Thulin in
Winter Light (1963)

The Shame (1968)

(Above left and below) Liv Ullmann and Bibi Andersson
in *Persona* (1966)

Max Von Sydow in *The Shame* (1968)

Naima Wifstrand and Max Von Sydow in *Hour of the Wolf* (1968)

Gertrud Fridh and Max von Sydow in *Hour of the Wolf*
(1968)

(Above right) Bibi Andersson and Max von Sydow in
A Passion (1969)

(Below) Liv Ullmann in *A Passion* (1969)

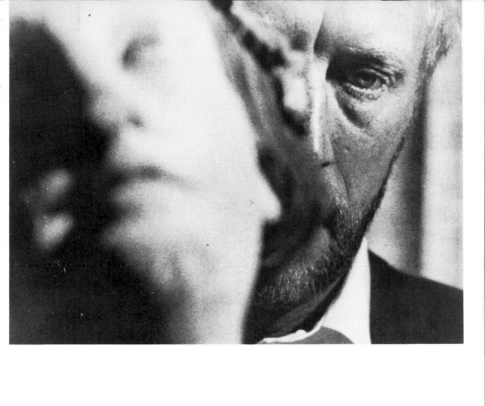

when seriously broached, as a clinical one and really quite wracking to observe in process. In *Through a Glass Darkly* the combined subject seems to me to be introduced only to be evaded with a ramshackle theology that sweeps it into the nebulous realm of the All.

Further, the credentials of David, father to Karin and ''Minus,'' for illuminating his son's life with a spiritual credo are far from respectable. He is himself a nervous casualty and an intellectual fraud; in one part of the scenario Bergman quite unnecessarily (unnecessarily because since we can't read it, the point should have been made clear in the dramatization) describes his novel as consisting of ''circuitous sentences, hateful words, banal situations and characters with a poverty of dimension.'' Presumably the author does acquire a sudden insight into his artistic insipidity, for he throws the manuscript into the fire. But he has already told Martin, Karin's husband, that after a suicide attempt in Switzerland, something was born out of his emptiness, something to which he does not dare to give the name of love—love for Karin, for Minus, and for Martin. Surely this is confusing. He is endowed with a vision of love before the events shown in the film, yet until the fruit of that vision is needed, after Karin's crisis, it has not given him sufficient clarity to see through his dishonesty as a writer or his frigidity as a parent. Probably the reason for this delayed revelation is Bergman's necessity for using David as an object lesson in the coldness of the artist, since David sees in his daughter's cyclical madness only the literary values he can exploit. The accusation is contrived; it would be as instinctive for a writer to observe symptoms under the aspect of literature as it would be for the husband, a doctor, to observe them medically and store the observation for future diagnoses.

This would not, and does not, as far as we can tell, vitiate Martin's love for his wife nor should David's awareness inhibit his love for his daughter. David is shown as diffident if not selfish, and as a writer he craves prestige, not the self-satisfaction of the creative act. But these traits were arbitrarily pinned on him as those of a writer because, as I see it, Bergman was undergoing qualms about a level of coldness in his own creative observation. No other conclusion is feasible, since what goes on in the film is an inadequate demonstration of the themes proposed in the dialogue.

Ingmar Bergman (1969)

The characterizations do not work. Here is a key interchange, between Martin and David; the former is reproaching his father-in-law for keeping a diary on the progress of Karin's disease.

In your emptiness there's no room for feelings; as for a sense of decency, you have none. You know how everything should be expressed. At any moment you have the right word. But there's one thing about which you haven't the foggiest idea: life itself. . . .

Are we not entitled to some evidence of this talent for meticulous verbal expression on David's part? Up to then, he has shown no disposition whatever for the *mot juste*; nor does he thereafter. Bergman may even have been confused as to whom he was going to award the merciless attributes of fine articulation, for in another sequence Karin tells her husband, and he's not a writer, "Funny thing about you. You always say the right words and do just the right things. Yet they're wrong, even so. . . ." Since Martin has just expressed his love for Karin with total sincerity, if with no special adroitness, we are perhaps asked to believe that her retort is paranoid; it's an odd coincidence, just the same. To return to Martin's charges:

> *M*: You have a God you toy with in your novels. I'll tell you something; you and your faith are equally bogus. What strikes one most is your staggering inventiveness.
> *D*: Don't you think I know?
> *M*: Then why go on? Why don't you do something respectable for a living? [Echo of Mrs. Borg in *Wild Strawberries*.]
> *D*: What could I do?
> *M*: Have you ever written as much as one true word in any of your books?
> *D*: I don't know.
> *M*: You see! The worst of it is, your lies are so subtle they resemble truth.

In the first place, these powers of invention and subtlety do not fit the description given in the script of David's writing. Obviously, the dialogue here, which will be in effect repeated both in *The Silence* and in *Persona*, is plainly Bergman talking to himself; consequently the illusion of a film dealing with potentially viable characters is shattered. It could only survive if these characters were in their own right credible and vivid. To my view they were not, for Karin alone had personality. The mad do impose themselves; but Harriet Andersson's performance was impressive; it might have been more so if she had been given any prior dimension, so to speak. I didn't get her when she wasn't in a state of dementia. David is inscrutable when not confused and Martin doesn't cut much of a figure. If you specify a doctor in your film and you're not familiar with doctors—but who on earth wouldn't be?—should you not ask yourself, "What would a doctor who is also in love with his wife-patient, really say?" Martin only says what Bergman wants him to say, which is not enough for Karin; it could never be enough because Bergman distrusts words. I must assume he also distrusts doctors when I remember the spurious psychiatrist of *Thirst*, the clownish Erneman (his name was *David!*) of *A Lesson in Love*, half of Isak Borg of *Wild Strawberries*, and Vergerus in *The Magician!*

Minus lives up to his name; there isn't much of him, poor chap. At that stage Lars Passgard was not sufficiently mature as an actor to give the role any appeal; that role was anyway rather insecure. Considering the boy's normally inarticulate character, it was difficult to accept the clarity of the play dialogue he writes, and with Karin performs, in which he exposes his father's pretensions without ruth. If this is supposed to be the circumstance that ignites David's self-knowledge, it is not presented with the dramatic emphasis it should then have. After the hideous crisis with Karin, Minus cries, "Reality burst and I fell out!", which is a good line but not quite in his style. And when he announces, at the end of the film, after the terraqueous sermon on Love delivered by David, "Daddy spoke to me!" (i.e., God spoke to him), the more sublime reference is lacking in force; it is oblique, since it was Karin who wanted God to speak; Minus' problem has been principally sexual. If God who is Love has spoken to him through incest with a schizoid sister interpreted by his neurasthenic father I am not, to put it mildly, impressed.

The only moment for me when the film came alive was in the incest embrace; this was projected with tact and intense feeling and with a real-Bergman sense of the right setting, in this case the womb-like interior of a stranded, rotting boat. Characteristic for this phase of Bergman's filmmaking, sexually motivated violence is much more convincing than the would-be conversations and normal contacts of four people living under the same roof. You may read the script; it is available in book form with pages of unalive dialogue which, even allowing for the demands of naturalism, no BBC television writer would be permitted to retain. Swedish critics received the film with a gasp of relief, as if they had been afraid Bergman might return to the world of baroque poetry. To my complaint that the characters were really quite drab, I received the assurance, "That's just the point! These are normal Swedish people". Thus, when a visiting friend of mine from overseas saw the film with me on my second trial, and flatly observed afterward, "I just don't believe that the people in this film ever existed," all I could answer was, "You're in for a surprise, old man. Don't look now, but they're all around you".

Winter Light

"For now we see through a glass, darkly; but then face to face; now I know in part; but then shall I know even as also I am known." The text from Paul's First Epistle to the Corinthians could just as well be the keynote to *Winter Light*. Perfect knowledge of God remains a deferred promise. Indeed, Pastor Tomas Eriksson has long since abandoned David's faith in God as Love. That he is played by the same actor, Björnstrand, lends a quirk of continuity to a situation which in essential matters echoes plangently the desolation of *Through a Glass Darkly*. The setting is another island of a sort; the parish of Frostnäs (literally, frost-*neck* or *isthmus*), between marsh and pine woods, is equally isolated. *Certainty Unmasked* was the subtitle given to this work in the published edition of the script.

An unidentified wit[81] once wrote that Bergman only made vertical films, up to God or down toward the Devil. *Winter Light* is the last of Bergman's films to date which, owing to its subject, might be described as vertical. The moral effort is upward but the formal movement, as in most of the Chamber films, is circular. *Winter Light* is a more attractive title than the accurate one, *The Communicants*. The former conveys the Northern chill, the latter has the asset of irony; there are so pitifully few communicants at Eriksson's church services and in the secular sense of the word the characters, even though articulate, can barely be said to communicate with each other. This movie is as uninflected as *Through a Glass Darkly*. In the former film, Bach's Suite No. 2 for Unaccompanied Cello was the sole, stern punctuation, imported from an *ultima thule* of culture; in *Winter Light* there is only the music provided by the church organ.

We begin to understand that Bergman intends his reduction to be comprehensive. From *Through a Glass Darkly* to *The Silence*, the very titles announce a glacial advance so inevitable as to be predictable. Thereafter, no subtraction of setting, sound, or passion is altogether surprising. In the same period, Antonioni has undertaken his own somewhat glib passage from the Lipari islands to Death Valley. The writer David in Bergman's first film of the series is seen shearing a sentence of everything but its descriptive meaning—from "She came toward him, panting with anticipation, scarlet-faced in the keen wind" to "She came running toward him" to "They met on the beach". Presumably we are being instructed in the principles of craft, even though, as I have said above, the writer is not otherwise shown as a model of artistic integrity, but the demonstration of such unvarnished syntax acquires another meaning; unconsciously, while implying the classical virtue of understatement, Bergman is prophesying the death of language. The bleak Northern ethos, identified by Anthony West in the review cited earlier, is being conveyed here. One often has the feeling that logically the Swede would prefer "The quick brown fox jumped over the lazy dog" to the language of The Song of Songs which is Solomon's. To its advantage, however, *Winter Light* has far less dialogue than *Through a Glass Darkly*. *The Silence* has half as much again. As the Chamber films become more "filmatic," they tend to become at the same time decreasingly accessible and human.

Winter Light is still clearly postulated on personal pain and on the unshakeable visitations of fear, loneliness, and love. For this reason I find it more sympathetic than the others. Like Erland in *Sommarlek,* Pastor Eriksson is unable to reconcile himself to the death of his wife but his position is more seriously equivocal; Uncle Erland was dead in life, Tomas is still struggling, and his struggle is given a cruel obliquity by the cynical view of Blom, the organist, that the late Mrs. Eriksson was an unloving horror, "a proper woodlouse". But I can best represent the tone of the film by reproducing here the compressed review I wrote when I first saw *Winter Light*; there is no point of my laboring to reword that statement when I find myself in substantial agreement with the position I then took.

I think *The Communicants* is no end depressing and I can understand that few friends of mine are willing to take the subject as seriously as Bergman: the secondary subject, that is, for the film is plainly about people suffering —to a degree anyone else is at liberty to consider morbid or in the service of something he may feel is in excess of the amount of anxiety engendered. That's as may be. . . . I'm not easily harrowed by Bergman these days but I'm ready to call *The Communicants* a masterpiece. Bergman is the only practising director who can make an elequent film from a rag, a bone and a hank of hair. Bresson can't. Antonioni can't now. Bergman can. Everyone (well, most of the "critics," let's say) thought he had done so with *Through a Glass Darkly*. I stand on my previously forwarded objections, that in the earlier film Bergman failed to distinguish between the necessarily arid and the factitiously tedious. . . . *The Communicants* is the film people thought he then made; there's faultless and almost intolerable harmony here between the major theme—God is silent—and the environment. Within a span or hollow of time little more protracted than the running time of the film, the pastor of an area (you can't call it a community) in north-central Sweden presides over Communion for a congregation of nine, is asked to comfort a man on the brink of suicide with faith he doesn't himself experience, confesses to the woman who loves him that he loves neither her nor anything save his dead wife, listens wearily to plaintively mumbled burdens or to inarticulate fervor with a face of crumbling stone and three slate-gray, graceless hours later begins another service of High Mass with only one auditor— the woman he has tried to cast into outer darkness. "Holy, Holy, Holy," he announces. 'God is all Mighty. [The earth is filled with his glory.]
. . . . The intimate agonies of three or four people fill an hour and a half with a nagging simulation of eternity. Nothing in this exiguous world is more present than the closeup tormented face: the few alternative images remain on the eyeballs and in the tympani like the hallucinations of a man in solitary confinement: a Lubeck altarscape or a Baroque pulpit glimpsed in an otherwise unadorned church; the feverish clamor of a dammed-up river under a pewter sky when the dead man is carted away; a key to the toilet-door in the schoolhouse, absurdly notable, labelled *pojkar* (boys).
Bergman could lay claim to genius for no other achievement than wringing from Ingrid Thulin such deeply-dredged pain and exaltation. For no one else has she given such a performance, for no other director could she so strip herself of all aids to glamor and drain her poor native capability to find at the bottom these dregs of an uncompromisingly authentic expression. Un-

precedented in the history of film, if elephant-memory serves, is the juncture at which she talks in mercilessly held closeup for what seemed to my unclocked sense well over four minutes. . . . But by now it's surely not contestable that Bergman knows unerringly how far he can ask any actor to go, how much more he can dig from their already excavated talent. Everyone in this film is better than he has been under anybody's direction: Gunnar Björnstrand as the doubting Thomas (when life does terrible things to you, said Dostoievsky, you do terrible things to others) ; Alan Edwall, the crippled sacristan whose secular apprehension of time convinces him that he suffers more than Christ did on the cross; Olof Thunberg as Frederik Blom, the hired organist, who performs a modest miracle of his own by converting the five barley-loaves of his tippling into a perennial repast of facetiousness; Max von Sydow as Jonas (Jonah?), the terrified fisherman drowned by his own irredeemable solemnity, while begging to be told he can walk on the waves. . . ."

For the purposes of a review in which I had neither the space nor the desire to be exhaustive, I omitted certain auxiliary observations which it may not be superfluous to add in the present context. I think it is interesting to know that before shooting this film Bergman, by way of getting in the mood, studied Bresson's film *Diary of a Country Priest,* which also concerns an intense soul-searcher, a young man, who is troubled by his loss of faith. Excepting the theme, there is no shadow of resemblance between the two films; they are models of two distinctly opposed ways of making movies. Bresson's is looseleaf, as if he had shot thousands of feet aimlessly, then edited, not too strictly, from the sum what he needed to tell his story within feature-length limits. The whole is held together, despite its crude literary transitions of entries from a diary, by the sheer ingenuous beauty of the young French actor's performance and by Bresson's usual sincerity of purpose. Bergman's film is as dangerously close to static theatre construction as Bresson's is to being an over-faithful transcription of novelistic details (the original was a fiction by Georges Bernanos).

It cannot have escaped notice that, objectively or whimsically, Bergman tried to see his own answers in *Through a Glass Darkly* as pure cant by having Blom sneer at Eriksson's beliefs, when he warns Märta not to sacrifice herself for Tomas. What he quotes are exactly the words of David in the previous film. "God is love; love is God. Love is proof of God's existence." "I know that jargon by heart. I've been a close listener to the pastor's outpourings, as you can tell.'' Arthur Gibson finds this self-revulsion on Bergman's part evidence of his advance from the conception of a personal God whose eye is on every sparrow to that of a more impersonal, suffusing and majestic God glimpsed by Tomas at the end of the film when he ends the ordeal of that wintry day, alone in the church with Märta and the faithful sacristan, pronouncing the omnipotence of the supreme being.[83] Given the situation, I found those words cruelly ironic rather than hopeful. However, I believe now that Gibson was closer to Bergman's intention, since the published script is preceded by a dateline, ''Torö, August 7, 1961. S.D.G.'' The initials stand for *Se Dei Gloria*, ''To the Glory of God''. Further, it is a fact that following *Winter Light*, while the questioning of an ultimate cause remains, like the memory of an amputated limb, the problem of God's presence recedes to the background. As with certain other questions Bergman had not so much resolved this one as he had exhausted it at the level of dramatic expression. Tomas prone on the church floor moaning, ''God is silent,'' is the furthest incarnation of the Knight in the chapel with Death saying the same thing.

For my personal estimation of the film as a whole, the word masterpiece which I employed seven years ago is perhaps grandiose. I would still rank it as one of Bergman's most scrupulous works; in it he made the most of what he decided strictly to include, without quite cutting off all air in which to breathe. Yet I am not eager to see it often; it is far too little cinematic, in my feeling for that term. It is possible to respect a film without liking it. *Winter Light* is not a film to which I can say *du*.

The Silence

Nor is *The Silence*, but it is a work I am forced to admire for its infernal compressionism. This is a film that transparently means something other than what you are seeing and this has become a jagged problem for critics who do not care for art as cryptology. I do not myself in numerous instances. I have seen many movie riddles not worth the unriddling—that of *Marienbad*, for one, the sleeveless errand of all time

—but I think *The Silence* rewards effort; at its core there is a rancid integrity which compels one's recognition, if not one's affection. A widely disseminated rumor slavishly believed, notoriously by Bergman himself, holds that a critic arrives at his judgments by scientific induction; it may help to scotch such nonsense if I here try to restate the process of intuition and recall by which I arrived at my conviction of what, in *The Silence*, Bergman was saying. It was something after this way, to use a Kiplingism.

I was first startled by the analogy in part with Sartre's *No Exit*, in which play, more lurid than profound but fascinating for its moral *mise en scène*, an Empire-period suite in a Paris hotel is represented as Hell. Here the man, the woman, and the man-woman are condemned to endure each other's vigilant and scabrous company eternally. Some years earlier, as I've recorded, critics had quoted from this play to explain another Bergman film, *Prison*, "Hell is other people". In *The Silence* two women are placed in a hotel room in a foreign country where one abuses the other, defies her by an act of sodomy with a bartender she has picked up, and finally leaves her to die. Bergman's film is even more abstract than Sartre's play for in it there are no connections, I now feel sure, with socially actual society—as there were in *No Exit*, memorably through the hero's political dilemma. Bergman had said, however, that when Ester looks apprehensively from the window in the place he called Timoka, this was how he felt in Paris in 1949. And in Paris he conceived the original version of the piece that became the radio play, *The City*; as I commented earlier, the location might as well have been Uppsala as any French town.

The weather in the city of *The City* was sultry, oppressive, electrical, with thunder on the left and dire premonitions of an engulfing catastrophe. David in *Through a Glass Darkly* was afraid of thunder; this was probably a bogey of Bergman's childhood as it was of Luther's. In *The Silence* the weather is also hot, the air is fetid, the sunshine harsh; the hotel room is stuffy, in the corridor a moldy chill reigns. Army tanks occupy the siding as the train arrives in Timoka; they rumble through the street. A siren wails. The two sisters wrangle about Father. If, in *Through a Glass Darkly*, Father was a surrogate of God, it might well be God again now dead and buried who is the subject of their contention.

God's Silence, The Negative Impression is Bergman's subtitle for the published text. One must ask the right questions to get pertinent answers. Who are these sisters? One is a translator, a mental occupation. The other has no professional identity; she has a boy and she is uncontrollably carnal. Are they indeed in a foreign country? The language, contrived by Bergman, is unknown to them; there are tanks in the street.

This is a city with the threat of war hanging over it, a city in which nobody can communicate successfully with anyone else, a city in which music is the sole language of exchange—the name, J. S. Bach, is all Anna can read in the paper; Bach is the only source of verbalized empathy between Ester and the floor waiter[84]—a city in which intellect cannot translate the few words it has learned for the enlightenment of a bewildered boy, a city in which the halves of an organism, the sisters, are hostile and mutually uncomprehending. Where is the puzzle? Given Bergman's antecedent and undiminished fears, the inference is plain. This is the City of Man, of Man divided from himself.

The sisters are Mind and Body. Ester, mind, is sick; she is self-generating; the first Timokan words she learns are for face, herself, and hand, with which she performs onanism. Anna is body, trying to shake off the mind's dominion; her insurrection is chiefly pornographic. Ester is shocked but yet sympathetic with the concupiscence of her other self. With this reading of the central, bisected image everything else in the film falls logically into place, logically, that is to say, as in a poem, not as in a mathematical equation. Thenceforth all fretting over peripheral meanings such as Lesbianism, the location of Timoka, and the boy urinating in the corridor of a grand hotel is superfluous and irrelevant. To look for a one-to-one correspondence is idle. Ester describing Father as in her memory huge and humorous need not puzzle anyone; to an older belief, as to that of a child, God is larger than life-size and sometimes jolly like Santa Claus. But consider the following speech of Anna to Ester with the above premise in mind.

> When Father was alive he decided things. And we obeyed him. We had to. When Father died you thought you could carry on in the same way. You went on about your principles and how meaningful everything is, how important! But this was just nonsense. (A pause.) Do you know why? I'll tell you. It was all in aid of your self-importance. You can't live without a sense

of your importance. That's the truth. You can't endure it if everything isn't "a matter of life and death," "significant," "meaningful"—I don't know what!

And Ester asks in reply, "How do you want us to live, then? After all, we own everything in common".

Anna's viewpoint here is of course Bergman's, previously anticipated in *The Magician* whereby Vogler, now that Granny (religion losing its force) is dying, thinks he too can "carry on in the same way," with mere magic, i.e., art. Bergman has often quoted O'Neill's belief that the relationship between man and God is the only important subject. We need not concede to this opinion to perceive its presence, but in *The Silence* it is not the artist but the intellectual who is accused of secular pride. In the passage quoted, body charges mind with conceit in its own powers, much as Marianne had challenged Isak Borg and Martin had called David to account. Or listen to this exchange:

> *Ester* (coldly) You can't manage on your own.
>   *Anna* You think you can make my decisions for me, just like Father.
> *Ester* (silent)
>   *Anna* You think I'm stupid, eh?
> *Ester* (smiles) I don't think you're stupid.

Further; when Anna begins to make love to the bartender, she says, "I wish Ester was dead". She wishes she could put her mind to sleep.

The body affronts the mind, the mind fights fear of extinction with reason and brandy; the child of the body wanders in an unpeopled world where the few inhabitants are grotesque and cannot speak to him. Since the total atmosphere is one of *reduction,* it follows that all phenomena will be reduced. The hotel, designed for the capacious life with many guests, is virtually unoccupied; it harbors only a literally shrunken company of dwarfs. Ester tries to leave the boy a last testament in a new language she is learning from an old servitor who is pretty clearly, I would say, a kindly forerunner of death; he has no desire to frighten the boy, but to beguile him he can produce only pictures of bygone scenes and people, one of them a woman in a coffin. Like Death in *The Seventh Seal,* he has no answers; he only does his duty. At the end, mind in its agony confesses its futility. Ester cries desperately in words that echo Strindberg: "We try them out, one attitude after another, and we find them all meaningless. The powers are too strong for us; I mean the *monstrous* powers.'' Since the body has its own life to live, it leaves the mind to die, as the sirens howl and the landscape darkens, at two in the afternoon, and the boy, once more in that train we never see from the outside, tries vainly to decipher the message left him by his dead aunt. *Emptiness under the moon, my lord.*

An extraordinary achievement in its way. An almost indefinable cloud of terror is shaped around a lacerating cloven image, the two lethally divided women, sweating in the mothless dark of ignorance, bickering and bleeding, the one coupling without joy, the other self-manipulating without passion. Ester in her death-throes is perhaps the most intensely revolting spectacle with which Bergman has confronted us. I intend that as a compliment to Ingrid Thulin; her's was an obediently savage performance, an unsparing threnody of masochism. This film is not an ingratiating experience. Personally, if I must have versions of dualism, I much prefer the sensuousness and wisdom of Thomas Mann's *The Transposed Heads*. I cannot share Bergman's lack of confidence in the mind, nor his puritan nervousness about the body.

For there is no doubt that over and above, or below, the appalling accuracy of Bergman's metaphor in terms of the contemporary world, *The Silence* betrays a grindingly personal animus and incidentally a bias of the national temper. When we imagine hell, we extend the worst we already have. Most of us in the Western world would envisage social chaos. Who but a Swede would have a nightmare of body and mind totally irreconcilable, projected into a milieu dwindled to fewer than a dozen people who can't talk to each other, with the sun setting at two P.M.? It is a moot point whether this film is conspicuously about the dessication of man in our time or the dessication of Bergman's film cosmos. Intended consciously or not, *The Silence* exploits a significant demise— I mean more significant than any visible demise—the death of the male principle; there are no men, only a faceless stud bartender, a funereal waiter, a small boy, and a bevy of midgets. Let it be said that even Bergman's reductions of his world obey a deadly artistic consistency. Here, in micro-format, are some of his principal themes. The train journey, once a characteristic passage, is now contracted to a masterful simulation without the necessity for photographing a train. His troupe of migratory players is a vertical third of its former self; it is not given that these mites have any audience, even, before which to perform. The play-within-a-play, staged last in somewhat tentative manner in *Through a Glass Darkly*, is a Punch-and-Judy show pathetically attempted by the boy Johan, broken off because Punch stammers in the unintelligible language of fear. The world out there is more baleful than ever, the indications of it more terse; a single tank on the Timokan street does duty for all those earlier occasions when a haunted Bergman character had trembled at the thought of corpses in the Baltic. To observe a carefully degraded proportion in the contemplation of one's willed impoverishment is an expression of genius.

One vital force remains and will remain: hate. Despite the omnipresence of love as at least a forlorn hope in the Chamber films and the wistful belief in the power of love which Bergman has professed in interviews,[85] it is hate that provides any dynamic principle to his films of the last decade. *Winter Light* crackles into life like a smoldering log over which you have tossed kerosene in the terrible schoolroom episode when Tomas tries to reject Märta in a climax of scorn. *The Silence* is entirely animated by the tempest of Anna's self-inflicting rage and lust. *Persona*, in its last half, is nothing but recrimination raised to the ninth power. *The Hour of the Wolf* is hate from beginning to end, more parody than paranoia. The most convincingly human moment of *The Shame* is the blowup between Jan and his wife in the field. And in *A Passion* the only clearly comprehensible episode is that in which Andreas beats his wife nearly senseless. I feel as if I am making a gratuitous observation if I add that this insensate fury seems to reach beyond the exigencies of whatever filmatic theme is being supported. Erik Erikson has explained, in his psychobiography of Martin Luther that a great creative man

> carries the trauma of his near downfall and his mortal grudge against the near assassins of his identity into the years of his creativity and beyond, into his decline; he builds his hates and his grudges into his system as bulwarks—bulwarks which eventually make the system first rigid and finally brittle.[86]

"*A Snakeskin Filled With Ants*"

Dr. Erikson's thesis may help us to understand the compulsion under which Bergman made his next film and, at another level of compulsion, the next. *All These Women*, 1964, to give it the mercifully short United States title, was his first feeble attempt to settle accounts with that hydraheaded monster, the critic, without whose indulgence in the Forties, admiration in the Fifties, and incense in the Sixties he might have remained an anonymous theatre director in Malmö. Bergman, not alone among contemporary artists, makes great demands on his idolaters. It is not enough to pay him gratified attention; you must love him though in love he disbelieves. It is not enough to expand your choicest words on his best work; you must never suggest that he does anything less. It is not enough to imply that he is the best living film director; you must insinuate that he is divine, though in divinity he disbelieves.

I said that *All These Women* was his first feeble attempt. There has been a rumor, perhaps initiated by the late Marianne Höök, that with the character of Vergerus in *The Magician* Bergman had intended to crucify the critic as he saw him personified by Harry Schein who once wrote film criticism for a Swedish literary quarterly, *BLM*. I cannot confirm the rumor. If Bergman really cannot distinguish between art criticism, a branch of aesthetics, and medical analysis, the inability goes far to explain his confusion about the professional man in many of his incarnations, for rarely in a Bergman film is a man with half a mind given a shred of positive sense or dignity. As for Mr. Schein, we trust that when he assumed the directorship of the Swedish Film Institute and hence heavy responsibility for the economic fortunes of Swedish film he thereupon exempted himself from any further suspicion of exercizing critical capacity.[87]

Now about all these women and their master, and his parasite, the critic. Henri Montherlant, the novelist and playwright, has had something to say on this general subject.

> Those who are creative in literature like to speak of critics as parasites on the creators. But the creative writers, though their works are self-justifying, grow and prosper in renown thanks to the studies which critics devote to them. Since these studies are soon forgotten, are not the creators to some extent parasitic on the critics? In other words, can one describe as a parasite the critic who dies leaving nothing behind him because his substance has become part of the creative writer's fame?[88]

Nonetheless, I can see that the possibilities which surround the theme of the artist's relation to his critic and through him to his public are, if not infinite, pretty numerous. If anyone believes he can surpass Thomas

Mann in his short story *The Infant Prodigy,* I'll be the first to applaud his intrepidity. Even the opportunities for satire or, less than that, comic abuse are enormous. I exploit such opportunities myself as often as possible, but to ridicule something effectively you had best know something about it. Bergman seems to know nothing whatever about the critical process; what he does know he doesn't understand that he knows. When, for example, he directs someone else's play, it is necessary for him to appreciate it, to analyze it, to interpret it, and to weigh its strengths and its weaknesses in order to stage it in such a way that he evokes its essential style and content. This is a critical act but he evidently doesn't know that; he conceives of criticism in italics, as a special application of the critical experience, a negative performance and an act of violation especially directed at him. Some of this attitude he comes by naturally; it is a generally Swedish prejudice that to be critical means to be adversely critical. It is impossible for Swedes to conceive—save for a quarter-hour when you are explaining the principle to them—that, as our own T. S. Eliot said, ''Criticism is as inevitable as breathing''.

I have always felt it a pity that Stanley Kauffmann's criticism of Bergman's more fruitful films was ungenerous but on the subject of such fruitless ones as this he has my support.

> A master cellist is in his gorgeous summer villa surrounded by women: a wife, a sponsor, a maid, a mistress, a student. To the villa comes a critic who also composes, intent on writing a biography of the master. We never see the cellist; we see a great deal of the critic and the ladies. There are many attempted jokes about the master's venery and veneration; there are various adventures of the critic in seeking admission to the presence. One route leads through a boudoir.
> All is in flashback; we open with the master's funeral and recount the last four days of his life. There are subtitles, tinny phonograph music; there are pratfalls, transvestism, comic tangos, custard pies, fireworks, explosions— all the mechanics of physical comedy. (There are also some unamusing broad jokes, particularly one about how the master teaches the ladies the cello.) But it is all apparatus. There is no wit in the film's conception, no humor in its execution. We seem to be expected to admire it because in it we see a Great Man unbending, acknowledging human frailties. . . .[89]

I cannot improve on this denigration and I do not believe *All These Women* requires any lengthier notice.

Within a year Bergman was provided with an opportunity to insult even more eminent admirers. He was awarded, together with Charles Chaplin, the Erasmus Prize for Cultural Achievement. Before examining his reaction to this honor, it may be pertinent to review what had been happening in the world of film since his apotheosis at the end of the Fifties. To muster the outstanding films released between 1959 and 1964 is to understand that Bergman had to share his glory with many, many formidable rivals. This period is one of the most extensively rich in the history of film production. At the center, that is, in Italy and France, two masters of European movie expression, Fellini and Antonioni, had reached their apex. Their work was no less marked by definitive power than Bergman's. A score of young and not so young French directors were turning out film art with a new spontaneity, a limber charm, and civilized intelligence—films very often derived from their sheer love of a world which Bergman was more darkly than ever consigning to perdition. Among these films from France were also not a few grave and meditative items worthy of that high seriousness which more solemn critics believe to be the *only* credentials for decisive art.[90] With an infallible taste for charlatanry, however, critics at large, which is to say the mob of journalists that dominates film festivals waiting for the signals, shouted down the poised or profound efforts by lionizing the most plebeian and morally incompetent sensibility among them, that of Jean-Luc Godard.[91] For a decade thereafter, Godard, more than any single figure, came near to destroying the richer values of cinema flowering elsewhere.

For from other countries beside France and Italy a super-abundance of seeable films was arriving every year from formerly peripheral countries such as Argentina, Greece, Poland, and Czechoslovakia, in most cases sadly defining themselves before expiring, and from Japan and India. Luis Buñuel, having occupied a lugubrious rear guard since *Los Olvidados,* made his greatest film, *Viridiana,* which expressed a crucial if Goya-black statement about the historical process in our century with elemental gusto and a gallery of luminous rogues whose vitality transcended the symbolic function assigned to them. A fair notion of what was transpiring internationally can be conveyed by noting that in the year 1961, when *Through a Glass Darkly* had its premiere, the world was seeing *Lady with A Dog* made the year before, *La Ciociara, L'Avventura,*

La Notte, The Bandits of Orgosolo, Viridiana, Jules et Jim, and *Summer Skin.*

Bergman was not unaware of his threatened position, of the indisputable fickleness of critics and audiences and of the implication that sackcloth was not the only wear. While making *The Communicants,* he remarked on the fact that *L'Avventura* had been reviewed on the culture page of a Stockholm newspaper while *Såsom i en Spegel* had occupied the normal niche in the Theater and Cinema columns. There is something degradingly sad in Sjöman's further report in *L 136* that he and Bergman methodically read the Swedish, not the international, reviews of *Winter Light* and Bergman in effect graded the critics on their relevance. The pueblo is the world. The fact was that Bergman was becoming an institution; this is a perilous thing for an artist to become, for it means he is being taken for granted. *The Silence* was a record success with critics and public alike but Bergman could not have been innocent of the knowledge that audiences thronged to it precisely to enjoy scenes which he had intended as cautionary visions of the schizoid human predicament.[92] How far this consciousness troubled him, how much a personal something in his life was responsible for the sequel, I have no final knowledge, but from a sickbed allegedly, he wrote the incredible address delivered for him by Kenne Fant, president of Svensk Filmindustri, at Utrecht on February 16, 1965. This message was entitled, then or later, after its repulsive leading image, which he had resuscitated from his film *Thirst,* "A Snakeskin Filled with Ants"—denoting the condition of art in our time.

To paraphrase his argument, literature, music, film, and theatre breed and are nourished on themselves. New mutations, new combinations come and go; seen from outside, the sheer busy-ness gives an impression of nervous vitality. But in fact art, with its new-found liberty, is shameless and irresponsible, is a snakeskin filled with ants. The snake itself has long been dead, eaten out, robbed of its venom, but the skin is animate, filled with busy life, the movement of the ants. Since he himself is one of these ants, he asks himself if there is any reason for his continued activity. He answers himself, affirmatively,

> even though theater is an old loved-out cocotte [en gammal älskad hålldam] who has seen better days, even though many beside myself find a Western more stimulating than Antonioni and Bergman, [*sic*] even though the new music,

mathematically rarefied, gives us a sense of suffocation, even though painting and sculpture are sterile and waste away in paralyzing freedom, even though literature has been transformed into a cairn of words without inspiration or intrepidity. The arts are no longer necessary. People have no need of music; their ears are every minute bombarded by hurricanes of sound. They have no need of poetry; the new world-picture has reduced them to functioning animals with purely metabolic problems—interesting, but from a poet's vantage useless. Religion and art are kept alive to serve as a sentimental shell, a conventional civility towards the past.

Ergo, if he, Bergman, continues even so to create art he must have a plausible motive apart from material profit. His reason is curiosity,

. . . . an unbounded, never-satisfied, ever renewed and unbearable curiosity that drives me on, unresting—curiosity, which has completely replaced my old hunger for fellowship. I feel like a released prisoner suddenly tumbled out into the world, the crashing, howling, snorting world. I am gripped by ungovernable curiosity. I note, observe, stay alert; everything is unreal, fantastic, terrifying or absurd. I catch a flying speck of dust, perhaps it's a film—what does it mean? Nothing at all, perhaps, but it interests *me*. I get busy with my captured figment. . . . I jostle with the other ants. We make a stupendous effort. The snakeskin begins to move.[93]

Numerous avenues of inquiry, which I have no wish to explore, are suggested by this extraordinary testament. The assertions about the incestuous, abstract, and cacophonous nature of modern art I would not dispute; they are self-evident, general propositions, familiar since T.S. Eliot wrote *The Waste Land,* Spengler *The Decline of the West,* and Ortega y Gasset *The Revolt of the Masses* and *The Dehumanization of Art.* And since the condition is such, one would suppose that more than ever people do need art which does not answer to this deviscerated condition. That such people exist was clearly demonstrated, I would say, by the gesture made in offering Bergman the Erasmus Award. It casts a curious light on his remarks if we remind ourselves to whom this award had been given previously. I quote descriptions of four of the recipients from the brochure for this occasion, which was printed in Dutch and English.

The Erasmus Prize was first awarded in 1958 to the Austrian people for the determination shown by them under difficult circumstances in their fight to preserve their European character and culture.

In 1959 the German philosopher Karl Jaspers and the French statesman
Robert Schuman were honoured. . . .as living symbols of the unity of Europe
on the philosophical and political planes.
The Erasmus Prize was awarded in 1962 to the Christian Humanist Romano
Guardini of Munich "for his many-sided contribution towards the preserva-
tion, cultivation and intensification of European spiritual life".
In 1963 the award went to the Jewish theologian Martin Buber "because he
has splendidly served the cause of European culture for more than fifty years
in many domains".

The gentleman of the committee must have been considerably dismayed
to realize that the distinction accorded to humanist scholars and even
to a people had now been bestowed on a man who in effect denied that
any European culture existed; who was relegating their concern for
cultural values to ''a sentimental civility''; who, they should have known,
had never in his films, where other splendors were happily paramount,
spoken an admiring word for learning or for any representative of
it he had cinematically invented and who was now declaring, with
boorish disregard for the community of ideals implied by the award, that
he created art from no other cause than a compulsion to express his
personal curiosity. He could not have more plainly rejected the European
idea if he had appeared at Utrecht in person to spit in the faces of the
foundation members. I think this is perhaps the most sovereign dis-
courtesy publicly committed by an artist in our time.

The question lingers. Why had Bergman accepted without comment
scores of film-festival prizes only to use this occasion of the most meaningful possible recognition to sound forth in trumpet accents his persecution
by the *zeitgeist*? Yet again, in gigantic relief, the silhouette of Strindberg
can be descried, like a mountain behind a mountain when the sun sets
over a misty lake. Maurice Valency has appositely uncovered the nature
of the Strindbergian dilemma:

.... Since it was [also] necessary for Strindberg to be loved and admired, he
was compelled to exhibit his grievances in detail, to justify and to rationalize
his actions and, in order to evoke universal sympathy for his sufferings, to
call, not merely on the neighbors, but upon all the world to witness the
injustices to which he was subjected. Strindberg's sufferings were no doubt
intense; but they certainly involved some element of showmanship. In order
to suffer properly, it was necessary for him to have an audience of thousands,

of millions; and even this did not suffice. His pain must be abstracted, generalized, universalized, until by a Christ-like effort he concentrated in himself all the suffering of mankind. Even so, it was not easy for him to reach the ear of God. For this it was necessary that his complaints be transformed into something so poignant and so beautiful that they could not possibly be disregarded.[94]

Persona

I might not describe *Persona* as poignant and beautiful but I am bound to recognize it as a film Bergman had to make. Dedicated is the fashionable word the artist likes to employ for his endeavor; it is a prettier word than condemned. Nothing in that Utrecht speech is stranger than its conclusion, Bergman's picture of himself as a curiosity-driven explorer who chases any will-'o-the-wisp in the hope that it might be the germinal moment of a movie. I gather he needs this illusion, *comme tout le monde*; we all need illusions to sustain actions for which in fact we can find no alternative. However you see Bergman, I don't think you would summarize him as being impelled by curiosity, not in any ranging sense; there is nothing Sagittarian about him. He is a man encaged from the beginning by an invoked set of obsessions which he submits to a perennial disarrangement and rearrangement, sometimes with a master's skill. But curious he is decidedly not. His expressive strength depends on his not being curious about anything or anybody outside his pueblo. It is comical when a hedgehog sees himself as a fox.

Bergman is not free to examine this speck of dust and that; he is pledged to exhaust a limited, personal line of inquiry, to move within an inscribed circle of concepts and images until he has played them out. Probably a metaphor from chess would be appropriate here but I don't play chess. In this phase of Bergman's art, the face is his omnipresent form; the face as such, irregardless of what is behind it. It means as much as, and at times little more than, for example, a guitar, a woman's body, or a bull has meant to Picasso: an infinitely plastic figure which he is under creative sentence to reproduce, reflect, frame, distort, double, halve, supplement or oppose. At some point it becomes united with didactic content, that is, with a story and this is where the viewer must move with caution; he may underrate the purely visual showmanship of Bergman's art.

I remember the press conference Bergman held before going into production with *Persona*; it was a thoroughtly depressing afternoon engagement. In the middle of a vast studio stage at Svensk Filmindustri, which someone had vainly tried to make cosy by fencing off an area with flats and a semicircle of chairs, Bergman sat at a table backed by the flats, confronted by mute members of the press and flanked by Miss Andersson and Miss Ullmann. The atmosphere was the very opposite of intimate. I imagined the midgets from the hotel in *The Silence,* stranded in the world's largest gymnasium with neither net, ball, nor spectators. Since Swedish critics had been by now fairly intimidated by Bergman and since on such occasions anyway they take an hour to thaw out and ask a burning question, the style of that meeting was, as I say, excruciating. I felt especially sorry for Misses Andersson and Ullmann who had nothing to do but sit there and be Bibi and Liv. After all, what can you ask an actress about a film in which she has not yet appeared?

Bergman explained that *Persona* was not connected with his trilogy, that it had replaced a scenario idea he had abandoned, that he had sketched out this idea in hospital and that the chief inspiration had come from his noting a sort of resemblance between Bibi Andersson and Liv Ullmann in a Norwegian film in which they had appeared called *Short is the Summer,* 1962, from the novel, *Pan,* by Knut Hamsun. If the man said that, it's a point of immediate departure but not in itself too helpful ultimately. From the moment Bergman set foot in the theatre, the *doppelganger,* the twin, the fraternal emblem, the complement and the rival, the *personae* (masks or persons), the mutually hostile or infatuate genders had constituted his world, as, at the risk of being tedious, I have been relentlessly pointing out. As far back as *The Murder at Bajärna*—probably further, if I had the photographs to support me—you can trace, in visual terms, a succession of duplicates, counter-faces, counterfeits and, so to speak, dissolves.

In that particular play, the mask-like face of Naima Wistrand, framed by a kind of witch's or executioner's close-fitting hood, predicts Death in *The Seventh Seal.* Teodor and Albert in *The Naked Night* were projected with no facial or physical features in common, but in his production of *Ur-Faust* Bergman had interpreted Faust and Mephistopheles as divisions of a single psyche and not only made up the faces of the actors, Von Sydow and Toivo Pawlo, accordingly, but spotlighted them in such a way as to make them loudly rhyme. Step by step we move into the dark; the mask is the only truth. Spegel and Death, Vogler and Spegel, Vogler and Manda, Vogler and Vergerus, the blind Tomas seeing only his wife instead of the closeup yearning face of Märta; from thence it is but a quick step to Anna and Ester in *The Silence.* Thus any incidental similarity between Bibi and Liv is a contingency in a lifelong subjection to the undislodgeable image, like a sty in the devil's eye?, of duality, duality, duality!

Caveat emptor. In *Persona,* which is almost as compacted a vehicle as *The Silence* of Bergman's all-and-sundry beliefs, at least three principal themes are mined simultaneously. Any prose attempt to explain these lucidly in A-B-C fashion will inevitably tend to falsify the movie you see, wherein these themes are interlaced, even interlocked, and not separate, linear and exclusively labeled. For one, there is the reality-and-illusion, life-and theatre conflict, enforced and exaggerated in this case by the device of harshly interrupting the action to remind you, as if you needed the reminder, that you are seeing a film. This is an involution by which Bergman was impressed when he made *Prison,* 1949. Second, we are presented with a split-image gambit, exceedingly tricky, the nature of which can only be interpreted with any hope of accuracy if you take the names of the antagonists as your inescapable clue. On this one point, I am dogmatic; beyond this, I have no complacent belief that I have exhaustively interpreted the film. Finally, there is the biographical stratum—for the sake of convenience, I am making a false distinction by so isolating it—which is to say, the portrait of the artist as alternatively victim and cannibal, as evinced by what happens to Elisabeth Vogler, no less than by what happens to Alma the nurse.

I maintained earlier in my pages on *The Magician* that Bergman's nervous remarks on the subject of film art as a fraud, in his 1960 preface to *Four Screenplays,* sounded much like Pirandello on the same subject. Here is the pertinent passage I had in mind, from the novel, *Shoot!,* 1925:

We do not play at our work, for no one has any desire to play. But how are we to take seriously a work that has no other object than to deceive, not ourselves, but other people? And to deceive them by putting together the most idiotic fictions, to which the machine is responsible for giving a wonderful reality?

There results from this, of necessity, and with no possibility of deception, a hybrid game. Hybrid, because in it the stupidity of the fiction is all the more revealed and obvious inasmuch as one sees it to be placed on record by the method that least lends itself to deception: namely, photography. It ought to be understood that the fantastic cannot acquire reality except by means of art, and that the reality which a machine is capable of giving it kills it, for the very reason that it is given it by a machine, that is to say by a method which discovers and exposes the fiction, simply by giving it and presenting it as real. If it is mechanical, how can it be life, how can it be art?. . . .[95]

Today, we can reply to Pirandello's rhetorical question, "Paradoxical, is it not? But it *can* be life, it *can* be art, with a totally respirant conviction you could not have possibly conceived when you wrote those brilliant paragraphs!" If anyone recalls the state of filmmaking in Italy in the early Twenties, and the generally "paleotechnic" stage of film apparatus in most countries, he will readily see that the incongruity remarked by Pirandello might well have appeared to be overpowering and the problem of removing that incongruity insoluble. But it was removed. Pirandello's question was ironic, however, not ingenuous, and the grounds of its express incredulity were aesthetic. The doubts phrased by Bergman in 1960 when he claimed to feel like an impostor because he was deceiving people with an apparatus were belated, even in his own career; they had an air of windowdressing about them and if intended seriously they were puritanical, for in no other sense could they be thoughtfully entertained, not after sixty-five years or so of the movie as a fact and forty years later than the film as a legitimate subject for Pirandello's skepticism.

The consequences are enjoined in *Persona* whereby the consciousness of art as a fiction (what else can it be?) is utilized, to a maddening degree, as a technique in the narration of the work of art. This is by no means novel, either in theory or practice. Unknown to Luigi Pirandello, the challenge to his "stupid fictions" had already appeared in the work of Dziga Vertov in Soviet Russia, an hysteric with original cinematic genius, and in 1926 the manifesto for Bergman's *Persona* had been virtually expressed by a Russian critic, extolling Vertov. "It is necessary to get out of the circle of ordinary human vision; reality must be recorded not by imitating it, but by broadening the circle [*sic*] ordinarily encompassed by the human eye."[96]

We have long ago passed the juncture in cinema where this point needs to be made, though our self-styled avant-garde is unaware of the fact. In Bergman's film, I find that where his shock-method serves the subject of psychological fission—the fractured, fused, and superimposed faces—it exerts a legitimate fascination; where it is used for the purpose of reminding us that all art is vanity in a cruel world it is trite, it is déjà vu, above all it is a barbarous attack, sadistically motivated, on the nervous system. Heretofore Bergman had been a cat that walked alone. Up to 1964, his films had rarely called attention to themselves by exhibitions of outré technical virtuosity. With *Persona,* he came in from the cold. Shortly before denouncing modern artists for their inbred obscurities, he produced this film, exploiting the whole range of the new cosmopolitan film semantics: the hopscotch à la Godard, a disjunctive explosion of thematic images before the introductory titles, frequently interspersed glimpses of a movie camera and sounds of the "silence" horn that announces a take, a narrator who abruptly introduces the single change of setting, simulations of frayed or burning celluloid in the projector, and stray footage from other films, principally his own.

The most abusive device here is that violent interruption of the continuity, sufficiently oblique as it is, with snatches of filmmaking (or film-wrecking). This is curiously in line with the savage practice of defeated artists in our time who look to avenge themselves for their own impotence by turning their rage onto the audience in the form of refusals to make sense, in obscenity—either verbal or dramatized—by a general display of temper tantrum, like that of a child who can't solve his long-division sums or correctly remember his Latin declensions. Films have a rhythm of life; the rhythms vary widely among individual directors and our own are adjusted accordingly. But this ruthless destruction of the art-flow, which is the lifeflow, this switching off the current, as it were, is an unmistakeable affront, a suicidal impulse diverted resentfully toward a faceless legion of surrogates called all those others. The sensation I personally receive from such an atrocious strategy is comparable to that of having someone cut off the light when I'm absorbed in reading a book, or ruining the Mozart I'm listening to by interjecting another program from a tinny transistor. Even closer to the synapses affected, it is like being curtly interrupted in the rapt and reverent act of making love. For this profoundly physiological reason, I find the film unseeable. I could scarcely sit it through twice in order to take notes. The ingenuity that distinguishes the Elisabeth-Alma embroilment is for me seriously minimized by the intermittent outrages which no pretense of artistic license can fortify. If I am nonetheless willing to devote several pages to a patient exploration of what I think Bergman is otherwise saying, it is in the interest of clarity, not of hospitality towards the whole.

Strindberg's one-act play, *The Stronger,* in which a psychological duel between two women reveals that the one who remains silent is the stronger of the two, pointedly offers itself as a source of *Persona.* The situation in the film, however, is represented in a psycho-symbolic manner, highly allusive, mutable, surreal, and far more insubstantially than the configured world of *The Silence.* That the attitude of Alma, the nurse, towards her patient, Elisabeth Vogler, is increasingly during the action that of Anna towards Ester in *The Silence* is the first pitfall to avoid. *Alma* recognizably stands for soul, which may deceive one into contending that Elisabeth is body and that in the course of Alma's long trial by silence the roles are reversed. In one sense the reversal does take place. Alma sucks Elisabeth's blood, in one of her aggressive onsets; Elisabeth robs Alma of her self-possession. Alma becomes a physical wreck, losing her power of speech; Elisabeth recovers so far as to say, "Nothing". But one should not expect complete consistency to follow these exchanges. Any sentimental or lofty interpretation of soul should be avoided. In common if slightly old-fashioned parlance, a soul is simply a person, a unit, as when one speaks of a village numbering two thousand souls. Alma, the creature you see at the natural level, has a rather drab soul. I doubt that one can appreciate the sardonic beauty of Elisabeth's relationship to Alma if one commences with the notion that we are dealing with a single divided psyche. Once I suspected so. I abandoned the theory because it didn't work without forcing and there are too many other things it does not explain. I am far from insisting that every detail be explicable but the value of certain nuances need not be avoided.

Initially, to face the fact that Elisabeth has the name Vogler, that of the artist from *The Magician*, secures one strand for certain as we advance into the labyrinth. Vogler, too, was silent as part of his mystery. Elisabeth is silent for another reason; according to the doctor who knowingly describes her predicament for her at the beginning of the film, she was suddenly overcome in the middle of a performance in the theatre by the falsity of always playing a part, tortured by "the hopeless dream of *being*; not seeming, but being". She retreated into silence to obviate the need for playing any part at all on stage or off. Ironically, she will be asked to play a part for Alma; when she refuses, Alma must play out her own, with devastating consequences. But this is to anticipate.

Mrs. Vogler, listening to the radio in her hospital room, hears a woman's voice delivering the following speeches, after each of which she breaks into laughter, more pitying than derisive.

> Forgive me, forgive me, my darling. You must forgive me! Your forgiveness is all I crave. Forgive me—and I can breathe.
> What do you know of mercy? What do you know? What do you know of mercy?

In the original script, Arthur Gibson has reported, there is yet another speech, not in the Svensk Filmindustri script I have consulted. Here my memory sticks. I do not believe it was in the film as shot. "O God, you who are somewhere out there in the darkness that surrounds us all, have mercy on me. You who are love, pure love." Whether or not it is in the film is no matter, if it had once been intended. For this is obviously the old outcry of Bergman's Jack and of the Knight, Blok, combined with David's formula of *Through a Glass Darkly* (God is love), already repudiated or at least put to question by Blom the organist in *Winter Light*. Taken together, these speeches in context are versions of histrionic anguish that arouse the mirth of Mrs. Vogler. Later that evening, she watches the television; when she sees a Buddhist monk burning himself alive in Vietnam, her eyes fill with tears. The banality of the personal turmoil expressed in the radio-play speeches, by contrast with the television image, the absurdity of verbal fiction faced by silent life, is soon reenacted by Alma and it is to her progressively vocal role we must now turn. During the radio sequence, Alma comments that while she too is interested in films and theatre, she doesn't know much about them; but she thinks "art is terrifically important in life". She blunders on: "I shouldn't be talking to you about that sort of thing. It's treading on thin ice, isn't it?" Indeed it is and she is the one who is treading.

They move to a villa at the seashore to speed Mrs. Vogler's convalescence; there the monologue is resumed. Alma talks with no vocal reciprocity from her patient. Soon she is retailing a sordid little sex encounter on a beach where she and a girl friend, lying naked, had been surprised by two boys with whom they had coupled as thoughtlessly as rabbits; following which, Alma went home to her lover, Karl-Frederik. After dinner and a bottle of wine she went to bed with him. "We've never had it so good together, before or since! Can you imagine?" She became pregnant and a friend of Karl-Frederik got rid of the foetus for her. "We were both equally pleased. We didn't want children". She tries to carry this off impassively, dismissing the idea of a bad conscience, but in a minute she is desperately crying.

The continuity here is especially important. Alma is shortly telling Elisabeth that after seeing her performance in a movie one evening she came home, looked in the glass and thought how much alike they looked. Elisabeth was prettier, of course; still, "I think I could change myself into you. If I tried hard. I mean inside me." This wishful resolution is followed by the brief strange halucination of Elisabeth visiting her in the night.

Can we by now ask who Alma is as an ostensible person? She has a basic misconception of herself, an ideal psychic costume of which, under the pressure of Elisabeth's silence, she is being rapidly divested. First she describes herself as a good little bourgeois who had one great love but will settle down to marry her dear Karl-Frederik. Next she discloses that she has no real feelings, that feelings overtake her without moral sequence or value. Nevertheless she is cracking; she begins to discover her own unreality and the shape of a bad conscience. To repair her image she begins to identify herself with Elisabeth, revealing that she believes she might very well become Mrs. Vogler, which can only mean at the mundane level that she, once given the chance, could be a great actress. Where does she fetch her ideas, such as they are, and her false views of herself? Spengler called Ibsen's Nora "a bourgeois derailed by reading". Alma is a bourgeois derailed by theatre, specifically by film, I would say; a romantic nonentity, an Emma Bovary corrupted by fictions. She imagines Elisabeth coming to her in the night, i.e., being touched by Art.

When, the following day, she reads an unsealed letter Elisabeth has written, she is quickly deflated; the actress has confided to her correspondent that she finds Alma amusing and that the girl's ideas are divorced from her behavior. "She's fond of me, even a tiny bit in love, in an unconscious, charming way. It's fun studying her." Alma tries to conceal her knowledge of the letter's contents but her bitter insecurity is uppermost. Determining to break Elisabeth's silence, she tries appealing to her calmly; when that brings no result she loses control, accuses the woman of exploiting her, confesses that she has read the incriminating letter, shouts wildly: "And you got me to talk. You got me to talk of things I've never told anyone!" One cannot help but remember that in *The Magician* Sara the maid, same actress, claimed she had been seduced by Simon, the Vogler Coachman—seduced by the theatre—and that Mrs. Egerman, who thrust herself on Vogler, afterward tells her husband that Vogler had undermined her resistance! At a pitch of frustration, Alma theatens Elisabeth with a potful of scalding water, finally eliciting from the mute actress a scream of fear—"No! Don't!"—the only words she utters before the last. Alma is for the moment proud of herself and mollified. The truce is brief, but before she mounts to her next crescendo of reproaches there is an interlude, during which the two women are visited by Elisabeth's "husband". We are not to imagine this is a literal visitation.

Why is Mr. Vogler there? Who is he? On my sustained assumption that the sex of Elisabeth is essentially unimportant, since the name Vogler is the key, I would revert to Bergman's previous and repeated reference to the theatre as his wife or, in another mood, as a wornout mistress. Now, if Mrs. Vogler is, so to speak, the Bergman mouthpiece, mask, *persona,* her husband would be the theatre. Early in the film, Alma reads a letter to Elisabeth, purporting to be from Vogler, her husband, who can't understand why she has left him or what the trouble is.

Have I done you wrong in some way? Have I hurt you without knowing it? Has some awful misunderstanding come between us?. . . .We've been so close to each other. . . .You have taught me that we must see each other as if we were two children full of kindness, but ruled by forces we can only partly control. . . ."

The theatre is a child-like, well-intentioned activity, nonetheless governed by larger, worldly considerations.

On the verge of her most intensely suppressed confession, which erupts from her in the form of a transference, Alma invokes, is perhaps possessed by, theatre, illusion, the protective lie, in the person of this alleged husband who cannot conceivably be a material Mr. Vogler, needless to say. Elisabeth watches in a detached way as the man—her husband?—mistakes Alma for his wife and makes love to her. Here, the dialogue is wonderfully at cross purposes, for the man is all the time addressing Elisabeth, while Alma, answering the man, is really talking to a romantic simulacrum—Karl-Frederik—in theatrical language. She is already half out of her *persona,* moving into the truth about herself which she will speedily impose on Elisabeth as *her* sins. A reader who has not seen the film must imagine that this is no mere exchange of theatre lines; the scene advances by stages of visual metamorphoses and voices not quite anchored to their respective vessels. The husband, in short, is trying to coax Elisabeth back by assuring her that if she loves her work, her craft, she will be loved in return. Thereby, *"you form a small fellowship. It gives security,* you see a chance of holding out". (Italics mine.) Alma picks up his cue to interpolate, "I love you as much as ever. Don't be anxious, my darling. We have each other. That's so, isn't it?"

Mr. Vogler, still speaking to Elisabeth, answers, "Yes. And the important thing is *the effort itself. Not what we achieve.* To think of each other as children. Tormented, helpless, lonely children. . . ." And Alma immediately babbles, in Elisabeth's person, about her little boy. She is now sliding out of herself. even as she disgorges herself. "Tell your little boy that Mummy has been ill but she's longing for her little boy." This is an extraordinary sequence: for Alma, it is surely clear, all terms that have a dedicated application are erotic, all emotional affirmations are addressed to her personally. Art is saying something to the artist which cannot possibly be understood by the Almas of this world.

The husband vanishes and Alma is unleashed. Beginning with the words, "It was one evening at a party . . .", she launches into a vociferous accusation. Elisabeth, she asserts, unsatisfied with her art, realized she lacked the maternal spirit and allowed herself to become pregnant. Faced with the prospect of motherhood, however, she was afraid:

> afraid of responsibility, afraid of being tied, afraid of leaving the theatre, afraid of pain! But all the time playing a part, that of the expectant mother, meanwhile trying several times to get rid of the foetus, wihout success. When you found there was no going back, you began to hate the child and you hoped it would be stillborn!
> You hoped the child would be dead!
> You wanted a dead child!

Her tirade climbs to a level of insistent hysterical torment in which she recapitulates the shameful details, always attributing the deeds and the emotions to Elisabeth. (Note the change of tense toward the end.)

> After a long, difficult delivery. . . .you looked with disgust and horror at your pulsing, deformed baby and whispered, "Can't you die soon, can't you die?" But it survived, screamed day and night and you *hated* him. . . . The boy was taken care of by relations; you could leave your sick-bed and go back to work. But your suffering was not at an end. The little boy was seized by a violent incredible love for his mother. . . .You've tried and tried to return this love but it's no good—your meetings with the boy are cruel and clumsy. . . .he loves you and he's so soft and you want to hit him for not leaving you alone. . . .You think he's repulsive and you're afraid.

Alma breaks off, changing the focus of her attention for a moment. "What are you hiding there? The snapshot of your little boy. The one you tore up! We must talk about that. Tell me about it, Elisabeth! All right, then I will!" Now she repeats the foregoing tirade all over again, in the same words, beginning, "It was one evening at a party. . . ." I have heard the view expressed that in this outburst Alma has been telling Elisabeth Vogler the naked truth about her concealments, exposing the secret life of the actress. I cannot accept this explanation. On the contrary, I believe she has been ranting about herself, desperately trying to unload her own guilt onto the artist. There are three principal reasons, supplied by what one sees, for my so believing.

First, I find no justification for the inference that Elisabeth Vogler has a boy. She is supposed to have torn up a picture of that boy but surely if Bergman had intended us to think of a literal child, he would have provided the "husband" with a single line or a phrase, at least, about "our child". There is no such reference, either in the letter which Alma read in the hospital nor from Mr. Vogler in person. The "snapshot of a boy" may simply mean a reminder of life. Secondly, Alma, as I said, repeats her tempestuous rehearsal of attempted abortion and hatred of the child. Why, if she is not frantically seeking to convince herself that it is Elisabeth she is talking about by reiterating doggedly the whole story? Finally—and this seals my conviction—after the duplicated recital, her next speech is a last-ditch grasp of her own identity. "*No*, I'm not like you! I *don't* feel as you do. I am Sister Alma. I am only here to help you. I am *not* Elisabeth Vogler. I'd like to have— I have—I love—I haven't. . . ." This broken sentence tells her story, does it not? Then at last she swerves into sheer incoherence as she moves around the villa, gathering up her belongings. Scraps of her speech isolate the several subjects of the film: pain, identification with Elisabeth, even snatches of what sounds like film-production talk. Here is how her jabberwocky is translated in the dialogue script I have from the Svensk Filmindustri language department.

. . . .You can do what you like with me. You'll never get at me. Say defend nothing—Cut a light—A sort of other. Not now no. No, no. Warning and without times. Uncounted. When it should happen it didn't happen as a failure—yourself where you are. But I ought to do it. . . .Takes, oh yes. . . . but where is nearest. . . .it's called what—no, no, no—us—we—no—I. The words many and then disgust. . . .incredible pain—the throw.

For a lucid moment, nurse and "patient" are back in hospital. Elisabeth's face is sweating. Alma patiently asks her once more to speak, to repeat after her the word, "Nothing". Elisabeth does so. Alma is purged. Mrs. Vogler has seemingly recovered, nourished on Alma's misery. She has nothing to offer in return, no consolatory answer.

The story part of the film ends with Alma walking unsteadily with her suitcase to the bus, thoroughly voided, having forced Elisabeth Vogler to destroy her by evoking her life lie. According to the original script, Bergman had intended a narrative voice to announce that Mrs. Vogler, the actress, had recuperated and returned to the stage. In the film we hear nothing more of her. I think we might assume, if we demand such conclusions, that she has learned there is no escape from theatre in life. Alma's escape is fatal. The end returns to the beginning. A strange, fragile boy, sitting on a cot or slab, repeats his preliminary gesture of incantation, bringing into shape on the surface of a milky screen the face of a woman which suggests, but is not distinctly, Mrs. Vogler. Then the empty-frame end of a filmstrip runs through a projector, and the director's voice is heard, off-track. The reality of theatre has the last word.

I do not know precisely who that boy is; to try identifying him as a substantial son of either woman will, I'm sure, lead you nowhere save into a boobytrap. What does one bring into being on a screen? An image, a *persona,* the film itself. What would be the issue of the artist and his medium—Elisabeth and Vogler? Art, not a human child, is the created offspring. And it may be that at the same time this boy expresses the childhood sense of wonder at images magically thrown, Bergman's cardinal experience as a boy, which he was now feverishly trying, amid fierce self-denials, to recapture. That he did not intend to have us accept the boy literally is surely indicated by his not listing the character in the credits of the film.

I think it is far from irrelevant to observe that Bergman himself, after a long absence and a crisis of allegiance, returned to the theatre as Director of Dramaten in 1963.

If there is a theological dimension to this film, I did not strongly feel it. Those who prefer interpretations that transcend the tiresome tread of quasihuman problems and the importunate personality of the self-conscious artist are referred to Mr. Gibson's vision of this film.[97] (See also, Appendix I.) For myself, I have learned in Bergman movies always to look for the personal involvement first. His subject, whatever ramifications and ideal extensions may be suggested, is forever himself. In *Persona,* among a diversity of excursions, he does seem to have faced the devouring necessity of the artist, as he sees it, to exploit the feelings of others; he states further, with even more merciless finality than in *The Magician,* the pitiful need of ordinary souls to be exploited, to empty themselves into the rhetoric of art so that they are left at the last with nothing of themselves. Their small vengeance is to repudiate their guide into the abyss.

"No, I'm not like you. I don't feel as you do. I am Sister Alma. . . .
You are Elisabeth Vogler". And Mrs. Egerman had finally said to the
other, unmasked Vogler: "I have never seen you before"

The Hour of the Wolf

Penelope Houston, one of the few critics writing in English who has not
been overpowered by Ingmar Bergman's invitation to anxiety, expressed
doubts on the subject of *Persona* in *The Spectator* of September 29, 1967,
that summarize admirably my case against all Bergman's later production.

> His films look progressively more hermetic—a hospital without visiting days,
> where surgeon Bergman and matron Bergman brood over the condition of
> patient Bergman. . . .Maybe one's quarrel with Bergman has to do with a
> feeling that even austerity begins to look like a special kind of emotional
> self-indulgence.

Much of the special interest that adheres to this film, as well as to *The
Silence* is, of course, the not entirely fortuitous nature of its "modern-
ity"; it is in harmony with our disharmony; it is without foundations,
febrile, technically high-strung; it is the thing we know we are and
may suggest that Bergman has keen insights into our condition. I think
he has stumbled into contemporaneity. While still asking the nineteenth-
century question of Does God exist?, he begins to ask in The *Silence* and
Persona the question nearer to us of Does Man exist? After the modern
ordeal of discovering by what numerous inner and outer determinisms
man is governed and of what ignoble stuff he is made when you remove
him not so much from religion, itself, that *sine qua non* of Bergman for
the secure life, but from the sanctions of a social commonwealth, the
guarantees of justice, the intricate, self-preserving defense of manners,
the scale of values which, however imperfect and arbitrary, gives his
life dignity by lending it aspiration, then what kind of figure does he
cut? Lamentably often an hysteric, a modish barbarian, a fractional
organism. Bergman has no intellectual clue to this condition; he glimpses
the ruin but cannot understand how it got there. The West is sapped by
moral anarchy; he seems to think that the devil in his cupboard is
responsible. His conception of evil is intense but provincial; his concep-

tion of possibilities is equally limited. Our sense of tragedy comes from our profound recognition that we are not free. For Bergman, tragedy seems to consist in what freedom we have. He should have been a Calvinist.

In what I am forced to call his Middle Period, from the present perspective, Bergman's films expressed a nostalgia for Europe, if only a Europe of the mind; they were thereby humanized. After *The Virgin Spring*, the more he cultivated the home scene and that island beyond, the more abstract he became, the more his sympathies withered. Much has been made of his pessimism. He is a pessimist in his nerve-ends, chiefly; there is nothing liberal and large about his pessimism because his spectrum is limited. He is a seismograph, merely trembling at the shocks he receives but there is in him no comprehension of any least cause of man's behaviour. This is why, when he has managed at times, with a great intuitive leap, to objectify his own anxiety in a single form that authentically suggests the universal ailment, he immediately flees the implication, collapses into solipsism or allows himself to be diverted by some peripheral nastiness or grudge. He is almost unique in the consistency with which he fails to shed his sicknesses by expressing them, generally conceded to be a blessing of the artistic process; almost it seems as if by expressing them he compounds them.

Any expectation that *Persona* was more than a skirmish in his inconclusive battle with the duplicity of the artist was certainly frustrated by *The Hour of the Wolf*. This film is almost pure dementia. The chaos of *Persona* is an irritating but relatively ordered choas made brittle by the exacerbated will behind it but yielding, at least, an optional set of configurations which could be related to the psychic life within a discernible, if not fully defined, duo of personalities. *The Hour of the Wolf*, chronologically trackable, never rises to the level of any implication you can invent for it, never becomes definition; in it Bergman explores nothing, creates nothing; this is wholly a disintegration product, replying to no serious question; it is theatrically shoddy and built on an ill-bred premise. The tone is that of polemic and self-pity. One feels that this is a movie which a man made instead of going mad. From the point of view that respects life, that is not an unimportant strategy. Still and all, a movie is made to be looked at.

Transactions between the entertainer and his public and the agents thereof are almost always ironic. At this hour of the wolf, by all means, when Bergman was less than ever attempting to ingratiate an audience of any size, United Artists secured the world rights to distribute *Persona,* along with an option to distribute a forthcoming Bergman film. The exact terms arranged are already a subject for secrecy and wild allegation, but I was openly informed at the time that a half million dollars to Svenskfilm was a modest estimate. Half a million dollars to watch a man putting on a hair shirt in an upper berth! Persona set Bergman right with critics of the advanced-purism wing, but since he hates critics as he hates happiness this could have been little consolation. And the fortune earned by the film, however much was left for Bergman after state taxes had reduced his share, was probably no comfort either. No rewards from plutocracy or acclaim from the loges cheer him; if there is any chance of his being bucked up, Bergman will spurn it. H. L. Mencken has classically defined puritanism as "the haunting fear that someone, somewhere, might be happy."

The most interesting thing about *The Hour of the Wolf* is its title, the dark promise never fulfilled. Bergman coined a saying with an antique air. "The hour of the wolf is four o'clock in the morning: the hour when most people die and most babies are born". In the Bergman universe nothing is certain but death and babies, tomb and womb, death and birth. The film has two framing devices, both of them superfluous. The techniques that reveal technique in *Persona* might be considered organic, as Susan Sontag believed,[98] even as they demolish the art to which they are calling attention, but Bergman himself doesn't seem to know when he has invented something propitious and when he has a gimmick. He employs the same kind of introduction to *The Hour of the Wolf,* without those thematic details of suffering and cruelty featured in the previous film. We hear the voices of the director, the cameraman, the sound technician, and the clapper (inclusion of the scriptgirl was somehow overlooked), and we shortly learn that this has nothing to do with anything in the movie. If this is going to be a signature, reminding us that we are in the presence of make-believe, it is pretty fatuous; repetition will make it a convention which will be accepted as part of the make-believe. Enclosing the narrative is another parenthesis. Alma,

the wife of the subject, her husband, who has vanished into thick air—
something sulphuric about it—is first shown after giving an offscreen
narrator Johan's diary on which the film is supposed partly to be based;
in a face-front. Dutch-door shot, she explains the little she knows about
the *untergang* of Johan Borg.

I suppose the names given to the characters in this film have a meaning for Bergman. They do not stimulate our interest in the people we
see, however, since nobody in this movie has any dimensions. Johan
Borg does not seem to invite comparison with Isak Borg and perhaps
by now Bergman just liked the name Alma. Veronica *Vogler*, with whom
Johan has had an affair—during which, we are told, he was afflicted by
jealousy as manic as that of Marcel Proust when infatuated with Al-
bertine—is at present the mistress of an art-fancying creep, the Baron
von Merkens; this may very well signify that the artist has become the
whore of collectors but I'd rather not follow that lead because it takes
us nowhere we haven't all been.

Crack-up is the subject of the story. Concentration is almost entirely
on the unattractive and paranoid figure of the painter, Borg, who for
no adequate reason given or for so many reasons that they are collec-
tively preposterous is taking leave of his senses, within the setting,
mainly, of his own mind but nominally situated on an island which
Bergman in the script bothers to identify as Frisian. Borg is hemmed in,
by his own choice; surrounded by a company of decayed upper-class
specimens who never existed outside Strindberg's *The Ghost Sonata*.[99]
Since Borg hates his neighbors at the outset—early on, he knocks down
a gossiping curator whom he considers tiresome—there is no justification for his accepting a dinner invitation from the von Merkens, except
Bergman's need to display everyone present, in the film's showcase scene,
as a figure from Madame Tussaud's waxworks. This is an exhausted
exercise, even in Swedish literature; the possessing classes have been
incessantly washed up, post-Strindberg, by Hjalmar Bergman, Olle
Hedberg, Agnes von Krusenstjerna, and Sigfrid Siwertz. At this bizarre
gathering, Johan Borg is intended as a model of the crucified artist.

> Forgive me. I call myself an artist for lack of a better name. In my creative
> work there is nothing implicit except compulsion. Through no fault of mine
> I've been pointed out as something extraordinary, a calf with five legs, a

monster. I have never fought to attain that position and I shall not fight to keep it. Oh yes, I have felt megalomania waft about my brow, but I think I'm immune. I have only to think for a moment of the utter unimportance of art in the world of men to cool off. But the compulsion is still there, all the same.

"There speaks an artist!" applauds Corinne von Merkens, without irony. And "A real confession!", cries Ernst von Merkens.

At no common-sense level does the film work and it should if it is by initial implication about a human relationship. Johan tells Alma at fair length that story, which by now everyone knows, about being locked in the closet when he was a boy; the details have become lurid in the retelling. What is so bald in this version is the unlikelihood that he wouldn't have told Alma the story long ago, for they have been married for some time, thus obviating the step-by-step recital we hear. At the other extreme, in the scenes at the castle, there is no normally pedestrian conversation at all. Everyone says exactly the speech which will consort with the label already pinned to him. Corinne says things like this as she shows her leg to the Borgs. "It's a scar from another man's, shall we say, advances. A perpetual source of renewed excitement. It's all very trivial, of course, but to me it is stimulating. Soon I'll have to think up something new." Time-honored Bergman interludes obediently reappear in the form of the puppet show and the editorial music. Mozart's *The Magic Flute* is called upon to revive the Jack lament. "O eternal night, when will you vanish? When will my eyes discover the light?" Lindhorst explains: "Mozart, seriously ill, feels the words with a secret intensity. And the chorus and orchestra answer with, 'Soon, soon, stripling—or never!' " The fact that Lindhorst, an archivist, is a fake scarcely gives weight to whatever conviction we are supposed to share.

Bergman's manufacture of these dummies, most of whom have a "von" before their names, is a piece of plebeian spite as unworthy as anything the cinema has spawned. It is as tedious as a similar onslaught in Luis Buñuel's *The Destroying Angel*, in which the point was made within a half hour and the remainder simply drove spikes into a corpse. I can think of only one film from a great artist which is as contemptuous and as contemptible; and that is Charles Chaplin's *A King in New York*.

This kind of class-baiting is one of the most cowardly phenomena of our age, a flogging of dead horses. We are not in danger from a declining class puttering over its porcelain and its flowers. The world at large is characterized by a petit-bourgeois collectivism threatened by a horde from the deserts with sand in their eyes. To employ a group of has-beens, inartistically caricatured, as a scapegoat for nebulous grievances is an unmanly and unintelligent gesture. Bergman would not have the courage to pillory a houseful of mediocre officeholders, union officials, and sycophantic newspaper editors. To be sure I am begging a question, since a critical portrait of society was hardly what Bergman in this film was attempting to perpetrate.[100]

A general inference does follow, however. This film reminds one, if in the grossest form, that Bergman's social antenna has an extremely limited range. There is little point in criticizing what an individual artist cannot do until he tries to do it. Believable social intercourse is the most deficient area of Bergman's film world, inevitably, since he is the citizen of a country with a thin texture of social differentiation. The assets of social shading which one finds in English and French films, in the earlier works of Antonioni, in Cacoyannis' *A Matter of Dignity*, a film Bergman liked and persuaded Kenne Fant to import, with disappointing results, or in Torre-Nilsson's *Fin de Fiesta* where the intersections of political and sexual morality are brilliantly analyzed —these are beyond his command for they are beyond his ken. Where a classless norm is the ideal, interpersonal subtlety becomes a lost art; realism must find other outlets and abandon a world in which conversation and the right wine count. Bergman today is a symbolist or nothing.

Before the film is far advanced, Johan is the center of an uninventive whirlpool of hallucination, during which he walks upside down on the ceiling, all this mechanically cruder than the triple-exposure delirium of such German films in the Twenties as *Secrets of a Soul*, *Warning Shadows*, *Variety*, *The Last Laugh*, *und so weiter*. An old woman puts in a perfunctory appearance at the Borg cottage, a kind of clairvoyant; Borg makes a real or introjected flashback confession, but it leaves one cold, of having murdered a boy clinging to him among the rocks. (This is that same pale, tubular child he always features, which is no doubt a parable of Bergman's vain efforts to drown the memories of his childhood.) Ultimately, he vanishes, as we had learned earlier, and Alma delivers another speech to the us-narrator, which might have seemed reasonable and thought-provoking if we had cared enough about her husband or been introduced intimately to the springs of their strained relationship. She is puzzled by her part in Borg's dissolution. When a woman lives with a man she loves for a long time, she grows to be like him, to think and see the way he does.

> Was that why I began seeing those others? Or were they there after all? I mean, if I had loved him less and not bothered so much about everything around him, would I have been able to protect him better? Or was it because I didn't love him *enough* that I grew jealous? Was that why those cannibals, as he called them. . .was that why we came to such grief?

It's a speech for a movie Bergman didn't make—not then, at any rate. This one ends in the studio again with an offmike voice saying, "That's all for today". I swear I heard a sigh of relief.

Bergman has been quoted as saying, "*Vargtimmen* är fruktansvart personlig". "*The Hour of the Wolf* is horribly personal". The adverb was well chosen.[101]

The Shame

The Shame is personal too. The further Bergman's career advances, the higher rises my esteem for the text of *The Magician*. The world, it seems, is full of Egermans and Antonssons. Ingmar Bergman says, I have made a film about the absence of God and everyone agrees, Yes, God is absent. Mr. Bergman announces, I'm going to make a film that declares God is love and the same people chorus yes, God really is love. Bergman tells them, this film exposes the illusion that God is love. They cry out yes, it's nonsense. The master says this film is very personal. And his disciples confide, you can't hope to understand this film altogether, for it's highly personal. He says, I am making a film against the indignity of war because I can't live with this crime of humanity on my conscience. All the critics who have been complaining that Bergman was inhuman now write Ingmar Bergman has made a film which spoke to his conscience; it speaks to the conscience of us all.

After completing production of *The Shame* (*Skammen*) on Fårö in November, 1967, Bergman was interviewed by Lars-Olof Löthwall in Stockholm. The following testimony, taken from that interview, is the best possible introduction to the film itself.

> *Löthwall*: You have often mentioned the moment of pain which is the kernel of a film's inspiration. Can you trace *The Shame* back to such a moment?
>
> *Bergman*: No, that's a long tangled thread. It's an experience of humiliation. A long, painful experience of man's humiliation. For some time, since the moment of recognition, I have wondered how I would have sustained the experience of a concentration camp, of being forced into such a damnable position.
> How noble would I have been?
> At the bottom of everything there lies this abomination to which man is exposed, the world over: they club his head in, they scream at him, they assault him, they terrorize him.
> The older I get, the more ghastly it seems to me. And the harder it is for me to live with it in my conscience.
> This is what we are attempting, modestly, in *The Shame*: to show how humiliation, the rape of human dignity, can lead to the loss of humanity on the part of those subjected to it.[102]

From the witness point of his films, we are justified in reacting skeptically to Bergman's representation of himself as having for any considerable period of time concerned himself with man's humiliation beyond the province of personal agitation, the hunger for love and incapacity for loving, and the endless transactions of the famished spirit with a silent God.

The world of large conflicts, battles, and martyrdoms has never intruded on the neurotic-spiritual obsessions of his encapsulated characters who, since 1960 especially, have shown no interest whatever in the fate of mankind and, insofar as they have been tangible enough for us to expect opinions from them, have betrayed little deference toward its select representatives. The impending clouds of universal trouble have been but a gloomy *frisson* to enforce the one-track conviction that if man is not governed by divinity, neither his intelligence nor his courage can support him. Through the mouth of Johan Borg—let us have no qualms when attributing his views to those of his characters if the correspondence is as bright as noonday and virtually confessed—Bergman had said, "In my creative work there is nothing implicit except compulsion". His declaration in the interview quoted above confirms the remark. The long meditated theme of man's humiliation is a smoke screen. *Bergman's* humiliation, past and possibly to come, is the source of whatever emotion went into *The Shame*, the fear of what kind of figure he, Bergman, would present if placed in the position of millions of others on this earth in our time and in all our yesterdays. This is an understandable fear; most of us share it, but we don't nurse it! My contention here is that Bergman did not make of it a creative point of departure. His covering subject, "to show how humiliation . . . can lead to the less of humanity on the part of those subjected to it," is the vulnerable assumption on which the film is built, barely protected by the wording, "can lead". The film, in central effect, says that war does lead to the loss of humanity.

Ingmar Bergman lived through the Second World War directing plays in Sweden. Everywhere east, west, and south of Sweden people ⁚. ⁻ ⁚ millions were uprooted, ravaged, blown to shreds, tortured slowly, crippled for life, incinerated in cells, block-busted, and set on the roads homeless, their cities destroyed, sometimes in a night. Coventry, Hamburg, Rotterdam, Monte Cassino, Stalingrad, and Dresden were ravaged; one has only to name them to hear the bell toll. Did the survivers lose their humanity? Norway was invaded, Finland fought two armies, and Denmark was occupied. Did Norwegians, Danes, and Finns lose their humanity? What is it that conserves humanity? Fighting for it or remaining neutral? The truth none of us likes to face because it puts us in a seriously awkward position, strapped by our fears, harried by our consciences, prompted by our intelligence but as much by our horror, to assert that nothing good can come of war, the truth is that some people, under duress, lose their humanity and others do not. Others find their humanity. The truth is that if you search the annals of history you will come up with the inordinately disturbing answer that life has an unfailing and miraculous way of renewing itself through catastrophe, though at a moment that seems eternal war leaves nothing but scorched earth and a pile of skulls.

If the answer were simple, man would have stopped making war long ago. Clearly—this may be the most sinister aspect of the subject —even in our age when we have the power and, from what one sees around one, the unconscious wish to destroy all life on the planet in order to still forever the unsatisfied envy and the itch to violate without which man seems incapable of existing, war still has its appeal. In a shorter view, regrettably, it is a necessary evil. Ask the Israelis or the Vietnamese, North and South, if they think the only issue of war is loss of their humanity. Some will say yes; many will laugh in your face. How much humanity have the Czechs lost by not being able to make war? Anybody can Wagnerize his imagination with forecasts of doom; anybody can earn applause easily by announcing that he is against violence in any form. Odd, is it not? Never before have so many people protested their hatred of violence; never, perhaps, was violence so endemic, and never have people so deceived themselves about their feelings. Tens of thousands who self-righteously inveigh against bull-fighting, boxing, crime on the street, and the war in Vietnam or the Middle East believe absolutely in reforming society by wrecking as much of it as they can lay hands on in the hope that they will inherit what they will in fact have destroyed. Thousands think nothing of violating their neighbors with impositions of public pornography—precisely the people who applaud Bergman's humiliation anxiety and his spurious film.[103]

For spurious it is, even if we acknowledge that it does depict a kind of suffering. The premise is as humiliating as any experience named by Bergman. For he takes his stand here on an *imagined* humiliation; his film is not even about suffering which people living among us have undergone in wartime; it is a projection of suffering which might overtake people imagined, rather poorly, by Ingmar Bergman. When reporters asked him if a parallel with the Vietnamese might be drawn, he did not say no; he thought it might have that application. An honest answer would have retorted, "Of course not! I know nothing of those people, the sound of their prayers, the taste of their rice, their powers of resistance or their timeless expectations". To take credit for such an analogy is paltry and undiscerning. *The Shame*, a regional film, patently pleads in advance for sympathy not earned and, if the Swedish government is as wily or as lucky as it has been before, will not have to be earned. I find this motivation, unconscious or not, radically unadmirable. This is the familiar spectator neurosis in full flower, projected at just the right psychological, internationally nervous moment to receive compliments for its essential trepidity.

Why Bergman made this movie would be consummately irrelevant, I agree, if the film stood up under scrutiny. Be it noted, first, that in the treatment of *The Shame* there is no nonsense about the duplicity and imposture of cinema art. When it suits his convenience, Bergman believes that art can and should mirror "reality," if it is a reality that is making him sufficiently uneasy. Miss Sontag's belief that in *Persona* Bergman was enlisting the eloquence of silence against the impossibility of assimilating the global outrage in art was not confirmed by a sequel.

When we accept the empirical terms with which we are expected to be content, then, the conception of *The Shame* is shorn of nearly all veracity by which you can adequately criticize it; the film is placed at an imaginary hour on the rim of an imaginary war on an imaginary island, inhabited by fairly unimaginable people. At the start, a central problem was raised and never solved. Bergman and Svensk Filmindustri had expected the production to be heavily supported by an American film-company investment. The invaders of that island, plausibly, were to be indistinctly foreign, with Anglo-American to be employed as the international patois. As I understand the sequence, the American investors wanted the film to be in color. Bergman said no, he wanted it gray, psychologically and chromatically grey. I respect that conviction. The potential producers did not. If any other factor was in dispute, I am ignorant of it. The offer was withdrawn. Svensk Filmindustri and Bergman made *The Shame* with a more limited budget than the action thereof required. They had a red-tape time of it trying to procure airplanes, tanks, and a submarine; they settled for less. This is why the invasion, the whole commando engagement and pseudo-terror has a spare look, not because Bergman was creating a microcosm of war with intentional understatement. (The explosions were very well managed). And this is why there were no foreigners. With no foreign investment, there was no obligation to use foreign actors. Logical enough, but in my opinion it didn't come off. We are cajoled into accepting an invading army that speaks Swedish. Whether or not this sort of thing is done in the films of other countries is beside the point; here it was dreamy, especially since, however well Swedes may be able to mime other emotions, they are emphatically unable to simulate belligerence. Never for one moment did I believe that dangerous men were abroad on that island, but a casting problem was solved.

Bergman made it easy for himself all along the road to commitment. With a completely defensive action he would have found it harder to wheedle sympathy. His population—the character of it we never really catch, because this is not a film about a people, it's a film about three people—is represented as having no cause for which to fight, no allegiance. They are doing no harm. The world, so far as we are informed, has been at war for years; these people expect to remain unmolested and in that ridiculous night interrogation, conducted by the director of *I Am Curious*, the only vocal victim, Eva Rosenberg, almost comically maintains that they don't know what is going on because they haven't listened to the broadcasts and they can't tell one side from the other. Is this supposed to win our sympathy?

Who are Jan and Eva and what do they want? They are musicians, first violinists from a disbanded symphony orchestra; they play no music because "music is dead". Another problem is solved. They have been musicians all their adult lives, we infer. But I don't believe it. How does an actor persuade you he is a musician, without an instrument? That's his problem. I only know that once I saw Charles Bickford, an actor consistently taken for granted by snobs, play a blind painter. He was not only believably blind but acceptably a painter and I can't now recall if in the film he even lifted a paintbrush. Bickford had the kind of physical relatedness to things which is less common than you might suppose if you haven't been looking for it. When he took an ax down from the wall, you felt he had taken down that ax every day for twenty years; when he removed a cork from a jug, he didn't just perform business; he focused the scene; when he was supposed to tie a knot in order to secure a packed pile of rawhides, he tied the knot. This is what I mean. If you have ever spent any time in the company of a musician, as Bergman certainly has, you could hardly escape noticing that surreptitiously he is always manipulating his hands by relaxing his wrists, pecking at a chair-arm or table-top to preserve his striking or fretting plasticity or, if he's a guitarist, to keep the fingertips hard. This is creative fidgeting, just what Jan or his wife never do, and I don't think they had been truck-farming long enough to lose the occupational reflexes of a lifetime. I don't know why Max von Sydow was plodding around with feet wide-spread, like a boob farmer. Jan had been exempted from service for a bad heart, not flat feet.

I stress such detail because Bergman announced so solemnly in interviews that the film was to have the feel of reality. Unreality begins here, in the physical fact. Psychologically, the solecisms are more serious. I said a moment ago that we presume the Rosenbergs have been farming a long time. It's hard to say. In contradistinction to many of Bergman's films that take place in a specified twenty-four hours or fewer, *The Shame* is hazy in its duration. But the behavior of Jan under pressure is very much dependent on the length of time he has presumably been demoralized by living in a state of siege. We are asked to believe that this man, who is shown as a hypochondriac but not as a jackal, would so far collapse out of himself as to shoot another man on order— he who has never used a gun, can't bear toothache, nor bring himself to kill a chicken—and subsequently to shoot a second, defenseless man voluntarily, in order to steal the fugitive's identification with which to escape in a boat to safety. I submit that this is inconceivable unless we have been convinced to begin with that Jan has no moral equilibrium at all, or that the time lapse is infinitely longer than implied. In conditions such as those of the Thirty Years War or those faced by villagers at the mercy of the Viet Cong, let us say, people are no doubt reduced to the status of animals that would turn on their own kind.[104]

Yet it appears as if with the first serious threat of violence this gentle invertebrate turns into an armed Goth. Is this not what a nonbelligerent neutral would like to assume, in order to ratify his neutrality? There was not a Swedish critic who objected to the imputation that given the circumstances the generic Swede contrived by Bergman would go to pieces and readily be a Judas. Is this not also the view of someone ignorant of the physical life who believes that a necessary consequence of physical action is naked aggression? Given as much as I have to go on about Rosenberg, I think he would have groveled on the ground before ever shooting Major Jacobi and that his assailants would have contemptuously left him there, or shot him in the head. There is even a doubt if the efficiency of war would have dictated the sadism of compelling an amateur to execute Jacobi. Again, Bergman played safe. He supplied a half-motive for Jan in his sexual jealousy of the Major. The wife in question, Eva, is fairly noble and, except for that violent domestic outbreak in the field, the only passionate moment in the film, stoical. She survives the ordeal with her humanity intact. I wonder, though, if she would have been quite so chummy with her husband at the end, after fully realizing she was married to something with the guts of a bat. In any case, she defends Bergman, for many critics, from the charge of having been equally ungallant to womanhood under the hypothetical conditions of disaster. With all Bergman's films in one's head, however, one gets tired of this irksome masochism by which his men always fold up and his ideal women have the patience of Griselda and the endurance of Mother Courage. He lines it up too neatly; at every stage Jan consistently retreats from the air raid, from the interrogation, where he faints, and from the pleas of Jacobi, which makes it the more unlikely that later having tasted blood he quickly becomes a carnivore.

There are too few characters who make their presence felt in this film to convey an authentic demonstration of what war might do to a community. Jacobi alone is believable, as the committed but secretly blasé Major who is destroyed by someone of half his stature, chiefly because Gunnar Björnstrand played him and Björnstrand, stout man, is always credible. I don't know why Filip shows up in that boat at the end of the film or why he drowns himself. Is he afraid of dying the slow way or is he being sacrificial so that there will be more room at the inn at Timoka? His face told me nothing.

The unreality is almost total. What is that set-piece doing there at the beginning, when Jan and Eva visit their friend, Lobelius, at his shop in Visby?[105] This sponge-cake mortal trots out his Meissen-ware music-box, or whatever it was, and the three sit and sip in that *främmande* (foreign) fashion of Swedes (apparently a long war has not improved anyone's gift for communication), while the whole film staggers to a halt before it is under way. Is he supposed to represent the remains of culture, this maidenly art dealer in an old curiosity shop? I wonder if Bergman really believed that the moment, as a scene, as cinema, as reality, as character exposition, was, even in the margin, illuminating.

Following this static scene there is another—the whole construction of this sequence is an error in film dynamics—between Jan and Eva at a table outdoors where, with the perversity of a Godard, Bergman decided to shoot, or later to edit, the entire scene, nearly, with his camera focused on Eva alone. This is the sort of thing that sticks out from a movie like a sore thumb and an infallible sign that a director is losing his hold on the content. There's a similar curiosity in *The Devil's Eye*, when the camera starts circling for no indisputable reason. Not surprisingly, this is just the moment when defenders of the film for other reasons will rush forward to repair the damage with a kind explanation. Mr. Stephen Farber who, with good intentions, misunderstands the late-Bergman as totally as anyone I have read, produced the following rationalization:

> Early in the film there is a very long scene, done in a single take, all shot from behind Jan's shoulder and looking at Eva's face as they have dinner together and she tells him of her strong desire for a child. We do not see Jan's face at any time during the scene, and so Bergman subtly reinforces Jan's isolation from Eva, his unwillingness or inability to pay attention to her and identify with her dreams.[106]

If we do not see Jan's face at any time, how can we arrive at a firm conclusion about his reaction? This is not subtle reinforcement; it has no psychological justification I could think of inventing. The perspective is so arbitrary it startles instead of preparing you for a subtlety. I suspect it was an idiosyncratic decision on Bergman's part, perhaps an affectionate prolongation of a Liv Ullmann closeup, for he made much of improvisation and departure from the script when he was interviewed about his method in this film. If he had clearly intended what Farber proposed, it seems to me he would have used nearly the opposite strategy: established Eva's sentiment, then cut to Jan's face so that while Eva was talking we would have noted the inattentiveness Farber claims to have deduced from the back of Jan's head.

Farber suggests that a later scene between Jacobi and Eva, which has a balance of shots from each witness point, strengthens his claim. I fear this is an earnest search for a justification of his first statements. His whole analysis of the film, which is methodical, seems to be based on an admiration for Liv Ullmann, for he is determined to make out that Eva has a fundamental change of role after the murder of Jacobi, from being the stronger of the couple to depending on Jan, who has now become the stronger because he has learned to kill. If she is dependent on him, that is only because by then she has nobody else in the world. But I saw no sign of her believing she was now protected by a resolved, if maniac, husband. Farber, like so many critics, takes Bergman, therefore the film, at face value. "The capacity to destroy lies dormant in the artist's nature, Bergman seems to say; it is only a terrifying extension of the qualities of narcissism and detachment that make him an artist."[107] Does Bergman seem to be saying all that in *The Shame*? If he does, I think it's a critic's job to question him. The capacity to destroy may lie dormant in the nature of some artists, among them Bergman, as I shall shortly illustrate, if I haven't; it may lie dormant in numerous contemporary artists, for reasons that have more to do with the exhaustion of their idioms and their consequent feeling of inadequacy than with any innate tendency to kill. An artist is a maker; *self*-destruction is his more common fate. All of us are consumed by the process that gives us identity; the price of style, too, is death. On the artist in war, Farber approves Jacobi's sneer too readily: "The sacred freedom of art; the sacred slackness. . . ." Since musicians are the involved parties here, we would do well to consult the record of their activities in the Second World War. We might begin with those of Myra Hess and Yehudi Menuhin.

No, I don't think Bergman tells us anything in this film about the artist, about a crisis situation, about political neutrality, about any sacramental human engagement. Louis XIV, in a film made by Christian-Jacque, was made to say, "I think war is far too serious an occupation to be entrusted to the military". War is too serious an occupation to be entrusted to a film director with no faint experience of it. *The Shame* is nothing but a fright product. At the center there is a triangle situation, closely resembling those in *The Hour of the Wolf* and in *A Passion;* it is likely they have the same provenance in Bergman's mind. They constitute the only clarified human relationships to be found in these films; they substantiate the only unqualified subject, at the secular level, remaining to Bergman, the hopelessly vindictive opposition of man and woman. *The Shame* needed no war, and the story could have been told without the pretense of Bergman's vaguely afflicted consciousness of universal cruelty. If you were not told that Jan and Eva were musicians, you might fancy them a failed lawyer and his wife, or the proprietors of a *Tobak* shop in Visby, trying to go back to the land. Under the alien life burden, the man breaks, the woman does not; since she is sustained by the interest of another man more worldly, the husband finds a way, sanctioned by society, to kill his rival.

Bergman's imagination is often imperiled by his easy infatuation with the abyss, by the melodrama of the moral absolute, by the loss of heart, brain, and courage: the polar image, people drifting in a boat to nowhere. He simply had to get those floating bodies back into the Baltic; he couldn't wait for history to put them there. For Bergman, to imagine trouble is always to imagine the worst. Yet his worst here, in terms of the subject he proposed, is mild. When the time comes, there may not even be a boat.

The interview from which I quoted, preceding my remarks on *The Shame*, is a rich source for studying Bergman's serene belief that at the moment of interrogation he has reconciled himself with life, art, and criticism. If I return to that context it is because there are two prologues in it, so to speak, of his subsequent performances. The first of these performances was literally on stage; the second was the creation of his next film. With expansive toleration, Bergman expressed these disclaimers.

> I used to be very dependent on peoples' opinions of me. I was tyrannically vulnerable to criticism and was unhappy for days if anyone said anything wounding to me or about me. Today I don't care about anything except the life I have with friends and the work I have to do. This is the only thing that's important to me.
> I have no need of power.
> I have no need to be influential.
> I have no need to be a participant in, or a shaper of, Swedish cultural life.
> I have no desire to justify myself before criticism.
> I have no need at all to strike out or to be aggressive. I hate that.[108]

On February 27, 1969—February seems to be an upsetting month for

Ingmar Bergman—he was conducting an open rehearsal in a Stockholm theatre. A certain drama critic whose reception of Dramaten plays, and especially of the actors, had been far from hospitable was conspicuously in attendance. Bergman, according to the explanation he later gave to a newspaper editor, from whom I have the information, decided he would give this wasp "something to remember". As the critic made to cross the stage afterward, Bergman intercepted him and gave him a provocative shove in the chest. The critic paled, offered no resistance, and fell to the floor. Seeing blood in Bergman's eye, he remained there. Realizing that the man was not going to satisfy his need to punish him, Bergman desisted from the attack. But the most was made of the episode, of course. *BERGMAN ATTACKS DRAMA CRITIC!* The critic was persuaded to take Bergman into court, the director paid a fine, posed happily for press photographers, and announced that he had perpetrated this aggression for the sake of his actors and in their defense would do so again. The incident, at the physical level, is ludicrous; it is like an early Bergman film comedy with Björnstrand as the director and Åke Grönberg as the critic. Pro-Bergman Swedes assure me that the critic on the floor had been persecuting the actors. I know enough of the cultural scene to construe persecution as well-deserved criticism. I know nothing of this reviewer's work. When in Sweden since about 1963 I have ceased with a few exceptions to patronize the theatre; its standards have in my opinion fatally deteriorated. And the lack of a bracing, adverse criticism is the first reason I would give. On the other hand, I am not familiar with the details of the feud in question. The critic involved may have been out of his depth or unnecessarily personal. This is not the real point, is it? The point was symbolic. Bergman made the point—the final, outward token of his inner frustration. At this stage, the reader will need no interpretive guidance from me.

A PASSION

sthetically, *A Passion*, 1969, is both curious and dazzling, for it consists of a chain of self-justifying monologues from the principal characters, during which, more intensively than ever before, Bergman, via Sven Nykvist, photographs his select colony of faces in closeups prolonged to the limit, as if he thought he might finally break through to a previously inaccessible answer to human existence. These closeups are interconnected with just enough action of coming and going, brief outbursts of violence, or the aftermaths of violence to give the film, apart from any paraphrasable interest, a quite unique form and rhythm. In the hands of someone less skilled than Bergman, it is not a form I admire; it is closer by association to photo-fashion reporting than to the art of the motion picture. But the suave surface of Bergman's frames, in which faces are isolated in cameos or in nests of warm, birds-egg color, conceals an abyss which everyone (in Sweden, at least) I listened to or read on the subject, had managed to skirt without noticing its presence. The film had not been reviewed elsewhere when I wrote the following pages. As it meets the eye, *A Passion* does seem to be another consummation of what Dilys Powell of the London *Times* once and

".... The words many and then disgust. ..."

Alma (*in Persona*)

"My whole life .... is like a book of fairytales. But although the stories are different, one thread ties them all together and the same leit-motif recurs constantly."

Hummel (in *The Ghost Sonata*)

memorably called "the desperate clarity of the Swedish film".

Bergman has arrived at a point of no return. The content of this film is wholly allusive; the images are symbolic deductions from origins invisible, a choir of meanings unheard, an anthology of hints from nearly every motif he has expressed before, a gallery of icons, unidentifiable without a catalogue that names the sources and the conventions which alone give these icons viable significance. This is an arcane performance to which, if I were Catholic, I would point, as to a sin of pride. It is as-if Bergman had spent a lifetime making a rainbow, then in despair, because it always faded or returned in an arch to earth, split it into a thousand pieces. *A Passion* is a jigsaw puzzle of those pieces, an assembled mosaic, schematically incomplete, but with sufficient pictorial interest apparently to satisfy many spectators that they know what they're looking at, and if they do not it is no matter, for it is all so pretty. Surprising it was to see Swedish critics, with a single exception, embrace this film with superlatives that emphasized its "humanity" or its "new hope," to see it advertised with a quotation from a reviewer, "Bergman's most human film," an assurance that did little for the public attendance,

I might add. No doubt the guild was seduced by the chromatic charm of the movie, by the glimpses, actually few in number, of earth and sky which afford this work a radiance absent from the lenten cast of Bergman's preceding films to the number of six[109] and further by something they sensed as a social accusation—that somnambulist cliché—directed at people who "live against society".

Superficially, these elements are salient. Bergman must in truth be a magician, since the presence of them seems to have hindered most from observing that *A Passion* sums as a total, hopeless ambiguity wherein nothing is finally and endurably explicable: the central vision is one of an eternal reign of inscrutability, deceit, "humiliation," and indifference, with a saving proviso, reduced to code. It is the despondent modern subject. *The Ghost Sonata, Ash Wednesday, The Castle,* and *Waiting For Godot.*

In the first major interview that Bergman granted, in 1956 (from which I have before quoted), he said of the camera:

> I can't help thinking that I am working with an instrument so refined that with it it would be possible for us to illuminate the human soul with an infinitely more vivid light, to unmask it even more brutally and to annex to our field of knowledge new domains of reality. Perhaps we would even discover a crack that would allow us to penetrate into the *chiaroscuro* of surreality. . . .[110]

Allowing for the Faustian pose which was part of Bergman's earlier utterances, there is something altogether disregarding and sadistic in this expression of the lust to expose, to unmask brutally, to annex, to penetrate. These are infinitives that describe rape; they are sexually defined substitutes for the will to breach heaven. A disingenuous reproach to the above manifesto is given by Elis Vergerus in a speech which is the formal key to *A Passion,* not to the subject of the film but to its method, to its raison d'être at one level of artfulness.

> I don't imagine that I reach into the human soul with this photography. For God's sake don't think that. I can only register an interplay and counterplay of thousands of forces, large and small. Then you look at the picture and give rein to your imagination. Everything is nonsense. Games and fancies. You cannot read another person with the slightest claim to certainty.

The moral point of the film, in its peculiar way, is that you cannot read another person without adequate love or knowledge and the point for us, looking at the film, is that you cannot read its story with the slightest claim to certainty if you only look at the succession of shots Bergman has taken. Since the only way to get into a visual work of art is through its images, a subtle bit of cheating was involved here. The dialogue seems to be of little consequence in much of the film, partly because everyone appears to be talking to himself (the replies are often oblique), partly because the visuals are so luminous and dominant. Yet the solution to the whole, for the film is recondite, is given in its dialogue; if there were none, the film would be incomprehensible. One way of conceiving this work is to view it as a number of concentric circles. As I said on the subject of *Persona,* a written analysis can only take the prosaic way of articulating one circle at a time. Before proceeding to a synopsis, the purpose of which is thereafter to inform you that you should disbelieve most of what you have seen, it may be convenient to provide a rough index to the characters.

There are five of importance: Andreas Winkelman, described by Ingmar Bergman, on the sound track, as forty-eight and living alone in an island house with a leaky roof; a sick farmer, Johan Andersson, who eventually commits suicide because he is suspected of having murdered animals on the island; a self-righteous woman, Anna From, allegedly damaged by a car accident and ostensibly a widow, who lives with Andreas during much of the film; Elis Vergerus, an architect and amateur camera enthusiast, who appears to have fotogen rather than blood in his arteries, and his wife, Eva, adrift and unwanted because Elis is indifferent to the love she is prepared to give. To think of the relationships among these five as if they were established and developed in an anticipated psychological fashion is to misinterpret the film from the beginning. I am only erecting a temporary scaffold. Relationship is accurate enough, in the sense that one element in a grouping relates to another simply by being there, as a unit occupying the space with another unit. As I recite the sequences, I shall interpolate the indispensable questions that must be asked.

Andreas comes down from his rooftop, cycles to the postoffice, and greets old Johan, trudging by, asks after his health, and offers him cough medicine if he needs it.

Outside his house, he meets Anna From, who limps up, introduces herself, and asks if she can use the telephone. Andreas pretends to leave her alone but listens curiously to her conversation with Elis, who is in Stockholm at the moment. She is upset; she wants Elis to find out about some money deposited for her in Basel by her husband, also named Andreas, when her boy was born.

Immediately after she leaves, Max von Sydow (as himself) is asked by Bergman, offscreen, what personal view he has of Andreas Winkelman.

Andreas in his house finds the handbag Anna has left, opens it, and reads a letter from her husband refusing to renew their relationship and asking her not to try to get in touch with him.

Returning the bag to Elis and Eva Vergerus, where Anna is staying, Andreas is invited to return another time. In Sweden, there may be nothing odd about this vignette; anywhere else there might be a question as to whether the manner of these people suggests they are meeting for the first time or already acquainted.

In the interim, Andreas finds his small dog, which he loves, hanging by its neck in a tree, half choked to death. He soothes the animal.

Andreas goes to dinner with Elis, Eva, and Anna at the Vergerus house. Over the meal, three of the four chat of belief and disbelief, of what values they hold and what they live by. Elis refers cynically to a culture center he is designing for the city of Milan, "a formidable monument of cultural affectation. . . . a mausoleum for the utter meaninglessness with which people of our kind live". Anna indignantly reproves him for doing something in which he disbelieves, to which he retorts that if he did otherwise he would be idle. "What do *you* do?" he asks her pointedly. She explains that she tries to live in a form of truth and gives a complacent account of her marriage with her ex-husband, Andreas. They had lived truthfully with each other; if she now had the attitude toward her marriage that Elis has toward his culture center, she would have nothing in which to believe. Andreas Winkelman has contributed little to this conversation. Eva has amusedly recited the nature of her childhood belief in God; when pressed, she confesses that she still believes.

Andreas stays over at the Vergerus house. The next morning Elis asks

Andreas if he had been disturbed by anything in the night. Anna had called out "Andreas" during a nightmare. Andreas answers that he had awakened once but immediately slept again. Elis explains that Anna "still has nightmares after that accident". Andreas agrees absently, "I can imagine". (Which accident? Nobody has informed Andreas before that Anna was in an accident!) Vergerus shows Andreas the property and takes him to his studio in a converted mill, where he keeps a huge photo collection of clippings from magazines and newspapers, photos by the hundred he has taken himself of people eating, people sleeping, people in the grip of violent emotions. He shows Andreas a picture taken of Anna some years ago and one of her husband. To Andreas' uneasy question, "What sort of person was he?", Elis answers that he was a scientist of unproven ability, "a strange mixture of warmhearted good nature and ice-cold ruthlessness". He had been no good for Anna and, diffidently said, he had had an affair with Eva for a year. In the next short sequence, Andreas, helplessly drunk, is taken care of by Johan Andersson.

Eva, left alone for a few days while Elis is away, visits Andreas. She tells him the rest of Anna's story, adding that at the moment Anna is in the hospital having another operation on her leg. There had been a car crash in which husband and child were killed. Apologizing for being personal, Eva asks Andreas about his wife. (How does she know he had a wife?) She has left him, Andreas tells her, and he doesn't really expect her to come back. We learn for the first time, here, that Andreas is a geologist or has been one; he mentions the nightmares he used to have at the thought of going down into those French potholes. Eva, in her turn, admits without self-pity that Elis is tired of her; for him she is just part of the general weariness. The mood becomes hushed and amorous and at last they go to bed together. Very late, remembering a promise, she telephones Elis, long-distance, pretending that she is at home. Later still, Elis phones back, blandly explains to Andreas that he has not been able to rouse Eva with a phone call at home, that perhaps she fell asleep, and would Andreas mind going to see if anything is wrong? If there is not, he need not call Elis back; just explain to Eva that he was worried. The next day [?] Eva leaves on a ferry; she will be away for three weeks. (But she wasn't going anywhere!)

Narrator Bergman announces, over shots of butchered sheep, that a madman is amok on the island killing animals.

Elis, conversing with Andreas, informs him that Johan Andersson is suspected by the islanders of being the sheep murderer; he lives alone, he has no animals of his own, he has been in a mental hospital, and re- mained moody following his loss of a suit at law. This reminds Elis that Andreas had asked for a loan, which he now agrees to grant him and to draw up a statement with a lawyer so that Andreas can repay him in installments. (Have we heard Andreas ask Elis for a loan?) Since he needs money meanwhile, perhaps Andreas would like to write out the notes he has made for a gigantic survey of that confounded culture center in Milan. During this dialogue, some of the most pregnant in the film, Elis is rapidly taking photographs of Andreas and it is in this scene where he speaks the disclaimer I quoted above. "I don't imagine that I reach into the soul with this photography. . . ." The session is interrupted by Eva, asking Elis if he will take care of a thermostat. In the brief while before his return, Eva assures Andreas that she knows about him and Anna; though she is not jealous, she does feel that he should be warned. "I can't explain what I mean, but you must be careful." (*She* knows about Andreas and Anna? WE don't know about Andreas and Anna! Where is this film taking place? Offscreen?) The Elis-Andreas conversation is resumed, in the course of which we learn that Andreas has been in prison for forging cheques, speeding under the influence of liquor, and hitting a policeman.

With the next transition, we are smoothly informed by narration that Anna and Andreas have now been living together "for some months". He is assembling the Milan notes; she is engaged on a translation. She repeats her story of the complete affinity she had enjoyed with her hus- band. It was not an ideal marriage, as everyone thought; they did quar- rel, but never seriously. Once Andreas was unfaithful to her, but he came to her straight away and told her about it. She felt how much he really loved her and she felt better. Then came the accident. She relives the terrible details. She was driving, the road was slippery, the car skidded, and Andreas grabbed the wheel in vain. They plunged across a ditch and into a stone wall. Husband and child were killed. "They found us a few hours later. I didn't think life could look like that. I didn't think life would be a daily suffering".

Andreas meets Johan again. The old man is afraid he will be killed by the islanders. A note attached to a rock thrown through the window warns him that he will meet the same fate as the animals he has killed.

At the Winkelman house, a bird flies against the house wall, and is badly injured. Andreas quickly kills it to put it out of pain. Anna abruptly asks him if he had an affair with Eva last autumn when she was alone. He denies it.

Anna has a dream in which, after arriving somewhere in a boat, she is wandering, lost. She wants to take refuge with a girl she meets; the girl refuses, fearfully, with the explanation that it is forbidden for them to have guests any more. A woman in the dream is identified as a mother going to her son's execution.

Johan Andersson hangs himself. Before doing so, he had written a note to Andreas, which the police now deliver. Andreas, said Johan in the letter, had always been kind to him. He describes his last hours; some roughs had attacked him, beaten him unmercifully, threatened him with worse if he did not confess. In his terror he confessed and they knocked him down again, urinated on him, broke his spectacles, and kicked him. When he recovered, he felt he couldn't go on living. Andreas is unbearably affected by this letter but becomes enraged when he finds Anna praying, as she insists, for Johan. She is a hypocrite, he taunts her —she prays for her own sake, it's all acting!

There is a brief scene at Johan's cottage, where his property is being divided.

"Anna and Andreas have now been living together for a year in comparative harmony", says I.B. (For a year altogether, or since we last saw them?) They bicker a little from time to time. In the odd scene that follows they are pictured as working in separate rooms, very still, visible to each other. Andreas is in the grip of a sexual fantasy, which is visualised and directly associated with illness. "What are you thinking about?" asks Anna. "I'm thinking about cancer. And it terrifies me. What are you thinking about?" "I'm not thinking of anything". She amends her response. "I'm thinking of the lies." Andreas asks, "What lies?" He receives no answer.

A long sequence follows, apparently unconnected with the preceding scene, (it is shot against a non-objective background) in which Andreas complains of not being able to get through to Anna. A wall separates him from her. "I want to be warm and tender and alive. I want to make a move. You know how it is, don't you?" She understands what he is trying to say. He continues to protest his misery and his feelings of humiliation. She repeats that she understands. He lowers himself into a deep pit of abasement and resentment in words that concretely refer to nothing ever related before, to humiliations which have sunk into him and remained, to the well-meaning contempt of others, to the feeling of being half stifled and spat upon. "Do you understand me? Can one be sick with humiliation? Or is it a disease that we have all caught? Isn't freedom a terrible poison? For anyone who is humiliated?" His dirge ends with a vision of depressed acquiescence to silence and captivity, to the cold that comes, the darkness, the heat, the smell. "We can never leave here. I don't believe in any move. It's too late. Everything is too late." (Why should he want to leave there? Why is it too late?)

Erland Josephson, the actor, explains affably that Elis Vergerus thinks it's hypocrisy to be horrified at human folly; he has made up his mind not to let the sufferings of others keep him awake at night.

The film moves toward the climax. Andreas and Anna have a violent quarrel that moves from the house into the yard where he begins to cut wood. She accuses him of lying about his marriage and about his divorce. (Have we heard him tell Anna anything about his marriage or his divorce?) She knows the truth and it is hell living with him. "Poor Anna," he tells her sarcastically. "You were so happy and every-thing was so fine before we met." She agrees, as the scene mounts in belligerence. "I had at least something. I had a happy memory of my husband and our love. . . . I believed in the truth. I lived in the truth! You've destroyed that with your goddam lies!"

Andreas tries to quiet her by shouting her down. Anna defies him. He aims a blow at her with his axe, but she sidesteps. He beats her; he beats her in what is surely the most sustained attack on a woman in a Bergman film.

She goes into the house and lies down.

There is fire at a stable, where a horse has been virtually burned alive.

Final scene. Anna and Andreas drive away from the scene of the fire. He demands his freedom; she must know he can't go on living like this.

They don't really love each other anyway, do they? It would be more truthful, wouldn't it? One must live in truth; that's the way she sees it, isn't it so? "Why don't you answer?" Andreas continues scornfully, reminding her of the time she left her handbag; he read her husband's farewell letter. "Poor Anna, you haven't much success with your men. . . . You're always talking about truth! . . . What a ghastly deception, when you spoke of your marriage, of all the happiness, all the love! It was lies, Anna!" The car starts to veer off the road. Andreas grabs the wheel, shouts to her to calm down. "Are you going to kill me just as you kil. . . ." He does not complete the sentence. The car stops. He climbs out, telling her she is out of her mind. "Anyway, why did you come to fetch me at the fire?" She replies, "I came to ask your forgiveness". This is more than he can bear. He waves her on. She drives away. He staggers around indecisively. The landscape is aqueous. Andreas walks back and forth, uncertain, trying to find dry land, seeking a clear firm path around the water. The film goes out to white as Bergman's voice says, "This time he was Andreas Winkelman".

The last clue repeats the first. If that uninflected statement at the end is translated correctly, it may provide the inkling by which the viewer has not been visited before. "This time he was indeed Andreas Winkelman" is a broader reading of it.

Bergman the magician has here discovered a brilliant way to take devilish advantage not only of the film-scenario convention in which ellipses of time, place, and explanation are readily accepted but also of the degenerated attention which has come about, partly because of that convention, partly because of the sheer saturation bombing of civilians by visual tokens everywhere to which, finally, they have become corruptly indifferent. The film and television gaper has made it clear that he will now swallow any possible mode of montage organization, any element of film vocabulary without questioning its literacy, any short-cut, parenthesis, bridge passage, special effect, jump-cut, irrelevant or protracted closeup, frozen shot, slow-motion shot, impoverishment of spoken language, fish-eye-lens effects, flashbacks within flashbacks, sur-reality in a "naturalistic" context—in short, the whole gamut of the cinema alphabet in any order and combination whatsoever, without in the least understanding what, paraphrasably, is going on before his eyes and without turning a hair.

In fact, if you ask him, "Well, what do you think that film was about?", ninety-five times out of a hundred he will not know and he will feel no discomfort at not knowing; he will express, if anything, a tired resentment at being expected to know and among certain echelons of the educated he will have the ready answer, "Art can be experienced on several levels," which plainly means that he is quite prepared to occupy the lower level of merely retinizing, having now shifted the responsibility of experience to the critic, whom he regards, generically, as a necessary evil.

Bergman's *A Passion*, although it is dedicated to a far different and even more mortifying aim, is incidentally the most audacious answer to this universal indifference to meaning which, to my recognition, has been conceived. For if anyone can accept the audiovisual chronology of this film, which with reasonable accuracy I hope I have reproduced, he has fallen easy and complete prey to the invitation of Elis Vergerus to make his own movie with the shots he has absently recorded. In which case, he can take scant credit for creative montage; he has merely received a continuity which has little temporal or moral order and he will in vain attempt to narrate that order with any support from the continuity fashioned by Bergman.

Let us examine a single example of the equivocation through the character of Andreas Winkelman. After at least nine episodes we learn, suddenly and casually, that this man has been in jail for, among other offenses, forging checks. Our tendency is to let this information go by until something is made of it. Nothing is made of it and I gather that most witnesses to the film find nothing morally odd about the disclosure, as if forging cheques were something one does every week. Up to this point and beyond it, perhaps to the end of the film, the gullible by and large accept Andreas as an exemplary man. This appearance is by Bergman very skillfully camouflaged. After a brief introductory definition of him as forty-eight and living alone, Andreas pays neighborly attention to old Johan, asks after his health, and offers him cough medicine. When Anna From leaves his house, we are confronted with the genial Max von Sydow chatting about the character of Andreas with his offscreen creator. We all know Max von Sydow. It is much easier for us to associate him with *The Greatest Story Ever Told* than with *The Kremlin Letter*. Upon leaving the Vergerus house the first time—so the chronology at least appears to say—he finds his puppy hanging by its neck and is naturally upset and solicitous when he soothes the animal. A man who likes dogs is a good man, no? Yet, earlier, immediately after being von Sydow, he had read Anna's private letters; before that, he listened to her telephone conversation.

However, these hints drive on by and all the way thereafter it seems to be the general tendency to accept his oddities of behaviour, such as his being found helplessly, boorishly drunk on the road by Johann, his odd admission to Elis that he is a whipped cur, his sex fantasies while in the same house with Anna, his lies, the verdict he pronounces upon Anna, his plain attempt to kill her with an axe, his violent and prolonged slapping of her, his stupefied outrage at her absence of response in the car, and his final, bleached-out isolation in the empty landscape—certainly, perhaps calculatedly, modeled on the closing shot of *La Strada*.

Who is Andreas Winkelman? And who is the other Andreas, to whom Anna was married before?

They are one and the same; there is only one Andreas. That is my belief.

The place to recognize this fact is precisely where it is given: at the beginning when Anna uses the telephone, calls Elis, and refers to ''Andreas''. If you let this go by as if it were a coincidence, then simply decide later that you are seeing a kind of fatal retake of a previous relationship between Anna and another Andreas, you will never get untangled. What Bergman has done in this film is to abdicate from the conventional conception of time and duration, even more radically than he did in *Persona*. This is *limbo* or, if you like, purgatory. This has all *happened before. It will happen again. Time. is spiral.* Andreas and Anna and the others are *reenacting* a convoluted, unending torment, out of the time-space continuum we are prepared to accept. Bergman deceives us first of all with the simple circumstance of Anna and Andreas meeting stiffly as if they haven't met before. Yet does he deceive us? Is it not conceivable that after a deadly separation a man and woman would meet stonily as if they did not know each other? At once he compensates us for our credulity by handing us the key to the entire film. Von Sydow, explaining Andreas Winkelman, says, "His unhappy marriage and his legal difficulties have driven him into a blind alley. . . ." Since we are not yet concentrating, we are unlikely to think quickly, "Oh, I didn't know he was married"; nor are we likely to associate these "legal difficulties" with those of the Andreas briefly mentioned by Anna.

Observe the adroitness with which Bergman reenforces the deception while all along providing us with the answers. Andreas meets Eva and Elis. The exchange as seen and heard could denote a completely fresh acquaintance; then again it might be false affability between cool neighbors. I have said that the ceremonies of worldly society are beyond Bergman's scope; but he sometimes cannily observes the temperature readings of the society he does inhabit.

On the morning after the second visit, "Anna has nightmares after that accident". "I can imagine". He certainly can, for he was involved in it.

At the mill studio the dialogue is especially cogent, shaped with subtle ingenuity. When Elis gets to the subject of "the other Andreas," he is offering Andreas Winkelman whisky and ice, refilling his glass and so forth. Andreas is ostensibly saying "Please" and "Thank you" to Elis's ministrations as a host. These courtesies are also wry rejoinders to Elis's statements.

> ". . . .He [Andreas] was a mixture of warm-hearted good nature and cold-blooded ruthlessness. Would you like a drink?"
> "Yes please". [Yes please, do go on.]
> "For Anna he was a disaster for obvious reasons".
> "Thanks". [Thanks for no compliment.]
> (After another speech, Elis switches to the subject of his wife, Eva.) "For a year my wife was his mistress. I'm not complaining. It was quite above board. Then one day she left him. I still don't know why. I haven't dared to ask."
> "Thanks". [Thanks for being so tactful.]

It should be noted that Elis says, "I *haven't* dared to ask", not "I *didn't* dare to ask". Does this not suggest an action in the present perfect tense, as it were? Yet just here is where Bergman cheats or is indifferent to visual logic. Of the photos Elis shows to Andreas, that of Anna is clearly a likeness, whereas the other does not resemble Andreas at all. But it makes no sense to suppose that "the other Andreas" was merely a namesake, else all these strategies of time and dialogue are misplaced and it is precisely after this revelation, as if he were thereupon exposed consciously to his identity that Andreas enters a cycle of moodiness and of frankly unspecified despair. In the next scene he is drinking heavily. All but insensible as he staggers about in the woods near his house, he addresses himself as if recalling himself, "Andreas! Don't you hear what I'm saying? Goddam it, Andreas. . . . Andreas—Winkelman . . . Winkleman! *Andreas!* Can't you hear?"

Eva comes to visit Andreas, a very long sequence which is preceded by flames from the bonfire of leaves Andreas is burning upon her arrival. I would say that damnation rather than passion is suggested by this image. Elis is away, Anna is in hospital, Eva is bored. She recounts the history of Anna's accident, adds that of course Andreas knows all that, for it happened very near here, crowds the reference by asking him, "Is this where your wife worked?" [i.e. this room] To her pointed question, "Do you miss her very much?" and her light kiss of apology for being personal, his only rejoinder is, "Are you hungry?"—a fine double meaning.

When she leaves him it appears to be, for we are given no direct clue to another possibility, the following morning. She has been left alone by Elis, she had said; there is no necessity for her to go anywhere. Yet she says goodbye and assures Andreas she will see him in three weeks, a departure and a prospect which have not been introduced until that moment. This sequence is surely a composite, a foreshortening, of many meetings, of a progression during many months. Elis has already said that Andreas had an affair with his wife for about a year. To speculate on where the elisions are placed is not necessary here; I want to suggest only that one probably comes at the end of reel five; directly thereafter Eva recounts her pregnancy—fatal to the child because she was given too strong a sedative—when Elis cried for the first and only time in her knowledge of him. This confession is far too intimate and disturbing, I would say, for her to have advanced it before a seasoned stage of her relationship with Andreas. The sequence ends with Andreas' return to his house after seeing Eva off and giving her his dog so that she will "sleep better". When he lies down he emits an indescribably agonized sound, as if everything were too much for him. The next cut pictures the slaughtered sheep.

Now that we are in another realm of time and logic, Elis and the loan, the shady past of Andreas disclosed by Elis as he "snaps" Winkelman with a powerful, inquisitorial light in his eyes, Eva's knowing about Andreas and Anna, the narrator's mild announcement that Andreas and Anna are living together, all should fall into place—more or less. Next, Anna's assertion that "the other Andreas" was unfaithful but confessed his infidelity to her stands exposed as a lie, for later in the film, after the death of the bird, Andreas does not admit his affair with Eva when Anna confronts him. The climax, if a cycle can have a climax, must appear differently to us now—differently, yet by no means transparent!

Anna screams that she knows the truth about him. He returns the knowledge to her when they are in the car. To be sure, he knows more than he had learned from that letter; he has all the while been reliving it. "Are you going to kill me just as you killed. . . ." *What?* "our marriage"? "the other Andreas"? "the child?" "This time he was Andreas Winkelman". There is no doubt for him of his identity. He is indeed Andreas one and the same.

Do we then have the truth about Andreas and Anna? Far from it. How else might Andreas' words be augmented? He could scarcely be saying, "just as you killed me before". Too melodramatic. To what extent are we seeing a recapitulation of the previous "accident"? Obviously it can't be the crucial one, since Anna is not hurt and there is no child to be killed. Was there ever a child? Who says so beside Anna and Eva repeating Anna? Who was driving at the fatal moment? We have learned that Andreas was jailed for speeding and for driving while drunk. Does this prove anything? Certainly not, yet it is suggestive. In Anna's account of that accident to Andreas at home she claims that since Andreas had been drinking he had allowed her to drive. Does our Andreas know this to be a lie which she tells to protect him and falsify her romantic desire to retain an unsullied memory of him? This would account for the nausea he expresses when faced with her lies of marital bliss. But all contingent questions remain unanswered. What sort of man is Andreas? He is kind to dogs, kind to old men—at least to Johan. When the farmer is driven to hang himself, Andreas is genuinely affected. He kills a bird to spare its suffering, yet Anna looks at him doubtfully. Might this be an illustration of Elis's description of him as cold-blooded? That depends on how cold you think the act is, for it is not so depicted; he wears a compassionate expression but in any case the episode has a further content, as we shall see. Andreas is crafty and haunted by peculiar fears. Let me say right here that to identify him, if one could, in civic terms is quite beside the point. To decide who was responsible for the accident is equally beside the point. The uncovering of an event as if it were an element in a sophisticated detection story is not the task required by the film's obscurity. Events in this film are but shapes of a universal moral ambiguity. With this observation, we are already within another of the concentric circles; we must ask questions with another purpose in mind.

Why is Andreas described as a geologist, curious occupation for the Bergman-surrogate, and why did he have bad dreams "about going down into one of those deep French potholes"? The geologist analyzes, among other things, the age of the earth's crust and his findings on this subject, as much as any other discoveries in the natural sciences, have been instrumental in destroying belief in the divine origins of mankind. Andreas is frightened by these literally rock-bottom answers. He experiences claustrophobia when he imagines penetrating that deeply, and without consolation, to the furthest layers.[111] Andreas never asks a question. He only expresses dread. He has gone as far to the base of things as he cares to go; at the bottom there is nothing. But it should be noted that his bleakest expression of futility follows the death of Johan.

Has it never occurred to you, Anna, that the worse off people are, the less they complain. At last they are quite silent. Although they are living creatures with nerves and eyes and hands. Vast armies of victims and hangmen. The light that rises and falls, heavily. The cold that comes. The darkness. The heat. The smell. They are all quiet. We can never leave here. I don't believe in any move away. It's too late. Everything's too late."

There is another answer to which he would like to break through, an affirmation he would like to make. Earlier in this dialogue he had told Anna, "When you speak of going away, I want so much to say yes. . . . At the same time a wall grows up. I cannot speak. I cannot show you that I am glad." Are we sure he is speaking to Anna? Andreas wants to be a believer but he won't tell the necessary lies to himself. He tells other lies, as we note; he conceals and prevaricates, but he is disgusted when Anna tells the big lie—that her life with him is [was] wonderful, that they lived in the truth. He knows how sordid his own life has been; we receive hints of that by way of Elis. This will be clearer when we know who Elis is.

Andreas believes too little. Anna believes too much. She believes too eagerly in the ideal nature of things; she falsifies the reality of her relationships.

Keeping this much in reserve, shall we turn to Eva? With the knowledge that the names Bergman awards his characters are frequently, if not invariably, connotative, we need not balk here. Eva is Eve is Woman. If one were to accept the domestic situation in this film as belonging to the mode it superficially suggests, sophisticated amoral drama like Antonioni's *Story of A Love* or Joseph Losey's *Accident,* one might think of Eva Vergerus as of that patented type, modern woman. She is unwanted by her husband, she is bored, she is barren, she goes to bed easily, and she is too indifferently amused by life to pass reproving judgments on others. Such a view is totally modified by the context, by the particular, ingenuous personality of Bibi Andersson and by the irrefutable undertones in collaboration with, of course, what we know to be Bergman's prevailing views.

Eva reproaches no one seriously; she warns Andreas to be careful about Anna, but this is not necessarily a criticism of Anna. Eva suffers from not being needed, she is fruitless, her progeny has been killed by those who would spare her pain, she states quite simply that she believes in God, and in the Bergman cosmos the believer is not wanted. She is primal woman for whom there is no Adam; this is part of the suggestion. Her issue has with good intentions been killed by science, shall we say, by knowledge?[112] Miss Andersson is given the explanation to give us that if Eva does not commit suicide she may take up useful work like teaching the deaf, who live in an even greater isolation. The fate of the Christian religion has been to become social service.

To be sure, Elis Vergerus is nominally half of Anders Ellius, the husband of Cecelia in *Brink of Life* (played by the same actor), and half the rational anatomist, Vergerus, of *The Magician*. In *A Passion* he is an architect, building something in which he doesn't believe. Why it was necessary for him to be as well a candid cameraman belongs to the economy of casting, so that Bergman could combine the photographic anatomist with the sterile builder and ultimately serve two motifs. In any case, Elis takes thousands of pictures of human beings in crucial or basic situations such as sleeping, eating, or in acute distress, with no alleged curiosity about the moral nature of their existence. He disclaims any interest in the soul yet we are free to believe, as he sits and snaps Andreas mercilessly, that he has a pretty shrewd conception of Andreas' soul. With an assurance bred of knowledge he puts Andreas to work for him, typing multitudinous notes for the construction of his false temple. He is what remains of Bergman's old crony, the Devil. But we can get closer than that.

Let us return to the title. Everything is there. In the Fårö interview to which I had earlier reference, Bergman mentioned that he would like to use his greater leisure to study Bach's *St. Matthew's Passion*. This is not esoteric information. My memory of the occasion simply sharpened my attention when the title of this film was announced. If the filmgoer allows himself to be sidetracked by the secondary meaning of the word passion as a state of strong feeling, associated commonly with anger or with sex, he will get further than ever away from the film. Passion is *passio*, quite simply, to suffer. The subject of the passion, whether or not you think of Bach, is the suffering of the Lord: the agony in the garden, the betrayal, the crucifixion. As this film opens, we hear a tinkling of bells before there is an image. The first shot is of sheep in a pastoral scene which might be that of the Holy Land. Most of Bergman's late films might, with no undue frivolity, be described as an agony in the garden; betrayal is clearly the theme of the relationships in this film, and there is a form of crucifixion in the hanging of Johan. It is *a* passion, not the Passion. The characters circle as in a timeless round of torture, lassitude, leaden expectation, and punishment. To a professing Christian, the events of the passion did not merely take place in history, once for all, then freeze into chronicle and doctrine. Nothing is annulled, everything is reenacted; every day, everywhere, the passion is performed —persecution, betrayal, death and atonement.

The matter of *A Passion* is the drama of the Christian text. As in *Persona*, however, we need not expect to trace every detail consistently with the master theme. There are simply some meanings which emerge unmistakably once you are in the ambience. The moment of the film is the moment of the betrayal and its consequences. The atmosphere is premonitory; signs of cruelty and disaster appear throughout the film. But the pellucid color, the absence of chiaroscuro, the offhand, daylight interviews with the actors, the seemingly concrete interplay between Elis and Eva and Andreas and Anna muffle the intimations of doom. Andreas, at the beginning, is patching his leaky roof. Why patch a roof when a tempest, before which nothing can stand, is on its way? As he scrutinizes the horizon, strange atmospheric effects are conjured: impalpable clouds gather, the sun is eclipsed, a wind begins to stir. In the Gospels, the crucifixion is accompanied by earthquakes and the opening of graves; the veil of the temple is rent. Bergman's catastrophes are of a different order. The Nordic, pre-Christian blood-sacrifice breaks into the scene. The hanging of the dog does not forecast the hanging of Johan so much as it predicates the slaughter, thereafter, of the sheep and the burning of the horse. A horse was traditionally sacrificed to Odin.

Elis is Pontius Pilate. He asks what truth is and does not tarry for an answer. Actually, it is only in *St. John* that Pilate asks "What is truth?" In *St. Matthew* he washes his hands after delivering Christ to the multitude. He explains to Andreas that Johan is suspected of killing the sheep, cooly presenting only the circumstantial evidence which has been assumed by the islanders. As for his other aspect, he is an architect of the Empire, on the subject of which, culturally, he has disdainful reservations.

If we now think to bring Eva closer to the New Testament scheme, it may not be too much of a gloss to suggest that she has been prepared for so immaculate a conception that no conception is forthcoming. She is a madonna without child. There is a beautiful touch at the dinner-table scene early in the film, when Anna asks her if she believes in God. Eva turns to her husband amiably and asks him, "Do I believe in God, Elis?"

She asks the sanction of science, you might say. We recall the ending of *Viridiana*, when the nun demurely knocks on the door of Liberalism, asking to be included. The killing of the dazed bird can now be explained by its exact place in the continuity. Misleadingly, it follows the Vietnam images on the television screen, an unnecessary emphasis on suffering, since the moment is already loaded with other references. More importantly, in the scheme of the Passion, it follows the threat of death to Johan—the Crowning With Thorns. We are on the way to a place called Golgotha. Also, it precedes Anna's direct questioning of Andreas about his relationship to Eva. "Eva is utterly defenceless. She can't protect herself." The meaning would appear to be : was Andreas serious in his attention to Eva? He denies Eva. He repudiates the Christians. To allay the bird's suffering, he kills it. Eva, remember, was victim of a mercy-killing before and note that in the film she has abruptly disappeared from the action.

Anna has more than a little of Mary Magdalen about her, has she not? She sins but asks forgiveness. Twice she asks; once in her dream, once of Andreas. Both times she is rejected. The dream enforces this stratum of the film's meaning with finality, although Bergman again detracts from the Crucifixion reference by introducing that shot of Anna arriving in a boat, an image of desolation which appears to have been a memory of *The Shame*. Otherwise, the sequence is explicit. "Anna had *a coherent dream at Easter*", Bergman informs us on track. (Italics mine.) In that dream, lost, she asks the girl if she can go home with her and receives the apprehensive answer. "We musn't have guests any more. It's forbidden. We've changed the locks on all the doors." "Why?" "I don't know, it just is so." The Christian movement has been crushed. No fellowship, no conspiratorial assembly. Anna asks who the woman is over there. Someone tells her—"Her son is to be executed. She is on her way to the place of execution." Anna (Magdalen), the repentant believer, cries out, "Forgive me! Forgive me!" And the directly ensuing scene announces the death of Johan.

The analogy is not *en face*. Johan is Christ-like, perhaps; he is not in any particular the Christ. He has no doctrine to preach, no disciples. But on the wall by his bed there is a painting of Christ (I could not make out its details) and at the moment in Andreas' long speech when he invokes the cold, the darkness, the heat and the smell, adding "They are all quiet,'' an image of Johan is interpolated. There is at least something of the good Samaritan in the character of Johan—he helps Andreas when he is drunk and fallen by the wayside—and of the martyr, that's for certain; he is stoned nearly to death, urinated on, and beaten. As Johan Andersson, he is of course innocent; the stables are set fire to after his death.

''Now from the sixth hour there was darkness over all the land unto the ninth hour'' (*St. Matthew*, 27.45). After the bird blunders into the Winkelman house, like the warning rock tossed through Johan's window, Andreas remarks to Anna, when the execution is over, and he brings a lamp to their table, ''Now we can see better, anyway.'' Light and darkness is a leading theme in *A Passion*, a far echo from the cry for light in Bergman's maiden efforts for the theatre, a cry that rings out in several of his films. But the crucifixion of the messianic nuisance brings no light, only more darkness. With the death of the saving belief, Andreas inhabits a trackless and phantasmal world in which his own freedom is a burden to him.

''We can never leave here. I don't believe in any move anyway. It's too late. Everything is too late.'' We cannot now leave this prison of earthly existence. The so-called Redeemer was mortal. They crucified him. Andreas had been violently affronted by Anna's prayer for Johan, because he was still unable to give consent to the divinity of the man released by Pilate to the mob and crucified in his stead ''*Not this man, but Barabbas. Now Barabbas was a robber*'' (*St. John*, 18.40). And Andreas has been a forger.

Within this circle of the film's meaning, the attribution is self-revealed. It is doubly confirmed by a speech in Strindberg's *The Ghost Sonata* (*A Passion* is as permeated with the gospel according to St. August as it is by New Testament sources). The Student, in Strindberg's play, complains in words as desolate as those of Andreas:

> They say that Christ harried hell. What they really meant was that he descended to earth, to this penal colony, to this madhouse and morgue of a world. And the inmates crucified Him when he tried to free them. *But the robber they let free. Robbers always win sympathy.* . . . Woe to all of us! Saviour of the world, save us! We are perishing![113] (Italics mine.)

The act of forgery as an emblem of the guilt-laden secret which everyone in the Strindberg world conceals in his breast is notably employed in *The Ghost Sonata* as well as in *The Burned House,* another Chamber play which also features a mysterious case of arson. Sexual love linked with disease can be found in the same context; giving a literal explanation of his moribund Young Lady in *The Ghost Sonata,* Strindberg suggested she had cancer of the uterus. After Andreas' reminiscence, or fantasy, of a sexual encounter with a female who looked rather like a nurse in one shot, he tells Anna, in response to her question about his thoughts, that he was thinking about cancer.

But even more relevant to Bergman's film than these analogies is what we may call the superstructural subject of The Ghost Sonata. Strindberg had once intended to subtitle the play, *Kama-Loka,* a theosophical name for *Limbo;* and the equivocations of moral viewpoints in *A Passion* are distinctly recognizable in the words spoken by Strindberg's Student: "It is remarkable how the same story can be told in two exactly opposite ways".[114]

A Passion is an impressive tour de force if you allow that the object of an artist is almost totally to conceal his most authentic meaning and if you are willing to exempt the film from a primary purpose of a work of art, to arouse emotion. Since emotion is inseparable from at least a rudimentary meaning and since the meaning here requires a major effort of intuition assisted by research, the only emotion available for the untutored viewer, unless he is instantaneously aroused by closeups of Swedish actresses, is, it would seem to me, perplexity. You cannot legitimately suffer for characters whose plight has no emotional correlatives until seen from the perspective of the year 29 A.D. These people are dead in their skins; as so often in the late-Bergman film, they express agonies the sources of which are unclear. We never learn *why* Andreas feels humiliated and incapable. (Whether he is Andreas I or Andreas Winkelman is irrelevant to this question.) And if Anna is a liar, how can we concede to a chronicle of her suffering which may well be a prevarication? If you choose not to accept the analogy of the Passion as I have outlined it, you still have to explain at a mundane level the schematic ambiguity of the film as you see it, or admit that your emotions have been tricked by a cinematic play of magic in which plausibility is an unwelcome ingredient.

One thing is by now clear. Whenever Bergman declares an intention (concerning life or art) one should read into it a direct refutation of what he has said or implied. He moves to an island, where the winds blow freely, men are few, the dawn belongs to the gulls and his life, honored and harrowed on the mainland, is here an unfettered breathing, with books, music, and a wife and child. He produces films that continue, as of yore, to describe human existence as a suffocating City of Dreadful Night. He assures interrogators, from the press or elsewhere, a dozen times over, that he has done with all that superfluous questioning of God and the silence of God and the riddle of existence. His films become, ever more hermetically, like messages launched in sealed bottles, rephrasings of the original cry for deliverance.

He complains that the theatre is no longer negotiable because it is meaningless; it is "a luxury maintained by the state for a minority"; "It does not reach out." Theatre should fulfill "the need of the simple man".[115] And what does he produce in the period during which he is asserting this failure of theatre to meet the demands of populism? He produces Pirandello's *Six Characters in Search of an Author,* Ibsen's *Hedda Gabbler* and Strindberg's *A Dream Play.*[116]

He mistrusts himself, he confesses, because he makes use of an apparatus expressly designed to deceive people by exploiting optical illusions inherent in the process of human vision. Steadily he perfects his talent for such deception until in *A Passion* he has virtually realized his earlier goal, "to penetrate into the chiaroscuro of surreality".

Closer to our recent subject, interviewers asked him if *The Shame* was to be a continuation of *The Silence* or perhaps part of a trilogy. No, nothing like that. However, *The Hour of the Wolf, The Shame,* and *A Passion* do comprise an insecure and dolorous trilogy, each unit of which might bear the title of either of the other two. In *The Hour of the Wolf,* Johan, an artist, disappears in a clap of thunder, you could say, from an island and a semidetached wife. In *The Shame* he reappears as an artist whose art is of even less value to anyone, so much so that he has abandoned it. With his eternally recurring mate he vanishes once more into the gray, as the armies gather, and in *A Passion,* unable to rest in whatever outrageous haven he had reached, he is back again as a revenant, nominally not an artist at all, though as inadequate, shamed and guilty, rejecting his "wife," refusing solace and denying pleas for forgiveness.

Anna, too, in the dream sequence, as I said above, seems momentarily to be returning to the island of *The Shame*; beyond this, she reminds us of Alma in *The Hour of the Wolf*, her questions partially and bitterly answered, and is not unrelated to the Alma (played by Bibi Andersson) of *Persona*, asking life that it be compatible with the kinder view she has of herself. "I didn't think life could look like that," says Anna. "I didn't think life would be a daily suffering."

Henri Michaux once apotheosized the iceberg in a prose poem: "Icebergs, Solitaries without cause, countries barred-up, distant, and free of vermin!" *A Passion* is the cinema, *borealis*, in quintessential style; the impeccable one eighth glows above the water, sunset colors warming its opaque nudity; the body of it is below the surface and the deeper you go the colder it gets. *A Passion* is "the typical Swedish movie" transfigured because it was made by a master. His lesser national contemporaries utilize somewhat the same method: they proceed on assumptions not visibly present to the eye; they create a photogenic façade behind which there may be nobody at all; there may be a negative platitude masquerading as a universal truth. The Swedish filmmaker deems it unnecessary to dramatize the motivations of his characters. We are asked to take for granted that, being people, they will behave in prescribed ways, usually disheartening. They discover that "life" is empty, never asking themselves if it is not they who are empty. Man and wife will inevitably hate each other: this is a given; affection is incestuous or one summer long; suicide is the only alternative to failure of comprehension; the older generation (age thirty, fifty or seventy) is always obtuse or cruel.

These assumptions, as I suggested in the chapter, "Man Came Late," are the consequences of thin culture, an inbred and envious social scene informed by an unnourishing religion and a provincial absence of mental flexibility. Much of this heritage in modern times, when you might expect the severity of such limitations to have been mitigated, is palpably— at least among the expressive minority—the curse of Strindberg, a neurotic giant in everyone's path. For him, social life was totally a conspiracy, existence was an unending abuse suffered in a penal colony and clouds were clots of blood. One biography of the man begins with the apt sentence, "The most unfortunate event in Strindberg's life was the day of his birth".[117] This negative force is like an iron hand on the

Swedish spirit, more unshakeably than most Swedes of the latterday generations will confess. They share his ground; tacitly they acquire his conviction, if not to so maniacal a degree, that since nothing good can come of one's fellowmen he had best be cultivated as little as possible. Hence they incur hells of loneliness, from which the only escape is alcoholism, supression, or any other form of oblivion that offers itself, such as drugs or the false vivacity of the pornographic image.

The exception is the Dogged Believer, exemplified by Bergman, a desperate pilgrim on the road to Damascus; he is bound to be desperate, like Strindberg having eliminated the possible alternatives; he is forced to become cabalistic, like Strindberg, for he is the citizen of a via media, here-and-now community and he dare not too freely boast of his complete defection from the pragmatic commandments. The more he becomes convinced that God is nowhere, the less inclined he is to forgive anyone for presuming to take His place and the more earnestly he strives in his art to expound the secret doctrine, that man in his freedom is paltry and helpless. *A Passion,* insofar as it passes judgment on the human condition, resembles an epistle from one of the Twelve addressed to the elect, carefully coded lest it fall into the hands of a Roman procurator. It is not irrelevant to note that John the Divine received his *Revelation* on an island. But the tone of *A Passion,* when you get down to the tone, is closer to that of St. Paul.

Even so, I have been visited by the suspicion, while writing this book, that Ingmar Bergman is not an authentically religious figure, despite the evidential symbols in his films that accumulate to suggest he is. I would describe him as a retentive personality, in whom belief has been replaced by obsession. A religious personality, by the simple definition I understand, is one for whom there is something resident beyond him, in the natural world, something with which he can commune and which, in turn, communes with him. The ceremony is reciprocal and instills confidence. I feel nothing like this in Bergman's movies, nor do I see it hinted in a single avowal he has ever made. Except for *The Virgin Spring,* I would never dream that his films came from the mind of a man who believes in "Something far more deeply interfused". He has no love of *things,* he has no humble comprehension of the value of anyone else's activity, unless that anyone is an artist and he has no interest in the neutral universe except to shudder at its indifference. Not one of his characters is ever redeemed by focusing for five minutes on a world uncontaminated by the self and the greedy itch for providence. We may not, customarily, think of Dostoievsky as a blithe spirit, but again and again in the pages of that great writer, pathetic man, is a fabulously simple concession to the external world which asks nothing of our consciousness except a moment's pause in our ego-centered progress. Here is Kirilov talking to Stavrogin, in *The Possessed.*

"When I was a boy of ten I used to shut my eyes deliberately in winter and imagine a green leaf, bright green with veins on it and the sun shining. . . ."
"An allegory?"
"No—why? Not an allegory, just a leaf, one leaf. A leaf's good. All's good."
"All?"
"All. Man's unhappy because he doesn't know that he's happy. . . . He who finds out will become happy at once—that very minute. . . ."[118]

Bergman is not driven to find out. He is the victim and the beneficiary of a traumatic displacement, a shock of disbelief from which he has never recovered in his soul; that shock is responsible for his impetus and for the intense condensation of his art. He cannot now move freely save within the confines of the belief he has tried to repudiate, the symbols it provides, the rejections it assists, the polarities and correlatives of which it is composed. He must retain the belief, if only in a glass darkly, for it is the sole source from which his own creation is supplied; within its conventions he can move. And one has to respect the untiring sagacity with which he has incorporated himself; he has been able to enact his own father, his own erring son, his own wife, God, the devil, and the saints. He has become his own Passion.

Theologians in Sweden have been divided between those who are confident that *A Passion* prophesies an imitation-of-Christ phase and those who believe that Andreas' rejection of Anna signifies Bergman's harsh farewell to Christianity. When his Fårö documentary was shown on the television, there was less disagreement; the obvious deductions were made, especially by reviewers of the Social Democrat persuasion, whose opinions on such subjects can usually be written for them in advance. The film pointed to a new social orientation on Bergman's part, an interest in and love for the plain folk.[119] I do not care to speak as a prophet but

I doubt inferences so neatly drawn. Certainly Bergman has been looking for something, prowling that island with his camera as if it were a Geiger counter that might pick up ultimate signals. He is looking for something he dropped a long time ago.

The notion that to embrace one's kind, as if you could decide tomorrow, confers artistic validity is one of the sentimental deceptions from our contemporary slag-heap. It is no more necessary than it is likely for Bergman to love humanity or to take a sustained interest in social problems of the civic order. If next week he were to divide his cloak, give his Fårö house to the poor, and become a hedge priest, it might save his soul but not his art. The important thing for a filmmaker is to know where his subject lies and how to treat it. I wonder if any sounder advice has been given to the artist than that by Delacroix when he said that you should be able to draw a man in the time it takes him to fall from the fifth story.

To write a lengthy epilogue on the rank of Ingmar Bergman as filmmaker would be superfluous. I have been all along evaluating his work. Nobody can predict future opinions on so perishable an art as that of the motion picture. Nobody can predict, in our time, what people will celebrate or what they will destroy six weeks from now. I can only summarize the Bergman movie from my own witness point. Where Bergman's art represents decisively "the emotional equivalent of thought," it is preeminent, I think, in film history.[120] If I have been less than generous in receiving his thought when it is most naked, that is because personally I have no patience with his oracular diatribes or with the pre-Renaissance temper of his fanaticism. I believe in the power of the mind, provisionally at least, to make choices and to exercise discriminations. Bergman too often appears to agree with Heine's coachman that "ideas are those things they put into your head at school". To say this another way, Bergman is impressed by man's sinfulness; I am depressed by his ignorance. But when I'm at C Major I believe with Ortega y Gasset, "To say that we live is the same as saying that we find ourselves in an atmosphere of definite possibilities." After *The Virgin Spring,* in Bergman's canon, I feel exposed for the most part to a doctrine of existence that repels me. I can only resolve the problem by ironically conceding that the depletions of Bergman's art originate in cultural assumptions without which his art would not be.

To speak in any final way of Bergman's film style is simply to elucidate alternatives and individual preferences. Bergman's art has none of the baroque dynamics to be seen in the films of Max Ophuls, of Orson Welles at his best, of Kurasawa, in Sjöberg's *Miss Julie,* or in Alexandre Astruc's *Le Rideau Cramoisi.* Bergman was not a born filmmaker, as could be said of Eisenstein, Jean Epstein, Walter Ruttmann, Max Ophuls, and certain others. He worked his will with an inherited, popular medium, after a long and erratic apprenticeship. He has disciplined that medium within the range that has served his purpose, a purpose more austere than not, seldom free from theatrical sources; in many instances, of course, the retention of them was calculated. But in any case, and despite *Persona* or *A Passion,* we do not think of Bergman as primarily a virtuoso and innovator but as a poetic moralist. We think of him as a filmmaker of magic with an evangelical point of view—a Druid captured by Lutheranism.

You may be able to name other film artists who surpass Bergman in subtlety, in urbanity, in exuberance, in courtesy of heart, and in scope of social interest; you can choose directors whose styles you favor for their camera inflections, their tempo, their modes of composition, and their rhythms; you will find few who have anything like Bergman's obdurate and sustained integrity; none who has so artfully succeeded in displaying his temperature chart as a map of the world. In his own boreal and phobic way, Bergman has engaged that subterranean crisis of the spirit which we have agreed to call modern.

One thing more. While Bergman appears, at present view, to be characterized, intemperately, by excluding themes that give to all his late films a clothing of monotony—God's silence, man's degradation, love's catastrophe—he is in fact, when the whole body of his work is passed in review, incredibly various within the limits of his gospel. How many film artists could have made *The Magician* as well as *A Summer with Monika? Smiles of a Summer Night* and also *The Silence? The Virgin Spring* and *Persona?* His best films will, I trust, outlast all strictures placed on them by critics. So, I fear, will his worst.

The dog barks; the caravan passes.

FOOTNOTES

". . . . You idealize him, and make him too complex. You introduce something Freudian into him which I never saw a sign of: fixations, transferences, inhibitions, or whatever else you call them. To my mind, he was perfectly normal, only a little vague and undeveloped. He required a lot of time to mobilize his forces."

"Yes," I interrupted, "because his forces were very great and drawn from a vast territory."

"Perhaps: but then why do you make him so much more intelligent than he seemed? You endow him with altogether too much insight. In reality he was simply bewildered. There was a fundamental darkness within him, a long arctic night, as in all Nordics."

"But isn't the arctic night very brilliant? And after the aurora borealis isn't there an arctic day, no less prolonged? I think there is no great truth that sensitive Nordics don't sometimes discover: only they don't stick to their best insights. They don't recognize the difference between a great truth and a speculative whim, and they wander off again into the mist, empty-handed and puzzle-headed. . . . A moral nature burdened and over-strung, and a critical faculty fearless but helplessly subjective—isn't that the true tragedy of your ultimate Puritan?"[1a]

George Santayana
The Last Puritan

1a. When Santayana received the Swedish translation of *The Last Puritan*, in 1936, he made the following comment in a letter: ". . . I gather from what I can make out of the Swedish wrapper, and from other hints, that the interest taken in the novel by the Nordics is entirely scientific. Style, humor, etc., are beneath their notice: but they say the book is an important document on American life; and as America—I mean the U.S.—is important for them commercially and racially, they wish it to be studied in their country." *The Letters of George Santayana*. Constable, London, 1955.

1. "Shakespeare and the Stoicism of Seneca," in *Selected Essays* by T. S. Eliot. Faber & Faber, London, 1932.

2. *Ingmar Bergman* by Jacques Siclier. Editions Universitaires Paris, 1960.

3. The formula appears in Chekhov's letters, more than once. ". . . . the narrative form is a lawful wife, but theatre is a showy, noisy, impertinent and tiresome mistress". (Letter to A. N. Plescheyev.) "Stick to fiction writing. She is your lawful wife, the theatre is a powdered mistress." (Letter to I. L. Scheglov.) *Life and Letters of Anton Tchekov*. Trans. and edited by S. S. Koteliansky and Philip Tomlinson. Cassel & Co., Ltd. London, 1925.

4. "Qu'est-ce faire des Films?" in *Cahiers du Cinema* 61, July 1956. Much of the same material appears in "Self Analysis of a Film Maker" trans. by G. P. E. Burke and Britt Halvarson for *Films and Filming*, London, 1958. Also, translated by Royal S. Brown, in Geduld, *Film Makers on Film Making*, 1967 (see Note 25, *infra*.)

5. *L 136 Dagbok med Ingmar Bergman* by Vilgot Sjöman. Norstedt, Stockholm, 1963. A day-by-day diary during the shooting and aftermath of *Winter Light*. In the film, Tomas, the pastor, recalls a childhood terror when he was left alone in the house one evening and ran screaming through the rooms and outdoors, crying out for Father.

6. Four years later, he restaged the play at Hälsingborg: as before, with a declared anti-Nazi stress. In an unsigned program note, Bergman declared that the issue of *Macbeth* now cried out "with ruthless clarity: we must have a belief!" And in the scene of Lady Macbeth's death, Macbeth struggled with his conscience between the reinvoked Witches and a luminous crucifix.

7. That malice domestic was an impressive subject to the young Bergman is perhaps underlined by his producing both *Macbeth* and *The Pelican* twice. The latter, one of four Chamber Plays, I find impossible to take seriously. The pelican is a devouring mother (literally she is depicted as having taken the chil-

dren's food for her own nourishment) who drives her husband into the grave and cripples her children for independent maturity. And the daughter's suitor, it is implied, was the mother's lover. The play ends with the son setting fire to the house in which he and his sister, locked in each other's arms, perish, while mother jumps from the window. The son's all but last words constitute for me the most comical line in Strindberg. "Poor mother—she was so wicked!" It's the dramaturgy, not the psychology, that confounds me.

8. No relation to Ingmar. She was the widow of Hjalmar Bergman, novelist and playwright (1883–1931). Since the simple content of *Kaspar's Death* has been said to derive from H. Bergman, as well as from Pär Lagerkvist, this may be the place for me to mention that the alleged influence on I. Bergman of H. Bergman I have never been able to pin down. The assertion has often been made with no specific citations. Hjalmar Bergman was a writer of many moods and of ranging interests. Few of his books have been translated into English and Swedish critics find him difficult to summarize adequately; he evades the categories. His most admired vein was that of worldly disenchantment conveyed ironically, scarcely an attitude which I. Bergman could have authentically inherited. The only work by H. Bergman I know anything of which might have significantly disturbed I. Bergman is *Clown Jack,* clearly an autobiographical exercise in which the title character exploits his own terror when he discovers how delighted the audience is at his simulation of it. "I was born human", he confesses, "I lived as a clown, I sold my heart. I shall die poor." (Note Ingmar Bergman's use of "Jack"—in my ensuing text—and consider certain aspects of *The Naked Night* and *The Magician.*)

9. Rune Waldekranz, currently head of the Film Department at the University of Stockholm Institute of Theatre and Film, is the author of numerous books on international film and a contributor to *Enciclopedia Spettacolo.* As producer for Sandrews for 18 years, he was notably responsible for Alf Sjöberg's *Fröken Julie* (Miss Julie) and for Ingmar Bergman's *Gycklarnas Afton* (The Naked Night).

10. There were two principal "treatments": one was idyllic, a nostalgic glance at vanishing countryside customs; the other, politically critical of previous social conditions, with strong implications that under the Social Democrats rural life had been made bearable. Either type was likely to be infused with what came to be known locally as "Social-Democrat pornography". *One Summer of Happiness (Hon dansade en sommar),* produced by Nordisk Tonefilm, 1951, was a conscious attempt to capture the foreign markets with a nude swimming scene (in fact innocuous, and poetically directed by Arne Mattsson) introduced into a story of opposing generations which might have seemed socially critical in 1919! Until *Dear John* surpassed it, *One Summer* was the most profitable Swedish film ever made.

11. To those of us who loved him as an actor, the death of Anders Henrikson, in 1965, at the age of sixty-nine, was like the loss of a personal friend. Partly because he was an immensely subtle, subjective, nonrhetorical actor, partly because his career was confined to Sweden, he never acquired such fame as was bestowed on Lars Hanson or Victor Sjöström. For me he is one of perhaps a half-dozen of the most memorable actors in the history of film and memorable in the few of his stage roles I was privileged to see. Thoroughly dissimilar in approach and style, Hanson and Henrikson were paired in a Strindberg play for two characters which I saw in 1958, *Pariah,* as pure an example of give and take playing as I have witnessed on any stage. Henrikson also played the most extraordinary Polonius I have ever seen in Sjöberg's 1959 production of *Hamlet.* Among his best film roles I would instance The Lord in *The Road to Heaven,* the father in Gustav Molander's Defiance (*Trots*), 1952, from a script by V. Sjöman with assistance of Ingmar Bergman, and the husband in "For a Consideration," the second of two Strindberg stories combined in one film, *Married (Giftas),* 1955, which he directed brilliantly himself. Henrikson, in fact, directed thirty films but only those in which he, himself, appeared, have any claim on critical attention. He was perhaps too intensively and personably an actor to have been more than a competent director. The actor-director, with genius in both professions, is an exceptional phenomenon.

12. "*The Dream-Play* was followed by a series of what one is tempted to call 'scream-plays'." F. L. Lucas, *The Drama of Ibsen and Strindberg.* Cassell, London, 1962.

13. The play was rehearsed for production at Student Theatre, but for some reason there was a change of programming and another piece by Bergman was presented instead, a sketch called *Tivolit* of which I have so shadowy a synopsis it is not worth retailing. *Jack Among the Actors* was never professionally staged.

14. These are my versions of extracts given by Frederic Fleisher in an article, "Early Bergman" (Encore, March-April 1962, London), and by Fritiof Billquist in *Ingmar Bergman,* Stockholm, 1960.

15. From a rejected Preface. See *Phoenix* The Posthumous Papers of D. H. Lawrence. William Heinemann, London, 1936. Reprint 1961.

16. Sigmund Freud's personal exploitation of the Devil is analyzed by David Bakan, in *Sigmund Freud and the Jewish Mystical Tradition* (D. Van Nostrand, 1958). My quotation is taken directly from Mr. Bakan's excellent synthesis of this subject.

17. The German films I mention here were but the end-products of an obsessive subject in German literature since pre-War I years, much of it proto-Bergman, you might say, but important for consequences somewhat more far-reaching. In *Die Ursache* (*The Cause*) by Leonhard Frank, 1915, a man who returns to the school in which he had been tormented by a sadistic teacher finds

the same teacher still torturing small boys—and kills him! . . . In the play, *Der Sohn*, by Walter Hasenclever, 1916, the son in question refuses to pass his examination for fear of having to venture into mature life. The school as an epitome of German tyranny becomes, in *The Black Mass*, by Franz Werfel, 1919, the cosmic scheme, whereby the Creation is ascribed to the forcible overthrow of an aboriginal democracy of spirits by Jehovah (=Father=Headmaster=Kaiser) : hence, the original sin of German authoritarianism can be identified with God, himself, who established his regime "upon the police powers of terror and grace". The patriarchal family, together with the religion that sanctions it and the militarism that defends it must be destroyed. It is only a step from Frank, Hasenclever and Werfel to the Youth Movements of the Twenties and to Arnolt Bronnen's *Vatermord* (Parricide) in which a fifteen-year-old kills his father, a Social Democrat, rejects his concupiscent mother, and walks out boldly to embrace his "liberty". The author became a fanatical Nazi. If this subject interests the reader, the indispensable book is *The Writer in Extremis,* by Walter H. Sokel, 1959.

18. First of all, these prefaces by Anders Dymling, and Bergman, himself, give every evidence of an official smoothing over of any differences which had existed between the producer and the director and of a common policy of pacification. Bergman's remarks must have been made soon after completing *The Virgin Spring* : curious that he should have said, "Religious emotion, religious sentimentality [these are identical?] is something I got rid of long ago. . . ." The more curious when, in the same preface, he maintains that unsound thesis, "art lost its basic creative drive the moment it was separated from worship". On another subject, "I believe that reviewers and critics have every right to interpret my films as they like . . . each person has the right to understand a film as he sees it". Part of his charm is that he believes these statements at the moment he makes them. As for the concession to Sjöberg, he retracted it by implication in the 1967 interview I cite in the next sentence of my text. However, he has acknowledged, with repeated emphasis, his debt to Sjöberg in the theatre, in a long interview conducted by Henrik Sjögren, May 1968, published as "Dialogue with Ingmar Bergman" in *Ingmar Bergman på teatern,* Stockholm, 1968.

19. I was subsequently apprised of this studio joke. Naturally, in 1957, when I first saw this film, I was quite incapable of reading a headline in a Swedish newspaper, in a brief shot, probably upside down.

20. Sjögren, *op. cit.* (note 18). This very useful book is a chronicle of *all the* plays directed by Bergman in the professional theatre, from 1944 to April 1, 1967 (premiere of *Six Characters in Search of an Author,* in Oslo). Sjögren has judiciously edited the diverse critical opinions of each production and furnished the book with a unique selection of photographs—scenes from the plays and closeups of director and actors.

21. Sjögren, *op. cit.*

22. The film in which Sjöberg first systematically displayed his techniques of antithesis was *Iris och Löjtnanshjärta* ("Iris and the Lieutenant's-heart," a pun in Swedish, for *löjtnanshjärta* is the flower we call "bleeding heart"), 1946, from a novel by Olle Hedberg, reminiscent of Arthur Schnitzler's world, in which the scion of an upper-class family falls in love with the maid, Iris (Mai Zetterling). The young lieutenant (Alf Kjellin) is killed in an accident and his older brother (Holger Löwenadler) discovers, to his astonishment, that the youth and Iris had been genuinely in love. The film is characterized, over-broadly perhaps, by shots that underline the distinctions between youth and age, between class and class, between those who serve and those who are served. The lieutenant and Iris bicker across a table with a pair of crossed swords on the upstage wall (an effect Sjöberg had used in *The Journey Out*, 1945); Iris submissively serves a drink to the brother, a desert of carpet between them magnified by the camera angle; the same brother attempts to console her after the lieutenant's death and a glassed-in door separates each from the other; the young maid and the grand-dame of the household, loaded with jewels and wrinkles, are posed within the same mirror view and at another moment the lieutenant, from a doorway, greets Iris who is shown full-length in a mirror, which has the effect of framing them off from each other in the act of greeting. Bergman restated this motif in *Sommarlek*: the journalist (Kjellin, as it happens) stands in a doorway of the dressingroom, above the level where Marie, facing us, looks into a makeup mirror we don't see, and the stage manager with his clown's face is reflected in another mirror—three frontal planes, three orders of reality. Sjöberg, himself, then multiplied and subtilized the process in a pre-wedding shot in *Miss Julie*, wherein a mirror and a window enforce the feeling of numerous planes in depth. *En passant*, the simplified class conflict depicted by Sjöberg does not conform with Hedberg's novel, according to Alrik Gustafson, who states that "the class confrontation loses some of its force and validity when we discover that Iris herself is rather far from being a creature of disinterested idealistic motives". (see Gustafson's *History of Swedish Literature;* the chapter, "Modernistic Ground Swell and Social Criticism").

23. The excessive number of alibis for misery in Bergman's early scripts make of him the boy who cried "Wolf!" When an authentic calamity is noted, we've already lost interest. There were bodies from German destroyers washed up on Swedish beaches. During the last winter of the War, 1944–45, Russian submarines played havoc with German and Swedish shipping in that area. A single German ship carrying nearly 6,000 evacuees from Eastern Baltic countries was sunk with a loss of all hands.

24. Hereby hang an anecdote and a distinction. The source of Bergman's money for these purchases was David Selznick, who had commissioned Alf Sjöberg and Bergman to write a film script of Ibsen's *A Doll's House*. The

script was delivered, payment received; the film was never made. Bergman's rueful explanation: "Sjöberg had too many ideas. I had too few". It is incidentally amusing, in view of the snappishness with which Bergman has dismissed all suggestions of *tyskeri* (Germanness) in his work, to recall that when he staged *The Bridal Crown* in 1952 he was criticized adversely for his "Berlin Grössten-schauspielcomplex," and when he produced *Faust* in 1958 he was applauded by reference to Adolph Appia (Wagner's scenographer) and Max Reinhardt. (Sjögren, *op. cit.*) No recent production of Bergman I have personally seen, either on stage or on the television, carries any German suggestions to me. Latterday German theatre, in any case, does not strike me as being lavish; on the contrary, it is ascetic to the freezing point.

25. from *My Autobiography* by Charles Chaplin, Bodley Head, 1964; also in *Film Makers on Film Making* (p. 68), edited by Harry Geduld. Indiana, 1967.

26. Twenty-two years later, the incumbent Swedish government is not averse to the subject again reaching the screen. Svensk Filmindustri in cooperation with Swedish Film Institute, is preparing for 1970 release, the film *Baltutlämningen,* from the novel *Legionaire* by Per-Olof Enquist, directed by Johan Bergenstråhle.

27. "On the Sublime" by Nicolas Calas, in a defunct magazine, *The Tiger's Eye,* Vol. I, No. 6, N.Y. December 1948.

28. Perhaps the adjustment was made easier for him by his being enabled to stage, in November of 1952, Strindberg's *The Bridal Crown,* an epic and not unimpressive fantasy which should have relieved Bergman of any lingering lust for black magic and infanticide. Strindberg's play contains both; since its setting is also Dalarna, Bergman's Bajärna play may well have been incited by it to begin with. At one stage, Bergman hoped to make a film of *The Bridal Crown,* but by the time Nordisk Tonefilm had cleared the rights he had apparently lost interest or was otherwise taken up. One can't help wondering how his filmmaking continuity might have differed if in 1953 *The Bridal Crown* had become a movie. There might never have been a "Rose Period".

29. *The Social Meanings of Suicide* by Jack D. Douglas. Princeton University Press, 1967. See especially Part IV. "Official Statistics on Suicide and their use in Sociological Works."

30. Hendin's study might profitably have included the occupations of his suicidal subjects. I infer that the more responsible the subject's occupation the likelier he is to attempt suicide in a crisis, but I have no assurance from Hendin that this is so.

31. This statement may be misleading. There was a witches' trial in Sweden as late as the mid-eighteenth century but this was exceptional; during the

high tide of European trials and burnings, at the turn of the seventeenth century, Scandinavian countries were moderate by comparison. There is no analogy in Sweden with the excesses of torture and burnings which took place in, for instance, Saxony or Bamberg. See Robbins, *Encyclopedia of Witchcraft and Demonology,* Spring Books, London, 1959, under the appropriate headings.

32. *On Being Swedish.* Secker and Warburg, London, 1968. This passage was quoted from Mr. Austin's abridged version in *Industria,* "An Annual Report on Business, Industry and Culture in Sweden." Stockholm, 1966–67.

33. A study was made by Veli Verkko, *Homicides and Suicides in Finland and Their Dependence on National Character* (Scandinavian Studies in Sociology 3. G.E.C.Gads Forlag, Copenhagen 1951). I find his method dubious. He equated availability of alcohol with the homicidal and suicidal rates over the years, but since he was consulting figures, not people, he had no other circumstances or motives to qualify the statistical items he had arbitrarily chosen. Thus he arrived at an unflattering description of his countrymen which in fact he had already framed from the traits attributed to their prevailing physical type, in the language of constitutional psychology.

34. It will always be urged, despite the clear contrary evidence, that the multiplication of diversions and of travel opportunities will modify a people's temperament. In any individual case, the experience of being carried by jet plane to Kenya, Crete, or Lisbon in a few hours might change a man's life; it is the man who determines, not the transit unaided. Package tourism does not disseminate culture, it obliterates it. And two-channel television will only enforce the already sparse communication among Swedes, besides increasing their spectator neurosis by a barrage of international impressions to which they must either react, with consequences noted, or resist by willed indifference.

35. *Russians as People* by Wright Miller. Phoenix House, London, 1960.

36. *Essays in Swedish History* by Michael Roberts, 1957.

37. *English Villages in Colour* by Geoffrey Grigson. Batsford Books, London, 1958.

38. Roberts, *op. cit.*

39. Roberts, *ibid.*

40. See *A History of Swedish Literature* by Alrik Gustafson, in which the biographical material is candidly and amply documented. To be especially noted for their views, their way of life and their fate—beside Strindberg, of course—are Erik Johan Stagnelius (1793–1823), Carl Jonas Love Almquist (1793–1866), Victoria Benedictsson (1850–1888), Ola Hansson (1860–1925), Gustaf Fröding (1860–1911), Karin Boye (1900–1941), and Agnes von Krusenstjerna (1894–1940). This is not the whole story, to be sure, but it is an aspect rarely acknowledged in cultural surveys of Sweden's yesterday that imply an unimpeded evolu-

tion of social felicity, emphasize political reform, Swedish emigrant successes in the New World, Swedish industrial growth, and the international triumphs of Jenny Lind. (For that matter, the career of Ivar Kruger is too great an embarrassment to occupy more than a footnote.) It is an aspect that more pertinently explains the background for the ambiguities sensed by many contemporary observers when viewing Swedish films.

41. Interventionism, i.e., as distinct from unrestrained capitalism. "One of the aspects in which the Swedish experiment deviates from Marxism is its emphasis upon the consumer and the role played by the consumer cooperative, as opposed to the dogmatic Marxist emphasis upon production. The technological economic theory of the Swedes is strongly influenced by what Marxists would call bourgeois economics, while the orthodox Marxist theory of value plays no role in it whatever." *The Open Society and its Enemies* by K. A. Popper. (Vol. II, p. 335, note 10). Routledge and Kegan Paul, London, 1952.

42. Jean-Paul Sartre presided over that tribunal, the same Sartre who approved Soviet Russian intervention everywhere but in Hungary. Peter Weiss sat on that tribunal—as Marat? or Robespierre?—Weiss, who declined to attend an international writers' symposium in Prague, November 1967, on the grounds that he was a good Marxist and that the Czechoslovak manifesto of freedom was "a false alarm"; it "directed attention to state-power terror in socialist countries" but "ignored the massacres in Vietnam [presumably he did not refer to massacres by the Viet Cong], fascism in Spain and Greece, racism in the United States". He challenged the Congress not to waste its time by playing into the hands of "imperialist aggression," of which John F. Kennedy had been an agent, but to take up the theme of "the writer's position in a socialistic society". (His open letter was published in *Die Zeit* and quoted in *Dagens Nyheter* (Stockholm), September 16, 1967. We assume that since that date Czechoslovakian writers have learned with their stomach nerves what the writer's position is in a socialistic society. Naturally, both Sartre and Weiss, who know what's best for the captive mind, live safely in the bourgeois-imperialist West, royalty-fattened and Vogue-photographed.

43. Cf. "Myrdal's Mythology" (*Encounter*, July 1969), by Clifford Geertz, Department of Anthropology, University of Chicago. "For someone so intent on restoring sociological realism to economic analysis, Myrdal's portrayal of Indian culture and society is astonishingly abstract. Unnuanced and unparticularized, it is a thing of silhouettes and shadows—'caste', 'landlordism', 'superstition', 'the village', 'the masses', 'provincialism', 'nationalism', 'the state' —a civilization without qualities. It would seem impossible to write nearly a million words on a country with so rich a history, so profound a culture, and so complex a social system and fail to convey the force of its originality and the vitality of its spirit somewhere; but Professor Myrdal has accomplished it."

44. Austin, *op. cit.*

45. "The Loss of Innocence" by Anthony West. *The New Yorker*, May 3, 1969.

46. While *Aftonbladet*, once a conservative paper, now an organ of the workers' cooperative, represents, like *Dagens Nyheter* but at a considerably lower level of address, the Social Democrat position, *Expressen*, somewhat right of center, is fairly indistinguishable from it in tone. Both have a populist voice, both maintain an unflagging suggestion of daily crisis, both are more anti-American than not and you might say anticapitalist, which at this level means simply hate those richer than you are. *Dagens Nyheter* has by far the most abundant coverage and the greatest number of service features but if I were to read a Swedish newspaper for international news I would depend on *Svenska Dagbladet* (*höger*) for the most reliable, uncolored reporting.

47. Published as *The Road*, translated by M. A. Michael. Jonathan Cape, London, 1955.

48. Cf. "The Wilderness Art of Arne Sucksdorff" by Vernon Young. *Industria*. Stockholm, 1963.

49. John Russell Taylor, *op. cit.*

50. *La Grande Aventure du Cinema Suedois* by Jean Beranger, *Le Terrain Vague* Eric Losfeld. No date given. Paris, 1960. That it is possible to over-praise this film I am immensely grateful to M. Siclier (*op. cit.*) for pointing out. He quotes, for the confirmation of my worst suspicions about the mind of Jean-Luc Godard, a statement by the latter that "*Monika* is to the cinema of today what *The Birth of a Nation* is to the classic cinema. . . ." *Arts*, Paris, July 30, 1958.

51. This sequence was shot with special filters and the print was afterward "pressed," in order further to increase the appearance of chalkiness and of shallow dimension.

52. M. Siclier made the suggestive observation that Von Sternberg (from whose films, stylistically, *The Naked Night* does appear to have derived) created a world out of Marlene Dietrich, whereas Bergman created a world into which he fitted Harriet Andersson. The comparison is all in Bergman's favor, precisely because Dietrich, while beautiful to contemplate, was histrionically so inexpressive that all Von Sternberg's later films consisted of a montage in which nothing availed against the face and legs of Dietrich except the interior decoration. On the subject of *baroque*, the importance of which is of course in its principle of movement, Siclier supplies an admirable description of Bergman's style in this film. He calls it "*a somber baroque*". (Siclier, *op. cit.*)

53. *Swedish Cinema* by Rune Waldekranz. (Trans. Steve Hopkins) Swedish Institute. 1959.

54. "Yorick. An Essay on the Clown. A Fragment. *Verve*, Paris, 1939.

55. John Russell Taylor, *op. cit.*

56. There were special exceptions to the all but general obloquy received by the film in this period. In South America, where serious attention to Bergman preceded that paid to him in North America and most of Europe, *The Naked Night* was awarded the first prize at Sao Paulo, Brazil, 1954, and in Uruguay, 1957, the first complete Bergman filmography was published according to Marianne Höök in *Ingmar Bergman*, 1962. In 1957–58, on my first visits to Sweden, the film had a secure reputation within a minority group. In 1964, *Chaplin* magazine, No. 50, Stockholm, conducted a rather unusual poll to determine the ten best Swedish films, ever. Among those voting, regular film critics numbered only 50 per cent; the rest were archivists, film historians, filmmakers, professors in related fields, editors and so on. Four of the ten films chosen were Bergman's. The first six choices were: 1. *Miss Julie;* 2. *The Naked Night;* 3. *Raven's Quarter;* 4. *Wild Strawberries;* 5. *The Seventh Seal;* 6. *The Silence.* While opinion polls have little objective value, they do indicate the temper of the hour, among members of the category being polled.

57. Siclier, *op. cit.*

58. Quite the most unbelievable reaction to this film was that of Olof Lagercrantz, editor of *Dagens Nyheter*, who wrote on March 10, 1956: *"Smiles of a Summer Night* is a comedy without enough spirit or wit to fill a doll's thimble; jokes and dialogue, though dolled up in fancy dress, are suited to the stableyard. The characters are too meager to bear analysis. . . . There is an inflexibility of thought and imagination scarcely credible when coupled with such frilly pretension. What a desperate fate to work with films in our country if such pictures as *Smiles* are praised and rewarded! The prizes must be felt as stinging blows in the face by each and every person who attempts to give his best. . . . A pimply lad's base imagination, the shameless dreams of a callow heart, boundless contempt for artistic and human truth—these have created the comedy." (Translation by George Simpson.) Within two years, Lagercrantz had become a champion of "liberal" literature, promoting the merits of John Steinbeck and Henry Miller, and defending a Norwegian novelist who had encountered the censor for his pornographic content (I am told that Lagercrantz compared the writer with Homer). The above quotation sounds the authentic note and ratifies a principle I have long entertained: scratch a militant progressive and you find a witch-burner. When I asked an experienced American observer of the Swedish press and politics how he would define the political position of Olof Lagercrantz, I was amused to receive the answer: "He's a romantic Leftist".

59. *Trämålning* (Moralitet) by Albert Bonniers. Owl Books, Stockholm, 1956. The play is brief, intense, skeptical, with very little action. Jöns is the central character; the Knight's role is considerably less important. There is no Death,

but a Girl is his emissary: as the actor dies, she tells him he is needed by her "stern master". The young Witch is importantly vocal; when Jöns converses with her, at length, she is already "dead"; she eloquently recalls her suffering and is explicit about her tryst with the Devil. A Mary figure, with swaddled child in her arms, is frankly named Maria. Speaking for myself, I wish the film had followed the more sardonic example of the play, instead of neutralizing Jöns by shifting the main interest to the Knight and Death. Jöns' line, "I shall be silent but under protest" is in the play.

60. *Swedish Cinema* by Peter Cowie. London, 1966, p. 147.

61. Cowie, *op. cit.*, p. 145.

62. *The Silence of God: Creative Response to the Films of Ingmar Bergman* by Arthur Gibson. 1969. The films responded to are *The Seventh Seal, Wild Strawberries, The Magician, Through a Glass Darkly, Winter Light, The Silence,* and *Persona.*

63. "*What* Cocktail Party?" by James Thurber. *The New Yorker,* April 1, 1950, p. 26.

64. The composer was Johan Olof Wallin (1779–1839), poet, psalmist and church dignitary.

65. Gibson, *op. cit.,* p. 52.

66. "The Rack of Life," in *Film Quarterly,* Berkeley, Summer, 1959. Quoted by Cowie (*op. cit.*) p. 130.

67. Cowie, *ibid.,* p. 128.

68. My impression has been mainly formed by Anglo-American criticism. Europeans were far less grudging and hostile. *The Magician* took three prizes at the Venice Film Festival in 1959, which proves nothing about the merits of the film, true; but it points to a susceptible reaction. The best of all interpretations I know was written by M. Siclier for the penultimate chapter of his book (*op. cit.*). M. Siclier never forgets that he is writing about poetry.

69. To my knowledge, this point was first made by Jacques Siclier (*ibid.*).

70. *Four Screenplays.* Introduction.

71. *Reason in Religion.* Vol. 3 of *The Life of Reason* by George Santayana. Collier Books, N. Y., 1962.

72. The line was addressed to Laurence Harvey by Julie Christie, in John Schlesinger's *Darling,* 1965.

73. The source was first called to my attention by George Simpson. Marianne Höök (*op. cit.*) also mentions the play and further suggests that a work by Hjalmar Bergman, *An Experiment,* unknown to me, has certain parallels with the situation in *Ansiktet.*

74. *Comedie rosse*—i.e., corrosive comedy, wherein virtue is unrewarded and vice unpunished. The term seems to have arisen in the nineteenth century, to describe the plays of Karl Sternheim in Germany and those of Julien Becque, for example, in France.

75. History is sometimes artistic. Royal intercession is not a myth. A famous Commedia del'Arte company, captured by Huguenots, was ransomed by the French ruler who awaited a performance at Blois. The great Moliere was involved in a more abstractly gratifying rescue. Refused local burial by the Paris clergy, he was secretly interred by special request of Louis XIV.

76. See *Juliet of the Spirits*. Interview with Fellini conducted by Tullio Kezich. Orion Press, N.Y.

77. Nothing is more damaging to Mr. Gibson's seven-fold thesis than his purposeful omission of *The Virgin Spring*. In a book devoted wholly to the religious content of Bergman's work, he ignores—not a single mention—the very film in which, at least for a long hour, Bergman embraces the relief he has been seeking.

78. "Bergman about Bergman," based on interviews by Maud Wester, in *Vecko Jouranlen*. Stockholm, 1970. A comically Swedish strategy was involved here. After Part Four of this series had been published, Bergman, on television, complained that his privacy had been invaded and reproached journalists for assuming that because Liv Ullmann had gone to Denmark with the child there was something domestically amiss; she had merely gone shopping. A week thereafter, the news broke. Bergman and Liv Ullmann were separated.

79. *The Scenic Art: Notes on Acting and the Drama* by Henry James. Edited by Allan Wade. Rutgers University Press, New Brunswick, N.J., 1948.

80. Between 1925 and 1931, Carl-Theodore Dreyer defined three fundamentally separate cinematic styles. *The Master of the House*, 1925, was a kind of late-Bergman but unabstract creation, on silent film: an eloquent achievement of domestic tension, confined to a single bourgeois setting, in which Dreyer cut from half-length and closeup shots to objects in the home, building drama from an unspoken dialogue between people and their things. He distilled this method for *The Passion of Joan of Arc,* made in France, so that two-thirds of the film consists only of closeup faces (or even backs of heads) in a fantastic crescendo of speaking power (silent, of course). *Vampyre,* 1931, allegedly a commercial job, was nonetheless a brilliant synthesis of styles from Germany and perhaps from Jean Epstein. Here Dreyer used the camera with great flexibility: long tracking shots, placement of the spectator in the camera's witness point—e.g., we see the world from below as if we were in a coffin carried to the graveyard. But, from *Day of Wrath* on, Dreyer lost his life-rhythm, as I see it, and increasingly gives us, in *Ordet* fatally, long slow pedestrian scenes with long shots

of characters grouped as on a stage; we watch them cross the room for no dramatic or cinematic reason. Dreyer's disciples have been stubbornly reluctant to admit that these films are cinematically dead. As for Bresson, he began with such restriction of means he had nowhere to go before reaching stasis. He made his films depend exclusively on the face and presence of one player. This worked in *A Condemned Man Escapes* and in *Diary of a Country Priest*. It was disastrous in *Pickpocket* and *Joan of Arc*, where his actors were expressionless. But Bresson was intelligent enough, French enough, to feel his error. With *Au Hasard, Balthazar,* and *Mouchette,* while his souls were as predestined as ever (is he a Jansenist?), he made motion pictures.

81. Quoted in *Vecko Journalen, ibid.*

82. "Films to Confirm the Poets". *Hudson Review.* New York, Autumn, 1963.

83. Gibson, *op. cit.,* pp. 97–115.

84. Peter Cowie has pointed out, aptly, that Bach's *Goldberg Variations,* heard on the radio in *The Silence,* was composed to alleviate the insomnia of Goldberg's patron, Keyserling. (Cowie, pp. 181–182).

85. Cowie quotes an interview with Bergman in *Playboy,* in which Bergman said: "What matters most of all in life is being able to make contact with another human being. If you can take that first step towards communication, towards understanding, towards love, then you are saved". (Cowie, *op. cit.,* p. 166).

86. *Young Man Luther* by Erik Erikson. W. W. Norton, N.Y., 1958.

87. Harry Schein told Ken Annakin that *I Am Curious, Yellow* was one of the most important works in Swedish film history. (*Dagens Nyheter,* Feb. 17, 1968.)

88. *Carnets* 1930–44. Quoted by John Cruikshank in *Montherlant.* Oliver & Boyd, London, 1964.

89. *A World on Film,* pp. 289–290. Stanley Kauffman. Harper and Row, N.Y., 1966.

90. I have in mind, particularly, Claude Chabrol's *Le Beau Serge (The Friends)* and Francois Leterrier's *Les Mauvais Coups.* The former, while manifestly uneven in execution, is as purely Christian a conception as the screen has yielded in many years. It is most regrettable that Chabrol never found his way back to the sensitized and critical vision of his first two films. *Les Mauvais Coups,* directed with a master's touch (his first film) by Francois Leterrier (Bresson's actor in *A Condemned Man Escapes*) seems to be unknown outside of France: with a wonderful feeling for place and with no anxiety to overstress his points, Leterrier told the relentless story of a woman, played with tragic and aggressive subtlety by Simone Signoret, who destroys herself in an attempt to destroy her husband.

91. Jean Cocteau was the well-meaning villain. Of *Breathless* he generously said, "The most important film of the last ten years!" Nobody stopped to ask M. Cocteau how many films he had seen in the last ten years, beside his own. The news was out. Godard was in, like a burglar.

92. Typical, I suppose, was a conversation I overheard on a train somewhere in Europe. A young American girl was ecstatically describing *The Silence* to a ditto friend. "It was kind of fantastic! These two weird females fighting in a hotel!" Half covering her mouth, she hissed in a loud sotto voce, "One of them *masturbates!*"

93. My translation, from the version which appeared in *Expressen,* Stockholm, August 1, 1965.

94. *The Flower and the Castle* by Maurice Valency. 1963.

95. *Shoot!* by Luigi Pirandello. Translation by C. K. Scott Moncrieff. E. P. Dutton and Co., New York, 1926.

96. Geduld, *op. cit.,* p. 100.

97. Gibson, *op. cit.,* pp. 135–53.

98. "Bergman seems only marginally concerned with the thought that it might be salutary for audiences to be reminded that they are watching a film (an artifact, something made), not reality. Rather, he is making a statement about the complexity of what can be represented, an assertion that the deep unflinching knowledge of anything will in the end prove destructive. A character in Bergman's films who perceives something intensely eventually consumes what he knows, uses it up, is forced to move on to other things." "Bergman's *Persona,*" in *Styles of Radical Will,* p. 140. Farrar, Strauss and Giroux. N.Y. 1969. I would say that in *Persona* Bergman was much more than "marginally concerned," since the progress of the film is continually impeded by his reminders. "The complexity of what can be represented" is increased, not to say exacerbated, by the interjections. However, he is indeed asserting what Miss Sontag then claims —and clearly she approves of precisely the conclusion Paul Britten Austin questioned in *On Being Swedish*: that deep, unflinching knowledge destroys. Note that Miss Sontag says "a character in Bergman's films who perceives something intensely," intensely, not clearly! I think Miss Sontag fails to distinguish between kinds of objects supposedly consumed by perception. If you love something, you wish to know more about it; knowledge may increase your love (Leonardo thought so); it may destroy it; there are no laws. If you are destroyed by knowledge you have concealed, this means your resources have failed you and you are destroyed by insufficient knowledge.

99. The von Merkens party in *Vargtimmen* is almost a travesty of the Supper scene (2) of *The Ghost Sonata,* itself so far over the edge that it can only be

viewed without a quaver if you check your risibilities at the cloakroom. Baron Skanskorg, Beatrice Holsteinkrona and Old Hummel, on crutches, have their flayed counterparts in the film; Naima Wifstrand removing her rubber face is only funnier in a desolate way than Strindberg's Mummy who lives in a closet and talks like a parrot.

100. In a review of *Vargtimmen* which had bite and intelligence (*Chaplin* 80, Stockholm, March, 1968), Per-Olof Enquist criticized Bergman for doing nothing creative with the *aggressions* he obviously harbors. Bergman is like a Hottentot (*en svart mamba*), said Enquist, whom society has allowed into the salon, and what does he do when he is there? ". . . the only thing, the absolutely only thing he does is to lie in a corner, wrapped up and remorseful, sobbing over his aggressions and his neurosis, and about being stepped on when he was a boy and whether there is a life after death." In his films, he dissipates his aggression in "caricatures of private enemies"; elsewhere he retreats to his position as an artist, unidentified with "society". Enquist's critique was not pragmatic; he made no demands that Bergman should be *engagé*. He simply pointed out the falsity of his position. On this issue, I would agree with the critic. I think Sweden must be a difficult place for an artist because the environment is so passionless and there is such a dearth of external themes, but to revolt against an ethnic atmosphere is undirected madness. Insofar as Sweden means an organized society, I think Bergman has no complaint; the hindrances he has suffered are negligible. He has worked in greater freedom than any film director I can think of anywhere.

101. Quoted by Enquist, *ibid.*

102. *Three* Fårö interviews were conducted by Mr. Löthwall and included in a Bergman number of the short-lived *Film och Bio* magazine, January 1968. 1. A press interview before production activity. 2. A long, comprehensive series of interviews with Bergman, himself, and members of his company, entitled, "Four Days on Fårö," of concrete value as a record of filmmaking seen by those who do the jobs. 3. An interview with Bergman, alone, after completion of the shooting. I quote here and hereafter from translations I then made for Svensk Filmindustri.

103. I am in complete agreement with George Steiner. "The novels [films] being produced under the new code of total statement shout at their personages: strip, fornicate, perform this or that act of sexual perversion. So did the S.S. guards at rows of living men and women. The total attitudes are not, I think, entirely distinct. There may be deeper affinities than we yet understand between the 'total freedom' of the uncensored erotic imagination and the total freedom of the sadist. . . . Both are exercised at the expense of someone else's humanity, of someone else's most precious right—the right to a private life of feeling." "Night Words," in *Language and Silence* by George Steiner. Atheneum,

N.Y., 1967. The irony is that in cinema Bergman's tragedy of violation, *The Virgin Spring,* opened the way for the violation of everybody by everybody else.

104. The Japanese film, *Nobi (Fires on the Plain),* Kon Ichikawa, 1959, is probably the most extreme confrontation of such a condition ever reenacted for film. After cannibalism, Bergman's worst dreams of humiliation are but toys of the mind.

105. That Bergman enjoys mystifying people was apparent when Löthwall asked him (in Fårö 3) where we had met "Lobelius" before. Bergman chuckled that he had set many on their ear with that, and preferred not to answer the question. I don't want to spoil his pleasure. The Bergmanic reader can find that reference for himself, without tears.

106. "Artists in Love and War," *The Hudson Review,* Vol. XXII No. 2 Summer, 1969.

107. Farber, *ibid.*

108. Löthwall. Fårö 3.

109. Excluding *All These Women,* which did have a confectionery brilliance. Cowie reported that Sven Nykvist exposed 18,000 feet of Eastmancolor film in preliminary experiments. (Cowie, *op. cit.,* p. 139.) *A Passion* was the real beneficiary of these trials; the color, in the interior scenes, especially, is bewitching.

110. My quotation is from the Royal S. Brown translation, in *Geduld, op. cit.,* pp. 187–88.

111. If Bergman specifically intends a reference to geology here, he can only mean the theories advanced by French geologists over a century and a half ago, with the Auvergne caves as evidence. It is also conceivable that he may have shifted his reference to archaeology, with the caves of the Dordogne in mind, where the Magdalenian decorations were found.

112. Here, Mr. Cowie would be justified in citing Bergman's claim that science kills. As usual, Bergman's metaphor sidesteps historical complexity. Was the Christian belief killed by science or by experience with which it couldn't be reconciled? As for destruction at large, the simple belief of an inspired nomad, when codified by "organization men," helped to destroy the classical civilisation.

113. *The Ghost Sonata,* Scene 3.

114. *Op. cit.* See especially the excellent introduction and notes by Evert Sprinchorn in the edition I cite (Bibliography). Regarding the inspiration from Bach, it is pertinent to remember that Strindberg's play, *Easter,* which was presented at Easter, 1901, in Stockholm, was designed after Haydn's *Seven Words of the Redeemer,* the three acts corresponding to Haydn's three movements. I do not like to assist others in drawing a long bow and hence to aggra-

vate the credulity of my readers, but a speculation made by Hans Nystedt, a creditable Swedish theologian, in *Svenska Dagbladet,* December 1, 1969, seems, upon reflection, quite likely. Mr. Nystedt pointed out that *A Passion* was given its premiere the day following the Sunday when the twenty-fourth chapter of *St. Matthew* is the prescribed text in the Lutheran church. That chapter is the sermon on the Mount of Olives, apocalyptic in nature. Of equal, if perhaps frivolous, interest to me is the fact that the premiere in question was given on Martin Luther's name day.

115. Löthwall. (Fårö 1). Bergman's confusion of Sweden with the world (a confusion which non-Swedish critics have been quick to share) is revealed by the fact that during the years when the supposed divorce of theatre from the public interest was taking place (it couldn't happen overnight), Paris was still producing notable plays and London was burgeoning with theatre talent, with innovative productions of classics as well as of contemporary plays, and British television has been abundant with capital adaptations, splendidly acted. One of Bergman's desperate answers to the Swedish crisis was free theater or theater with a uniform low price so that anybody could attend, dressed anyhow; as if you could create theatre with the audience rather than with the plays; as if you could increase the value of anything by lowering its price: what people get cheaply, they honor cheaply. Witness the movies.

117. *Strindberg, An Introduction to his Life and Work* by Brita M. E. Mortensen and Brian W. Downs. Cambridge, Cambridge University Press, 1949.

118. *The Possessed* by Fyodor Dostoievsky. Translated by David Magarschack. Penguin Books.

119. *Fårö,* a documentary, feature-length (1 hour, 20 minutes), was not made for Swedish Television. It was an independent venture which developed into a social comment addressed to the State. It was premiered New Year's Day, 1970. (See further, Appendix II.)

120. Film history, as I have used the term, is pure hyperbole. Like M. Malraux's "imaginary museum," it is something each of us carries in his head. Film history for the spectator, in its living continuity, is wholly dependent on the whims of archivists, film-society organizers, commercial distributors and exhibitors. A history of the art of the film there never will be, in any language— for, excepting the special study, film histories are written by librarians or sociologists. Either film history is a living, if incomplete, body of film available to the filmmaker, who takes his hints wherever he finds them and thereby adds to the history, or it is nothing but the paper on which it is written. Film histories on our shelves, insofar as they exist by that classification, are notorious for the filmmaking talent their authors have minimized or ignored, or of which they are ignorant.

APPENDIX I.

On Extended Meanings in Four Bergman Films

The Naked Night (*Gycklarnas Afton*). I believe there is another dimension of meaning in this film, personal to Bergman; I explore it here because the film is a world in itself, with no other interpretation necessary. But I hope that my further deductions, if they are valid, will suggest how Bergman's mind works on his material—to what degree unconsciously, I have no certain conviction. I was puzzled by something which eluded me, arising from the fact that Bergman told me he dreamed the initial sequence of this film. Assuming that dreams have coherent meanings for us if we know how to interpret them (I respect the theory but my faith in it is not unbounded), I asked myself why Frost never smiles, and next asked what his name signified. Frost is obvious enough, merely descriptive—he has certainly been blighted—but Teodor? The name of the Director in *Jack Among the Actors* (see context) was *Teodor* (Skarp is simply sharp). We have already one director, Albert Johansson. He visits the theatre director in that town; his name is Sjuberg. This is almost too close for comfort to Alf Sjöberg, who was Director of Dramaten. I saw no point in underlining a local joke which nobody outside Sweden could be expected to appreciate. In any case, I didn't suppose anyone could miss the point that the theatre in relation to Johansson's circus was also the theatre in relation to filmmaking. Then, it seemed to me, the clue went further. Recall the sequence. Albert, rebuffed by the theatre and the community (the public?) turns to his wife as a way of escape from au ''art-form'' visited by virtually everybody but honored by none. But his wife will not have him : he has made his choice and she sends him back to his mistress. His mistress, Anne? ''The theatre is my wife, the film my mistress.''

Now, if Teodor Frost is a projection of what Albert may likely become, and the mistress becomes the wife, one day the ''circus director'' will find that he is married not to a Muse but to a painted hag whom he has constantly to rescue from public humiliation : a wife to whom he is chained by virtue of the commitment he has made, commitment which, to a director of ''the performing arts,'' becomes through the long years a burden which he carries down an unending beach while the crowd, visible yet undistinguishable vocally, turns aside, merely gloats, or laughs bawdily as he stumbles on his way.

The Magician, The Silence, and Persona

Regarding theocentric interpretations of certain other films (such interpretations are not the isolated concern of Mr. Gibson ; he has simply been more explicit, by organizing his responses at book-length), I want to say firmly that it's anybody's pleasure to see a work of art in the way he wants to see it, just as he sees the world in his own way. But written criticism carries the obligation of interpreting as far as possible what is demonstrable ; it is not your dream of the film you made while watching the one made by Bergman. In private conversation, I might tell someone that I see the subject of such and such a film as The Marriage of Heaven and Hell, or The Seventh Strawberry is silent ; if I am going to expatiate on my view in a critique I had better have evidence for it or be hanged for an impudent fellow.

In *The Magician,* I had long entertained the suspicion, which I guarded with my life, that since Bergman, through Vogler and Granny, implied the assertion he later made in print that art became dessicated when it cut itself off from religion—he might well be implying, when Vogler is saved at the last minute by the King, that the King = God, recalling the artist to higher things. Yet this seemed to me little more than a hunch, which didn't deserve being shown off. Imagine my astonishment when I find Mr. Gibson, to whom this sequel should logically appeal, wasting his time making Granny the God-mouthpiece, when obviously she is evangelism become Black Magic. He senses this, too, but he is unable to surrender his determination that every Bergman film he chooses for his Scripture must have an interrogated God-character. Five of these, incidently, are female, which raises very indiscreet questions in my mind.

However, in *The Silence* I am sure he is straining at a gnat when he picks Ester as God and Anna as the contemptibly human plaintiff. Putting aside the repulsiveness, to me, of conceiving God as a sick woman, the attribution is not logical. If Ester is God, who has been "willing to expose himself to our abuse" and is left behind by the carnal rebel to die in Timoka (you can see the appeal in this setup), then who in Hell would the Father of God be, whom Ester and Anna have in common? Directly you remove your attention from Ester-Anna in Mr. Gibson's scheme, nothing else in the film is thereby clarified.

Where he really misses the train is in his emphasis on a piece of dialogue, when Anna asks her boy, Johan, what he is staring at. He says, "I'm looking at your feet". "Oh? Why?" "They're walking around with you, all by themselves." Gibson sees this as an image of man, "destitute and forlorn". Yes, in a special sense. The key is closer to Mr. Gibson's hand than it is normally to mine. For the essential unity of Ester and Anna is pictured in the very context from whence came Bergman's through-a-glass-darkly figure: in Paul's First Epistle to the Corinthians. "For as the body is one and hath many members, and all the members of that one body, being many, are one body: so also is Christ" (Corinthians I., 12.12). And three verses later, "If the foot shall say, Because I am not the hand I am not of the body; is it therefore not of the body?" Ester and Anna are one; after that recognition, Mr. Gibson may take over, to see them as Christ in man, denied; but let us at least resume with a premise contained by the film and by what we know of Bergman's sources.

Similarly, other theologians (including Hans Nystedt, see Note 114) tend to feel that Elisabeth Vogler in *Persona* is God, or at least has a divine suggestion, being challenged by secular man with his piffling questions (Alma). Gibson is dogmatic on this score, but I must say his interpretation of the dialogue works better here than in his other cases. It still leaves a congregation of ambiguities. But if he wants overtones, which I would never flatly say are not there, he might manage to be more orderly about them. If Vogler in *Ansiktet* was sent for by the King, and Mrs. Vogler is presumably summoned to the theatre at the end of *Persona,* who summons her? Her husband. In which case, Mr. Vogler would be God, or his vicar, and everything I have said in my text about the small fellowship that gives security would then apply, rather than to the theatre (or, as well as to the theatre), to the community of Christians. I don't know why I should supply these chaps with their arguments, but this does make sense to me, the more so since Mr. Vogler refers to his confreres, in their work, as "tormented, helpless, lonely children" and John, the apostle, repeatedly addresses the bretheren as children, in his Epistles.

"My little children, these things write I unto you. . . ."
"Little chidlren, keep your selves from idols."
"The elder unto the elect lady and her children, whom I love in the truth. . . ."
"The children of thy elect sister greet thee. Amen."

Yes, I believe this whole level of presence hovers in *Persona;* since, in my case, I did not feel it when I saw the film, but came to it by deductive brooding, I have discussed it here out of context. And I don't think this level excludes the other, for if it did the very title and most of the allusions to theatre would be mere vanities. The two conceptions may be thought perhaps to verge, split, overlap, become one, and separate again like the faces of Elisabeth and Alma.

A Passion is a different matter. There is no possible other way of construing the work except as a parallel with The Passion. Once you move into the concentric circles, you can't stop and make any sense of the film. You must follow through to the final ironic encounter: that the movie Bergman has "really" made is not the one you see.

On Press. I learned later that this film has been distributed under the title, *The Passion of Anna,* a radically obtuse and inaccurate alteration which effectively eliminates the primary clue for interpreting the film, save for members of the press who should be well aware of the original title.

APPENDIX II

Ingmar Bergman and the Theatre, Radio, and Television

A full account of the intimate connections between Ingmar Bergman's theatre activity and his films is not likely now to be written; plays (I speak of them in performance) have an even more ephemeral life than movies; when they no longer exist before the eye, their details can only be recaptured, feebly, at second hand by reference to someone else's opinion and by whatever photographic record may remain. I have tried to intimate, wherever the connection seemed pertinent, and with what knowledge I have, the nature of that connection in Bergman's case. A field quite as fruitful because it is to an extent recoverable is Bergman's productions for radio; ironically, however, it is rendered inaccessible to most because of the language barrier. Since I have probably heard about the same number of plays for radio directed by Bergman as I have seen plays directed by him in the theatre, in neither case many, my judgment of him in both media is not founded on abundant evidence.

Bergman has not, in my opinion, original genius in the theatre. He has a personal touch of course with anything he does, but he has not the kind of imagination that makes a play memorable for a lifetime. I would say that he is too intent on accenting the themes he finds significant to reveal the spirit of another dramatist to its most spacious advantage. (Naturally, therefore, he does better with Swedish plays.) Some of his radio presentations, however, have been striking. There, his natural tendency to concentrate, to suggest, and to abstract is assisted by the medium. All requirements of time and place are abridged; he has only one element on which to focus, the individual human voice. Often, from that, he conjures an intensity as lacerating as, on film, he does from the closeup face. An outstanding example, to my ear, was his production of Hugo von Hofmannsthal's *The Old Play of Everyman*, in a superb translation by Bertil Malmberg, first transmitted in April, 1956, and replicated on Easter Sunday, 1970. This production had the same kind of singleminded, driving purity as had *The Virgin Spring* (the setting was, to be sure, comparable). Bergman's players conveyed a heard atmosphere, difficult to pin down concretely yet all the same present to other senses than hearing. Max von Sydow surpassed himself in all his other roles I have heard; his nuances of character and his pious emotional power were compelling.

Painting-on-Wood is, I should hazard, a vehicle ideally suited to radio. Essentially a debate among personalities who instantly define themselves by their convictions, with a voice from beyond the living, and a shape of the plague that needs no visual proof to induce a shudder down the spine, the play is almost predestined for a bodiless existence.

The television is another matter, for this is theatre again or film. So far, the productions of other mens' works Bergman has directed have been mainly those too brief or too evanescent in their quality to stand the open glare of a theatrical evening. Strindberg's *The Storm* (or *Storm Weather*), for example, is a thing of intimacy, of mood which can't be overstated or rushed or played too fully—and this, on the television, was a very special experience—*ganz fur sich*.

Bergman's own debut as a writer for the medium was not, for my mind, auspicious. *The Rite* seems to have been a spillover from the rancor of *Vargtimmen* (*The Hour of the Wolf*), the frustration of a man incensed because nobody will crucify him—though, in the film, Bergman personally played a species of inquisitor. The subject appeared to concern the persecution of the artist by society (which? when? where?); three actors, played by Thulin, Björnstrand, and Ek, form a self-hating triangle, among whom sex is as ever a tired and dirty act; they are being tried in a court for a crime which is never specified. Having seen it only once, I am to date in agreement with Leif Zorn, who described the film (in *Dagens Nyheter*, March 26, 1969) as frigid and obscure, the dialogue as scentless. ''It takes place where all Bergman's films take place . . . on the border between actuality and hell, in the same indefinable location outside history, an eternal Middle Ages." I think Mr. Zorn is closer than he knows; before having studied the dialogue closely, I suspect that the characters are not "really" actors. I think we have to adjust ourselves in future, whether we like the idea or not, to seeing Bergman as a Christian anarchist. My own interpretation grieves me but I cannot refute the evidence that he is increasingly confusing the company of actors with the company of the apostles, a conception I find dangerously sentimental or comic. "Why, Bottom, how thou art translated!"

As for the documentary, *Fårö* (see Note 119), the subject has scant interest for a non-Swedish viewer, which will not forestall attempts to acquire the film, if only because it was made by Bergman. (I have often believed that in the last decade or so Picasso has had a dwarf at his elbow; every time the master doodles on a serviette, the dwarf whisks it away discreetly and sells it for $2000). In *Fårö* there are some lovely views in color of sheep grazing and lambing—the interviews with the residents are counterpointed by shots of the passing seasons—but I have seen a hundred documentaries on the television more enthralling. The necessity for conducting long testimonial interviews with considerably inexpressive people is naturally not conducive to high-tension appeal.

Fårö has a purely academic interest for me; its structure is essentially that of *A Passion*: a sustained tatoo of monologues or duologues in closeup, with cuts to silent shots of the landscape or to quiet occupational actions. In his last three films, whatever reservations I have entered against them, Bergman has established his witness point consistently with his subject. For *The Hour of the Wolf* he took a prodigious number of closeups and cut from them into group scenes: Johan as antagonist against the upper-class mob. In *The Shame* he also shot an abundance of closeups, cutting often to participating movements, sometimes with handheld camera, which did provide whatever feeling of reality was present. *A Passion* is dominated by the closeup face, photographed frequently against a nonobjective background, just a field of color, and held to hypnotic length. The cuts to scenes of another kind are abrupt and infrequently on a movement, a process that ensures the sensation of discrete time sequences and hints at the disunion of physical and metaphysical duration.

A SELECTIVE BIBLIOGRAPHY

(This pertains directly to Swedish culture and Swedish film. Collateral reading is indicated in the Notes.)

Austin, Paul Britten   *On Being Swedish.* Secker & Warburg, London, 1968.

Beranger, Jean   *La Grande Aventure du Cinéma Suédois.* Eric Losfeld, Le Terrain Vague, Paris 1960.

Bergman, Ingmar   *En Filmtrilogi.* P. A. Norstedt och Söners Förlag, Stockholm, 1963.
(English Version) *A Film Trilogy.* The Orion Press, N. Y., 1967.
Four Screenplays of Ingmar Bergman. Tr. Lars Malmstrom and David Kushner. Simon & Schuster, N.Y., 1960.
Trämålning. Moralitet. Uggleböckerna: Albert Bonniers Förlag, Stockholm, 1956.

Billquist, Fritiof   *Ingmar Bergman.* Teatermannen och Filmskaparen. Natur och Kultur, Stockholm, 1960.

Cowie, Peter   *Swedish Cinema.* A. Zwemmer Ltd., London. A. S. Barnes and Co., Inc., New York, 1966.

Fleisher, Frederic   *The New Sweden.* The challenge of a disciplined democracy. David McKay Co., New York, 1967.

Fleisher, Wilfrid   *Sweden.* The Welfare State. John Day Co., N. Y. 1956.

Geduld, Harry (Ed.)   *Film Makers on Film Making.* Statements on their art by thirty directors. Indiana Univ. Press, Bloomington and London, 1967 (pp. 177ff.).

Gibson, Arthur — *The Silence of God.* Creative Response to the Films of Ingmar Bergman. Harper and Row, Publishers, New York, Evanston and London, 1969.

Gustafson, Alrik — *History of Swedish Literature.* American-Scandinavian Foundation. Univ. of Minnesota Press, Minneapolis, 1961.

Hendin, Herbert — *Suicide and Scandinavia.* Grune and Stratton, New York, 1964.

Höök, Marianne — *Ingmar Bergman.* Wahlström and Widstrand, Stockholm, 1962.

Kauffmann, Stanley — *A World on Film.* (Part II, pp. 270ff., Sweden.) Harper and Row, Publishers, New York, 1966.

Lucas, F. L. — *The Drama of Ibsen and Strindberg.* Cassell, London, 1962.

Roberts, Michael — *Essays in Swedish History.* Weidenfeld and Nicolson, London, 1957.

Samuelsson, Kurt — *From Great Power to Welfare State.* 300 Years of Swedish Social Development. George Allen and Unwin Ltd., London, 1968.

Siciler, Jacques — *Ingmar Bergman.* Classiques de Cinema. Editions Universitaires, Paris, 1960.

Sjögren, Henrik — *Ingmar Bergman på teatern.* Almqvist and Wiksell, Stockholm, 1968.

Sjöman, Vilgot — *L 136.* Dagbok med Ingmar Bergman. P. A. Norstedt & Söners Förlag, Stockholm, 1963.

Strindberg, August — *Chamber Plays.* Tr. and Edited by Evert Sprinchorn, Kenneth Petersen, and Seabury Quinn, Jr. Dutton, D 107, 1962.

Taylor, John Russell — *Cinema Eye, Cinema Ear.* Some Key Film Makers of the Sixties. (Chapter, "Ingmar Bergman"). Methuen & Co, Ltd, London, 1964.

Valency, Maurice — *The Flower and the Castle.* Introduction to Modern Drama. Macmillan, New York, 1963.

Waldekranz, Rune — *Swedish Cinema.* Tr. by Steve Hopkins. The Swedish Institute, Stockholm, 1959.

● ● ●

Svenska Dagbladet Årsbok. 1935 ff. (Annual surveys of events and personalities.)

Swedish Sound Pictures and Their Directors. A Checklist by Sven Winquist. Swedish Film Institute Publications, Documentation Dep't, 1967.

Theater and Ballet in Sweden. A Pictorial Survey. Text by Gustaf Hilleström and Bertil Nydahl. The Swedish Institute, Stockholm, 1956.

THE PLAYS OF INGMAR BERGMAN

A List of Premiere Production Dates

Date And Place	Title	Director
12.9.44 Malmö City Theatre	*Rakel and the Cinema Attendant*	I. Bergman
12.1.47 Gothenburg City Theatre	*The Day Ends Early*	I. Bergman
26.10.47 Gothenburg City Theatre	*To My Terror*	I. Bergman
January, 1948, Oslo (Complete dates unavailable)	*Hets* (*Frenzy* or *Torment*) Dramatization of film, by Bergman	Per Gjoersöe
February, 1948, London (Complete dates unavailable)	*Frenzy* (Dramatization of the film, by Peter Ustinov)	Peter Ustinov
8.12.48 Hälsingborg City Theatre	*Kamma Noll* (Draw Blank)	L. L. Laestadius
14.2.52 Malmö City Theatre	*The Murder in Barjärna*	I. Bergman
22.10.54 Malmö City Theatre	*Twilight Games,* a ballet by I. Bergman and C. G. Kruuse	I. Bergman, choreography by C. G. Kruuse
18.3.55 Malmö City Theatre	*Painting-on-Wood*	I. Bergman

Ingmar Bergman on Swedish Television

Author	Title	Date	Director
Hjalmar Bergman	*Mr. Sleeman is Coming*	18.4.57	I. Bergman
Anon. from sixteenth century	*The Venetian*	21.2.58	I. Bergman
Olle Hedberg	*Rabies*	7.11.58	I. Bergman
August Strindberg	*The Storm*	22.1.60	I. Bergman
August Strindberg	*The Dream Play*	2.5.63	I. Bergman
Ingmar Bergman	*Painting-on-Wood*	22.4.63	Lennart Olsson
Ingmar Bergman	*The Rite* (film for TV)	25.3.69	I. Bergman
Ingmar Bergman	*Fårö* (Documentary)	1.1.70	I. Bergman
Ingmar Bergman	*The Sanctuary* (Euro-vision-play for 1970)	(October, 1970)	Jan Molander

THE BERGMAN FILM
CHRONOLOGY: Principal Credits

SF = Svensk Filmindustri. Sc = Scenario or Script. Ph = Photography. M = Music. S = Sets or Art Direction. Ed = Editing.

Hets (Torment, Frenzy)
2.10.1944 SF. Direction: Alf Sjöberg. Sc: Ingmar Bergman. Ph: Martin Bodin. M: Hilding Rosenberg. S: Arne Åkermark. Ed: Oscar Rosander. Cast: Stig Järrell (Caligula), Alf Kjellin (Jan-Erik Widgren), Mai Zetterling (Bertha Olsson), Gösta Cederlund (Pippi), Olof Winnerstrand (Rector), Stig Olin (Sandman), Jan Molander (Pettersson), Gunnar Björnstrand (A teacher), Birger Malmsten (A student).

Kris (Crisis)
25.2.1946 SF. Sc: Bergman, from Leck Fischer's play, *The Mother Animal*. Ph: Gösta Roosling. M: Erland von Koch. S: Arne Åkermark. Ed: Oscar Rosander. Cast: Marianne Löfgren (Jenny), Inga Landgré (Nelly), Dagny Lind (Ingeborg), Stig Olin (Jack), Allan Bohlin (ulf), Ernst Eklund (Uncle Edward).

Det Regnar På Vår Kärlek (It Rains on Our Love)
9.11.1946 Lorens Marmstedt, distributed by Nordisk Tonefilm. Sc: Bergman, from a play by Oscar Braathen, *Good People*. Ph: Hilding Bladh, Göran Strindberg. M: Erland von Koch. S: P. A. Lundgren. Ed: Tage Holmberg. Cast: Barbro Kollberg (Maggi), Birger Malmsten (David), Gösta Cederlund (Man with an umbrella), Ludde Gentzel (Håkansson), Douglas Håge (Andersson), Hjördis Pettersson (Mrs. Andersson), Gunnar Bjornstrand (Mr. Purman), Åke Fridell (Pastor), Benkt-Åke Benktsson (public prosecutor).

Skepp Till Indialand (Ship to India)
22.9.1947 Lorens Marmstedt, distr. Nordisk Tonefilm. Sc: Bergman, from Martin Söderhjelm's play, same title. Ph: Göran Strindberg. M: Erland von Koch. S: P. A. Lundgren. Ed: Tage Holmberg. Cast: Holger Löwenadler (Captain Alexander Blom), Birger Malmsten (his son, Johannes), Gertrud Fridh (Sally), Anna Lindall (Alice Blom), Lasse Krantz (Hans), Jan Molander (Bertil), Naemi Brise (Selma), Hjördis Pettersson (Sofie), Åke Fridell (Vaudeville director).

Kvinna Utan Ansikte (*Woman Without a Face*)
16.9.1947 SF. Direction: Gustaf Molander. Sc: Bergman. Ph: Åke
Dahlquist. M: Erik Nordgren. S: Arne Åkermark. Ed: Oscar Rosander.
Cast: Gunn Wållgren (Rut Köhler), Alf Kjellin (Martin Grande), Stig
Olin (Ragnar), Anita Bjork (Frida, Martin's wife), Olof Winnerstrand
(Director Grandé), Marianne Löfgren (Charlotte), Georg Funkquist
(Victor), Åke Grönberg (Chimney-sweep), Linnea Hillberg (Mrs.
Grande).

Musik I Mörker (*Music in the Dark, The Night is my Future*)
17.1.1948 Terrafilm (Lorens Marmstedt). Sc: Dagmar Edquist, from her
novel of the same name. Ph: Göran Strindberg. M: Erland von Koch.
S: P. A. Lundgren. Ed: Lennart Wallén. Cast: Mai Zetterling (Ingrid),
Birger Malmsten (Bengt), Bengt Eklund (Ebbe), Olof Winnerstrand
(Minister), Naima Wifstrand (Mrs. Schröder), Bibbi Skoglund (Agneta),
Hilda Borgström (Lovisa), Douglas Håge (Kruge), Gunnar Björnstrand
(Klasson).

Hamnstad (*Port of Call*)
18.10.1948 SF Sc: Bergman, from a story by Olle Länsberg. Ph: Gunnar
Fischer. M: Erland von Koch. S: Nils Svenwall. Ed: Oscar Rosander.
Cast: Nine-Christine Jönsson (Berit), Bengt Eklund (Gösta), Berta
Hall (Berit's mother), Erik Hell (Berit's father), Mimi Nelson (Gertrud),
Birgitta Valberg (Assistant Vilander), Hans Strååt (Engineer Vilander),
Nils Hallberg (Gustav).

Eva
26.12.1948 SF Direction: Gustaf Molander. Sc: Bergman. Ph: Åke
Dahlquist. M: Erik Nordgren. S: Nils Svenwall. Ed: Oscar Rosander.
Cast: Eva Stiberg (Eva), Birger Malmsten (Bo), Eva Dahlbeck
(Susanne), Stig Olin (Göran), Åke Claesson (Frederiksson), Wanda
Rothgardt (Mrs. Frederiksson), Inga Landgre (Frida), Hilda Borgström
(Maria), Lasse Sarri (Bo, aged twelve).

Fängelse (*Prison, The Devil's Wanton*)
19.3.1949 Terrafilm (Lorens Marmstedt). Sc: Bergman. Ph: Göran
Strindberg. M: Erland von Koch. S: P. A. Lundgren. Ed: Lennart
Wallen. Cast: Doris Svedlund (Birgitta-Carolina Söderberg), Birger
Malmsten (Tomas), Eva Henning (Sofi), Hasse Ekman (Martin Grande,
film director), Stig Olin (Peter), Irma Christenson (Linnea), Curt
Masreliez (Alf), Anders Henrikson (Professor), Marianne Löfgren
(Mrs. Bohlin), Carl-Henrik Fant (Arne), Inger Juel (Greta).

Törst (*Three Strange Loves, Thirst*)
17.10.1949 SF. Sc: Herbert Grevenius, from stories by Birgit Tengroth.
Ph: Gunnar Fischer. M: Erik Nordgren. S: Nils Svenwall. Ed: Oscar
Rosander. Cast: Eva Henning (Eva), Birger Malmsten (Bertil), Birgit
Tengroth (Viola), Mimi Nelson (Valborg), Hasse Ekman (Dr. Rosen-
gren), Bengt Eklund (Raoul), Gaby Stenberg (Raoul's wife), Naima
Wifstrand (Miss Henriksson, ballet teacher), Sven-Eric Gamble (worker).

Till Glädje (*To Joy*)
20.2.1950 SF Sc: Bergman. Ph: Gunnar Fischer. Music of Mozart,
Mendelssohn, Smetana, Beethoven. S: Nils Svenwall. Ed: Oscar Rosander.
Cast: Stig Olin (Stig Eriksson), Maj-Britt Nilsson (Martha), Victor
Sjöstrom (Sönderby), Birger Malmsten (Marcel), John Ekman (Mikael
Bro), Margit Carlquist (Nelly, his wife), Sif Ruud (Stina), Erland
Josephson (Bertil).

Medan Staden Sover (*While the City Sleeps*)
8.9.1950 SF Direction: Lars-Eric Kjellgren. Sc: Bergman and Kjellgren
from a story by Per Anders Fogelström. Ph: Martin Bodin. Cast: Sven-
Erik Gamble (Jompa), Inga Landgré (Iris), Adolf Jahr (Iris' father),
John Elfström (Jompa's father), Märta Dorff (Iris' mother), Ulf Palme
(Kalle Lund).

Sånt Händer Inte Här (*It Can't Happen Here, High Tension*)
23.10.1950 SF. Sc: Herbert Grevenius. Ph: Gunnar Fischer. M: Erik
Nordgren. S: Nils Svenwall. Ed: Lennart Wallen. Cast: Signe Hasso
(Vera), Alf Kjellin (Almkvist), Ulf Palme (Atkä Natas), Gösta Cederlund (Doctor), Stig Olin (Young man).

Frånskild (*Divorce*)
26.12.1951 SF. Direction: Gustaf Molander. Sc: Bergman and Grevenius.
Ph: Åke Dahlquist. Cast: Inga Tidblad (Gertrud Holmgren), Alf Kjellin
(Dr. Bertil Nordelius), Doris Svedlund (Marianne Berg), Hjördis Pet-
tersson (Mrs. Nordelius), Håkan Westergren (P. A. Beckman), Holger
Löwenadler (Tore Holmgren), Marianne Löfgren (Ingeborg), Stig Olin
(Hans).

Sommarlek (*Illicit Interlude, Summer Interlude*)
8.10.1951 SF. Sc: Bergman and Grevenius, from a story by Bergman.
Ph: Gunnar Fischer. M; Erik Nordgren; excerpts from Tchaikowsky's
Swan Lake. S: Nils Svenwall. Ed: Oscar Rosander. Cast: Maj-Britt
Nilsson (Marie), Birger Malmsten (Henrik), Alf Kjellin (David),
Annalisa Ericson (Kaj), Georg Funkquist (Uncle Erland), Stig Olin

(Ballet master), Renée Björling (Aunt Elisabeth), Mimi Pollak (old lady), John Botvid (Karl).

Kvinnors Väntan (Secrets of Women, Waiting Women)
3.11.1952 SF. Sc: Bergman. Ph: Gunnar Fischer. M: Erik Nordgren. S: Nils Svenwall. Ed: Oscar Rosander. Cast: Anita Björk (Rakel), Maj-Britt Nilsson (Märta), Eva Dahlbeck (Karin), Gunnar Björnstrand (Lobelius), Birger Malmsten (Martin Lobelius), Jarl Kulle (Kaj), Karl-Arne Holmsten (Eugen Lobelius), Gerd Andersson (Maj), Björn Bjelvenstam (Henrik), Aino Taube (Anita), Håkan Westergren (Paul).

Sommaren Med Monika (Monika, Summer with Monika)
9.2.53 SF. Sc: Bergman and Per Anders Fogelström, from the novel by Fogelström. Ph. Gunnar Fischer. M: Erik Nordgren. S: P. A. Lundgren. Ed: Tage Holmberg, Gösta Lewin. Cast: Harriet Andersson (Monika), Lars Ekborg (Harry), John Harryson (Lelle), Georg Skarstedt (Harry's father), Dagmar Ebbesen (Harry's aunt), Naemi Brise (Monika's mother), Åke Fridell (Monika's father).

Gycklarnas Afton (The Naked Night, Sawdust and Tinsel)
14.9.1953 Sandrew (Rune Waldekranz). Sc: Bergman. Ph: Sven Nykvist, Hilding Bladh. M: Karl-Birger Blomdahl. S: Bibi Lindstrom. Ed: Carl-Olof Skeppstedt. Cast: Åke Grönberg (Albert Johansson), Harriet Andersson (Anne), Anders Ek (Frost), Gudrun Brost (Alma, his wife), Hasse Ekman (Frans, an actor), Gunnar Björnstrand (Sjuberg, theatre director), Annika Tretow (Agda, Albert's wife), Erik Strandmark (Jens), Åke Fridell (officer), Kiki (dwarf).

En Lektion I Kärlek (A Lesson in Love)
4.10.1954. SF. Sc: Bergman. Ph. Martin Bodin. M: Dag Wirén. S: P. A. Lundgren. Ed: Oscar Rosander. Cast: Gunnar Björnstrand (Dr. David Erneman), Eva Dahlbeck (Marianne, his wife), Yvonne Lombard (Susanne), Harriet Andersson (Nix), Åke Grönberg (Carl-Adam), Birgitte Reimer (Lise), Olof Winnerstrand (Henrik Erneman), Renée Bjorling (Svea Erneman), John Elfström (Sam), Dagmar Ebbesen (nurse), Sigge Furst (minister), Helge Hagerman (travelling salesman).

Kvinnodröm (Dreams, Journey into Autumn)
22.8.1955 Sandrew. Sc: Bergman. Ph: Hilding Bladh. S: Gittan Gustafsson. Ed: Carl-Olof Skeppstedt. Cast: Eva Dahlbeck (Susanne), Harriet Andersson (Doris), Gunnar Björnstrand (Consul), Ulf Palme (Lobelius),

Kerstin Hedeby (Marianne), Sven Lindberg (Palle), Naima Wifstrand (Mrs. Aren), Bengt-Åke Benktsson (Director Magnus), Git Gay (a lady in the atelier), Ludde Gentzel (Sundström, photographer).

Sommarnattens Leende (Smiles of a Summer Night)
26.12.1955 SF. Sc: Bergman. Ph: Gunnar Fischer. M: Erik Nordgren. S: P. A. Lundgren. Ed: Oscar Rosander. Cast: Gunnar Björnstrand (Frederik Egerman), Ulla Jacobsson (Anne, his wife), Eva Dahlbeck (Desiree Armfeldt), Naima Wifstrand (Mrs. Armfeldt), Jarl Kulle (Count Carl Magnus Malcolm), Margit Carlquist (Charlotte Malcolm), Harriet Andersson (Petra, Egerman's maid), Åke Fridell (Frid, a groom), Björn Bjelvenstam (Henrik Egerman, son to Frederik), Bibi Andersson (actress), Lena Söderblom (chambermaid).

Sista Paret Ut (Last Couple Out)
12.11.56 SF Direction: Alf Sjöberg. Sc: Bergman and Sjöberg. Ph: Martin Bodin. M: Erik Nordgren, Charles Redland, Bengt Hallberg. S. Harald Garmland. Ed: Oscar Rosander. Cast: Eva Dahlbeck (Susan Dahlin), Olof Widgren (Hans Dahlin), Björn Bjelvenstam (Bo Dahlin), Harriet Andersson (Anita), Bibi Andersson (Kerstin), Jarl Kulle (Dr. Farell), Aino Taube (Kerstin's mother), Hugo Björne (Lecturer), Nancy Dalunde (Mrs. Farell).

Det Sjunde Inseglet (The Seventh Seal)
16.2.1957 SF. Sc: Bergman. Ph: Gunnar Fischer. M: Erik Nordgren. Choreography: Else Fischer. S: P. A. Lundgren. Ed: Lennart Wallén. Cast: Max von Sydow (Knight), Gunnar Björnstrand (Squire), Nils Poppe (Jof), Bibi Andersson (Mia), Bengt Ekerot (Death), Åke Fridell (Smith), Inga Gill (Lisa), Erik Strandmark (Skat), Bertil Anderberg (Raval), Gunnel Lindblom (a girl), Inga Landgré (Knight's wife), Anders Ek (monk), Maud Hansson (a witch), Gunnar Olsson (painter).

Smultronstallet (Wild Strawberries)
26.12.1957 SF. Sc: Bergman. Ph: Gunnar Fischer. M: Erik Nordgren. S: Gittan Gustafsson. Ed: Oscar Rosander. Cast: Victor Sjöstrom (Professor Isak Borg), Bibi Andersson (Sara), Ingrid Thulin (Marianne), Gunnar Björnstrand (Evald, Isak's son), Naima Wifstrand (Isak's mother), Folke Sundquist (Anders), Björn Bjelvenstam (Viktor), Jullan Kindahl (Agda) Gunnar Sjöberg (Alman), Gunnel Broström (Mrs. Alman), Max von Sydow (Åkerman), Sif Ruud (aunt), Gio Petre (Sigbrit), Gunnel Lindblom (Charlotta), Maud Hansson (Angelica).

Nära Livet (*Brink of Life, So Close to Life*)
31.3.1958 Nordisk Tonefilm Sc: Ulla Isaksson. Ph: Max Wilen. S: Bbi Lindström. Ed: Carl-Olof Skeppstedt. Cast: Ingrid Thulin (Cecelia Ellius), Eva Dahlbeck (Stina Andersson), Bibi Andersson (Hjördis), Barbro Hiort af Ornäs (Sister Brita), Max von Sydow (Harry Andersson), Erland Josephson (Anders Ellius), Inga Landgré (Greta Ellius), Ann-Marie Gyllenspetz (social worker), Gunnar Sjöberg (Dr. Nordlander).

Ansiktet (*The Magician, The Face*)
26.12.58 SF. Sc: Bergman. Ph: Gunnar Fischer. M: Erik Nordgren. S: P. A. Lundgren. Ed: Oscar Rosander. Cast: Max von Sydow (Albert Emanuel Vogler), Ingrid Thulin (Manda Vogler, or Aman), Gunnar Björnstrand (Dr. Vergerus), Lars Ekborg (Simson, Voglers' cook), Bibi Andersson (Sara), Åke Fridell (Tubal), Sif Ruud (Sofia), Erland Josephson (Consul Abraham Egerman), Gertrud Fridh (Ottilia Egerman, his wife), Toivo Pawlo (Chief of Police, Starbeck), Ulla Sjöblom (Mrs. Starbeck), Bengt Ekerot (Johan Spegel, actor), Birgitta Petersson (Sanna) Naima Wifstrand (Vogler's grandmother), Oscar Ljung (Antonsson, Egerman's groom).

Jungfrukällan (*The Virgin Spring*)
8.2.1960 SF. Sc: Ulla Isaksson. Ph: Sven Nykvist. S: P. A. Lundgren. Ed: Oscar Rosander. M: Erik Nordgren. Cast: Max von Sydow (Herr Törre), Birgitta Valberg (Märeta, his wife), Birgitta Petersson (Karin, Töre's daughter), Gunnel Lindblom (Ingeri), Axel Düberg (the thin one), Tor Isedal (the tongueless one), Ove Porath (the boy), Allan Edwall (the beggar), Axel. Slangus (bridge-keeper), Gudrun Brost (Frida), Oscar Ljung (Simon).

Djävulens Öga (*The Devil's Eye*)
17.10.1960 SF. Sc: Bergman. Ph: Gunnar Fischer. M: themes from Scarlatti. S: P. A. Lundgren. Ed: Oscar Rosander. Cast: Jarl Kulle (Don Juan), Bibi Andersson (Britt-Marie), Stig Järrel (Satan), Nils Poppe (Vicar), Gertrud Fridh (Renata), Sture Lagerwall (Pablo), Georg Funkquist (Count), Gunnar Sjöberg (Marquis), Torsten Winge (an ancient), Axel Düberg (Jonas), Kristina Adolphson (veiled woman), Allan Edwall (ear-devil) Ragnar Arvedson (guardian devil), Gunnar Björnstrand (actor), Inga Gill (Sara), John Melin (beauty doctor).

Såsom I En Spegel (*Through a Glass Darkly*)
16.10. 1961 SF Sc: Bergman. Ph: Sven Nykvist. M: from J. S. Bach,

Suite No. 2 in D-minor for cello. S: P. A. Lundgren Ed: Ulla Ryghe.
Cast: Harriet Andersson (Karin), Gunnar Björnstrand (David, her
father), Max von Sydow (Martin, her husband), Lars Passgård (Frederik or "Minus", her brother).

Nattvardsgästerna (Winter Light)
 11.2.1963 SF Sc: Bergman. Ph: Sven Nykvist. S: P. A. Lundgren. Ed:
 Ulla Ryghe. Cast: Gunnar Björnstrand (Tomas Ericsson), Ingrid Thulin
 (Märta Lundberg), Max von Sydow (Jonas Persson), Gunnel Lindblom
 (Karin Persson), Allan Edwall (Algot Frövik), Olof Thunberg (Frederik
 Blom), Elsa Ebbesen (old woman), Kolbjörn Knudsen (church-warden).

Tystnaden (The Silence)
 23.9.63 SF Sc: Bergman. Ph: Sven Nykvist. M: from Bach's *Goldberg*
 Variations. S: P. A. Lundgren Ed: Ulla Ryghe. Cast: Ingrid Thulin
 (Ester), Gunnel Lindblom (Anna), Jörgen Lindström (Johan, Anna's
 boy), Håkan Jahnberg (Waiter), Birger Malmsten (Bartender), Eduardo
 Gutierrez (Impresario of the dwarves, the "Eduardini"), Lissi Alandh
 (Woman in the cinema), Leif Forstenberg (Man in the cinema), Nils
 Waldt (Cashier), Birger Lensander (usher), Eskil Kalling (bar pro-
 prietor), K. A. Bergman (paper-vendor), Olof Widgren (old man in
 hotel corridor), Kristina Olausson (Stand-in for Gunnel Lindblom).

För Att Inte Tala Om Dessa Kvinnor (Not to Mention all These Women)
 15.6. 1964 SF. Sc: Erland Josephson and Bergman. Ph: Eastmancolor,
 Sven Nykvist. S: P. A. Lundgren. Ed: Ulla Ryghe. M: Diverse. Cast:
 Jarl Kulle (Cornelius), Bibi Andersson (Humlan), Harriet Andersson
 (Isolde), Eva Dahlbeck (Adelaide), Karin Kavli (Madame Tussaud),
 Gertrud Fridh (Traviata), Mona Malm (Cecelia), Barbro Hiort af
 Ornäs (Beatrice), Alan Edwall (Jillker), Georg Funkquist (Tristan),
 Carl Billquist (Young Man), Jan Blomberg (English radio reporter),
 Göran Graffman (French radio reporter), Gösta Prüzelius (Swedish radio
 reporter), Jan-Olof Strandberg (German radio reporter), Ulf Johansson
 (Man in black I), Axel Düberg (Man in black II), Lars-Erik Liedholm
 (Man in black III), L. O. Carlberg (chauffeur), Doris Funcke (Waitress
 I), Yvonne Igell (Waitress II).

Persona
 18.10.1966 SF Sc: Bergman. Ph: Sven Nykvist. M: Lars Johan Werle.
 S: Bibi Lindström Ed: Ulla Ryghe. Cast: Bibi Andersson (Alma), Liv
 Ullmann (Elisabeth Vogler), Margaretha Krook (Doctor), Gunnar
 Björnstrand (Mr. Vogler).

Vargtimmen (Hour of the Wolf)
19.2.68 SF Sc: Bergman. Ph: Sven Nykvist. M: Lars Johan Werle.
S: Marik Vos-Lundh Ed: Ulla Ryghe. Cast: Liv Ullmann (Alma), Max
von Sydow (Johan), Erland Josephson (Baron von Merkens), Gertrud
Fridh (Corinne von Merkens), Gudrun Brost (the elder Mrs. von
Merkens), Bertil Anderberg (Ernst von Merkens), Georg Rydeberg
(Lindhorst, archivist), Ulf Johanson (Curator Heerbrand), Naima Wif-
strand (Lady with hat), Ingrid Thulin (Veronica Vogler), Lenn
Hjortzberg (Kreisler, conductor), Agda Helin (maid), Mikael Rundqvist
(boy in jeans), Folke Sundquist (Tamino).

Skammen (The Shame)
29.9.68 SF Sc: Bergman. Ph: Sven Nykvist. S: P. A. Lundgren Ed:
Ulla Ryghe. Military Adviser: Stig Lindberg. Cast: Liv Ullmann (Eva),
Max von Sydow (Jan), Gunnar Björnstrand (Jacobi), Birgitta Valberg
(Mrs. Jacobi), Sigge Furst (Filip), Hans Alfredson (Lobelius), Ingvar
Kjellson (Oswald), Frank Sundström (Interrogator), Ulf Johanson
(Doctor), Frej Lindqvist (cripple), Rune Lindström (stout man), Willy
Peters (older officer), Bengt Eklund (sentry), Åke Jörnfalk (condemned
man), Vilgot Sjöman (Interviewer), Lars Amble (officer), Björn Tham-
bert (Johan), Karl-Axel Forsberg (Secretary), Gösta Prüzelius (pastor),
Brita Öberg (lady at the Interrogation local), Agda Helin (market wife)
Ellika Mann (female gaoler).

En Passion (A Passion)
10.11.69 SF Sc: Bergman. Ph: Eastmancolour, Sven Nykvist. S: P. A.
Lundgren. Ed: Siv Kanälv. Cast: Liv Ullmann (Anna Fromm), Bibi
Andersson (Eva Vergerus), Max von Sydow (Andreas Winkelman),
Erland Josephson (Elis Vergerus), Erik Hell (Johan Andersson), Sigge
Furst (Verner), Svea Holst (Verner's wife), Annika Kronberg (Ka-
tarina), Hjördis Petersson (Johan's sister), Lars-Owe Carlberg and
Brian Wikström (policemen).

Beröringen (The Touch)
26.6.1971 ABC Pictures Corp., distributed by Cinerama Releasing. Produc-
tion, Direction and Scenario: Bergman. Ph: Sven Nykvist. S: P. A. Lund-
gren. Ed: Siv Kanalv-Lundgren. Cast: Bibi Andersson (Karin, Mrs.
Vergerus), Barbro Hiort af Ornas (her mother), Elliot Gould (David
Kovac), Staffan Hallerstam (Anders Vergerus), Maria Nolgard (Agnes
Vergerus), Max von Sydow (Dr. Andreas Vergerus), Erik Nyhlen (An
Archaeologist), Margareta Bystrom (Secretary to Dr. Vergerus), Alan
Simon (museum Curator), Sheila Reid (Sara, sister of David Kovac).

INDEX